Historical trauma and memory

Living with the haunting power of the past

Conference Proceedings

Pumla Gobodo-Madikizela,
Eric Ndushabandi,
Kopano Ratele

SUN PRESS

Historical trauma and memory – Living with the haunting power of the past
Conference Proceedings

First edition 2021

ISBN 978-1-991201-58-4
ISBN 978-1-991201-59-1 (e-book)

Cover design, typesetting and production by African Sun Media

This publication can be ordered from:

orders@africansunmedia.co.za
Takealot: bit.ly/2monsfl
Google Books: bit.ly/2k1Uilm
Amazon Kindle: amzn.to/2ktL.pkL
JSTOR: https://bit.ly/3udc057
africansunmedia.store.it.si (e-books)

Visit africansunmedia.co.za for more information.

Contents

Part III: Reparative Practice

Part IV: Empathic Encounters

Part V: Perspectives from Rwanda Community Researchers

Part VI: Coming to Terms with the Past: Film-based Interventions

Foreword

A Public Discourse Imbued with Moral Possibilities

Pumla Gobodo-Madikizela

The conference reported in this book brought together scholars and practitioners from nine countries to participate in a conference held in Kigali, Rwanda, titled Historical Trauma and Memory: Living with the Haunting Power of the Past. Besides myself, the co-hosts of the conference included Eric Dushabandi (Institute for Research and Dialogue for Peace, Rwanda), Kopano Ratele (Psychology Department, Stellenbosch University), with external adviser Christine Schliesser (Systematic Theology and Ethics Department, Zurich University). The multidisciplinary group of participants were from the following countries: Rwanda, Germany, the Netherlands, Northern Ireland, Slovakia, South Africa, Switzerland, the United States of America, and Zimbabwe. Each of the participants were involved in research concerned with a range of topics related to historical trauma, trauma's transgenerational repercussions, different forms of reparative practice and/or social transformation in countries where victims/survivors, perpetrators and bystanders continue to live together in the same country, including art practices. There are many similarities and some potentially instructive differences among the case studies presented at the conference. Our interest therefore, was also in using the conference opportunity to initiate an exploratory conversation about a comparative approach to articulate what some of the common problems are, and/or what are the problems unique to new democracies emerging after mass violence or older democracies with a history of prolonged oppression. We selected Rwanda for the conference as a special case study to explore these questions, and an important site to inspire critical reflection on the themes of the conference.

Rwanda stands alone as a country that has drawn from its cultural values and practices to implement strategies of bringing peace to communities even as victims live as neighbours with perpetrators. Initiatives that have been implemented in Rwanda to bring former enemies to live and work together productively as neighbours are unique among response to genocide and crimes against humanity. This makes Rwanda site for a profound learning experience for scholars and practitioners interested in deepening their understanding and critical analysis of strategies that help to sustain relative peace.

Each visit to Rwanda has deepened our understanding of how Rwandans are finding new ways of dealing with the past and building their communities for peaceful living together. The memory of the past is a constant presence, but it is tempered by a public discourse that is imbued with moral possibilities and a sense of responsible citizenship. The community dialogues in the reconciliation villages we visited where genocide survivor and perpetrator families live as neighbours are an innovative way that draws on age-old traditions of communal living, where there is an expectation of reciprocal mutual recognition, acting in a way that does not foreclose the human flourishing of the other. There is no doubt that this is not a simplistic "love one another" solution. It requires work, given the presence of the past and considering how it affects people differently. The community dialogues in the reconciliation villages and in other Rwandan communities, and bringing people from different sides of the genocide through collaborative community projects are some of the strategies we witnessed aimed at strengthening community bonds. The reality of facing historical injustices, particularly when victims and perpetrators have to live together in the same country, and often as neighbours, is that it is not always easy to reckon with the past. Facing the past requires confronting difficult truths. Avoidance of the past is not an option when one has to face one's neighbours every day.

The arts have been important in Rwanda's dealing with the genocide past and the quest for ways to restore human connection. The Rwanda Annual National Arts Festival, the *Ubumuntu Festival*, was inaugurated in 2015, and since its launch has attracted artists from around the globe. Described as Africa's premier performing arts gathering for social change, artists are invited to explore themes that centre on the question of historical trauma and restoration in trauma's aftermath. Theatre, music, film, and the visual arts offer an important alternative for engaging with the past. Engaging with the difficult past in creative ways can give shape to historical legacies and help to face the pasts while building bridges for human connection across diversity instead of breaking them down. We were fortunate that the presentations at this conference included work that illustrates the various ways in which the arts has played a role in facing past violence and its transgenerational repercussions in different countries represented at the conference.

Acknowledgements

We have to start by thanking Marietjie Oelofsen. From coordinating the compilation of the essays in this book to ensure that we kept to the timetable, she was important to the production of this book. A very special thanks to Landi Davidson, our ever patient Project Coordinator at the office of Studies in Historical Trauma and Transformation at Stellenbosch University. Always meticulous and paying attention to detail in whatever task she manages, Landi did an exceptional job on the complex logistical arrangements to ensure the smooth running of our conference. We are especially grateful to Landi because she insisted on seeing this work through to the end of the conference despite it coinciding with the dates for the University of Cape Town's graduating ceremony. This meant that she could not attend her own graduation to receive her Masters in Neuro-Psychology. We are grateful to Samantha Lakin, who at the time was affiliated with the Institute of Research and Dialogue for Peace (IRDP) in Kigali, for her invaluable support with logistical arrangements in Rwanda. Our appreciation also goes to Eunison Mugamu for stepping in to take over from Marietjie Oelofsen for coordinating the compilation of the essays for this project.

Financial support from the Centre for Collaboration in Africa at Stellenbosch University and the National Research Foundation (NRF) in South Africa made it possible to have a productive conference and to compile this publication. We thank them for their generous support.

Introduction:
Context of the conference

When victims break their silence

Pumla Gobodo-Madikizela[1]
Eric Ndushabandi[2]
Christine Schliesser[3]

In our work with historical trauma, we have interviewed women and men who told their stories to the Truth and Reconciliation Commission (TRC) in South Africa and testified at the gaçaça hearings in Rwanda. Both the TRC and the gaçaça are processes established to help these two countries to face the past. The question that has guided our inquiry is what makes it possible for victims of massive traumas to continue living with the memory of their traumatic experiences. And for those who engage in acts of forgiveness, what does forgiving a person who caused immeasurable pain mean – what does the process of forgiving look like, what is involved in it and what are the conditions that bring about the forgiving response? And for perpetrators who experience remorse, how does their journey of reflection on their deeds unfold?

These questions are as relevant for South Africa as they are for other countries with histories of violence. In Rwanda, a country where victims live with perpetrators as neighbours, and Germany, where descendants of Nazi perpetrators have been engaged in dialogues with children of Holocaust survivors[4] are important sites of investigation in this work.

Again, the question that guides this work is: how do the new subjectivities in victims, perpetrators as well as in witnesses and implicated others, to borrow a term from Michael Rothberg,[5] emerge? What can we learn about human relationality in the immediate aftermath of historical traumas and intergenerationally?

In this introduction, we will attempt to make more explicit some of the dynamics that play out when victims break their silence. In the first part, we will draw from the work of the TRC in South Africa and commemorative events in Rwanda to show that narrative in its spoken or written form is not the only appropriate way of bearing witness to the suffering of the traumatised subject. We make a mistake by

1 Research Chair, Studies in Historical Trauma and Transformation, Stellenbosch University.

2 Executive Director, Institute for Research and Dialogue for Peace, Professor of Political Science at University of Rwanda.

3 Christine Schliesser is a theologian and an ethicist at the Centre for Ethics at Zürich University, Switzerland.

4 Hammerich, B., Pfäfflin, J., Pogany-Wnendt, P., Siebert, E., & Sonntag, B. (2008). Handing Down the Holocaust in Germany: A Reflection on the Dialogue between Second Generation Descendants of Perpetrators and Survivors. In C. Van Der Merwe & P. Gobodo-Madikizela (Eds.), *Narrative and Forgiveness: Perspectives on the Unfinished Journeys of the Past* (pp. 27-46). Newcastle: Cambridge Scholars Publishers.

5 Rothberg, M. (2014). Beyond Tancred and Clorinda: Trauma studies for implicated subjects. *The future of trauma theory: Contemporary literary and cultural criticism*, 2076-0787.

focusing only on narratives presented through textual and oral testimony as the only valid form of witness to traumatic historical events. The body is a powerful site of witness. Paying attention to this communicative form may deepen our understanding of the transformative possibilities that unfold in the encounter between victims and perpetrators.

In the second part of our introduction, we will advance a general theoretical argument that in Rwanda and in South Africa, the cultural ethic that defines human relationships offers an over-arching moral framework that was not destroyed by the violence and trauma in the two countries. In other words, the restorative approach to dealing with the past in Rwanda and in South Africa was in part made possible by the cultural and moral framework of the processes of gaçaça and Ubuntu, respectively. This cultural and moral framework therefore facilitated the emergence of forgiveness and a shared moral vision between victims and perpetrators.

We begin with a story from the opening public hearings of the South African TRC. It is a story of 'the cry' of Nomonde Calata, one of the widows of the brutal murder of a group of activists known as the 'Cradock Four'. Mrs Calata's scream as she gave testimony about the murder of her husband was elevated to iconic status as Archbishop Desmond Tutu (1999) referred to Calata's scream as "the defining sound that characterised" the TRC.[6] And long after the TRC hearings, her iconic scream was adapted and used as a central feature of a musical performance created from voices of witnesses who appeared before the TRC. With this example we want to illustrate the diverse possibilities of bearing witness that emerge from the public testimony presented at the South African TRC, and to reflect on this testimony as a performative speech act that inspires a response from others who are witnesses, listening to it.

At the opening of the public hearings of the TRC, the large city hall in East London, a city in the Eastern Cape province of South Africa, was filled with a predominantly black audience interspersed with a few white TRC commissioners and some reporters as the only visible white people in the audience. Then the audience rose to sing a song that was at once a poem and an anthem of black pain, sung throughout the years of apartheid repression by black people at mass funerals, political rallies, and peaceful protests, the song, *Lizalis'idinga lakho Nkosi* (Fulfill your promise Lord), reverberated into the large hall, carrying the hope that the moment promised.

Narratives of re-enactment of the past

This was the same moment into which Mrs Calata screamed her own pain. She 'dared' to wail her pain and the suffering she was subjected to into the large hall, giving voice

6 Tutu, D. (1999). *No Future without Forgiveness*. London: Image.

to it, bearing witness for all to hear, beyond the walls of the public hearings space in East London.

It is this wailing voice that South African composer, Philip Miller, resurrects from the archives of TRC narratives. One of South Africa's celebrated soloists, Sibongile Khumalo then picks up Mrs Calata's crying voice and re-presents it through her magnificent and electrifying mezzosoprano. Later in the song, several other voices emerge and merge in a choir with different levels of intensity, male and female voices, singing this wailing cry – a chorus of collective voices, bearing witness to this human cry. The effect that the music produces is a seamless repetition that reverberates like a re-enactment of a wound that refuses to be silenced – history playing itself out, confronting the audience with the reality of the fact of the living memory of this past. The piercing scream seemed to shatter the magnificent walls of the East London city hall; a structure built in colonial times to celebrate Queen Victoria's Diamond Jubilee. The building still houses memorial plaques for some of the fallen British soldiers when the British and the Afrikaners fought to take over South Africa.

Individual narratives and experiences recounted in front of a public audience carried an extra weight because they went beyond the individual to capture a larger story of collective trauma. The testimonies were an important source of history, and of historical reflection on the significance of traumatic pasts for memory, its reconstruction as victims and survivors tried to make sense of their traumas and to reclaim their sense of agency. Thus, as a public process 'performed' on the national stage, both the TRC and gaçaça processes served a narrative function that went beyond the individual victims' testimonies. It is in this context of remembering that a collective working through of the past can take place.

Philip Miller called the musical he produced from the testimonies of the TRC, *Rewind: A Cantata for Voice, Tape & Testimony*. The title is drawn from the words of a mother who tells the Commission how she discovered the murder of her son in the evening news on television that day. Sobbing uncontrollably, she told the Commissioners: 'I wanted the newsreel to re-wind, I stayed on to watch, wanting it to rewind the story ...' As an artwork, Miller's Rewind, as its title suggests, represents a telling of events that are not so much remembered as such. It represents, and becomes, an articulation of a recurring 're-memory' – in Toni Morrison's parlance[7] – that re-appears as embodied fragments of memory.

A similar example from Rwanda that addresses traumatic memory is the musical theatre performance of the production, *Shadows of Memory*, by Hope Azeda. A stirring performance of the genocide against the Tutsi at the 20th commemoration of the genocide in 2014, the cast of more than 800 actors re-presented every detail of the genocide – the killers, the UN Peace Keeping Force and its abandonment of the

7 Morrison, T. (1987). *Beloved*. New York: Plume.

Tutsi, leaving them at the mercy of the murderous *interahamwe*, the streets riddled with bodies, the rescue by the Rwandan Patriotic Front – all these elements were present in the performance and the story of the genocide powerfully and evocatively depicted. The performance itself was a kind of a re-enactment of the painful past and the articulation of the memory of the horror of the genocide through the movements of the 800-member cast, each standing for, representing a particular memory aspect from the past.

Miller's *Rewind* and Azeda's *Shadows of Memory* communicate trauma in ways that evoke an embodied response. The performances themselves involve enactment through the body and therefore demand this kind of response, inviting the listener or viewer to remember the past in all its painful and horrific details. It is in fact 're-membering' the past, putting together the dissociated fragments in order to make sense of the re-emergence of the trauma in the present.

Even with the power of artistic representation, however, there are limits to the capacity to adequately represent historical trauma. In other words, at the heart of attempts to represent historical trauma lies a paradox. This is captured in the notion that trauma shatters all frames of understanding, including the arts, and it calls to mind Theodor Adorno's famous dictum that 'there can be no poetry after Auschwitz'.[8] Read as a metaphor, Adorno's statement may be true, pointing to the fact that even the artistic form falls short of adequate portrayal of the magnitude of the human cost and all the complex layers of these historical traumas.

In Rwanda, the arts have been central in both commemorative and educational projects that involve dialogue about the genocide. How can the immeasurable human cost of the genocide be represented? Even with a large cast, such as the performers of *Shadows of Memory*, how can the many layers of suffering be portrayed – the suffering of the victims, and the suffering of their descendants who have now come of age and participate in the commemoration events every year? The complexities of the story of the genocide also mean that suffering goes beyond Tutsi victims who were the main targets of the genocide. The children of victims, the children of perpetrators, Hutus who resisted or played the role of rescuers, and perpetrators who have returned to their communities and are now involved in restorative dialogue and rebuilding projects in their communities, all add to the complexity of the story told through representational form. Having said this, the arts does open up a space for reflection on the multiple dimensions of historical trauma.

A return to witness testimony

So, we return then to the sites of witness, to the actual stories presented by survivors themselves as they paint a clear picture of their pain and communicate their lived

8 Adorno, T., W. (1963). Kulturkritik und Gesellschaft. *Prismen. Kulturkritik und Gesellschaft*, 7–26.

experience of loss and sense of brokenness. Narrative testimony brings us closer to victims' 'shards of pain', and to witness what Homi Bhabha has described as the experience that speaks 'to the condition of the marginalized, the alienated, those who have to live under the surveillance of a sign of identity and fantasy that denies their difference.'[9] Below, is a mother's story of the loss of her son during the apartheid army's invasion of black residential areas.

The story further illustrates Bhabha's point about narrative that communicates trauma's re-membering as 'shards of pain':

> He came home during school break at 10 o'clock. I was sitting right there where you are sitting, just sitting exactly where you are sitting in that chair. He walked in dressed in his school uniform and went to the cupboard over there and cut himself a slice of bread. He is doing all of this in a rush. He is like that when he comes home during break. He spread peanut butter on it and then put the rest of the bread back, leaving the crumbs all over the cupboard, and the knife, still smudged with peanut butter. He ran out. He is still chewing his bread and holding it in his hand. It wasn't long – I heard shots outside. Some commotion and shouts. Then I'm hearing, 'uLuthando, uLuthando, nank'uLuthando bamdubule! [This is Luthando. They have shot Luthando!]' and then someone calling out for me: 'mama kaLuthando! [Luthando's mother!]' I went flying out of this house. Now I am dazed. I ran, not thinking. My eyes are on the crowd that has gathered. ...

The mother's recollection of the events has a visual and embodied quality to it: a young boy in school uniform; returning to class with a slice of bread that he had only moments before smeared with peanut butter. She wants the interviewer to picture the moment – to witness it and to feel it in the body as it were – the moment when she was called out by a crowd who witnessed the shooting of her son. Listening to this story and others like it gives one a clear sense of the dangers that young people like Luthando faced, how vulnerable they were during the anti-apartheid struggle, and the fear with which parents lived, that their children may not return home alive. It invites us to put ourselves in the mother's shoes and to feel with her.

Describing the moment of her loss, the mother recalled the final moment when she arrived at the scene and saw her son's lifeless body: 'Here is my son,' she said, gesturing with her hand toward her kitchen floor. She continued:

> It was just blood all over. My anguish was beyond anything I ever thought I could experience. They have finished him. I threw myself down on him. I can feel the wetness of his blood – I felt his last breath leave him.

9 Bhabha, H. (2010). *The Location of Culture*. New York: Routledge, p. 90.

As she said these words, she placed her hand on her chest. The listener is drawn to this moment – to that moment. The 'here' in her words – 'here is my son' – is evocative. It points to a specific place that resides not only in terms of its physical location 'there' in the streets of the past where her son was killed, but more significantly for her, here in its embodied state of her body and her mind. The events recounted cannot be understood to be 'in the past', but events experienced as in the 'here' of now. Thus, from this we may conclude that to suggest that people should 'forget the past and move on' creates great conceptual mischief. The past is an embodied psychic reality for many people whose lives are marked by violence. Or histories of violence. The narratives gesture toward the sites of the theatre of the original violence, but their recollections also evoke the mental landscapes where the scenes of violence re-play in unending re-enactments of the original scenes.

Gaçaça and the TRC facilitating a shared moral vision

Rwanda and South Africa have created spaces of victim-perpetrator dialogue in an effort to open up transformative possibilities that might contribute to rebuilding communities in the aftermath of historical trauma and violence. Engaging with the past in this way is an imperative in countries where victims, perpetrators and their children live together as neighbours. The processes of the TRC and gaçaça set the tone for how the two countries might face their tragic histories with a vision to rebuild human bonds. We want to turn our attention for a moment to the concept of Ubuntu, or Ubumuntu in Kinyarwanda. When we say in the Xhosa language of South Africans, *umntu ngumntu ngabanye abantu*, and in Kinyarwanda, *Umuntu Agirwa n'Undi* (which, loosely translated, means 'a human is made by another human'), we imply an ethic based on the understanding that one's subjectivity is inextricably intertwined with that of others in one's community through reciprocal recognition of the other's human dignity. In other words, a person is a person through being witnessed by, and engaging in reciprocal witnessing of other persons. Alternatively, human subjectivity is defined by the multiplicity of relationships with others. The meaning conveyed by the expression is twofold. First, human subjectivity depends on being witnessed; the richness of subjectivity flows from interconnectedness with the wider community, and from the reciprocal caring and complementarity of human relationships. Second, the phrase conveys the kind of reciprocity that calls on people to be ethical subjects.

Mutual recognition inspired by Ubuntu/Ubumuntu is fundamental to being a fellow human being, a relational subject in the context of community. This becomes an experience that allows entry into the other's life in a way that makes it possible to reconstitute the other's experience within the self. In this sense then, recognition is not simply recognition of the physical face of the other – it may not even be about the other's physical presence. But rather about something more subtle, less visible than any of the physical elements of the encounter. It is about seeking to know the other's identity as part of a wider human community and already creates the possibility of crossing any boundary that may separate the self from the other. In contrast to the Cartesian 'I think therefore I am' philosophy that positions the self at a distance from the other, Ubuntu/Ubumuntu is a stance that allows the self to feel the other, and to stand within the other's historical circumstances in order to evoke a sense of shared humanity across time and place.

This, in our view, is what drives the stories of reconciliation between survivors and victims that seem to defy comprehension in Rwanda. An example from research in Rwanda offers another illustration: young Rwandan researchers presented their research at a research workshop on various aspects of the post-genocide period in their country. One of the studies described an encounter in a facilitated group process between a woman survivor of the genocide and one of the men who perpetrated this crime. The woman described the horrific scene of mass killing that she survived during the genocide in Rwanda. She then told the group that the last time she saw the man was in a church where he shot and killed families who had sought refuge in the church. 'His hands are full of the blood of an incredible number of the Tutsi he killed in the church', the woman said. 'He was like a killing machine ... and I am sure he honestly does not know how many Tutsi he killed'. Her testimony led to uncontrollable sobbing in the room. The man then crawled out of his chair and went to kneel in front of the woman, sobbing and asking for her forgiveness. After some relative calm, the woman, now standing next to the kneeling man, extended her hand and helped him to get up. She then embraced him and told him that she wanted to forgive him and not to think of him as a killing machine, but 'as a fellow human being and brother'. Hyppolite Ntigurirwa, the researcher reporting on this encounter describes the moment as follows: '[They] stood in an embrace with arms folded tight across each other's backs.'[10]

This is recognition of the other not from the distance that bestows such recognition from a position of power, but one that does so from a place of proximity to the other's lifeworld. It is an 'experience-near'[11] that opens up the possibility of an embodied recognition that seeks to repair the brokenness of the other – because now it has become [it is like] one's own brokenness. In the aftermath of historical trauma, restoring human bonds requires a new vocabulary of re-humanisation. This new mode

10 Ntigurirwa, H. (2018). *The Dilemmas and the Cost of Re-humanisation*. Paper presented at the Post-genocide Rwanda: Research Workshop, London School of Oriental and African Studies / Aegis Trust.

11 Kohut, H. (1978). Introspection, empathy and psychoanalysis. In P. Ornstein, H (Ed.), *The Sense for the Self: Selected Writings of Heinz Kohut: 1950-1978* (Vol. Vols. 1 and 2, pp. 205-232). New York: International Universities Press.

of being human, what has been referred to as a 'reparative humanism',[12] opens towards a horizon of an ethics of care for the sake of a transformed society.

If the level of depravity that has been captured most compellingly with the phrase 'the banality of evil' is fostered in an environment in which inhumanity against others thrives, then it should be possible that relationships that foster thoughtfulness and a sense of being human reproduce themselves in our relational world. In this sense then, it seems to us that a word that best captures what is needed is not 'forgiveness', but rather 'empathic repair'.[13] The notion of 'empathic repair', points toward not only one's healing, but also one's responsibility to participate in the building of a society in which people can come together and be fellow human beings – 'to touch the other, to feel the other'[14] – sharing in the vision of a more humane society. The potential for the unexpected, unforeseen and thoroughly creative, endemic to the human condition is always present when victims and perpetrators and their descendants encounter one another. These are precisely the ideas that were embodied in the TRC and gaçaça processes, in order to foster the possibility of human encounters that were not possible in the past that was characterised by dehumanisation and hateful engagement designed to deepen ethnic and racial divisions. Sustaining the emergence of new forms of subjectivity, of closer relationships that begin to close the gap between these old divisions requires attending to issues of social and economic justice in order for victim groups to experience a sense of real transformation of their lives and to be able to enjoy the freedoms that come with changes in the post-conflict environment.

12 Gobodo-Madikizela, P. (2010). Reconciliation: A call to reparative humanism. *In the Balance: South Africans Debate Reconciliation*, 133-139.

13 Gobodo-Madikizela, P. (2008). Empathetic repair after mass trauma: When vengeance is arrested, *European Journal of Social Theory*, 11(3), 331-350.

14 Fanon, F. (2008). *Black skin, white masks*. Grove Press.

Keynote address

1. Beyond trauma? Notes on a word, a frame, and a diagnostic category

Nancy Rose Hunt

History happens, history may cut, and sometimes history kills. How a next generation deals with death and terrible wounds is critical. What can be transmitted to or remade the *generation that follows* may be bound up with suffering and forgetting or with narratives of resolve and refiguration.

So, it is important to ask: What work does the word *trauma* do? Sometimes too much work: in the sense that the word may conceal persons within a diagnostic category or confine them to sensations of hauntedness. Some speak of pathological and psychic *wounds* instead of trauma (as Vincent Crapanzano did recently). Rather than bodily trauma, psychoanalytic and psychiatric definitions focus on psychic injury and emotional shock, with memories of the injury often repressed and unhealed. Usually, such injuries relate to an event of catastrophe or disaster. Fassin and Rechtman have shown how contemporary trauma's 'language of the event' goes with victims and victimhood, especially within humanitarian economies.[1]

The event-based nature of trauma usually goes with the *historical*: most psychic injuries are related to a time and place and to generations formed around experiences and their senses. The word trauma may be bound up with narratives, forgetting, and remaking. How may *the trauma word* frame or distort history? May it position subjects to see pasts, futures, and each other? Awful, oppressive, and murderous times and places produced in memory and as history and event, go with wounds and memories, collective and enduring. Thus, why might we want to avoid the trauma word? That it works to produce victims via pity and diagnostic categories is an important reason. The category also easily becomes a technology, producing and naming subjects as damaged.

When can historical memory of wounds embolden or inspire, rather than cripple and disturb? Terrible histories may inflict confusions and disorientation on those who experienced them and the others who follow. A catastrophe, disaster, or set of events of this stature often involves a terrible rupture in being as well as in a milieu, community, family, or network. A surrogate frame may be helpful if it repositions

1 Vincent Crapanzano, *The Harkis: The Wound That Never Heals* (Chicago: Chicago University Press, 2011); and Didier Fassin and Richard Rectman, *Empire of Trauma: An Inquiry into the Condition of Victimhood* (Princeton: Princeton University Press, 2009).

harm away from victim production. Ghastly injury and memories may remain, suffering, disability, forgetting too, but the very process of reframing may bring human wits, creativity, and generative discord to the fore.

Has a *spectral frame* – feeling haunted – always been kind, capacious, and just toward those living in post-conflict settings, whether in a here and now or over longer durations? The word *aftermath* flattens and encumbers, as does the pair *event-aftermath*. Not all conflict or mass violence is the same. How wounds from a previous generation may weigh on children and grandchildren contains much of interest. Yet if we unpack the ghostly, the eerie, and the spectral in transgenerational hauntings, if we allow for the suffering or the disturbed to forge social links, such contacts may enable breaking into reconnections and afterlives. And here is a starkly different word from *aftermath*.

Françoise Davoine and Jean-Max Gaudillière devised a clinical method aimed at discerning broken social links among those striving to heal wounds following violence and conflict. Marianne Hirsh speaks of similar matters through visual sources and her concept of post-memory generations. The differentiation between first-person survivor memories – whether spoken or unspoken – and the next generation's sense of things matters. In interviews with serial female migrants, Valerie Walkerdine developed a method for working with stories, attending to embodied manifestations of complex experiences associated with slavery, colonialism, poverty and migration. Importantly, her aim was 'a mode of working which did not pathologize'. Instead, it dissolved, while she 'recognized the transmission of suffering and distress,' while noting complex 'twists and turns across generations'. This interest in intergenerational transmission goes with a politics that glimpses refractory sites of power. It aims to 'radically reject any split' between a 'psychic/personal' and a 'social/historical realm'.[2]

How these two realms are conjoined is vital to any consideration of catastrophe or disaster in history. My contribution lies in an insistence that historians avoid simplistic forms of *event-aftermath* narration, forms that tend to place the injured inside a *trauma box*. The idea is to enable affective and concrete approaches that are open to spirited, feisty, and unruly *afterlives*.

The trouble with the trauma word is not its literary or psychoanalytic uses or meanings, but rather how it may yield ways of reading the archive or engaging subjects in memory mode. How may we detect insurgency, daydreaming, or courage? A different scaffolding, away from that pathologising word trauma, may enable perceiving forms of life, recognition, or dissent. Alternative words may begin with

2 Françoise Davoine and Jean-Max Gaudillière, History beyond Trauma (New York: Other Press, 2004); Marianne Hirsch, *The Generation of Postmemory: Writing and Visual Culture After the Holocaust* (New York: Columbia University, 2011); and Valerie Walkerdine, Aina Olsvold, and Monica Rudberg, 'Researching Embodiment and Intergenerational Trauma using the work of Davoine and Gaudilliere: History walked in the door,' *Subjectivity* 6 (2013): 272-97.

futures or reverie. Sidestepping trauma, whether in narrative, politics, or clinical work, may embolden, letting wits, creativity, and generative discord come to the fore. Trauma as frame may weaken, diminish, or limit, while a surrogate frame may reposition harm and wounds away from pity, with memories remade via forms of alertness, daring, and inspiration.

Genocide, colonial violence, and mass killings harm those who survive, just as catastrophes may come back to life within descendants, generations later. Sometimes persons carry within them an experience they do not understand; one that erupts within them as memories, perhaps of a delirious quality. Still, next generations (or a historian) may rework these memories and traces, less as sensation or narrative of paralysing trauma, than as urgent matters excellent to rework. One only needs to think of the near epidemic of rape in South Africa to sense violent hypermasculinity erupting as madness, mediated by a history of brutal, racialised reduction. But it is also important to move beyond the brutalities and madness, to consider the individual and collective refigurations surfacing out of layers of catastrophe.

There is no denying the theoretical power of the word *trauma*. It opens up matters of repetition, harm, and the eerie across time and generations. The problem is that all too often a heuristic (in narrative and historical writing) or a diagnosis (in a clinical context) takes over, flattening available interpretative schemes. A *trauma frame* has not always been kind or just to those living in post-conflict settings, whether in the here and now or over long durations. As a diagnostic category, trauma tends to fix persons and subjects, as if locking them down.

Calling for trauma to be used more capaciously, the remainder of this paper turns to two Congolese examples, widely separated in time: a time of atrocities and death in the 1900s and a time of a new trauma-focused psychological technologies in the 2000s amid Congo's Kivu warzones.

Not aftermath

A Nervous State is the title of my work in history that interweaves war, healing, and rape, as well as the festive.[3] Its context begins with the strongly violated region of King Leopold's Congo (1885-1908), which produced 'shock'-mutilation photographs still seen worldwide. Death and rape were rife in one region in the 1900s: southern Equateur. Moods and metrics followed in the Belgian Congo (1908-1960), suggesting a low birth rate, widespread barrenness, and remedial forms of development.

It is important to ask: Who was witnessing what, when, and how, and who was able to act as a witness, and in what capacities, through what kinds of media and venues, and for whom? What happens to Congolese suffering, perceptions, and dissent in

3 Nancy Rose Hunt, *A Nervous State: Violence, Remedies and Reverie in Colonial Congo* (Durham: Duke University Press, 2016).

the process? Who felt the weight of painful pasts in Equateur from the 1910s on? Congolese in this region did not forget. Songs signalling awareness of an older rubber-working generation tell that some of the mutilated were still present and visible, noticed, and heard. A priest organised an essay contest, alert to the kinds of memories that would come in. These essays in the Lomongo language had many authors in 1953–54. Congolese wrote down accounts some 40–50 years after the terrible violence that beset this area, which resembled a warzone in the 1890s-1900s. The priest asked late colonial subjects, in sum, 'to name the disaster'.[4] Some wrote about charms, or a suicidal white man with contested, music-making *fanfare* though also baskets filled high with smoked human hands. Many wrote as if past events were legible, detailing battles, massacres, rape, and mutilation. Some regretted Mongo reproductive troubles as a consequence of ongoing colonial hardships. Quite a few compared past and present, using the occasion to critique the colonial production of suffering during the Second World War. A wartime return to rubber collecting had been as bad, some accused, as what their parents and grandparents endured during the time since known as that of 'red rubber'.

My historical narrative avoids traumatic, event-aftermath logic. It instead tackles a range of perplexities in relation to colonial extinction fantasies, guilt, harsh labour regimes, and also economies of pleasure. To do so, it mines security, poetic, acoustic, and visual sources, whether produced by state agents, missionaries, doctors, travellers (Roger Casement to Graham Greene), or Congolese literati, along with song and memory texts. A two-faced heuristic of a biopolitical state sand a nervous state culminates with a developmentalist infertility clinic and a securitising penal colony. The heuristic ensures that epidemics come to the fore, along with vernacular and securitising dynamics, beside much therapeutic insurgency and its policing besides. The two bleeds by the close, when motion of the imagination and the body emerges as a set of diagnostics by which to sense Congolese autonomy, energy, and deeds.

A narration that simply went from event to aftermath would distort; it would also overlook much. Novel concepts in A Nervous State that evade trauma include Canguilhem's shrunken milieu and latitude, Bachelard's reverie, yet also Balandier's pointing at colonialism itself pathological. Historiographically, the way histories of imperial medicine have been limited to the biopolitical is rejected. Africanist public healing may be widened to practices of making war and making joy within everyday life with mobile religious movements organised around charms.

Everyday privations fuelled daydreaming in reverie. A spectrum ranging from violation to enchantment returned more than once, whether in cut-off body parts in war tactics, monstrous ogre tales, or a battered wife meeting the sounds of feuding within a song, or a stolen baby and its fictional birth. With layers of perceptibility, *A*

4 Maurice Blanchot, *The Writing of the Disaster* (Lincoln: University of Nebraska Press, 1986), 4.

Nervous State aspires to suggest a history of a mood. Nervousness *evokes*. It unfastens dispositions, like bitterness, wonder, dread, even joy. In making health embrace dance and distraction, pleasure, fashion, urbanity, and sexual economies bleed into this interpretation of energetic afterlives in one iconic imperial region.

Colonial nervousness morphed and grew in all kinds of directions. The book enters into matters of mental health while hardly mentioning the term. In jettisoning notions of aftermath, attention turns to sensory registers instead. The narrative strategy insists on going beyond *certain* knowledge about the past: there is much we cannot know or that bore no retrievable trace. The insistence is on wonder, on telling micronarratives with a spilling forth of details that found their way into a state, missionary, or memory archive. Hints of laughter, terror, dread, amusement, and nervousness surface.

My conceptual and narrative choices emerged as traces from a post-conflict situation in the Belgian Congo. A fresh scaffolding, with other categories and points of view, enabled Congolese subjects to emerge well outside of victim categories. There is a method to the links made between threads, subjects, and situations. I muse at length over order and duration. There is a trajectory about visual and other forms of witnessing that links with memory, forgetting, traumatic form, and emotions; it goes with 'trauma' – feeling scared, anxious, guilty, even numb.

What is the importance of avoiding a trajectory or words of trauma in writing such a history of violence? *A Nervous State* insists on the value of skirting a narrative arc that would go event | *aftermath* for King Leopold's Congo, a colony replete with terrible rape and mutilations. With religious imaginations at work double-time, dance, song, and possession became vital modes of being. They suggest horizons of expectation as much as traces of pain. I located dissent, recognition, and reverie, a form of imagination and dreaming. The book frames pleasure widely, aligning it with the festive and distraction. The ways places of leisure allowed for anticipation and daydreams pushed historical narration away from a segmented event-aftermath arc, and away from locating next generations of colonial subjects as under the imprint of trauma or within a surfeit of distress.[5]

Global mental health's 'trauma'

Psychological matters were at play in Belgian colonial logics, and interventions came in the form of development projects: better health care and schools in the 1950s. Yet diagnostic categories were rare, while trauma was rarely an explicitly part of vocabularies. If Equateur was a war zone in the 1900s, war zones returned in Congo's eastern Kivu provinces after nearby Rwanda's genocide in 1994. It is interesting to

5 Hunt, *A Nervous State*.

think about how trauma and PTSD have become key words since this time and with what effects.[6] These reflections also call for new kinds of history and anthropology.

Two facts have combined since 1989 to make a history of mental health in Africa urgent. First, the continent became a place of war, trauma, and humanitarianism and in global eyes. Images of suffering coincided with the arrival of new expertise from the North. Secondly, Global Mental Health (GMH) emerged as a major movement and industry. It is still wending its way into Africa's slums, gated communities, and clinical trials. The gulf between rich and poor may be seen in patterns of resort and arrangements for becoming research subjects. Such contemporary forms may be rendered as zones. If one tracks websites and global mental health meetings – peering in on specialists working in Africa, many of them African – one may determine potential field sites. Current patterns in the mobility of expertise, the instrumentalities of research, and social inequalities often had colonial counterparts.

What was *new* in this 1990s trauma-focused phase of mental health expertise and programming was the reliance on one diagnosis – PTSD – while providing kinds of psychosocial care. This neoliberal, humanitarian era was mixed up with weak states, shadow economies, war, and myriad NGOs. A second difference was that most *trauma talk* in the 1990s and 2000s went alongside human rights and efforts to alleviate social suffering. Many of those labelled as traumatized underwent brutal violence. All of this was so for countless women raped under war conditions in eastern Congo since 1996. This same space became a humanitarian zone, and a good share of assistance came in as psychosocial care.

Through its creation, archiving, and transnational circulation, the diagnostic object, PTSD, may make trauma and mental illness legitimate within an immediate clinical encounter and for global policy audiences. It also produces new categories of subjects, whether a young psychiatric patient or say a 'problem' street child. PTSD also figures potential political crisis, in and through the subjects imagined on the verge of crisis.

Global mental health is creating a new diagnostic culture with effects, with some subjects becoming consumers or recipients of *psy* care while also coming to understand their bodies, health, and states of being through care received in clinical sites. They participate in global processes as they engage trained, expatriate, and national humanitarian mental health experts. The 1990s was a decade when the terms *trauma* and *psychosocial* entered into discussions of all manner of new developments on the continent, from the Truth and Reconciliation Commission, in South Africa, to the genocide and its consequences in Rwanda, and difficulties for refugees and others

6 Allan Young, 'Posttraumatic Stress Disorder of the Virtual Kind,' in *Trauma and Memory: Reading, Healing, and Making Law*, eds. Austin Sarat, Nadav Davidovitch, and Michal Alberstein (Stanford: Stanford University Press, 2007); and Fassin and Rectman, *Empire of Trauma*.

displaced by war. Trauma often emerged in Congolese humanitarian documents, websites, documentary films, and the like.

Global mental health has also generated debates. It is the latest addition to 'global health', wedged as it is between being an entrepreneurial *psy* industry, a new academic field, and new career options. It is somehow an outgrowth of the huge growth of trauma-based psychosocial work done in war and disaster zones since the end of the Cold War. Indeed, GMH seemed a reaction to that decade and a half of work where the psychosocial especially had the upper hand. The field is contested terrain, either seen as salutary or as a new imperial menace. The GMH agenda has attained an immense policy influence, while debates about the universal validity of psychiatry continue in expert circles.

There is surely room for GMH discourses and practice to be reformulated on the ground, but there are few studies of these processes at work. By about 2000, the Congolese emergence of messy, twenty-first-century wars of shadow networks, nasty sexual violence, and securitisation was clear. In 2007, 2010, and again 2019, I discovered that many Congolese I met claimed to feel traumatised, not by rape or war, but by the ubiquity of the word itself. At the same time, the opened doors to services for some (in the Kivus, mostly women) and excluded others (men) struggling with precarity and anger.

Trauma zones

Getting a handle on Africa's trauma zones and their embeddedness in conjoined agendas of humanitarianism and securitisation takes time and patience, while new agendas are announced on a regular basis. A trauma zone is a laboratory of psychological, psychiatric, and PTSD experimentation. These zones are places of war, disaster, and human rights language and claims. What feeds them is not only human need but career ambitions of expatriate and national or local experts from the *psy* sciences.

Where are Africa's trauma zones? We do not yet have a full map or timeline regarding their emergence, but this would be a valuable project in digital geography and digital history for someone. Regardless, it is important to question what is producing and happening inside the world's and the continent's trauma zones today. Do we have a history about the mobility and pathway of PTSD diagnostic use and psychosocial technologies in relation to say Bosnia, Sri Lanka, Sierra Leone, Angola, and South Africa since 1989? I think not, though we need one in relation to global warscapes not only since 1989 but also since the First World War. Interviewing experts who developed psychosocial interventions for the Rwanda-Congo border regions or other zones since 1994 would illuminate.

Wounds are simultaneously political and intimate, and they may fester in terrible ways. Just think of rape in South Africa or in Congo's Kivu provinces. What do social and individual pathologies have to do with violence in a previous generation? If the word *trauma* is there, it is in good part because it has been deployed by experts who arrive from the outside to help, teach, do research, and dispense psychosocial care.

Congo's Kivu region became a zone of war, rape, and of gender experimentations from about 1994 on. All kinds of new medical, 'psychosocial', and 'confessional' technologies have been interjected to mend persons, bodies, and families, and to secure funds for large and small NGOs working as far west as Kisangani. Most rape-related experimentation took place in North and South Kivu, especially in two hospitals I visited in 2010, one in Goma (called Heal Africa), the other now world-famous in Bukavu, the capital of Sud-Kivu Province. Bukavu has at least a quarter of a million people, with another quarter million living in nearby towns and villages. The city is now famous for its Panzi Hospital, whose award-winning director Dr. Denis Mukwege innovated in the way he provided gynaecological care to rape victims. He became famous in humanitarian and global health circles, in the *Economist*, in documentary films and television channels around the world, before receiving the Nobel Prize.

In 2010, these rape hospitals were transferring out a handful or two of women a year to sites of enclosure that also provided medication. Yet for the most part, it seemed worthwhile where the pharmaceutical companies were. While Mukwege and staff were keen to add psycho-pharmaceuticals and psychiatric nursing to treatment protocols and staff training about 2011, it is less clear how far these ideas went.

Yet since the Kivus became a rape zone, it became a place of experimentation with psychosocial treatment modules arriving from Geneva, New York, Uppsala, and Konstanz, Germany. An important result was the parachuting in of expertise from the outside, aimed at knowing and relieving trauma. Experts came from other war and refugee locations in the wider world, where psychosocial technologies had been developed to help large numbers narrate, work through, and cope. By 2010, in the Kivus, psychosocial care became fundamental. So did a gender skewing of the public health system with much resentment building up among men who would say to me: 'we are all traumatised'.

In 2010 Goma and Bukavu, I talked with Swedish, Italian, and American expatriates working in communications, trauma care, and rape hospital administration. One had been in Congo since the 1970s. The others were in their thirties with 1-3 months experience in Congo. Most intriguing were conversations with Congolese and Rwandan psychologists and counsellors, mostly women. Some were lay counsellors, (not unlike the way a TBA is a lay midwife). One Congolese woman psychologist in Goma backed up to her university education in Kisangani in the 1970s, and then came forward to her supervision of dozens of lay rape counsellors in Goma's Heal Africa hospital and its network of rural clinics and waiting houses.

She pulled a series of bound booklets from her shelves; each one had her telling about another segment in her autobiography, often about a European or Kenyan psychologist who introduced a new treatment *module* and its contents. She spoke about how she felt during training sessions. Her pride in being a paid professional was palpable. These conversations suggested that war, gender training, and gender *parité* are producing a small revolution in who may hold what job.

Since about 2004, Narrative Exposure Therapy (NET) became one of the therapeutic technologies to reach Rwanda and Congo. NET psychologists claim to reduce PTSD symptoms among war, refugee, and migrant populations. They involve 'lay counsellors' in therapeutic work. Thus, the subaltern listens and speaks in NET therapy. The idea is to anchor 'hot,' destabilising memories into a 'cold,' firm, coherent, contextualized, and *autobiographical* – also chronological – narrative. At the same time, the therapist's role is to ensure a correct chronology of events.[7]

NET has advocacy and heritage dimensions. Chronology and historicisation tighten within a simplifying, linear grip, it seems, in this experimental practice where the therapist works to 'ensure the correct chronology' of events, while individualizing them, too. The founders aspire to document human rights abuses, reduce 'the silence which often surrounds such painful violent events,' and provide – not unlike many 1970s historians of Africa – 'a voice for the victims'. How all of this works on the ground, away from the scholarly literature praising NET, would be fascinating research. That patients are drawn to the NET method because they may receive a testimonial book as a tangible result of the therapeutic process is telling. It is theirs to keep and share with their children.[8]

The absence of psycho-pharmaceuticals yet the presence of Narrative Exposure Therapy and other inexpensive, apparently quick-acting, cognitive-expressive therapies in Rwanda and eastern Congo calls out for more attention. So do masculine counterpoints in and outside of armies and militias. Some well-planned humanitarian gestures for emasculated, recuperated, perhaps 'traumatised' soldiers suggest that not only women were receiving attention. Without barracks or respectable salaries for troops, and with most money going to separating, housing, helping, and empowering women rape survivors, it is not difficult to see that gender-specific experiments may produce tensions. Men seemed only to receive more emasculation, precarity, and punishment. Women may find forms of empowerment, an Eve Ensler-inspired 'city of

7 Maggie, Schauer, Thomas Elbert, and Frank Neuner, *Narrative Exposure Therapy: A Short-Term Intervention for Traumatic Stress Disorders after War, Terror, or Torture* (Gottingen: Hogrefe & Huber, 2005).

8 Katy Robjant and Mina Fazel, 'The Emerging Evidence for Narrative Exposure Therapy: A Review,' *Clinical Psychology Review* 30 (2010): 1030-39.; and Ulrich Schnyder, et al., 'Psychotherapies for PTSD: What do they have in common?' *European Journal of Psychotraumatology* 6 (2015): 28186-96.

joy', reinsertion kits, and PTSD therapy, but what about men? Perhaps some have been receiving new technologies of the self within some additional kind of psychological pipeline. NET has an advocacy organisation named Vivo with a motto suggesting the key impulses at play: to release 'the victim's voice'.[9] Social and symbolic *capital in suffering* is awkwardly integral to this kind of psychotherapeutic, trauma work.

Conclusion

I have been arguing for an approach to research and clinical interventions that accounts for the porousness and interconnections among the psychic and the social, the historical and the generational. It is a delicate, nuanced approach that takes time, reads for moods, distinguishes social categories, and seeks to sidestep the trauma word.

Personal or historical wounds are often first experienced in connection with a listening other, sometimes before the injuries can even be remembered. People tend to make the best they can of what there remains. A body may remember what is not spoken. What is passed on is largely transmitted through bodies and in affects, wishes, desires, or within modalities of masculinity and femininity. What is passed on may become sedimented into memories, silences, and cultural practices. Still, in a *shrunken milieu,* one may find pleasure, practices of freedom, and active or wrathful imaginations, with daydreaming and futures at the fore. The advantage of reverie is not just temporal, its orientation toward futures rather than pasts. Reverie may enable repair to a subjectivity and social links within collective or individuated daydreaming or healing labours.[10]

Critical engagement of these processes is needed and within various frames. This essay has reacted against the 'trauma turn,' which accompanied the 'social studies of suffering' approach to affliction, misfortune, and violence. Social and symbolic capital in suffering may become hollow or a pernicious game, or it may yield relief or ruses. The global is never a view from nowhere; someone is always presuming or discarding that standpoint, and from within spaces of global mental health among others. A global scale may make specific actors and technologies visible while erasing others, producing hierarchies and inequalities in the process.

Global mental health practices, not unlike histories of catastrophe, need to be sorted and made in relation to such visibilities, erasures, and rankings. The uses of

9 Katharin Hermenau, et al. 'Addressing Post-traumatic Stress and Aggression by Means of Narrative Exposure: A Randomized Controlled Trial with Ex-Combatants in the Eastern DRC,' Journal of Aggression, Maltreatment and Trauma 22 (2013): 1545-083X. See too: F. Neuner, et al. 'Treatment of PTSD by trained lay counselors in an African refugee settlement: A randomized controlled trial.' *Journal of Consulting and Clinical Psychology* 76 (2008): 686-94; S. Schaal, T. Elbert, and F. Neuner, 'Narrative exposure therapy versus interpersonal psychotherapy. A pilot randomized controlled trial with Rwandan genocide orphans. *Psychotherapy and Psychosomatics* 78 (2009): 298-306.

10 Hunt, *A Nervous State.*

Global Mental Health, a still novel experimental kind of research and care, take place on vernacular ground, within everyday lives, and surely always via forms of subterfuge. Are people sometimes domesticating these new so-called global trauma manifestations as their own? If so, let us learn more about when and how. All these aspects need sustained and nuanced examination.

Part I:
Memory and Time

2.
Remembering forwards: Managing the burden of the future after conflict[1,2]

John Brewer

This lecture concerns itself with how we remember and what we remember. Rethinking these things helps us manage the burden of the future after conflict. The burden of the future concerns the problem of how we learn to live together in tolerance despite the divided pasts that continue to live in us. It poses the question of how we can manage a past that always lives in us yet avoid living in that past. How we remember is through an approach I call here 'remembering forwards'; what we remember involves the virtues of truth, tolerance, togetherness and trajectory.

Let me start, however, by reiterating the problems that can arise in post-conflict societies when we only remember backwards and exclude the future.

There is a prosaic truth central to the field of memory studies: conflict is in part constituted by memory. Divided and contested memories are wrapped up in the process of identity formation, which ends up sculpting mutually exclusive identities. Nations, societies and groups have always been defined in part by their collective memories, which disclose images, narratives and representations of the past that assist in constructing moral boundaries and senses of solidarity. Any collectivity is in large measure defined by its shared memories. Where nations, societies and groups are divided within and between themselves, this division is to some degree always constituted by contested memory.

Remembering backwards gives us two maxims for thinking about the past. First, the present is lived through the past. People locate themselves in historical events of which they have no direct remembrance because these travails are foundational to the groups with which they identify, resulting in them being perceived as personal. In this way people can appropriate history to affirm collective affronts and hurts as personal ones, or experience group triumphs as individual achievements and honours.

1 An earlier version was delivered as a plenary lecture to the Church of Ireland Theological Institute and Edgehill Theological College, joint integrated seminar for Anglican and Methodist ordination students, Church of Ireland Theological Institute, Dublin, 17 May 2016.

2 This presentation is being adapted for publication in the forthcoming book, *Post-Conflict hauntings: Re-imagining the ghostly for societies dealing with collective memories of violence and historical trauma*, edited by Kim Wale, Pumla Gobodo-Madikizela and Jeff Prager, published by Palgrave MacMillan.

Secondly, the past is understood through the present. People appropriate selectively from the past in order to comment on current events that dominant their personal concerns and group loyalties, making the past a tool for mobilisation.

From the vantage point of post-conflict societies therefore, remembering backwards can, if not actually invent tradition ex nihilo, falsify actual events, for representational memories can distort and misperceive them, nourishing anger and resentment and encouraging false aggrandisements. It is for these reasons that memory is integrally tied to conflict and for these reasons also that memory can be problematic in peace processes. This defines the 'burden of memory' after conflict, as Soyinka calls it based on work in Sudan, a term reminiscent of Miroslav Volf's idea of 'the end of memory', developed from his reflections on the negative aspects of memory following the Balkan wars. The suggestion that remembering painful and hurting memories of conflict turns memory into a burden forms the basis of David Rieff's popular argument in praise of forgetting, Connerton's sympathetic distinctions between types of forgetting according to their social functions, and Linden and Rutkowski's edited collection on the 'beneficial forgetting' of hurting memories.

The theoretical problem that provokes this lecture, however, is that remembering backwards also distorts the connection between memory and the future. Two problems arise with respect to the future when we only remember backwards. First, continuity between the past, present and future is broken as the actual past is replaced by social and collective memories of the past that are distorted. Secondly, remembering backward by means of social memory can make the past an arbiter of the future burden of the future. It bears saying very strongly therefore, that forgetting is impossible and cannot be a way to deal with the burden of the future. The empty chair at the dinner table, the constraints of the prosthetic limb or wheelchair, the annual painful anniversary, the constant media coverage that makes entertainment or political capital out of victims' pain: these are constant reminders that make forgetting impossible. To forget is to excise from memory; to wipe out and to destroy. You cannot tell a bomb victim, or someone brutally raped to forget; it cannot be excised from memory. Nor should it be; and the memory certainly should not be destroyed. To forget victims is to victimise them twice.

Remembering forward offers an approach to memory that places the past in the context of the future – that is, it offers a way of how to remember, thus dealing with the burden of the future – and an approach to re-imaging the past, that is, to what we remember.

The key to remembering forwards is to deliberately remind oneself not to recall; it is to remember to cease to remember. Failing to remember, in other words, involves a conscious act of remembrance in a way that forgetting does not. It involves memory in a future-oriented act: avoiding repetition of the past by remembering to cease to remember the past. This is what I mean by remembering forwards. It is releasing the memory, not forgetting it; letting go of oppressive and haunting memories so that they no longer have power over the person. It is their hold over us, not the memory itself, which is released by non-remembrance. Remembering forwards is a way in which we can progress to the future while still living without common memories.

Remembering forward, however, is only part of the solution to the burden of the future; we need to rethink the divided memories that will persist into the future. In fleshing out how we might rethink the burden of memory in remembering forwards, there are four features that need to be isolated when re-imagining the enduring divided memories that will persist within remembering forwards. In a fondness for alliteration, I call them truth, tolerance, togetherness and trajectory. These virtues define what people should remember. They are not necessarily easily practised, but they point a way forward.

Change develops at the pace of truth; truth is essential if the burden of the future is to be met and untruth delays the pace of change. Truth, however, is about remembering events as they occurred, not as they are selectively perceived in subsequent symbolic representations of the past. Untruthfulness does an injustice to memory, for as Volf puts it, untruthful memory is unjust memory, and without it, victims can be peripheralised. Accuracy is important for victims, Blustein informs us, because perpetrators and their supporters typically attempt to justify their actions by demeaning victims and falsifying and misrepresenting the past.

Truth, however, must be tempered with tolerance, for evil things actually happen in conflict, as shown in people's torn bodies and torn minds. Tolerance moderates the consequences of truth. Tolerance requires respect for competing narratives and acceptance that others will see these events differently, allowing us to recognise that this selectivity of memory is normal and should not be amplified into sculpting mutually exclusive identities. Tolerance is not about seeing the past through another's standpoint – near nigh impossible in the aftermath of conflict – but accepting that the other's standpoint is as valid to them as yours is to you. Tolerance is about respecting differences rather than eliminating differences.

Tolerance balances truth, but truth and tolerance can be accelerated by togetherness. There are two features of togetherness that are relevant to divided memories; togetherness in the act of remembering the past, and togetherness in what it is that is remembered. Remembering together is a liberating form of memory, for sharing divided memories *together* facilitates acceptance of the other's standpoint and encourages the tolerance I have just advocated.

Another part of togetherness, however, also concerns what it is that is remembered. The past can be excavated for 'joint remembrances' as I have called them elsewhere;

that is, historical events that exemplify togetherness rather than apartness. Joint remembrances describe historical events that we can now see were shared rather than separated, reflecting common experiences rather than divided ones.

Truth, tolerance and togetherness, however, all need to be contextualised by trajectory. Trajectory is about looking forwards rather than backwards. What we remember and how public commemorations are practised should reflect that we all have to inherit a shared society in the future. Remembering in ways that keep us in the past will only delay that future. Trajectory is about remembering to cease to remember the divisiveness and contentiousness of disputed memories, reminding us not to live in the past but to remember the future. It is precisely this trajectory that distinguishes what I have called remembering forwards.

3.
Scars, marked bodies, and suffering: The Mulele 'Rebellion' in postcolonial Congo[1]

Emery Kalema[2]

> *Papa, [in 1970], when I came out of the bush, the first thing I had to ask for when I got in Kikwit was a mirror. I did not want people to continue telling me stuff about my scars I wanted to see with my own eyes what my face had become ... I wanted to see myself and understand I asked for a big mirror. Not only that I wanted to see my face, I also wanted to see my back and all the marks that my back was carrying. In the bush, people used to tell me. But I was sick of them always talking about me. ... This time, I wanted to see myself and understand. ... I wanted to have a clear idea of what my body had become in its entirety. ... After locking myself into the house, I took off my clothes. ... Papa, it was horrible. I assure you that it was horrible to see my face in the mirror. ... People used to tell me, but now I could see for myself what my face had become I did not believe at all that it was me, Kitoto. ... I could see scratches all over my back. ... On my buttocks, you cannot even describe. Besides, you can see how scars abound on my legs, just to show you these ones.*[3]

These are the memories of Eugène Kitoto, an 82-year-old man I first met in November 2013 in Kikwit, a town 500 km east of Kinshasa in the Congo. In 1964, he was arrested by the *militaires* during the Mulele Rebellion. He was shot in the cheek. Some of his nerves were affected and, as a result, he does not speak well. Apart from the shooting, Kitoto was badly beaten by the same *militaires*.[4] They cut his testicles off and burned

1 This paper was subsequently published in the *Journal of African History*, 59:2, (2018), pp263-82.

2 I am grateful to Achille Mbembe, Catherine Burns, Eric Worby, Maria Suriano, Pumla Gobodo-Madikizela, Ruth Sacks, and two anonymous reviewers for *The Journal of African History* for their enormously helpful comments on earlier drafts of this article. I also wish to thank the Ford Foundation for a PhD scholarship awarded through the Wits Institute for Social and Economic Research (WiSER) at the University of the Witwatersrand. This scholarship made the research for this article possible. Lastly, I would like to thank the Mellon Foundation for a Postdoctoral Fellowship, and the National Research Foundation, both of which allowed me to undertake the revision work at the Studies in Historical Trauma and Transformation Unit at Stellenbosch University.

3 Interview with Eugène Kitoto, Kikwit, 7 Aug. 2015.

4 The Congolese/Zairian Army responsible for the atrocities described in this article grew out of the colonial Force *Publique* and came into being as the enforcers of the 'red rubber' regime under King Leopold II and the colonial project more broadly. See A. Hochschild, *King Leopold's Ghost: A Story of Greed, Terror, and Heroism in Colonial Africa* (Boston, 1999); J.-J. Wondo Omanyundu, *Les armées au Congo-Kinshasa: Radioscopie de la Force Publique aux FARDC* (Saint-Légier, 2013).

them. They mixed them with water and forced him to drink the mixture. The morbid spectacle of his being cut up, thus, was an indication of the transition of human being into animal, meat, and nothingness. The fragments of testimonies he provides are painful, full of emotion, and regret. To a large extent, they shed light on the new form of life that took shape when disruptions and reductions – aiming to reduce everything that was corporeal to 'pieces, fragments, folds', and wounds difficult to seal – were introduced into the continuousness of the corporeal. It is this new form of life, which I deliberately call the life of scars, which constitutes the subject of this article.

The Mulele Rebellion was a guerrilla war. It was led by Pierre Mulele and his companions in the Kwilu region – and beyond – between 1963 and 1968. Pierre Mulele was one of the founders of the Parti Solidaire Africain (PSA), established in 1959, and served as the Minister of National Education for the Lumumba government from July 1961. He was violently murdered after being tortured by the Congolese Army in October 1968.[5]

Destabilised in the Congo's violent nineteenth century, the groups most implicated in the Mulele Rebellion were subject to colonial violence relating to the Unilever plantations, where coercion was used to secure wage labour for what was then the largest palm oil exporter in the world, with Kwilu being William Lever's 'brutal' state – within a state.[6] The area supported politicians from the 'radical nationalist' pro-Lumumba faction who won the elections at independence in 1960 – but who were then pushed out of power in a Western-backed coup.[7] The aim of the rebellion, which broke out during Cold War, was to reconquer the Congolese state from what the rebels called 'Belgian neo-colonial domination'.[8] This form of 'neo-colonialism', which in the view of the rebels was more insidious than traditional colonial rule, operated through Congolese intermediaries.[9]

Over the past years, academic research in the fields of body and disability have shown how scars – or effects on the body, following a gruesome treatment of the latter – may become sites of alternative readings: that of resistance through memorialisation and commemoration, as well as a potential currency for reading one's experiences as righteous.[10] Inspired mostly by the Foucauldian notion of the 'body as the inscribed surface of events', a number of these research projects have treated scars and marks as

5 See L. Martens, *Pierre Mulele ou la seconde vie de Lumumba* (Bruxelles, 1985).

6 See J. Marchal, *Lord Leverhulme's Ghosts: Colonial exploitation in the Congo* (London, 2008).

7 A.-R. Ilunga and B. Kalonji, 'Les événements du Kwilu', Etudes Congolaises, 6:3 (1964), 8-9; I. Ndaywel è Nziem, *Histoire générale du Congo: de l'héritage ancient à la République Démocratique du Congo* (Bruxelles, 1998), 610-19.

8 S. Kiangu, *Le Kwilu à l'épreuve du pluralism identitiare* (1948-1968) (Paris, 2009), 228.

9 Ibid.

10 See E. Cole, *Theorizing the disfigured body: Mutilation, amputation, and disability in post-conflict Sierra Leone* (Trenton, NJ, 2014); T. Meyer-Fong, *What Remains: Coming to terms with Civil War in Nineteenth-Century China* (Stanford, 2013).

a text – that is, a character, something that can be read, a site from where narratives can emerge – or a 'fixed sign of identity'.[11]

My goal in this article is not to reiterate these works on scars and marked bodies; but to show the signifying capacity of scars, their relationship not only with the body but also with time, the arresting of time, and the annihilation of future time.[12]

The central argument that drives my analysis is that the scars that people bear on their bodies can produce or reproduce suffering in the *longue durée*, as long as those who bear them live. To be tortured during the Mulele Rebellion in the 1960s was unimaginably terrible. But the suffering did not stop there. There was something beyond that, something even more important that caused a kind of psychic suffering that not only exceeded the physical, but also extended across time.[13] In what follows, I will demonstrate this by discussing first the production and reproduction of suffering in relation to the body, the self, the image of the self, and the gaze of others. In the second part of the article, I will take up these themes in relation to time (the future past), the arresting of time, and the annihilation of future time.

Living with scars: self, image, others, and suffering

To live with the scars of the rebellion is to permanently live in a state of self-questioning, or self-interrogation, about the transformations that the body has undergone. It means, to a large extent, continuously and critically looking at one's body as a shapeless mass that has undergone a series of mutilations and destructions,

11 R. Samolsky, *Apocalyptic futures: Marked bodies and the Violence of the text in Kafka, Conrad, and Coetzee* (New York, 2011), 11,13. See also P. Brooks, *Body work: Objects of desire in modern narrative* (Cambridge, 1993); Cole, Theorizing; R. Garland-Thomson, *Extraordinary bodies: figuring physical disability in American culture and literature* (New York, 1997); and T. Hollander and B. Gill, 'Every day the war continues in my body: examining the marked body in postconflict Northern Uganda', *The international journal of transitional justice*, 8:2 (2014), 1–18.

12 The materials that form the core of this article are fragments of words. They are fragments of evidence. One of the questions this kind of evidence raises is: what kind of interpretation does one get from them? The interpretation one can get from fragments can only be fragmentary. Fragments do not allow for total interpretation. Ultimately, the knowledge that one can build from them will, out of necessity, be an incomplete kind of knowledge, a position that needs to be embraced as such.

This should not be considered a lack, but the most logical approach. My interpretation of these fragments comes from a close reading of them. This attempt at close reading builds from theoretical insights gained from the work of Jean-Paul Sartre, Jean Luc Nancy, Sabine Melchior-Bonnet, Jean-Pierre Vernant, Reinhardt Koselleck, Jacques Derrida, Walter Benjamin, Nancy Rose Hunt, Achille Mbembe, and Martin Heidegger. These fragments of words come from a series of interviews I conducted with witnesses and survivors of the rebellion in Kinshasa, Kikwit, and Idiofa in 2013 and 2015.

13 The analysis proposed in this article could be useful to think about – and understand – (among others) the long-term personal, emotive, and temporal effects of mutilations in other contexts, in Africa and elsewhere.

in order to grasp the nature of the terrifying act that led to these bodily reductions.[14] As many people from the contested region remembered, this is what was happening in everyday life, both during the rebellion as well as after it had ended, and stability had returned.

> This is exactly what we experienced ... My cousin, a very grown and strong man, was arrested by the *militaires* on the night of [30 June 1964]. They cut off his right arm from here [elbow]. ... And then, they cut off his left hand ... One can only imagine the kind of trouble he went through! ... I can see how he was howling that day. It was not different from the howling of a beast ... All the time we spent in the bush, he could not stop looking at himself... Whenever we got somewhere after many hours of wandering, he would prefer to withdraw and be alone... He would constantly raise the stumps of his arms and look at them. It was painful. One could read the pain on his face... At the end of the rebellion, he could not do anything. He would stay in the village from morning to night, regretting all the time... One day, after having looked at his arms, he turned to me and asked me sadly: 'What did I do to deserve all of this? ... Is there anyone out there who can give me a clear explanation?' Papa, looking at his body and asking himself a bunch of questions had become his new life. As he could not bear the pain and the humiliation anymore, he died prematurely in 1968.[15]

But, to have a look over one's own body is more than this gesture of self-questioning. In *Being and nothingness*, Jean-Paul Sartre states that this gesture requires one 'to stand' in front of someone or something that is being questioned, interrogate this person or thing about his or 'its ways of being' and, based on a 'pre-interrogative familiarity' with this person or this thing, 'expect' an unveiling of his/'its being' or his/'its way of being'.[16]

To have to look at one's own body means turning this body into an object of knowledge and creating a discourse on it. It implies rejecting how others represent one's body, even when one knows that in situations such as these, where one cannot see the deformities of his/her own body, one has to rely on others to describe these deformities; or, as Jacques Lacan states, 'the image of my body passes necessarily through the one imagined in the gaze of the other'.[17]

---

14 Telephone interview with Balingite Osam, Kikwit-Idiofa, 8 Aug. 2015; telephone interview with Evariste Nzonzele, Kikwit-Idiofa, 8 Aug. 2015; telephone interview with Palmie Andiang, Kikwit-Idiofa, 8 Aug. 2015; telephone interview with Placide Ngay, Kikwit-Idiofa, 8 Aug. 2015; and interview with Adolphe Kuma, Kikwit Sacré Coeur, 6 Aug. 2015.

15 Interview with Georgine Mankieta, Kikwit Sacré Coeur, 6 Aug. 2015. See also interview with Adolphe Kuma; interview with Ernest Kiangu, Kinshasa, 14 Dec. 2015.

16 J.-P. Sartre, *Being and Nothingness: An essay on Phenomenological Ontology*, trans. H. E. Barnes (Secaucus, 1956), 4-5.

17 Lacan, cited in S. Melchior-Bonnet, *The mirror: A History*, trans. K. H. Jewett (New York, 2001), 6.

Looking at one's own body also means confirming for oneself that bodily disruptions are concrete and cannot be restored by adding up the individual parts of one's body that others – those who look at me – describe. Looking finally means that one can only accept the gravity or profundity of the reductions introduced to the body's natural life when one can see these disruptions oneself.

This opens the question of how one can assess the disruptions introduced to one's body while one is unable to see these disruptions oneself. How does one make the disruptions of one's body an object of consideration when one is unable to see them? How does one get a clear idea of the disruptions when one is deprived of the faculty that would enable one to grasp their essence? These are fundamental questions that most of the people who experienced violent disruptions to the continuity of their bodies posed to themselves in the years after the rebellion. A woman from Banda, whose uncle's body underwent a series of mutilations in Mukulu in 1965, remembered this questioning:

> He was arrested at night. The *militaires* waited until the first rays of the sun to dissect him... They stabbed his right thigh with the bayonet. The man began to shout... They seized his right eye. They stabbed it with their bayonet. We were standing in front of the *militaires*, [who were] watching and applauding how they were dissecting my uncle. ... They seized him again. They gave him a blow of the bayonet in the left eye. There was blood... After all of this, they decided to release him. They asked him to run away... How could he run away while he could not see anymore? ... It was so sad ... The man lay down on the ground. His body was covered with blood... He could barely speak... After the departure of the *militaires*, he tried to open his mouth and speak, but he could not. You could tell that the man was deeply racked by pain. In the following months he would ask himself: "Oh the world, why?... Why me? How could they take everything away from me? Even my own body, I cannot see it anymore." It was hard. He would not let anyone tell him anything about his body. He died five months later because of the pain.[18]

All these questions – the ones this man was asking himself as well as those I raised above – have two implications. Firstly, they led the subjects to reject any mediation or evaluation by others, as they considered the comments as nothing more than the product of the others' construction. Phrases such as: 'I did not want people to continue telling me stuff about my scars'; or 'I wanted to see with my own eyes what my face had become'; or 'Please stop bothering me with your words, I cannot even see what you are talking about' all illustrate this rejection of mediation by others.[19]

18 Interview with Marie Nzamba, Kikwit, 9 Aug. 2015.
19 Interview with Eugène Kitoto, 7 Aug. 2015; interview with Marie Nzamba.

Secondly, these questions led the subjects to search for tools that could help them receive a visual image of themselves and thus make this mediation unnecessary. Hence there was an increasing desire of victims to have access to a mirror.[20] But, what would happen in front of this polished and metallic glass, believed able to capture what one really looks like and place it in front of oneself? To use Achille Mbembe's vocabulary, it is precisely the 'divorce between seeing and touching', 'a discrepancy, a gap between the subject and his/her representation, a space of intrusion and dissonance between the subject and its fictitious double [double fictive, in French] represented by the shade' that these women and men experienced in front of their mirrors.[21] Kitoto's fragments of testimony, which highlight how he saw a new geography of his body represented through the mirror, are evocative of this. The most difficult part of the engagement with the mirror was, however, confronting the image that appeared in it and its surprising and appalling appearance. The moment when the subjects step in front of the mirror, appearances were transcended. The subjects went beyond the boundaries between sight and touch and reached a point where their psyches cast aside their corporeality.[22] They questioned the images in front of them and tried to grasp the reality that the image in front of them seemed to suggest.[23]

> Papa, ... I was surprised when I saw the scratches all over my back. I could not believe that it was me. I thought it was someone else [tears] People used to tell me, but it is only when I looked at myself in the mirror that I came to understand what I went through. ... My cheeks were completely distorted. The scars from the stitches were still there. You can see them, can't you? It was terrible. I remember spending hours and hours in front of the mirror. I was crying. I was saying to myself: "If only I could change what I see into something else!" Papa, I could not stop wondering if what I saw in the mirror was me. I could not believe. It was so painful for me.[24]

We can see how the process of self-examination could also become an act of self-torture. However, the images that the subjects saw in the mirror surprised them. This surprise lies, essentially, in the monstrous character of the image. Yet it also goes beyond this monstrous character. 'The image', writes Jean-Luc Nancy, 'disputes the presence of the thing. In the image, the thing is not content simply to be; the

20 Usually, during the rebellion, people used to look at their reflections in water when they wanted to carry out self-examination. Bathing, under these conditions, became a moment of self-torture. Those who had no injuries on their bodies would splash into the stream without hesitation, while those with bodily disruptions would stop for a moment to look at their reflections to see if the wound was healed or not. Interview with Ernest Kiangu.

21 A. Mbembe *Critique de la raison nègre* (Paris, 2013), 202-03. See also F. Frontisi-Ducroix and J.-P. Vernant, Dans l'œil du miroir (Paris, 1997), 222–4.

22 On this phenomenon, see J. Starobinski, The Living Eye, trans. A. Goldhammer (Cambridge, MA, 1989), 4.

23 A reality whose reading was hitherto only possible through the mediation of the other.

24 Interview with Eugène Kitoto, 7 Aug. 2015.

image shows *that* the thing is and *how* it is. The image is what takes the thing out of its simple presence and brings it to pre-sence, to *praes-entia*, to being-out-in-front-of-itself ... The image is of the order of the monster ... [I]t is outside the common sphere of presence because it is the display of presence. It is the manifestation of presence, not as appearance, but as exhibiting, as bringing to light and setting forth'.[25] But the image of Kitoto's deformed body, and his encounter with this image, is of a qualitatively greater and different degree than an encounter with any image, as he, himself, shows in this testimony:

> I spent hours and hours in front of the mirror... Thoughts began to multiply inside of me when I saw the image of myself in the mirror... What could I do?... I was crying. I could not believe that... The hardest part was when I looked between my thighs. I came to understand that I had become worthless ... I held my [penis]... I raised it. ... I looked at it through the mirror. Papa, what a pain! It was terrible. I hit my hands against each other... It is true that when I was in the bush, I would touch my scrotum and my genitals.... But in front of the mirror, things were different... I could see that my scrotum had lost its [normal form]... I could not stop thinking about what the *militaires* had done to me.[26]

The surprise caused by what the subjects saw in the materiality of their mirrors was also because their reflections brutally interrupted the ignorance in which they had hitherto been able to live with regards to their bodily deformations.[27] And yet, while disturbing and troubling the subjects, the images also revealed some truths. As the testimonies above show, the truths revealed by the images were unsettling and shocking insofar as they only came out of themselves to harm. This is what Kitoto points out:

> I was completely horrifed... Even though my [consciousness] reminded me all the time that it was me, still I could not believe that [the image] I saw [in the mirror] was me. ... Tears were spilling from my eyes. ... [Having a look between my legs] reminded me more than once that it was over. My marital life had no more meaning. A man without [testicles], was he still worth? ... I cried out: "Oh [my testicles], you are [now] gone! I will no longer have you."... Papa, I cried out. I asked myself: "The *militaires*, why did you cut my [testicles] off? ... Why? And yet you had already stabbed me everywhere, why could not you just leave me my [testicles]?"[28]

25 J.L. Nancy, *The Ground of the Image*, trans. J. Fort (New York, 2005), 21-2.
26 Interview with Eugène Kitoto, 7 Aug. 2015.
27 J.-L. Nancy, *Being Singular Plural*, trans. R. D. Richardson and A. E. O'Byrne (Stanford, 2000), 171–2.
28 Interview with Eugène Kitoto, 7 Aug. 2015.

The most striking element in this process of revealing the truth is the way in which Kitoko recounted scrutinizing his body as something alien, something strange, something over which he had no power; and, in the process of this self-examination, talking to parts of himself, to fragments, to his genitals: 'Oh... you are gone!' Of course, it is common among men to experience the penis as a self-animated subject, distinct, and autonomous from the body that bears it. But here Kitoto described it as a lost possession and an autonomous subject worthy of address, one whose gratuitous, inexplicable destruction at the hands of the *militaires* rendered him without 'worth'. This, as we can see, has some bearing on the question of the 'wholeness' and partibility of one's body as an object of examination by oneself.[29]

The image that the subject perceived through the materiality of his mirror, in which the body appeared in all its nakedness, reminded him that the body has been separated from its original form. It has undergone a becoming, a 'radical metamorphosis.'[30] It has become something else, something other than what it previously had been. Hence the shock, regret, loss of will, and negativity that is evident in the above testimonies. The same image that the subject saw in the mirror revealed the marks that a violent person, in this case the *militaire*, wanted to see on the body he attacked.[31] It revealed to the subject how this violent person was only preoccupied with seeing the externalization of the interiority of life principle;[32] and how, through this act of externalization, the same violent person wanted to grasp hold of death, not by looking steadily and intently 'into emptiness of the depths but ... by filling his eyes with red ... and with the clots [of blood] in which life suffers and dies'.[33] Kitoto remembers this double act of externalization of the interiority of life principle and appropriation of death by the *militaires:*

> When I saw my face in the mirror, I was shocked. My mouth opened widely, I suddenly remembered the young man that the *militaires* killed like an animal in Lutshima.[34]
>
> Instead of killing him far away, they preferred to kill him in the presence of his father. They took the bayonet. They began to stab the child. The child fled. They ran after him. They caught him. They opened his eyes widely. Two blows of the bayonet into the right eye: '*kiek, kiek*'. The eye burst. Blood flowed. They grabbed him again. They bayoneted him at the neck,

29 Here, of course, it is a question of gender/sexuality as indexed by parts of the body. This relates to literature on mastectomy following breast cancer. See, for example, S. L. Jain, 'Cancer butch', *Cultural Anthropology*, 22:4 (2007), 501–38.

30 On this concept of radical metamorphosis, see C. Malabou, *The Wounded: From Neurosis to Brain Damage*, trans. S. Miller (New York, 2012).

31 Nancy, *The Ground*, 20.

32 Ibid. 24

33 Ibid. 24-5

34 Interview with Eugène Kitoto, 7 Aug. 2015.

> 'kiek, kiek'. They began to turn the bayonet [in the neck of the child]. They moved the bayonet. The child shouted: 'Ah, ah, *munu!*' They pulled the bayonet out [from the neck of the child]. They gave him another blow to the chest, 'kiek, kiek'. Over. The child gave up his soul [*azenga ntima*, in Kikongo].[35]

> I was horrified. I could see how the bayonet blows would make the young man urinate. It was painful to remember all of this.[36]

This is where the obsession with looking at one's own image in the mirror could lead. But more than that, the image that the subject perceives through the materiality of his mirror revealed to him how violence alters, shatters, and annihilates that which it attacks;[37] and how the same violence, once it has intruded the body, carries off the shape and significance of that which it has assaulted, and transforms it, in Nancy's words, 'into nothing other than a sign of its own rage, assaulted or violated thing or being ... whose very essence now consists in its having been assaulted or violated'.[38]

> It [the image] also reminded me of [those terrible moments] when the militaires came towards me and caught me.[39]

> They took the bayonet. They wanted to kill me with the bayonet. I said to their leader: "Pardon, Lieutenant Nguya. I am begging you. Please shoot me. Don't kill me with your bayonet". The *militaire* replied: "No, you spent so much time deciding. You must die by bayonet as your comrades were. If you do not want to, you will die 'suffocated' like ... the other recalcitrants [have been killed].... The weapons will [only] [help] to kill Mulele. But you, you must die by bayonet". They decided to kill me. They asked me to pass ahead. They tied me up. I was shaking. They shot. The bullet penetrated my cheek. Then, it came out on the other side. ... I was bleeding. They left me naked. I managed to flee... I [reached ...] a village called Yongo ... My heart was overheating... Everyone was laughing at me as I was naked... It was painful. I [cried out] and regretted having been born.[40]

On reading these testimonies, one can see how images from the past, which the subject would not want to remember, are being crystallised again and again in his memory. But the same image in the mirror, that raised so many questions and thoughts in the subject, reminded him that violence, which unexpectedly intruded his body, is only 'stupidity'. It is 'stupidity' for, once it has intruded the body, it does

35 Interview with Eugène Kitoto, Kikwit, 1 Nov. 2013.
36 Interview with Eugène Kitoto, 7 Aug. 2015.
37 Nancy, *The ground, 16.*
38 Ibid
39 Interview with Eugène Kitoto, 7 Aug. 2015.
40 Interview with Eugène Kitoto, 1 Nov. 2013.

not want to substitute anything else other than itself.[41] Violence owns the body that it has invaded, and imprints itself on it. Instead of leaving those marks free, it assigns them new functions, that of producing and reproducing suffering.[42] A focus on the fragments of memories of those who experienced the relentless desire of violence, which makes it exclusively preoccupied with its own overwhelming obtrusion, can help to have a better understanding of how, in the longue durée, these marks imprinted on the bodies fulfilled this role of the production and reproduction of suffering assigned to them.[43]

> If I am miserable today, it is because of what the *militaires* did to me... When I came out of the bush [in 1970], it was very difficult for me... At the time, Mobutu did not want people to speak about the rebellion anymore. Talking about my injuries to strangers was really a problem. Whenever I was in front of a stranger, I would lie about the cause of my injuries, because you never know... I was a man of pride when I was born. But, today, I am worthless.... I am now the object of mockery for everyone because of what the *militaires* did to me. My voice, I no longer have it. And it has been years now. Along the way, people make fun of me... They say to me: "Look at this 'mute' [*espèce de muet]* walking up and down." 'Mute' is the name they gave me because of my voice. When I tell them that I have not always been so, no one understands me. When they begin to laugh at me, you have no idea! And when I see all of this, pain and sorrow multiply in me. Even when I politely tell them that I was not born with these deformities, nobody understands me. On the contrary, they laugh out loud at me. This is what I have been experiencing – and still experience – for years... It is painful![44]

Hence, to seize 'bodies' during the rebellion, to torture these 'bodies' until they are marked is to expose these 'bodies' to the perpetual renewal of humiliation, and to crush them into subjectivity across time. It is also to render the mobility of these people vulnerable within a political regime that is essentially preoccupied with liquidating its enemies. By grafting tightly on the skin, the marks imprinted on people's bodies automatically linked them to politics. This was particularly the case in the Mobutu regime, which, as the testimonies above suggest, often understood the scars imprinted on a body to suggest that its bearer had been part of the rebellion. The scars could thus lead to the arrest of an entire 'body' as they betrayed the bearer. People bearing scars could be dragged before military courts and condemned to a

41 Nancy, *The ground, 16*

42 After having seen his image in the mirror, Kitoto said: 'I concluded that the militaires cannot be anything else than dogs. They are... idiots. All they know is to destroy. ... They do not care about the consequences of their actions'. Interview with Eugène Kitoto, 7 Aug. 2015.

43 Nancy, *The ground, 16.*

44 Interview with Eugène Kitoto, 7 Aug. 2015.

violent death. They could be hanged in public, in front of everyone, without mercy.[45] The *raison d'être* of power during the Mobutu regime was decidedly *nervous*. It could get into the bodies of its subjects with extraordinary intensity. Once in the bodies, it would place the subjects in threatening and defenceless situations and produce in them various kinds of sensations.[46] This could go 'from physical pain to convulsions.'[47] It resulted from this nervousness that bodies were violently spread out, flesh and organs torn apart, and bones broken.[48] This man remembers what happened in 1965 near Kikwit Airfield:

> They [the *militaires*] began [the process of killing] the young man, who was arrested because of his scars, by giving him food. They gave him a lot of food and forced him to eat... [And then] they beat him heavily to the point where he could not rise anymore. [After that] they dragged him in front of the wooden podium that was there... They forced him to say in front of everyone why he was going to be killed... Afterwards, they placed the rope around his neck. They destroyed the plank [he was standing on]. ... The young boy began to swim in the air. His body was shaking. His tongue came out. The saliva was flowing from both sides of the mouth. The young boy died while he was still urinating and shitting.[49]

Beyond this humiliation caused by political power is the form of suffering created by the narrative construction by others. In the specific case of Kitoto, this narrative construction by others led to the attribution of degrading stereotypes such as 'mute'. Other victims were nicknamed 'eighteen' or *diboité* (dislocated), depending on whether they lacked two fingers or two toes, or they walked with a limp. As this woman recalls:

> The *militaires* arrested three young men. ... Papa, do you know what they did to them? ... They grabbed the first one. They stabbed his right arm [with the bayonet]. And then they cut his thumbs off. ... They caught the second one. They beat him up heavily. And then they cut his ears off They turned to the last one. They beat him as well and they cut his lips off. Afterwards they asked the three young men to walk away to the bush. ...

45 Interview with Jacques Kuma, Kikwit Sacré Coeur, 6 Aug. 2015.

46 A. Mbembe, '*Variations on the beautiful in Congolese worlds of sound*', in S. Nuttall (ed.), *Beautiful/Ugly: African and Diaspora Aesthetics (Durham, 2006), 74. A thorough analysis of the relationship between the scars of direct violence and other forms of bodily memory which encode violence, such as dance* (see N. Argenti, *The intestines of the state: Youth, violence, and belated histories in the Cameroon Grassfields* (Chicago, 2007); J.-P. Warnier and J.-F. Bayart (eds.), Matière à politique: l e pouvoir, l e s corps et l e s choses (Paris, 2004), could well be undertaken. It is, however, a task that goes beyond the boundaries of this article.

47 Mbembe, '*Variations*', *74*.

48 E. M. Kalema, 'The Mulele 'rebellion', Congolese political regimes, and the politics of forgetting', *Cahiers d'Etudes Africaines*, 4:233 (forthcoming, Dec. 2018).

49 Interview with Jacques Kuma.

> Do you know what people used to call these three young men? The first one people used to call "eighteen" as he lost both thumbs. The second they used to call *maseke* [horns], because he would put his hands around the eardrums to hear better as he had no longer had ear cups. The fact of continuously putting his hands around his ears gave the impression of someone who had horns. That is why he was nicknamed *maseke* [horns]. ... The last one people used to call *aseka kala,* meaning someone who always laughs, because he did not have his lips anymore. And having his teeth always visible gave the impression of someone who always laughs.[50]

'Mute', '*diboité*', as well as '*maseke*' are primarily words. 'A word', writes Mbembe, 'always refers to something. But the word also has a proper thickness, a proper density. A word is made to evoke something in the consciousness of that which it addresses, or who hears it. The more it has a density and thickness, the more it provokes sensation, a feeling, a resentment among those to which it refers. There are words that hurt'.[51] 'Mute', '*diboité*', and '*maseke*' are among those words. Worn permanently as an insult, the effects of their weight mark the consciousness of those who are sentenced to bear them unconditionally. As we can see, the words 'mute', '*diboité*', and '*maseke*' objectify, degrade, paralyse, amputate, and emasculate those who are forced to bear them, as Kitoto went on saying:

> When they insult me like that, I do not even know how to answer... Isn't it that you can only answer with words? I am deprived of those words. What do you want me to do? ... When I dare to speak, they multiply insults. ... They say to me: "Look at this mute who wants to speak. What is it that he wants to say exactly?" It is painful. Even my own son-in-law calls me 'mute'. Nobody has any idea of what I am going through... Those who cannot make fun of me openly, they do it through gestures What can I do? When I try to speak, my blood pressure increases, my body gets tired, I suddenly get breathless. And this is even one more reason for them to intensify the insults... How can I live in peace? How should I not be sick all the time?[52]

Apart from these degrading words, the narrative construction by others also led to the use of gestures as a way of making fun of the victims, as Georgine Mankieta explains below. It is within this economy of gestures that the marked bodies could become a fixed idea and, therefore, destroyed. When people could not make use of gestures to fix them, they would make use of metaphors from their web of words. People developed ways of separating words and sentences from their conventional meanings.

50 Interview with Georgine Mankieta.

51 A. Mbembe, *Critique*, 219. On 'words that hurt', see also D. Schoenbrun, 'Violence, marginality, scorn and honour: language evidence of slavery to the eighteenth century', in H. Médard and S. Doyle (eds.), *Slavery in the Great Lakes Region of East Africa* (Oxford, 2007), 38-75

52 Interview with Eugène Kitoto, 7 Aug. 2015.

They would use those words in contradictory ways and, in doing so, offended those living with disruptions inflicted upon their bodies.

> Papa, people suffered a lot... You get into a village to only find that some people do not have ears, others do not have legs, and some others do not have arms. ... You would not even be able to look at them... Once in front of them, all you could do is to pretend that you have not seen anything while actually you are watching them from the corner of your eyes... This is what we used to do... One day, my friends and I sat down on the edge of the road... We saw 'eighteen' coming... My friend touched me slightly on my thigh. She said to me in a low-pitched voice: "Georgine, look, 'eighteen' is coming towards us." I lift up my eyes. I saw the man coming. Quickly, I turned my eyes around in order not to give the impression that I was looking at him... My friend insisted. I pretended not to understand and did absolutely not want to lift my eyes... She dug her nails into my leg... And when I lifted my eyes, she stretched her mouth twice in the right direction, as to point the direction from which 'eighteen' was coming... After a few minutes we saw 'eighteen' stopping... He turned towards us and stared at us... We understood that he was aware that we were watching him. For a few minutes he stood in front of us. He shook his head and then left. You could tell that he was very depressed... Everyone had their own tips when it came to making fun of people... One could laugh in front of this man without lips to say that this man had been laughing forever.[53]

Confronted with such humiliation, the marked body could do no better than itself seek refuge in laughter:

> I was walking down the street. And suddenly, they began to laugh at me... I stopped and turned around... I saw them as they were laughing out loud at me... As I could not say anything, I just shook my head ... and laughed as well... I decided to go away as they were intensifying the insults. But all along the road I could not contain myself. I continued to laugh.[54]

What was this kind of laughter that captured and invested in the marked body, maintained and extended itself across time? Certainly it was not the laughter of mutual recognition, the one that happens when one suddenly encounters someone one knows but rarely sees.[55] It was not even the 'cackling carnivalesque laughter', the one described by Bakhtin and which, in the post-colony, has constantly been used

53 Interview with Georgine Mankieta.
54 Interview with Eugène Kitoto, 7 Aug. 2015.
55 G. Bataille, *Writings on Laughter, Sacrifice, Nietzsche, Un-Knowing*, trans. A. Michelson (Cambridge, MA, 1986), 69.

and mobilised by subjects in order to resist the dominant culture.[56] It was not even a laughter that scoffed, the one used by children when they witness the collapse of an authority, someone they fear.[57] It was rather something closer to what Nancy Rose Hunt calls 'the nervous', the 'agonised shaking', 'the trembling laughter'; one that emerges out of 'the unknowable' and 'anguish', in so far as 'the unknown makes' people 'laugh'; and one that comes from extended and unlimited suffering.[58] After having erupted, this kind of laughter usually involves a proliferation of thought that can no longer be stopped, not even by the person who is laughing.

> While I was laughing, I could easily think of the swarms of flies which swirled around the streaming blood of my wounds, when the *militaires* shot at me... I was asking myself if these people who were making fun of me have already suffered... I could not understand why they were taking pleasure in my suffering.[59]

Despite the excessive suffering caused by the laughter and gestures by others, the scars that the subject bears on his body never stop producing hardship and a particular state or kind of subjecthood. He is constantly immersed in asymmetrical relations of subordination. In contact with others, an atmosphere of submission has permanently been created because of the transformations that his body has undergone.

Within the deeply paternalistic society in which a man like Kitoto lives, having lost his manhood, his own wife speaks to him in the way one speaks to a child. He is deprived of any right to assert himself. His body is both the object of appropriation and rejection. He is constantly driven to question the reasons for his continued existence.

> We who were born very well have now become like kids because of the lack of testicles... Oh, the *militaires!* My wife can treat me as her child and give me orders: "Turn these cassava chips [*cossettes de manioc*]".[60] I have no other alternative. I must do it; otherwise, she will not give me food... If I dare to speak, she says to me: "Shut up, sterile. Have you got anything on your body that you can give to a woman? Your body has been dead a long time ago." This is my life. She and I, we never had children. The only ones that we have are those that she had elsewhere. When I look at those three children, I constantly cry out... Papa, since the day she discovered that I had no testicles we have no longer had romantic encounters. She has chased me from her bed. I sleep on the floor.... What can I say to her?

56 N. R. Hunt, '*An acoustic register: rape and repetition in Congo*', in A. L. Stoler (ed.), *Imperial debris: On ruins and ruination* (Durham, 2013), 51; A. Mbembe, *On the Postcolony* (Berkeley, 2001), 103.
57 Bataille, Writings, 68.
58 Hunt, '*An acoustic register*', 51.
59 Interview with Eugène Kitoto, 7 Aug. 2015.
60 He refers to his second wife here.

> When I tried to talk to her, she replied with brutality: "Open your mouth again, I will tell everyone here that you are not a man,... that you do not have testicles."... These days she is dating a young boy named Jonathan... What can I do?... Those who have the power to impregnate women have confiscated my wife. I do not have testicles, what can I do?... One day, I made her sit down and talk to me. She said: "Look at this thing that is telling me that [Jonathan] is a child! Do you think he is not a man?... In my opinion, Jonathan is completely a man. ... You, rather, you are not a man. Have you got anything on your body that you can give me?"... Papa, what a humiliation! Instead of going out with an adult like me, my wife would rather go with a child. Oh, the world![61]

This is how the violence experienced during the Mulele rebellion of the 1960s continues to produce and reproduce humiliation. For Kitoro, it is made far worse by his wife attributing to him a lack or failure, even though it is one for which he bears no responsibility. This is the life of scars.

Bodily disruptions, temporality, and suffering

> Seeing my child having [his arm cut off] ... was a big shock to me... I never stop regretting that. ... I remember one day [in late 1965], after leaving the *Hôpital Général de Kikwit*, I had to wash my child. I took his clothes off... I made him sit in his pond. Papa, I sprinkled water on his head. ... It was painful. I began to cry. And to rub soap on his amputated arm, it was a big problem for me. I could not bear the pain. ... My heart was burning. ... After many hesitations, I managed to wash him. I took him out of the pond. ... I made him sit on my legs to dress him, it was painful. I was crying... My right hand was holding his [amputated] arm. I was touching his scars. I was crying while I was looking at these scars... I was asking myself: "Now that he has got only one arm, what does the future hold for him?" I was so scared. ... I could not believe it... I could foresee all kinds of suffering that was awaiting him in his life. ... I could see my son suffering. I could see how his friends would laugh at him... Papa, looking at my child's arm was so painful to me. ... I was afraid to see my own child suffering.[62]

These are the memories of Angelique Niepela, a 79-year-old woman from Impanga Mbele, whose child experienced a terrible accident at the beginning of 1965.[63] On the one hand, these recollections highlight the tremendous and deep pain that a mother experienced at the suffering of her child. On the other hand, they show the

61 Interview with Eugène Kitoto, Kikwit, 7 Aug. 2015.
62 Interview with Angelique Niepela, Kinshasa, 3 Aug. 2015.
63 The accident took place in early 1965. Her son was shot, and his right arm was destroyed. He was three years old.

possibility of reading time – the future, in this specific case – from the scars that a person carries on the body. This is particularly true given the fact that, at the time, the issue of marked bodies and their well-being did not seem to be at the forefront of the Congolese authorities' agenda. For the Mobutu regime, the fact that someone was in the rebel zone at the time of the rebellion was an indication of collaboration with the rebels. Mobutu wanted to punish not only the marked bodies, but also the region as a whole, accusing everyone living there of supporting Mulele and his rebellion.[64] This had a huge impact on the imagination – and conception of life in general – of those whose bodies were marked. The way in which they conceived of time and, particularly, of the future was determined by their physical condition. Kitoto, for example, remembered projecting himself into an 'eternal' future on the basis of the scars of his testicles and thinking about how the life he had planned for himself would never come about.[65] Many others with injured bodies took the same approach. The following is the case of Adolphe Kuma Kuma's brother-in-law whose severe disfigurement was imposed on his body in the late 1960s. Kuma shows that people with marked bodies did not only perceive themselves to have no future, but that they were actively prevented from having a future by the central government, the community, as well as by local authorities.

> Papa may nobody delude you with persuasive speech.... One can somewhat give oneself the luxury – I insist on the word somewhat – of not worrying about what happened to one's body, or what this body has become, only if one knows that the injuries have been fully taken care of – either by the state or by the family... But when you have undergone [a series of mutilations] like my brother-in-law, and no effort is being made by the government or those in the immediate environment to guarantee his safety and life, he who has experienced these mutilations, how could you expect this person not to worry about his life and his future in general?... Georgine [my wife] has just told you about her cousin who, as she described, was a very strong and well-built man... His arms were [brutally] amputated by the *militaires*... Do you know how he spent the two years before he died? It was horrible for him. ... He would not stop complaining about his loss... He was always absent-minded.[66]

He continued:

> Georgine has just told you that he would not stop looking at the stumps of his arms. ... This is someone who was abandoned to himself... He did not receive any help, neither from the government, nor from the community...

64 Telephone interview with Ernest Kiangu, Johannesburg-Kinshasa, 28 Jan. 2016. This suspicion and related punishment did not abate during the rest of the Mobutu reign.
65 Interview with Eugène Kitoto, 7 Aug. 2015.
66 Interview with Adolphe Kuma.

> People could barely help him... His own wife left him behind with two children because of his disabilities.... At the time, we had just come out of the bush. We had almost nothing to eat. ... I guess you understand how difficult it was for a man without arms to feed two kids daily. ... He would cry every single day. ... He would think about his future and that of his children Whenever I visited, he would not stop sharing his fears: "Adolphe, I am scared about the future of my children. I know I will die, maybe this evening, maybe tomorrow morning, or late in the evening. But should I die anytime soon, please do not forget to take care of my children."...This had, practically, become his new life until 1968 when he passed away. ...Papa, ... may nobody convince you otherwise. The question of the future of these people was out of the agenda of the authorities. Nobody cared at all at the time.[67]

It is this active denial of a future that led most of those who suffered mutilations during the rebellion to use their scars to project themselves into the future and to imagine what could happen. The question now was to know how this imagined future, terrifying and full of fears and uncertainties, would come to fruition. A careful examination of the fragments of testimonies given by the injured people and their acquaintances shows that they could not attach a specific date to what they were fearing would happen in the future.[68] All of them, nevertheless, seemed to be certain that this terrifying future would come.

Niepela's testimony is clear in this regard. 'As a parent', she said, 'I could not wish anything bad for my child. But [my consciousness] would not stop reminding me that, one day, this thing would eventually end up [making its appearance]'.[69] As a result, the entire life, or the rest of life, was reduced to waiting for this terrifying future, this 'yet-to-come', to come into fruition.[70]

But how many presents needed to pass before this terrifying future would make its appearance? How long should one remain, to use Jacques Derrida's vocabulary, 'between what goes and what comes, in the middle of what leaves and what arrives' before this imagined future would make its intrusion? A focus on the fragments of testimonies of those onto whom this terrifying future had been projected since 1965 allows a better understanding of the realization of this 'yet-to-come'.[71]

> All started in 1968. ... I must have been five or six years old at the time... It was the first time that I came to realise that I was abnormal... I was playing

67 Interview with Adolphe Kuma.
68 This is not to say that this kind of imagined future did not come to pass.
69 Interview with Angelique Niepela.
70 J.-P. Martinon, *On Futurity*: Malabou, *Nancy and Derrida* (New York, 2007), 1.
71 J. Derrida, *Specters of Marx: The State of Debt, the Work of Mourning and The New International*, trans. P. Kamuf (New York, 1994), 29.

> with my friends. I was observing them. I could see that each of them had two arms while me, I only had one. It was painful for me to discover this truth. I began to feel ashamed... My friends began to make fun of me. They would single me out: "Oh, look at him. He has only one arm!" It was a big shock to me... Over the years, things got complicated... I was sad all the time, even though sometimes I would pretend that everything was okay. ... In 1975, when I went back to the village for the first time since 1965, it was even worse... People gathered around me. They wanted to see me, the child whose arm was taken away by the *militaires* during the rebellion. It was not easy for me because such attention caused emotion and pain in me. ... But it was at the age of 18 that I really felt the weight of my suffering. ... I came to realise that I was no longer this child who used to think that life was normal and that his parents would still be doing everything for him. I came to realise that I was becoming an adult and that I had to take care of myself... But when I turned to look at myself, all I could see was my deformity. And that made me feel terrible... I was so scared of my own future. I was asking myself: "What will the future hold for me, I who have this deformity?" I could not stop asking myself this question. This is what I was fearing most of the time. ... And the more the years went by, the more my fears intensified. I was so scared to face [this] future because of my disability.[72]

These testimonies identify the key moments in the chain in which the terrifying future projected in 1965 began to materialise. In the case of Alidor Muliongo (son of Angelique Niepela), for example, there are two key moments at either end of the continuum: five years and eighteen years of age. Each of these ends is dominated by the awareness of his physical condition. What was the future in 1965 became, as time passed, the present and then the present past or past present.[73] The fragments of testimonies of the child led to another reality: fear of his own future. His testimonies suggest that, as a state of mind, this fear gradually increased as he approached this 'new' future, the one that he posed, as his mother did long ago, as the 'yet-to-come' or that which 'comes towards us'.[74] He relied upon his present situation, as he went beyond perception and what could, to use Derrida's vocabulary once again, 'present itself in the present tense of sight'.[75]

72 Interview with Alidor Muliongo, Kinshasa, 3 Aug. 2015.

73 J. Derrida, 'A time for farewells: Heidegger (read by) Hegel (read by) Malabou', preface to C. Malabou, *The Future of Hegel: Plasticity, Temporality, and Dialectics*, trans. L. During (New York, 2004), xix. See also R. Koselleck, *Future Past: On the Semantics of the Historical Time*, trans. Keith Tribe (New York, 2004).

74 Martinon, On Futurity, 1.

75 Derrida, 'A time for farewells', xxii. On this emotional state, or this way of anticipating something detrimental, see M. Heidegger, *Being and Time*, trans. J. Macquarrie and E. Robinson (London, 1962), 179–80.

In this dreading, or 'bringing-close' of fearing, the self-reflective mind could not have other alternatives than to rely on his emotional states, and develop, at the same time, a variety of moods.

> It was not easy at all... Fearing my own future had brought a lot of trouble in my life. I would get angry easily. If I was not sad, I would become shy. ... I began to isolate myself from the people around me because of shame I could not stop looking at myself. ... My own life became boring... Evil thoughts would abound in my mind; you have no idea!... I would foresee situations where my friends would be working and getting money, while I could not do anything because of my deformities... Mentally, I was already limited... I could not spend a day without fearing my own future... I was so scared.... I would imagine myself working with friends somewhere. I would imagine them being aware of my incapacity to work like them, but none of them would help me... [or] say: "Let us give him at least 1 percent of our salary because his physical condition prevents him from working like us."... No one could give me anything because, physically, I was not in good shape; and that I did not work like them. ... These are the kinds of thoughts that were torturing me. ... I could see how I would already been dismissed from life whenever it came to work. ... This is [precisely] what was troubling [me] in my early twenties as a disabled person.[76]

But the most difficult moment in this process of dreading is the impression of passivity created on the side of those who were socially involved with the wounded child. In Muliongo's own words, it seems as if the others were unwilling to take any responsibility of avoiding this 'terrifying' future that was anticipated since 1965. It seems as though the others operated, in Slavoj Žižek's phrase, as 'passive aggressive' people.[77] They did nothing and thus actively ensured that nothing really changed. In an informal discussion, an interviewee, who wished to remain anonymous, strongly objected to this view, and accused the injured themselves of irresolution, passivity, laziness, and weakness:

> It is amazing to see how these people [the injured people] remained entirely passive... Normally, when I have anticipated my own future, and I have discovered that this future I have projected onto myself is not promising, I cannot just cross my arms and be relaxed about time. ... I must do something... I must think about the ways in which I can overturn this future that seems too unpromising... I cannot take pleasure in withdrawing myself from the battle, sit down and watch how I am going to fail. ... I must do something... I am greatly surprised that they remained passive

76 Interview with Alidor Muliongo, Kinshasa, 3 Aug. 2015.
77 S. Žižek, *The Parallax View* (Cambridge, 2006), 341.

> when they knew that the predictions regarding their future were not promising.[78]

This way of thinking, based essentially on a lack of consideration, is evidence of the kinds of encounters that the injured people continued to have on a daily basis.[79] The others, by reading passivity, irresolution, and laziness into the actions of the injured people, ignored, to a large extent, the efforts made by the injured to counteract this terrifying 'yet-to-come'.[80] Muliongo's parents, for example, worked laboriously to give him a better future. They sent him to school at a very young age in the understanding of the time that it was the best means of gaining social mobility.[81] Muliongo completed his studies in the early 1980s.[82] Unfortunately, when he began to search for work it coincided with a crisis of unemployment in wider Zairian society. By 1980, the country was experiencing the consequences of an economic breakdown that had begun in the early 1970s.[83] To avert the crisis, many individuals branched out into the more informal economy.[84] Similar to most of the young people of his generation, Muliongo felt compelled to participate in these informal activities. Yet it is exactly in this informal economy that all his thoughts and fears found their expression. In a long testimony, he provided an overview of his life trajectory and how, in his quest for constructing a meaningful and active life, he became involved in informal activities.[85]

> After leaving school in 1983, I embarked myself in the *libanga* [informal economy]... In 1985, I was going to buy goods in Brazzaville and sell them here in Kinshasa... Quickly, I stopped with it because we were treated like animals on the Brazzaville side. There was no respect for human rights. ... In the mid-1990s, my friends convinced me to join them in seeking diamonds at the Congolese-Angolan border. The deal was made. I went with them. ... In any case, I did not gain anything. I came back empty handed.... It was a bad experience. I would even say an ordeal. I could

78 Informal discussion with an anonymous interviewee, Kinshasa, 14 Dec. 2015.

79 On the recurrent absence of sympathy and literature that examines the deeper history of communities' treatment of the disabled or disfigured, see J. Livingston, 'Disgust, bodily aesthetics and the ethics of being human in Botswana', *Africa: Journal of the International African Institute*, 78:2 (2008), 288–307; J. Iliffe, *The African poor: A history* (Cambridge, 1987).

80 Martinon, On Futurity, 1.

81 Today, with the increasing number of unemployed academics, the school increasibly loses its symbolic value of social mobility. See N. Obotela Rachidi, 'L'université face à une jeunesse en quête de modèle', in I. Ndaywel è Nziem (ed.), *L'université dans le devenir de l'Afrique: un demi-siècle de présence au Congo-Zaïre* (Paris, 2007), 253–61.

82 Interview with Alidor Muliongo, 3 Aug. 2015.

83 Ndaywel, Histoire, 727-44.

84 Ibid. 745–50.

85 On the entrepreneurial use of handicaps by marked bodies, see D. Hoffman, *The War Machines: Young Men and Violence in Sierra Leone and Liberia* (Durham, 2011), 162–93.

> not work like everyone else because I was limited.... The diamonds having become rare, I had to dive into the river to get them.[86]

> With one arm, how could I swim? It was very hard for me. I felt useless and unproductive. ... Life became so difficult to the extent that I could not even afford to buy bread. ... Nobody would give me anything as I could not work like the others. I felt somehow like I was harvesting the fruit of my deformity.[87]

He continued:

> In June 2015 I was returning from Kenge. ... I had some merchandise... I took a large vehicle. When we reached Bukanga Lonzo, the vehicle was about to fall down a cliff. ... All passengers and the crew jumped off, except me... With only one arm, I could not grab hold of the crossbeams of the vehicle and jump like them. As a result, I went down together with the vehicle. My left foot was seriously injured. The heel was torn... The bone came out. It protruded from foot. Everybody could see it.[88]

> The nurses at Kenge Hospital did not suture my wound well. There was no difference between a beast and me.[89]

> It was painful. If I had both my arms, I would have jumped from the car as the others did... Now that I am talking to you, I am no longer walking. To get out of the house, I have to crawl like a baby... I am lost. What should I expect again from life?... First of all, I have one shortened arm; now that they are going to cut my leg off, what am I going to become?... I am already unproductive with one arm. With this... additional blow, it is clear that I am completely downgraded in life. What should I expect again from life now that I am 53 years old?[90]

Here are fifty years of a life trajectory, essentially dominated by an explosion of metaphysics of anguish, sorrow, and suffering, and the end of which – this is the arresting of time – Muliongo, the marked body, no longer expected anything, neither from time, nor from existence in general. Even the future, which, not long ago had made him tremble with fear, was no longer important. It was replaced with a lack of expectations. Time, as we can see, 'has gone farther away, leaving behind only a field of ruins, an immense weariness', and 'an infinite distress'.[91] At the heart of this

86 On the issue of diamonds, see F. de Boeck, 'Postcolonialism, power, and identity: local and global perspectives from Zaire', in R. Werbner and T. Ranger (eds.), Postcolonial Identity in Africa (London, 1996), 75–106.
87 Interview with Alidor Muliongo, 3 Aug. 2015.
88 Interview with Alidor Muliongo, 3 Aug. 2015.
89 Interview with Alidor Muliongo, Kinshasa, 19 Dec. 2015.
90 Interview with Alidor Muliongo, 3 Aug. 2015.
91 Mbembe, *On the Postcolony*, 199.

distress, the injured body can only discover the senselessness of the life he has spent on earth: 'I have wasted my life for nothing. What have I earned from all of this? Oh, life is unfair! It has no mercy at all'.[92] If not nullity, it is a combination of disgust, pain, and sorrow.[93] This relates to the kind of suffering that Ernest Kiangu referred to as 'supreme suffering' when he said: 'One feels like a wreck that was used and that has been subsequently cast aside, because it does not have any value'.[94] And, as a result, the injured body feels completely lost, and, at the same time, disconnected from the world, as Muliongo, himself, went on saying:

> Even in my family people usually do not need me because they know that I am worthless. When there are family gatherings, no one invites me. They know that I will not bring any money or any contribution to their reunion. ... I am the king of rejection. On more than one occasion I overheard my own family members saying: "Ah, what is it that Alidor is going to do again in his life?" Even my own nephews, they often repeat that: "It is over for him. He will no longer do anything in life." You see! Now, do you think there is anything else I can do to change their minds? What can I tell them to convince them, I who has already been downgraded in life? ... I am useless. [All of this is happening] because of this arm.[95]

Confronted with the proliferation and continuity of this 'metaphysics of sorrow', the marked body cannot do better than immerse itself into negativity and produce a critique of time – and the future more specifically:

> With all of these [pains and sufferings], why should I continue to believe in the future?... I am 53 years old now. I will be 54 years old next year. I am not married. I do not have a wife. I do not even have a girlfriend. Ladies do not like me. Even when I approach them for a simple friendship, they run away because of my arm. I do not have children. Why should I continue to believe in the future? My friends with whom I grew up are all married. They have children... Tomorrow, it is these children who will be helping them. For my friends, there is at least a hope for the future... The future means something for them. For me, however, it is nothing at all. ... Why should I continue to think about the future? Have I ever gained anything from this future for me to continue to believe in it?... My life is a mess. I have failed everything. I do not even have an offspring because of my deformities. Why should I again believe in the future? It is over.[96]

92 Interview with Alidor Muliongo, 19 Dec. 2015.
93 Interview with Alidor Muliongo, 3 Aug. 2015.
94 Interview with Ernest Kiangu.
95 Interview with Alidor Muliongo, 3 Aug. 2015.
96 Interview with Alidor Muliongo, 3 Aug. 2015.

To compensate for this lack of interest in the future, the marked body turns back to the past and lives in a mode of repetition. But in this movement to the past, he no longer sees 'the connected and sequential chain of events' he, as a 'forward-looking' person, used to conceive of as a future possibility.[97] All he can now see is one catastrophe; the thing that made part of his body, in this case the arm, prematurely lifeless; a material thing that brought an untimely experience of death, as well as an incomplete sense of time.

> I was a child at the time. I must have been two or three years old. ... I do not even know why the rebellion broke out... I never asked anybody because it is out of my interest... When I am deeply in my thoughts, all I can see from this past is only my wound. The rebellion has brought a lot of pain in my life; that is all I can see... When it comes to the rebellion itself, it is not in my interest. I do not even know why Mulele [took arms] and started the rebellion... All I know is that I got injured from his rebellion. And this has brought a lot of trouble in my life.[98]

This is the life of scars, a life that consists of navigating backwards and forwards in time, only to find oneself at the heart of disappointment, apathy, nullity, and inutility.

Conclusion

This article deals with scars, their signifying capacity, their relationship not only with the body but also with the apprehension of time, the arresting of time, and the annihilation of future time that the scars seem to both symbolise and put into effect by making the body useless, undesirable, even revolting to others. The main argument is that the scars that people bear on their bodies can produce or reproduce suffering in the longue durée, as long as those who bear them live. To be tortured during the Mulele Rebellion in the 1960s was unimaginably terrible. But the suffering did not stop there. There was something beyond that, something even more important that caused a kind of psychic suffering, which not only exceeded the physical, but also extended across time. This happened first and foremost when the self-encountered its image, a deformed image, an image it could not recognise, a representation, which, to a large extent, was also a monstrous version of itself.

Looking at one's deformed image – and self-conceptions in the face of the violence of truth brought into actuality by the same image – became an act of self-torture in itself.

Second, it happened at the moment in which the subjects were confronted by the 'nervous state' as the marks, 'the emblems of subjectivation' imprinted on their

97 I am drawing here on Walter Benjamin's conception of history. See D. C. Hoy, *The Time of Our Lives: A Critical History of Temporality* (Cambridge, 2009), 154.
98 Interview with Alidor Muliongo, 3 Aug. 2015.

bodies, linked them to politics and rendered them vulnerable to further abuse by the same state.[99]

Third, it made its apparition at the termination of seeing one's life continuously failing. It finally occurred when the injured people engaged in social relations with others. In this sense, the scars that people bear on their bodies register and condense a sense of hurt in the course of time. They bristle at the unethical treatment that the injured people receive from others and by the indifferent or cruel regard in which those who ought to exercise greater moral responsibility towards them hold. This only shows the extent to which the people whose bodies were disfigured during the rebellion are continuously being objectified by the gaze of others, the very same people who are supposed to help them reconcile their bodies with themselves. Because this process of reconciling with one's body never takes place, it is not possible to expect marked bodies to live in peace. Instead, one only finds frustration, desolation, and lack of interest in time and existence more broadly.

99 I borrow the concepts of 'nervous state' and 'emblems of subjectivation' respectively from N. R Hunt, *A Nervous State: Violence, Remedies, and Reverie in Colonial Congo* (Durham, NC, 2016) and J.-F. Bayart, 'Total subjectivation', in J.-P. Warnier and J.-F. Bayart (eds.), Matière, 217.

4.

Remembrance as 'normative bridge' between the past, present and future: Towards an ethics of remembrance

Christine Schliesser

Introduction

When Paul Ricœur calls for a *juste mémoire* – a just memory – he indicates that memory is not morally neutral. Rather, it can be just or unjust. It is my thesis that processes of remembrance and forgetting in their individual and collective dimensions constitute a 'normative bridge' between the past, the present and the future. As such, they are of fundamental importance to processes of healing and reconciliation after historical trauma. I will unfold my thesis in three consecutive steps. In a first step, I will sketch out the theoretical framework in which I situate the term 'normative'. A second step discusses remembrance – and forgetting – and their formative and normative impact on the presence and the future. A third and final step seeks to relate processes of remembrance to processes of healing and reconciliation, exploring paths that seem conducive and/or hindering to dealing constructively with historical trauma.

What do we mean by 'normative'?

A norm is commonly understood as 'a standard ... by which something can and ought to be measured'[1,2] i.e. a summary of those convictions that guide our actions. In the following, however,

I prefer a wider definition of norms. A 'norm' is a sign that establishes a demand within an ethical discourse; a demand that is directed at the behaviour of individuals or of groups. At the same time, this sign contains an ascription of value.[3]

Based on this understanding of norms, I would like to emphasise three aspects. *First*, any sign that entails a justificatory character for an ethical judgment can become

1 All translations by the author, if not indicated otherwise.
2 Härle, Wilfried. *Ethik*, Berlin 2011, p. 17.
3 Zimmermann, Ruben. *Pluralistische Ethikbegründung und Normenanalyse im Horizont einer 'impliziten Ethik' frühchristlicher Schriften*, in: Friedrich Horn et al. (eds.), Ethische Normen des frühen Christentums. Gut – Leben – Leib – Tugend, Tübingen 2013, p. 17.

a norm. Examples of such signs are: traditional moral authorities such as the law, habits and customs; emotions such as hatred or empathy; grammatical forms such as imperatives; terms that encapsulate moral authority such as justice; and people who function as role models. *Second*, norms are not static, but rather dynamic entities and entrenched in their respective linguistic and cultural communities. We always need to ask 'for whom'? with regards to the scope of a certain norm. From the rootedness of norms within a specific community follows, *third*, the necessity of a mediator that transforms signs into norms. Language is the most common mediator in this respect, yet my ensuing discussion will point to other mediators as well such as rituals, symbols or locations like memorials.

Norms are not synonymous with ethics, however. I understand ethics as a theoretical endeavour concerned with behaviour and actions.[4] Ethics thus deals with the convictions that guide our behaviour and actions, i.e. with norms, and with the evaluations connected with these convictions. The evaluation of a certain action as 'right', 'better' or 'wrong' is based on a hierarchisation of norms. Next to the importance of both actions and their reasons for ethics, I would like to draw your attention to two more dimensions of ethics, namely narratives and emotions. Moral orientation and ethical discernment depend on their narrative foundation.[5] It is the actual concrete situation – or its narrative representation – that affects us emotionally. Consequently, emotions manifest themselves in our behaviour and actions. We thus need to take the significance of emotions in processes of ethical decision making into account, as recent empirical moral research emphasises.[6]

In the following, I want to term 'moral significance' what is influencing and preceding our action. The question of *how* moral significance is generated is of special interest here. For Johannes Fischer, it is primarily 'the moral significance of the *experienced* [or narratively represented] situation that causes us to act.'[7] Yet next to the concrete situation affecting us, I argue that different norms, understood as 'signs', can also raise claims to validity and thereby create moral significance. For example, next to experiences or narratives of violence, moral significance can furthermore be generated through the law or what we think of as justice. Boundaries may be fluent, however, as different normative signs serve to interpret each other. Based on this framework, I return to my main thesis that remembrance functions as a normative bridge. In

4 'Actions are the specific subject matter of ethics. We understand actions as the self-aware, free choice of a consequential behaviour through personal individuals'. Herms 1991, p. 56.

5 Fischer, Johannes. *Zum narrativen Fundament der sittlichen Erkenntnis. Metaethische Überlegungen zur Eigenart theologischer Ethik*, in: Friederike Nüssel (ed.), Theologische Ethik der Gegenwart, Tübingen 2009, 75-100.

6 In this regard, cognitive theories of emotion are of special interest as they indicate that emotions encompass both cognitive and affective dimensions. Cf. Robers, 2003 and Nussbaum 2001.

7 Fischer, Johannes. *Ethik als rationale Begründung der Moral?*, in: Zeitschrift für evangelische Ethik 55 (2011), p. 195.

order to defend the plausibility of this thesis, we now need to ask if and in what way memories generate moral significance.

Remembrance as 'normative bridge'

I would like to begin my investigation with some fundamental deliberations concerning the phenomena of remembering and forgetting. We need to differentiate between two dimensions, *individual* remembering on the one hand and a collective culture of remembrance, a *collective* memory, on the other. Remembering, on both an individual and a collective level, is not simply the opposite of forgetting. Rather, remembering and forgetting resemble two sisters, different, yet related. Remembering presupposes forgetting. We cannot remember infinitely. While Friedrich Nietzsche hailed forgetting as the prerequisite to happiness,[8] Sigmund Freud and the school of psychoanalysis perceived of forgetting as in the proximity of highly questionable suppression. Suppression, in turn, was meant to be overcome through the well-known trilogy of 'remembering, repeating, working-through'. By means of this trilogy, 'un-pacified' forgetting was meant to be transformed into 'pacified' forgetting.

In respect of the development of any collective culture of remembrance, for instance, in present-day post-genocide Rwanda, cultural scientists Aleida and Jan Assmann's research on the formation of cultural memory can be helpful.[9] According to the Assmanns, *collective memory* is based on both our *cultural memory* (understood as the centuries-old tradition in us that shapes our perceptions of self and world) and our *communicative memory* (based on the oral tradition of the past three generations). Like individual memory, cultural memory constitutes a dynamic construct that is being constantly formed through manifold processes of remembering and forgetting. Aleida Assmann differentiates between 'active remembering', i.e., selecting memories for a 'canon', and 'passive remembering', i.e., accumulating memories in a 'storage', which would have to be reinterpreted on re-use. 'Active forgetting' involves the intentional destruction of memories, while 'passive forgetting' is related to non-intentional acts such as losing, hiding, and neglecting.[10]

Based on this background, we can now turn to the bridging functions of remembrance. Remembrance does not solely refer to the past. Rather, processes of remembrance link the past, present and future. 'The central aim of cultural memory, then, is ... the

8 Nietzsche, F. *Vom Nutzen und Nachteil der Historie für das Leben (1874)*, in: Friedrich Nietzsche, Sämtliche Werke Bd. 1. Kritische Studienausgabe, Giorgio Colli and Mazzino Montinari (eds.), Berlin 1988, p. 249.

9 Assmann, J. *Das kulturelle Gedächtnis*, in: Jan Assmann (ed.), Thomas Mann und Ägypten. Mythos und Monotheismus in den Josephsromanen, München 2006, 67–75.

10 Assmann, A. *The Religious roots of cultural memory*, in: Norsk Teologisk Tidsskrift 109 (2008), 274-280.

extension of the temporal horizon by creating links to a normative past.'[11] There are three aspects that I would like to draw your attention to.

First, the bridging functions of remembrance. Assmann speaks of a 'diachronic communication' that transcends the boundaries of time and space. 'By forging a link between a normative past and the present and by building a future on this link, cultures create horizons of "diachronic communication" between the living and the absent: God, spirits, the dead and the not yet living.'[12] Cultural memory thus functions as a link between times. It initiates a communicative process that not only serves to connect yesterday with today and tomorrow but to establish a relationship between them.[13]

Second, the nature of the relationship between times. Assmann speaks of a 'normative' past that is set into a relationship with the present and the future. Let me return to my question above: What do we mean by 'normative'? How can the past – and the remembrance focused on it – be normative with regards to the present and the future? In other words: What is the moral significance of the past? Both dimensions developed above come into view here: On the one hand, moral significance can be generated through concrete situations, either experienced by oneself or represented by a narrative, as emphasised by Fischer. On the other hand, moral significance can be created through norms, understood with Zimmermann as 'signs'. In view of post-genocide Rwanda, moral significance seems to emanate primarily from narratives (both experienced and recounted), often regarding unleashed violence, but also from traditional normative authorities such as the law or moral concepts like 'justice' or 'truth'. Moral significance arises further from individual people who either function as role models, e.g., heroes, or to whom we feel obliged, for instance, because they were killed.

Third, placing Assmann's analysis of cultural memory into a wider context. Cultural memory is 'the tradition within us; texts, images and rituals that have been imprinted on us for generations, through centuries or even millennia of repetitive cycles, thereby shaping our perceptions of time and history, of ourselves and our world.'[14] In addition to *cultural* memory, I want to include *individual* memory, in order to take into consideration as well their normative dimension and moral significance for shaping the present and the future. However, processes of both cultural and individual remembrance are closely connected, as can be observed in the current process of actively forging a collective memory in post-genocide Rwanda.

11 Ibid. p. 273.
12 Ibid. p. 273.
13 'Cultural memory creates an extended framework for communication across the existential limit of death and the abyss of time'. Assmann 2008, p. 273.
14 Assmann, Jan. *Das kulturelle Gedächtnis*, in: Jan Assmann (ed.), Thomas Mann und Ägypten. Mythos und Monotheismus in den Josephsromanen, München 2006, p. 70.

Before linking my discussion with the questions of constructively dealing with historic trauma, I want to point to one final aspect, namely the role of power structures in the formation of cultural memory. 'The items that have entered the canon have undergone complex operations of contestation, selection and ascription of value in the context of power struggles.'[15] Any culture of remembrance is prone to the dangers of abuse and exploitation. This is not least due to the inherent connection between remembrance and identity, as Paul Ricœur emphasises in his seminal work *Memory, History, Forgetting*.

Because of the 'fragility of identity' there is 'opportunity for the manipulation of memory.'[16] Ricœur points to different kinds of abuses of memory, namely thwarted memory, manipulated memory and enforced memory. Thwarted memory, according to Ricœur, takes shape in 'forgetting things, screen-memory, failed actions' and can 'take on gigantic proportions on the scale of collective memory.'[17] Manipulated memory is displayed in strategically selected and ideologically coloured memories. Enforced memory manifests itself as both active memory and active forgetting.[18] The active selection of certain memories for the official canon usually goes hand in hand with the destruction of other memories. 'The denial of memory'[19] gives expression to the attempt 'to silence the un-forgetting of memory'[20] and can hardly be differentiated from amnesia. Yet the 'greatest danger' for remembrance, according to Ricœur, lies in the 'handling of authorised, imposed, celebrated, commemorated history – of official history.'[21]

For a particularly 'devious form of forgetting' is taking place there, resulting 'from stripping the social actors of their original power to recount their actions themselves.'[22,23]

In view of the manifold ways to abuse remembrance, Ricœur calls for a 'juste mémoire', a 'just memory.'[24,25] Relating memory to justice, he understands 'the duty to remember [as] the duty to do justice.'[26] This gives material content to the normative dimension of remembrance. The significance of a 'just memory' becomes especially

15 Assmann, Aleida. *The Religious roots of cultural memory*, in: Norsk Teologisk Tidsskrift 109, 2008, 281f.
16 Ricœur, Paul. *Memory, History, Forgetting*, Chicago 2004, p. 448.
17 Ibid. p. 447.
18 Assmann, A. *The Religious roots of cultural memory*, in: Norsk Teologisk Tidsskrift 109 (2008), 270-292.
19 Ricœur, Paul. *Memory, History, Forgetting*, Chicago 2004, p. 453.
20 Loraux, N. *La Cité divisée. L'oubli dans la mémoire d'Athènes*, Paris 2005, p. 171.
21 Ricœur, P. *Memory, History, Forgetting*, Chicago 2004, p. 448.
22 Ricœur, P. *Memory, History, Forgetting*, Chicago 2004, p. 448.
23 Biblical scholar Jürgen Ebach emphasises three different, yet equally significant forms of remembering: objective representations, subjective narratives and ritual places. Ebach 2009:284f.
24 Ricœur, P. *Memory, History, Forgetting*, Chicago 2004, p. 68.
25 Abel, O. et al. (eds.). *La juste mémoire: lectures autour de Paul Ricœur*, Geneva 2006.
26 Ricœur, P. *Memory, History, Forgetting*, Chicago 2004, p. 89.

visible in processes of dealing with historic trauma and reconciliation, to which I turn now.

'Juste mémoire' and processes of reconciliation

Once primarily at home in religious context, the term 'reconciliation' has long been established in historical and political discourses. Societies-in-transition, in particular, rely on this concept to give expression to their quest for a new beginning, for stability and security after violent conflict. The most well-known example is the South African Truth and Reconciliation Commission (TRC). With theologian Stefanie van de Loo I understand reconciliation as a relational term that refers both to a procedure and a result. It is a 'reciprocal *process* between at least two parties, who in immediate or mediate contact with each other reflect on their mutual relationship, and who aim to design this relationship in a positive and new way by mutual acceptance, as well as the *result* of this process'[27,28] According to ethicist Fernando Enns, the process of reconciliation may include 'different elements such as the confession of guilt, atonement, asking and granting of forgiveness ..., up to a newly ordered relationship.'[29] For reconciliation processes, the underlying concept of justice is of special importance. Without justice, reconciliation cannot happen; reconciliation is 'reconciliation in justice.'[30]

Yet thoughts of reconciliation are preceded by thoughts of the injustice suffered. Due to its normative character, one can hardly overestimate the power of memory for the formation of the present and the future. Often enough, this power is a destructive one. Individual and collective identities as 'identities-in-enmity' are being 'nourished by memories, particularly memories of atrocities that have been committed by one group against the other.'[31] Yet I contend that the power of memory can be turned into a positive and constructive force that can be engaged for reconciliation processes – if the justice dimension of memory is attended to.

Even though I will not be able to engage with them in detail at this point, I would like to briefly point to three aspects in the relationship between justice and memory that seem crucial to me. *First*, the other. The virtue of justice is by its very constitution turned toward others. The duty of memory thus becomes 'the duty to do justice, through memories, to an other than the self.'[32] *Second*, the emergence of debt and

27 Van de Loo, S. *Versöhnungsarbeit. Kriterien – theologischer Rahmen – Praxisperspektiven*, Stuttgart 2009, p. 16.
28 My emphasis.
29 Enns, F. *Transformative Gerechtigkeit als Möglichkeitsraum zur Versöhnung*, in: Kirchliche Zeitgeschichte 26 (2013), p. 24.
30 Friese, S. *Politik der gesellschaftlichen Versöhnung*. Eine theologisch-ethische Untersuchung am Beispiel der Gaçaça – Gerichte in Ruanda, Stuttgart 2010, p. 212.
31 Falconer, A. *Erinnerungen zur Versöhnung führen, in:* Ökumenische *Rundschau* 45 (1996), p. 472.
32 Ricœur, P. *Memory, History, Forgetting*, Chicago 2004, p. 89.

heritage as significant categories. We are, as Ricœur says, indebted to those who have gone before us for part of who we are. 'The duty of memory is not restricted to preserving the material trace, whether scriptural or other, of past events, but maintains the feeling of being obligated with respect to these others, of whom we shall later say, not that they are no more, but that they were.'[33] This includes a self-critical dimension as it calls us to inventory our own heritage. *Third*, the moral priority of the other victims. Again, the focus is on the other. Ricœur cautions against 'the tendency to proclaim oneself a victim and endlessly to demand reparation.'[34] Rather, the issue here is 'the other victim,' besides myself.[35]

Preliminary conclusion

In my closing remarks, I would like to reflect on my discussion above in the light of the context of post-genocide Rwanda. As a European and an outsider from a different culture and with different experiences, I am aware of the limits of my perspective. These limits call for the utmost caution and modesty in my remarks. Yet I would like to pose the question of whether Rwanda's processes of remembrance truly resemble a *juste mémoire*. A just memory is characterised by a polyphony of perspectives, not merely one 'official history'. A just memory not only allows but welcomes deviant narratives as a means to do justice to someone other than the self.

Against this background, I would like to share one experience with you. When I came to Rwanda for the first time in 2014, I went to the genocide memorial site in Nyange. During the genocide, the Catholic church of Nyange, harbouring around 3.000 people seeking refuge, had been demolished with the help of bulldozers available from road building projects nearby. While my group and I wandered around the bleak space, where the outlines of the once magnificent church were still visible among the fallen rocks strewn at large, a man came to offer us his guidance. He introduced himself as the only survivor of the massacre, having remained close to the site where his wife and children had been killed, along with nearly everyone else inside the church. The priest of that church, we learnt on that day, had gone to the authorities to betray the ones entrusted to him. Two years later, I came back to the same site. I hardly recognised it. Instead of the austere space with scattered rocks and bent window frames, I now saw the beginnings of a smart new architecture. While my group and I ambled around, a man came to offer us his guidance. He introduced himself as a Belgian priest. What we saw here, we learnt, was to be the new memorial of the site of massacre. During the genocide, he explained to us, about 3,000 people had sought refuge in this church. Yet the priest helped to rescue almost all of them, except about 50 people.

33 Ibid. p. 89.
34 Ibid. p. 89.
35 Ibid. p. 89.

I am not in a position to judge whose story is true or even comes closer to the historical facts. Yet what I witnessed at the site of the demolished church was the open contestation of memories. History was being made into an 'official history' and I wondered if I encountered an instance of 'stripping the social actors of their original power to recount their actions themselves.'[36] Due to the normative function of remembrance and the close connection between remembrance and reconciliation, processes of active and passive remembering and forgetting are of crucial importance for the formation of the present and the future. *What* we remember (and not remember) and *how* we remember makes a difference to how we live today and tomorrow. A (self-) critical and just memory and a polyphonic culture of remembrance – on both individual and collective levels – are needed in order for remembrance to assume a constructive rather than destructive role in any country's quest for sustainable peace and reconciliation after historic trauma.

36 Ricœur, Paul. Memory, History, Forgetting, Chicago 2004, p. 448.

Part II: Transgenerational Memory: Trauma, Guilt and Responsibility

5.
Intergenerational nostalgia: Loss and longing in Bonteheuwel[1]

Kim Wale

This paper is based on research for the project entitled Trauma, Memory and Representations of the Past, which was conducted under the auspices of Studies in Historical Trauma and Transformation at Stellenbosch University. This research project broadly seeks to understand how societies characterised by histories of mass violence work through their traumatic pasts. The research was conducted in three communities in the Western Cape: Bonteheuwel, Langa and Worcester. These communities were selected because they share a legacy of mass violence during apartheid and also in the present context. Data was collected from life history interviews with the "first generation" who experienced apartheid-era violence, and the focus group research with the "second generation" who represent young people born after South Africa's democratic transition. The paper restricts its analysis to data from Bonteheuwel and focusses on the focus group research with the young generation. However, it is also underpinned by a contextual analysis of the life history narratives of the parents' generation. The central question that underpinned the analysis of the focus group interviews was how these young South Africans make sense of the memories of the mass violence of apartheid experienced by the parents' generation in relation to their experiences of the present and their views about the future.

Memory and violence in Bonteheuwel

In the life history interviews with the 1st generation, two painful memories of historical violence and trauma reoccurred in the personal life histories of the people of Bonteheuwel. The first was the forced removals under the notorious Group Areas Act. Bonteheuwel was declared a Group Area in 1965 and accommodated people who were designated as coloured and forcibly removed from areas such District Six, Claremont and Diep River, which were designated as white spaces.[2] The violent nature of the Group Areas Act had a devastating impact on the fabric of community and individual sense of home, economic security, personal safety and belonging.

1 This presentation is being adapted for publication in the forthcoming book, *Post-Conflict Hauntings: Re-Imagining the Ghostly for Societies Dealing with Collective Memories of Violence and Historical Trauma*, edited by Kim Wale, Pumla Gobodo-Madikizela and Jeff Prager, published by Palgrave MacMillan.

2 Tapscott, C. (1977). 'The Effects of the Structure of Local Government on Crime', Unpublished Masters dissertation, Department of Public Administration, University of Cape Town, South Africa, p. 143.

One of the legacies of this violence was the birth of gangs for alternative forms of livelihood, safety and belonging.

The second painful memory highlighted in the 1st generation narratives is the violence of the 1980s and the anti-apartheid struggle which turned communities into war-zones. One of the legacies of the struggle environment is that many of these young activists turned to drugs and alcohol to cope with the painful memories of this time, which has had a reverberating impact on their children and the broader community.

Within this knot of violence, a yearning or nostalgic relationship to the past emerges as one of the dominant modes of remembering for the 2nd generation. Two common sites for this nostalgic memory were the spaces such as District Six, which existed before the forced removals as well as the milkman and the sugar neighbour in Bonteheuwel during apartheid times. The 2nd generation affectively relates to the memories of the 1st generation in the mode of embodied longing, *'I can see it in their eyes, the longing for the past'*. At the same time, they retell sweet memories of milkmen and sugar neighbours in their recollection of apartheid times. This dominant nostalgic mode of 2nd generational remembering seemed very peculiar in the initial analysis of this data and begged the question why? Why would a dominant intergenerational mode of remembering a painful and violent past be nostalgia? This paper addresses this question through analysing the data on intergenerational nostalgia in Bonteheuwel in relation to the theoretical literature on nostalgia and the intergenerational transmission of trauma.

Nostalgia – an affective ambivalent concept

Nostalgia is a concept steeped in affect, a twinge in your heart far more powerful than memory. It is also an ambivalent emotion that co-activates both happiness and sadness at the same time.[3] Like the emotion, the concept of nostalgia etymologically contains this ambivalence. This quality is etched into the very etymology of the word divided into *Nostos* (the return home) and *Algos* (longing).

Svetlana Boym works this distinction into her characterisation of the two different types of nostalgia.[4] *Restorative Nostalgia* focusses on the restoration of a prefabricated notion of 'home' and 'the past'. This is the backward looking, ideological, dangerous and divisive connection to the past that people are willing to kill and die to restore. *Reflective* nostalgia represents the shared existential human experience of longing which welcomes the ambivalence that dwells within this experience.[5] It resists the urge to return home even as it longs for it. It welcomes the creative possibilities for the future that emerge from this space of ambiguity.

3 Sedikides, C., Wildschut, T., Arndt, J., & Routledge, C. (2008). Nostalgia: Past, present, and future. *Current Directions in Psychological Science*, 17, 304–307.
4 Boym, S. (2001). *The Future of Nostalgia*. New York: Basic Books.
5 Ibid.

Intergenerational trauma and nostalgia

The theorisation of intergenerational transmission of trauma stems from the work of Abraham and Torok and their concept of the psychic crypt that both protects and passes down the family secret. This secret is inaccessibly entombed in the ego in a 'special kind of unconscious' but is passed down to the following generations in the mode of haunting and experienced as a ghostly presence.[6] For Fresco,[7] Danieli[8] and Hoffman,[9] intergenerational trauma is passed down to the 2nd generation through silence and the absence of memory. Marion Hirsch, in her concept of post-memory, however, moves beyond this notion of silence and emptiness noting that the post-memory of the 2nd generation is sometimes felt as 'too many stories' and 'too much affect', it is as full as it is empty.[10]

The connection between nostalgia and trauma in the South African context is theorised in three articles in a special edition on nostalgia in *Peace and Conflict: Journal of Peace Psychology* (2012), which published the proceedings of the final conference of the Apartheid Archives project that was organised around this memory concept. Derek Hook[11] draws on Freud to conceptualise nostalgia as a screen memory hypothesising that: '*The "sweetness" of nostalgia perhaps has more to do with what it has enabled one to avoid, what is screened, than with the obvious content of what has been recalled*'. Pumla Gobodo-Madikizela analyses the memory narratives of white South Africans demonstrating how nostalgia is operating as a form of idealisation and denial resulting in an inability to mourn.[12] In their article about the stories that black grandmothers in Durban tell their grandchildren about apartheid, Frankish and Bradbury[13] emphasise an active silence around political trauma and the reconstruction of nostalgic narratives as a means to impart lessons from a longer past towards creating a meaningful future.

6 Abraham, N. and Torok, M. (1994). *The Wolf Man's Magic Word:* A Cryptonomy. Trans. Nicholas Rand. Foreword: Jacques Derrida. Minneapolis: University of Minnesota Press.

7 Fresco (1984). Remembering the unknown. *In International Review of Psychoanalysis* 11: 417-27.

8 Danieli, Y. (1998). Introduction: History and conceptual foundations. In Y. Danieli (Ed.), *International Handbook of Multigenerational Legacies of Trauma* (pp. 1–20). New York, NY: Plenum Press.

9 Hoffman, E. (2004). *After Such Knowledge: Memory, History and the Legacy of the Holocaust*. New York, NY: Public Affairs.

10 Hirsch, M. (1997). *Family Frames: Photography, Narrative and Post memory*. Cambridge: Harvard University Press.

11 Hook, D. (2012). *Political nostalgia and psychoanalysis: Screened history, fantasmatic memory and retroactive time. Peace & Conflict*, 18, 225–239.

12 Gobodo-Madikizela, P. (2012). *Re-membering the past: Nostalgia, traumatic memory and the legacy of apartheid. Peace & Conflict*, 18, 252–267.

13 Frankish and Bradbury (2012) Frankish, T., & Bradbury, J. (2012). *Telling stories for the next generation. Peace & Conflict*, 18, 294–306.

Intergenerational nostalgia in Bonteheuwel

While the 2nd generation in Bonteheuwel express a sense of silence around their parents' memories of the painful past, they nevertheless experience forms of embodied communication from their parents about the past. For example, respondents on the one hand say that there are certain historical memories, such as the 'army trucks' and the 'juicy bits' of history that are not shared with the younger generation:

> The army trucks, the army, whatever. They don't talk about that, man. They will say the trucks were here but they don't talk about what really happened. They keep the juicy parts for themselves. They want to bore you with the bits you don't care for.

Nevertheless, this generation viscerally experiences the pain that their parents are feeling about the past through embodied forms of communication. For example, a 2nd generation respondent shares how she experiences her father's sadness that is written all over his face when they pass the geographical location and houses in Cape Town from where his family was forcibly removed:

Whenever we go to Cape Town, my mom and dad and I, then I can see how my dad stares at the houses and the longing is there ... the sadness ... you can see it written over his face, he is sad about ... this is my place, but it's not my place anymore because this is where I want to be, but I can't be here, it's like taking a bone away from a dog.

Another memory of pain that is transferred to the 2nd generation via the embodiment of nostalgic affect is the memory of the milkman who would deliver milk to the neighbourhood. In the quote below we see how a grandmother has passed on the memory of the milkman to the granddaughter, however the granddaughter who 'has some wisdom' also sees the scars and burns that the grandmother carries on her body. The story of violence and pain of the student struggles is passed on beside the nostalgic memory of milkmen for the young granddaughter.

> My five-year-old daughter, **she has some wisdom** already, and she would sit there and listen to all **these stories about the milkman** that came around on a bicycle because that time, there weren't house shops. So it's already been passed on to her. And she's ... how can I say? **She's very inquisitive**; she would want to ask questions like "What did they do, Mamma?" Because my mommy was also part of the struggle and she went to school one day and a riot broke out, I don't know, and it was just chaotic and they threw her with a stone, **there was a hole in her head** and because she wears her hair short, you can still see the mark here. **She was burnt on her back**, so the mark is ... the scar is still there, so that is also already the story that has been told to her, so **it's already been passed on**.

These quotes demonstrate how intergenerational nostalgia in Bonteheuwel is communicating the traumatic memories of the past non-verbally. The nostalgia is thus acting more like a connecting channel memory than a defensive screen memory for these young South Africans. The bitter-sweet nostalgia complex is communicated in a combination of verbal, affective and embodied communication.

Nostalgia as critique of the present

Moving from an analysis of the form of nostalgic memory as channel to the content of nostalgic memory, this content is also important as it implies both critical and ethical claims. Whether or not the past was how it is being nostalgically remembered is somewhat beside the point for the more critical work and ethical call that are embedded in the meaning and feeling of the content of this nostalgic memory. Nostalgia as social critique of the present has been demonstrated by Jacob Dlamini in his controversial and path-breaking book *Native Nostalgia* in which he asserts: *These are people for whom the present is not the land of milk and honey, the past not one vast desert of doom and gloom.*[14] He reflects on native nostalgia as a counter-hegemonic work of memory that refuses to go along with the view that during apartheid townships were only sites of resistance or sewers of human degradation, while at the same time reflecting the sense of betrayal in the present context.

For the intergenerational nostalgia in Bonteheuwel, the memories of milk and sugar seek to critique a present sense of loss of community connection, safety, sharing and trust in the present context. At the same time, an ethical call for repairing the tear in the fabric of community is implied, which contains an important intuition for memory work in these spaces going forward.

> Bonteheuwel used to be a nice place to stay in. Like those who couldn't even wait for the person dropping the milk. That guy with the bicycle (laughter), he used to come and sell his milk and his juice and you were all excited, you want to go outside and wait for the guy. But nowadays we can't even go to the shop to buy milk. Because, it's like you're ... you're scared. Even if you have children or so ... uhm ... you don't want to send them outside or let them play outside. What I can say about Bonteheuwel, it used to be nice. But not anymore. I mean, we were so proud to say "I stay in Bonteheuwel". I mean, if I walk around the corner or maybe at work, I say I stay in Bonteheuwel then people say "What?! Daai plek wat vol gangsters is. Daai's dan deurmekaar." (What?! That place that is full of gangsters. That place is crazy). I mean, but then those days when you might have said you live here in Bonteheuwel, they were like, proud, man, yoh.

14 Dlamini, J. (2009). *Native Nostalgia*. Auckland Park, South Africa: Jacana, p. 12.

The symbol of milk is a powerful one carrying with it memory, emotion, critique and desire. At an archetypal level, milk calls to mind images of the mother and mother's milk. It also calls to mind biblical images of the promised land as a 'land flowing with milk and honey'. While participants do not mention honey, they do talk about sugar and remembering the past through the nostalgic lens of a time when neighbours shared their sugar.

> The neighbours looked out for each other. You wouldn't go and ask someone for sugar and the next minute they gossip about you. They shared with each other during apartheid, because everyone had it rough. During those years, no-one had money and you couldn't go everywhere because of apartheid. But they were like one big family, not separated like now, people acting whiter than you. Everyone stood together. And the gangsters during those years, they didn't just shoot to kill. They protected the elderly before doing their thing. And they had a lot of respect for each other's parents. If someone cursed someone's mother, they wouldn't leave it at that. You had to go apologise. And you would probably receive a couple of slaps. But no senseless killing.

In the nostalgic recollection of the younger generation, sugar represents that 'neighbours looked out for each other'. There is a sense that things were rough back then, but the destructive force came from outside rather than inside the community. The past is constructed as 'one big family', a caring collective and juxtaposed with 'separation of now, people acting whiter than you'. Today there is a sense that the destructive force is inside, internalised by 'people acting whiter than you'. The collective parent, and particularly the figure of the mother was cherished and protected, but in today's context the younger generation stress that this respect has been lost.

Conclusion: the call of nostalgia

Through these expressions of intergenerational nostalgia, it is not apartheid that is longed for, but something that was present during the time of apartheid and destroyed over time and is currently being further destroyed. Symbolised through milk (nurturing) and sugar (sweetness) it is a sense of care, community, solidarity that was strong in the face of collective hardship. The trauma, although not directly communicated, is pointed towards through the embodied nostalgia and the sense of loss it expresses.

What appears to be emerging from this nostalgic space is a call – a call for community connection, love and solidarity. Whether or not this was present in the way it is nostalgically remembered is somewhat beside the point, as this remembering directs energy into a desire for the future. The desire captured in this memory is also for the holding space of facilitative community that would enable the process of moving through the pain of the past in order to imagine and allow for a new future. The content of nostalgia points towards what has been lost through the violence of apartheid, and what is required in order to redress the impact of this past. While most of the work on redress, reconciliation and repair in the South African context focusses on the relationship between victim and perpetrator and black and white, this intergenerational nostalgia points us towards the loss of community care and solidarity that has resulted as much from the violence of apartheid as it has from experiences of post-apartheid neglect and betrayal.

6.
The Black Christ and white South African responsibility after 1994

Wilhelm Verwoerd

One evening in late December 1961, a 21-year-old Ron Harrison was lying in bed. Haunted by recent political events such as the Sharpeville massacre, the arrest of ANC, PAC and SACP political leaders, more and more apartheid legislation and 'the government's antipathy towards [ANC president] Chief Luthuli' he had become 'obsessed with the idea of taking some constructive action in the liberation movement' using his artistic talent. That evening 'a thought flashed through' his head: 'How could a government that professed to be Christian perpetrate such immoral deeds and inflict so much pain and suffering on its own countrymen simply because [they] were of another race, another colour, another creed? [Prime Minister] Verwoerd and [Minister of Justice] Vorster were wreaking havoc in their quest for white supremacy and Afrikaner domination, and in the process the black races – in fact, all races that were not classified 'white' – were being crucified'.[1]

The Black Christ and the white centurion

In his autobiography, Harrison then describes the birth of *The Black Christ*:

> The picture of a suffering Christ at the scene of His crucifixion surged through my mind, but the vision forming in my mind's eye was rather unusual in that the figure on the cross was a black man! I realised that I

1 See Davenport, T. R. H. 1986. *South Africa: A Modern History*. Johannesburg: Macmillan, Kenney, H. 1980. *Architect of Apartheid: H.F. Verwoerd – an Appraisal*. Johannesburg: Jonathan Ball, Biko, S. 2012. *I Write What I Like*. Johannesburg: Picador, Gilliomee, H. 2004. *The Afrikaners – A Biography*. Cape Town: Tafelberg.

could depict the suffering of the black people and equate this with the suffering of Christ.

After many rough sketches, I finally settled on the facial features of my Christ figure. Who better than Chief Albert Luthuli, who had just been awarded the Nobel Peace Prize ... Luthuli was a revered icon of the struggle against oppression... I decided that the architects of apartheid also had to be brought into the scene. I had it! Verwoerd and Vorster would be portrayed as two Roman centurions, the tormentors of Christ. Verwoerd would be piercing the side of Christ, and his henchman, Vorster, would be standing with the sponge of vinegar and gall. A coloured Madonna and an Asian St John would complete the scene.[2]

Oupa and *Ouma* Verwoed with grandchildren

Harrison expected the painting to be controversial. Though widely welcomed in anti-apartheid church circles, the (white) Dutch Reformed Church mouthpiece, Die Kerkbode, condemned it as blasphemous and the major Afrikaner newspaper Die Burger called for its banning. As expected, this happened soon, but by then The Black Christ had been smuggled out to the UK where it was used for a number of years to raise awareness and funds for the anti-apartheid struggle. Harrison was repeatedly and brutally interrogated and tortured to reveal the whereabouts of his painting, leaving permanent damage to his health. The painting somehow disappeared from the international scene only to be 'discovered' (hidden in a basement in London) and returned to South Africa in 1997.

My first encounter with the *Black Christ* at this point. While I was working in the Truth and Reconciliation Commission (TRC) office in Cape Town I regularly attended services at St George's Cathedral. After a special reconciliation service my attention was drawn to a big painting in one corner of the cathedral. It was indeed unusual to see the Christ figure depicted as a black person – rather than the typical Western portrayal of a 'whitey in a nightie'[3] I recognised the face of Chief Luthuli. But my eyes were drawn to a figure in the bottom left corner: a white soldier with a long

2 Harrison, R. *The Black Christ: A Journey to Freedom*. New Africa Books, 2008, p. 25-26.
3 Ibid. p. 26.

spear piercing the side of the black figure on the cross. This Roman centurion had a disturbingly familiar face. Pictures, paintings, statues of a revered Prime Minister Verwoerd featured prominently in my Afrikaner Nationalist upbringing. But we were not only members of the same 'white tribe', the Afrikaners. We belonged to the same church, the Dutch Reformed Church. And Dr. H.F. Verwoerd is *Oupa* Hendrik, my grandfather.

The subscript reads: 'Grandpa and grandma Verwoerd with their grandchildren, Pretoria, 8 September 1964'. In this picture, taken on the porch of the Prime Minister's official residence, Libertas, I happen to be the six-month-old baby on Grandpa Hendrik's lap.

By the time I encountered *The Black Christ* in 1997, I had already undergone a major political and religious transformation away from my earlier enthusiastic membership of the Dutch Reformed Church and proud membership of the Verwoerd family.[4] Still, the image of Verwoerd as the person piercing the side of Luthuli was and remains upsetting, especially when I also zoom in on the above family picture.

An irreconcilable contrast: Architect of Apartheid versus *Oupa* Hendrik

How can I look honestly, open-heartedly at both these images – the emotionless soldier and the smiling, caring grandfather? How do I face the truth of an 'iconic painting of the struggle for liberation' (Martin in Harrison 2008: xiv) and accept the intimate intergenerational connections symbolised by *Oupa's* smile and the unexpected milk bottle in his almost motherly hand? How have my bones – my deep-seated racialised prejudices and ethnocentric fears – been shaped by my grandfather's

4 Verwoerd, W. J. 1997. *My Winds of Change*, Johannesburg: Ravan Press.

'milk'?[5] And what is the relevance of this 'blood' connection in my relationships with those who still identify with Luthuli? These images – and the largely irreconcilable tension between them – are guiding my ongoing efforts to articulate and embody my shared responsibility as a former supporter and ongoing beneficiary of apartheid, as a 50-something white, Afrikaner.[6]

In what follows I draw attention, in broad brushstrokes, to some of the large themes highlighted for me by pondering *The Black Christ* in combination with this white *oupa*.

A double-edged spear

Ron Harrison's visual comparison between the apartheid era suppression of 'non-Whites' and the crucifixion of Jesus enabled his prophetic critique to transcend political and moral denunciation, to bring perhaps the deepest wounding of those represented by the Luthuli figure to the surface. As Archbishop Desmond Tutu put it in his preface to Steve Biko's classic *I Write What I Like:*

> Constantly, in the difficult days of our struggle against apartheid, I used to say that the Black Consciousness movement was surely of God. You see, the most awful aspect of oppression and injustice was not the untold suffering it visited on its victims and survivors, ghastly as that turned out to be. No, it was the fact that apartheid could, through its treatment of God's children, actually make many of them doubt whether they were indeed God's children. That I have described as almost the ultimate blasphemy.[7]

Of course, as pointed out by Biko, Black Theology and Liberation Theology, a system such as apartheid also raised doubts about God.[8] For example, while working on *Verwoerd: My Journey through Family Betrayals*,[9] I asked a fellow believer, Ashnat Adolph, how she made sense of the fact that white Afrikaners like me claimed to be Christians, while enthusiastically supporting apartheid.

> 'It didn't make sense!' she answered. 'At that time, we believed that God was a white person, that's why all this injustice is done to us as black people'.[10]

5 See Jansen, J. D. 2009. *Knowledge in the Blood: Confronting Race and the Apartheid Past*. Cape Town: UCT Press.

6 For earlier, more philosophical writing on my shared historical responsibility see Verwoerd, W. J., 2001. 'On Our Moral Responsibility for Past Violations', Alternation, 8 (1), pp. 219-242.

7 Biko, S. *I Write What I Like*. Johannesburg: Picador, 2012: ix.

8 Boesak, A. 1984. *Black and Reformed: Apartheid, Liberation and the Calvinist Tradition*. Johannesburg: Skotaville.

9 Verwoerd, W.J. 2019. *Verwoerd: My Journey through Family Betrayals*, Cape Town: Tafelberg.

10 In the mid-1970s Ashnat and her sister became part of a charismatic Christian movement. 'So, we thought, "this is cool, maybe God is not so bad after all, I see a different God. Maybe the god that we knew [before] was a white god, but this is a different God – it seems that this God is loving". So, our faith increased' (Verwoerd 2019).

How different would South Africa's history have been if members of the Dutch Reformed Church took John Calvin's theology of social justice more seriously. I am entering rather murky theological and political territory here, but I am struck by how 'Calvinist' *The Black Christ* is, at least according to Wolterstorff's Calvin.[11] He stresses that for Calvin claims of love and justice towards other human beings is grounded in the *inalienable* iconicity of *all* human beings as being created 'in the image of God'. Therefore, 'to treat unjustly one of these human earthlings in whom God delights is to bring sorrow to God. To wound his beloved is to wound him.'[12] Calvin's discussion of the Eucharist brings Christ explicitly into this radical picture:

> We shall benefit very much from the Sacrament if this thought is impressed and engraved on our minds that none of the brethren can be injured, despised, rejected, abused or in any way offended by us without at the same time injuring, despising and abusing Christ by the wrongs we do (Institutes, IV 8:38)[13]

In other words, Harrison's painting presents a radical questioning of *Christian* Afrikaner Nationalism. It confronts someone like me with a profound, painful truth: what Verwoerd and his supporters did to Luthuli and his people, we also did to Christ (Matt. 25:38-40, Acts 9:4-5); even though I was *sincere* in my Dutch Reformed, Christian nationalist following of (a white) Jesus, I thus remain complicit in the deepest wounding of fellow human beings and, therefore, the re-crucifixion of Christ.

Why is it so painful for me to really look at *The Black Christ*? Partly because of an empathetic connection with the visible, bloodied point of the spear – the 'suffering with' of (growing) compassion for those on the receiving end of the multi-layered violence of apartheid.[14] There is also the intense discomfort accompanying the moral emotions of guilt and, especially, shame evoked by accepting that I also held that spear.[15] But I sense that there is yet a deeper kind of (self-inflicted) pain at stake.

In working with ex-combatants from the conflicts in and about Northern Ireland, Israel-Palestine and from the USA, I became intensely aware of the human cost of direct involvement in violence.[16] Especially in the US context, the language of 'moral

11 See also De Gruchy, J. 2009. *John Calvin: Christian Humanist and Evangelical Reformer*. Wellington: Lux Verbi.

12 Wolterstorff, N. 1987. 'The wounds of God: Calvin's Theology of Social Justice', *The Reformed Journal*, 37 (6), p. 20.

13 Quoted in Wolterstorff 1987:20

14 See Orange, D. 'Traumatised by Transcendence: My Other's Keeper' in Eric Boynton & Peter Capretto (editors), *Trauma and Transcendence: Suffering and the Limits of Theory*, New York: Fordham University Press.

15 On guilt as a moral emotion associated with particular actions in contrast to shame arising from a sense of failure in one's being, see Klaassen, J. A. 2001. 'The Taint of Shame: Failure, Self-Distress, and Moral Growth', *Journal of Social Philosophy*, 32 (2), 174-196.

16 Little, A. & Verwoerd, W.J. 2013. *Journey through Conflict Trail Guide: Introduction*, Trafford Publishing.

injury' has become prominent to try and capture an inner wounding that cannot really be addressed by psychological diagnoses and interventions associated with 'post-traumatic stress disorder'. 'Moral injury' usually designates 'the violation, by oneself or another, of a personally embedded moral code or value resulting in deep injury to the psyche or soul. It is what used to be called sin.'[17] Typical war-related moral injuries include the witnessing of or being involved in the killing of children and women, even if the soldier believes in the 'rightness' of his side's overall cause.[18]

Drawing on his academic training as a classicist and many years of helping to address the moral injuries of US veterans, Meagher carefully applies ancient notions of (moral) pollution ('miasma') in his nuanced critique of the 'just war' tradition. Given my personal and professional journeys, his claim, that the killing of another human being leaves 'blood' not only on the hands of the killer (even if the killing was not intended), resonates with me. Morally and spiritually speaking, the hands of those who directed and supported the killing are also stained.[19]

When I look at *The Black Christ* through the lens of 'moral injury' I see an invisible part of the spear, the sharp point at the bottom end, which actually is deeply buried in the soldier figure. I see that part of the apartheid spear because I can also feel it entangled in my guts.

My hunch is that the repression of *this* pain – the violation of our core moral and religious values by the political system we supported (and still benefit from) – lies at the heart of the (ongoing) 'banning' of Harisson's painting from white Afrikaner enclaves, such as the Dutch Reformed Church. This avoidance of the truth symbolised by *The Black Christ* raises the urgent question: how can I (and people like me) constructively address the realities symbolised by this double-edged spear?

A good place to start, I believe, is to take our shared historical responsibility as white South Africans much more seriously.[20]

White responsibility after 1994

The figure of the soldier with a spear in *The Black Christ* can also be seen as a representation of shared responsibility. A close look reveals the elderly, wrinkled face of an elected, revered/hated political leader, but the body is that of a muscular, youthful soldier. For me, this unusual combination is a warning against a too easy

17 Meagher, R. E. 2014. *Killing from the Inside Out: Moral Injury and Just War*. Eugene, Oregon: Cascade Books, xvi-xvii.

18 On 'perpetrator trauma,'see Eyerman, R. 2018. 'Perpetrator trauma and collective guilt: My Lai' in Eric Boynton & Peter Capretto (editors), *Trauma and Transcendence: Suffering and the Limits of Theory*, New York: Fordham University Press.

19 An obvious pitfall with this relational approach is destructive guilt by association, as demonstrated by cases of 'ethnic cleansing', blood feuds etc.

20 Accepting responsibility can help to make the blanket ascription of guilt-by-association less tempting and at the same time help heal moral injuries.

scapegoating of a particular political leader. While I acknowledge the large individual responsibility, H.F. Verwoerd carries as former Minister of 'Native Affairs' (1950-1958) and Prime Minister (1958-1966), I also accept that the most visible faces of the apartheid state, apart from political leaders like Verwoerd, were fellow Afrikaners in the bureaucracy and the police. But there were many other white South Africans who, in effect, were also holding on to that long spear. I recently found a telling reminder of the less visible support of (many) English-speaking white South Africans in my grandmother's diary from the 1960s. On 1 September 1963 Betsie Verwoerd wrote:

> The day before yesterday we returned from [the National Party conference] in Natal. I was a bit sceptical about reports of a turnaround in Natal. The reality was overwhelming.
>
> Already at Monday evening's dinner it was surprising: around 480 people, more than half English-speaking. H[endrik] received a standing ovation.
>
> After H's speech on Tuesday evening – City Hall filled to capacity – Mrs Hattingh told me what someone next to her had said: 'I am rooted to the spot, I can't move'. Nearby a group of three English people, one said: 'Oh, if only I could touch his sleeve!' And then they started to sing 'For he's a jolly good fellow!'

This disturbing picture reminded me of a statement by a senior military person, Craig M. Williamson, at the Military Forces hearing of the TRC (Cape Town, October 1997):

> South Africa's weapons, ammunition, uniforms, vehicles, radios and other equipment were all developed and provided by industry. South Africa's finances and banking were controlled by institutions that went so far as to provide covert credit cards for covert operations. South African chaplains prayed for 'victory' and South African schools and universities educated for war. The media carried propaganda and the enfranchised white community voted the former government back into power, time after time, with ever-increasing majorities.[21]

In a sub-section on Responsibility and Reconciliation, the TRC Report begins to draw out the implications of the above spiral of responsibility by stating that '[t]he emergence of a responsible society, committed to the affirmation of human rights (and, therefore, to addressing the consequences of past violations), presupposes the acceptance of individual responsibility by all those who supported the system of apartheid (or simply allowed it to continue to function) and those who did not oppose violations during the political conflicts of the past. It is, therefore, not only

21 Williamson, C.M. Quoted in TRC Report, Vol 1:131, Cape Town, October (1997).

the task of the members of the Security Forces to examine themselves and their deeds. It is for every member of the society they served to do so' (1:131).

I fully agree with this statement. However, the responsibility of someone like me goes beyond my individual acts of support and omission before 1994. My strong personal connection with the Verwoerd figure in *The Black Christ* draws my attention to a more relational, identity-based understanding of my shared historical responsibility.

To begin to flesh out this understanding I would like to quote from a reflective conversation amongst peace practitioners, as part of an international Beyond Dehumanisation research project.[22] I greatly value the practical wisdom brought by all the participants, but here I would like to focus on an interaction between three South Africans present – myself, Brandon Hamber (from an English, anti-apartheid background) and Themba Lonzi (a former anti-apartheid youth activist):

> I'm thinking if, under Apartheid, I did something directly to you Themba, it would to some extent have been easier for me to say today, "I'm sorry, Themba, for what I did." And then together we figure out a way to address that wrong. One of my difficulties is that what happened to you and your family and your community is also because of what my grandfather did, what my family did, what my community did – what I did *as a member* of the Afrikaner community – what my church did, what white South Africans did.
>
> Take Alistair's question this morning: "What does it *really* mean to accept responsibility for the suffering of your enemy?" Yes, Themba, I would have regarded you as part of a group that I saw as an enemy of white Afrikaners. I've moved beyond that perception, but what is my shared responsibility for what we Afrikaners did to our enemies, to you and your group? I'm not sure how the language of "I am sorry" or even "responsibility" helps me to grapple with that bigger, shared responsibility. What would be enough? What can I do – as a white South African, as an Afrikaner, as a Verwoerd, as a former member of the Dutch Reformed Church, as a former supporter, as an ongoing beneficiary – that will really be meaningful restitution?

Alistair was the first to respond:

> Wilhelm, why do you want to know "what is enough"? Let's say *nothing* will ever be enough. Why can that not be ok? Because it's not about un-doing,

22 From 2012 to 2014 my colleagues Alistair Little (from a Loyalist, ex-paramilitary British background), Brandon Hamber (Professor of Peace Studies, Ulster University) and I brought together small, diverse groups of experienced peacemakers from the conflict in and about Northern Ireland, from the Israeli-Palestinian conflict and from South Africa, to reflect on the challenging journeys of humanisation between (former) political enemies. Funding was provided by The Fetzer Institute.

> it's not about making right what can't be made right. It's about what can I do with my life now, for the rest of my life, that might make a difference. Knowing that no matter what you do will ever be enough. Because the question "what is enough" points to the danger of putting some kind of value on people's suffering. There is the risk of wanting to find out "what's enough so I don't have to do it anymore"; "what's enough so I can forget and let go?"
>
> Maybe we're never meant to forget, or to let go. But it does mean that the way you live the rest of your life is about making that small difference.

Brandon also challenged me:

> Wilhelm, when you were speaking, there was a part of me that just wanted to say to you: "this is something you need to let go of: you don't have to represent the whole of Afrikanerdom in South Africa because of what your grandfather was. You should be measured on what *you* do *now*, not about what *he* did *then*". Maybe that's me speaking to myself: as an *individual* white South African I have to let go, I shouldn't have to pay the price for *everything*.

Then it was Themba's turn:

> The fact that Wilhelm is part of this kind of work, it means a lot to me. I mean, his grandfather was the leader of the Apartheid system, but personally he made a different choice in his life. I know he is a Verwoerd. That fact will never change. He is a grandson of H.F. Verwoerd – someone responsible for a lot of damage caused in South Africa and to my people. But Wilhelm has made a choice to become part and parcel of processes of healing and reconciliation. The fact that he is able to acknowledge things that went wrong, that, yes, he benefitted from Apartheid simply because of the colour of his skin, for me, that means a lot. The moment people are able to acknowledge – and not only acknowledge, but take steps, take actions that are trying to seek redress – for me it means a lot ...

With a lump in my throat, I responded to Themba and Brandon:

> For me there is something very profound about what Archbishop Tutu and others call "Ubuntu". This means I cannot fully be myself without a relationship with you Themba. It was only through relationships with black South Africans – them being willing to listen to me and accept me for who I was – that I became liberated. I couldn't "let go" on my own.
>
> And yes, I'm an individual. But I'm also in relationship with many people. That is why I think the relationship with my grandfather, with my family,

> with my community, is not some kind of taking on of everything. It is about honouring the relational connections. It is about knowing that people are still suffering because of what he did. And understanding that my **acknowledgement** of past wrongdoing *because of my family connection* can still make a small difference to that suffering.

In this conversation I was challenged, on the one hand, by Alistair Little to be (more) honest with myself, to investigate more deeply the motives behind my question 'what would be enough'? How much self-interest is lurking behind my concern about too much shared responsibility? Am I trying to mark out a sustainable share, or am I actually trying to get rid of a heavy burden? To the extent that the latter desire is playing a role my 'enough' question becomes a symptom of my underlying tendency to accept too little responsibility.

In the process Alistair also confronted me with this uncomfortable truth: compassion across conflict boundaries cannot be quantified; even if I accept 'too much' responsibility, it will still not be enough. No matter what I do it will still be inadequate restitution for my share in a crime against humanity. Accepting my shared responsibility is also about learning to live with this fathomlessness.

He also pointed, on the other hand, to a form of complicity that I've not considered before. It is possible for me to take too much responsibility on my shoulders. If I highlight my shared responsibility too brightly, then I am in effect contributing to scapegoating. When I am not prepared to challenge fellow Afrikaners and other white South Africans to also accept shared responsibility, then I am making it easier for them to place the sins of the fathers on me as an individual.

As far as my shared responsibility as a grandchild of Dr. H.F. Verwoerd is concerned, I do agree with Brandon and Alistair: I don't want to allow Oupa Hendrik's sins from the past to smother my creative contribution in the present. He must take responsibility for his actions. I don't want to turn him into a scapegoat, but neither can I carry all the pain caused by him. I was two and a half when he was assassinated. I did not do what he did.

I do realise, however, that the division of responsibility in my Verwoerd family is not that clear-cut. Whether I like it or not, a part of me still feels co-responsible for what Dr. Verwoerd did as politician. After all, he remains my grandfather. There is a relational dimension to my shared responsibility that cannot be reduced to causal agency.

People like Themba Lonzi, ironically, continue to be midwife in my attempts to embody my shared responsibility, in particular as a grandson of H.F. Verwoerd. In a recent follow-up conversation Themba stated:

> In life and death, one is connected to your ancestors. They are still around. One needs to talk to them, or to him, though not confrontationally. You ask him to remove the burden of his actions from you. One should not be burdened by the deeds of forefathers. You can also ask other ancestors to help with this lifting of the burden ... It is more complex when it comes to those who are still suffering. *Given the blood connection they will always see you as a representative of your ancestor.* When they see you, it will trigger the association with what he did ...

I asked him whether it is possible to do some kind of public ritual, so that [those who are still suffering] are aware of the difference between me and this ancestor? 'Is it not possible for me to distance myself from what he did and to acknowledge their suffering'?

'Yes,' he answered. 'But this is not going to be easy, especially if those who are still suffering don't know you.'

So, this is what Themba is telling me: Wilhelm, accept that your grandfather is your ancestor. This is a bond of blood that cannot be broken. Because you are a blood relative, you will remain a representative of your deceased forefather for the rest of your life. The question is: how do you act as a representative of Verwoerd?

(White) resistance to shared responsibility

When I try to respond to Themba's call I am disturbed to notice that a part of me continues to resist, the same part that still tries to shy away from the political blood on the hands of the soldier-with-a-spear in *The Black Christ*. What is going on in me?

I suspect that more than the intense discomfort of shame and 'moral injury' is at stake. Neither does being a 'blood relative' fully explain my inner resistance, even though I must face the likelihood that the 'milk' from Oupa's hand and especially my father's 'unbreakable' loyalty to *his* father probably soaked more fully into the marrow of my bones than I would like to acknowledge.

A different kind of blood tie is also involved. A close look at the oupa-with-a-milk-bottle family picture will not show visible scarring on Verwoerd's face, even though a few years before this picture was taken, on 9 April 1960, he was shot twice in the face, at point blank range by David Pratt. His full recovery was a medical rarity and unsurprisingly was interpreted by religious family, friends and the Dutch Reformed Church as a 'miracle from God'. Two years after the grandparents and grandchildren photo was taken, on 6 September 1966, Prime Minister Verwoerd was assassinated by Dimitri Tsafendas in Parliament. Among his many supporters his death was sanctified – 'he sacrificed his life for our volk (ethnic group)'.

This inherited, inner circle *meaning* given to the spilled lifeblood of a beloved leader became an invisible, 'sacred bond' between Verwoerd and his followers.[23] It is this bond that probably is the main source of my persistent reluctance to name the political blood on his hands. For this naming feels like a betrayal.

During the Beyond Dehumanisation reflective process, in the context of a conversation about 'sacred bonds' between the living and those who 'sacrificed' their lives, Alistair Little gave this graphic input:

I think this notion of sacredness and bonds also has something to do with how we've been conditioned – going along with the group or going along with the cause. Betraying all of that, betraying all of what you've been conditioned to believe is the right thing to do, feels like breaking "sacred bonds". If you speak out against this conditioning you're "supporting the enemy" or you're "agreeing with the enemy". *And therefore, the blood of your friends, your community is not only on the hands of the enemy, this blood is also on your hands, because you're supporting those who did the killing.* (My emphasis).

By critically pointing to the blood on Verwoerd's hands there is a sense in which his sacrificial, sanctified lifeblood is now also on my hands. No wonder my father and those who still share his views see me as a traitor of family and *volk*?

To make some sense of this visceral dynamics of betrayal and its contribution to my inner resistance to the truth represented by *The Black Christ*, I find it helpful to draw on Margalit's key distinction between 'thick' and 'thin' human relationships.[24,25] The latter refers to the basic, unconditional respect one owes to all persons in their capacity as human beings; the former points to the multidimensional, limited nature of relationships of mutual care. These 'thick' relationships are characterised by an interwoven sense of belonging (versus achievement), the sharing memories and the provision of existential meaning. The main paradigms or metaphors for thick relationships are **family** and **friendship**. Margalit's central claim is that the home of betrayal is thick relationships; betrayal involves the undermining, the breaking of thick relationships.

In other words, to fully understand the dynamics of betrayal one must appreciate the 'thickness' of the (**intra**group) relationships that are under threat when a member of a tightly-knit group reaches out to the Other. In the process of untangling the strands of family type relationships, one also gains a clearer picture of why it is so difficult to move beyond an initial sense of family/fraternal betrayal. Thus, Margalit helps me to see that what is also at stake in 'reconciliation' between (political) 'enemies' is the

23 Verwoerd, W. J. 2019. *Verwoerd: My Journey through Family Betrayals*, Cape Town: Tafelberg.
24 Margalit, A. 2002. *The Ethics of Memory*. Cambridge, Massachusetts: Harvard University Press.
25 Margalit, A. 2017. *On Betrayal. Cambridge*, Massachusetts: Harvard University Press.

transformation of thick relationships with one's own group, with one's (literal and/or figurative) family and friends.

There is of course a huge risk that too much attention could be given to intragroup dynamics, as highlighted by some 'single identity' peace work in Northern Ireland.[26] But in my experience the complex challenge of transforming 'thick' intragroup relations tends to be neglected in mainstream reconciliation discourse with its typical focus on restoring or healing **inter**personal or **inter**group relations between 'victims' and 'perpetrators'. This focus is typically accompanied by an emphasis on the need for forgiveness and apology, without addressing the 'dilemma of apology' – the sense of betrayal of comrades, cause, community that may arise from the acknowledgement of wrongdoing coupled with the fear that *not* acknowledging wrongdoing will add insult to injury.[27]

Embracing *The Black Christ?*

The unavoidable tensions between Verwoerd-as-soldier in *The Black Christ* and Oupa-with-a-milk-bottle in the family photo highlight for me the messiness and the conflictual nature of deep reconciliation in, for example, post-1994 South Africa. I deliberately do not refer to 'post-apartheid' since the legacies of decades and centuries of systematic racial discrimination are still so present in South Africa, 25 years after our first democratic political election. I am also very cautious to use the language of 'reconciliation' given the tendency among people like me to embrace the undeserved generosity of spirit of so many black South Africans far too easily. I therefore hesitate to draw out some of the implications of putting a Chief Luthuli in the place of Christ on the cross, especially when it comes to Jesus' 'Father, forgive them ... for they do not know what they are doing' (Luke 23:34).

Before South Africans who look like me can explore the latter implication, we firstly need to spend time owning our presence in another painting, which for many black South Africans, in my experience, truly represents the face of most white beneficiaries of apartheid, before and after 1994. White South Africans need to critically revisit our European roots, aided by a visit to the Arena Chapel in Padua, Italy. There, in the centre of a series of paintings depicting vices such as anger, envy, pride, we will find Giotto's *Inguistizia.*

His portrait suggests how injustice looks to victims. The face of Injustice has a male profile that looks to the right. Small, fanglike teeth at the sides of the mouth and the chin thrust forward speak of coldness and cruelty. In his right hand is a nasty pruning

26 Church, C., Johnson, L.S. & Visser, A. *A path to peace or persistence? The single identity approach to conflict resolution in Northern Ireland. Conflict Resolution Quarterly* Vol 21 (3) Spring 2004.

27 Verwoerd, W. J. & Little, A. 2018. 'Beyond a Dilemma of Apology: Transforming (Veteran) Resistance to Reconciliation in Northern Ireland and South Africa', in B. Kröndorfer (ed.) *Reconciliation in Global Context, SUNY* (State University of New York) Press.

hook, not a sceptre; his left hand holds a long sword, pointing downwards; he wears a ruler's or a judge's cap, but it is turned backward. Around him is a gate in ruin. The trees surrounding him are rooted in soil where there is a theft, a rape and a murder. The scene is watched by two soldiers, but they do nothing; neither does the ruler.[28]

Giotto's *Inguistizia*

'Ordinary' white South Africans might struggle to identify with the fangs and the coldness of the ruler but a common refrain in my current engagement with black South Africans is their experience of typical white South Africans as 'arrogant' and 'indifferent'.[29] When beneficiaries of systemic racial injustice 'do nothing', look away, or hide behind the pointing of (historically unaware) fingers at the (serious) shortcomings of current black rulers, the need for 'white work' – for the self-critical examination of 'whiteness'[30] and the pervasive power of the 'ignorance contract'[31] – is highlighted. For a critical feature of shared historical responsibility is the fact that apartheid wounding is not restricted to once-off acts at a particular time and place; the quality of subsequent responses to what happened in the past has the potential to wound again or to help heal in the present. As Paul Ricoeur put it succinctly: 'by remembering and telling, we ... prevent forgetfulness from killing the victims twice.'[32] That is, my (and my children's) responses to what our forefathers did has the ability to crucify black South Africans again, or to be part of the slow intergenerational process of (re)humanisation.

Returning to *The Black Christ*, I am struck by the contrast in vulnerability between the white soldiers and the black person on the cross. My facilitation practice has taught me the critical importance of spaces of shared vulnerability and deep listening. For me, this painting has become an invitation to lay down the white spear of defensiveness and forgetfulness, to remove outer and inner armoury that laagers our compassion and humbly to open hearts and hands to black pain.

28 Shklar, J. 1990. *The Faces of Injustice*. New Haven: Yale University Press, 46-7.

29 In the 2017 South African social attitudes survey 64.8% of white South Africans disagreed/strongly disagreed with this statement: *'It is essential that all white South Africans take action towards repairing the damages of the past'.*

30 Snyman, G. 2011. 'Empire and a Hermeneutics of Vulnerability', *Studia Historiae Ecclesiasticae*, 37 – Supplement: 1-20.

31 Steyn, M. 2012. 'The ignorance contract: recollections of apartheid childhoods and the construction of epistemologies of ignorance', *Identities*, 19:1, 8-25 (DOI:10.1080/1070289X.2012.672840).

32 Ricoeur, P. 1995. *'The Memory of Suffering', Figuring the Sacred*. Minneapolis: Fortress Press, p. 290.

The Black Christ ultimately leaves me with a sense of hope that there is indeed new life after the crucifixion of apartheid. This hope is largely rooted in my own experience of real Ubuntu when I accept my 'cross' as a white, Afrikaner, Verwoerd; an experience mediated by the undeserved welcoming arms of black South Africans.

7.
Memory holes and impoverished democracy in South Africa and Central Europe[1]

Dagmar Kusá

Memory holes and democracy

> Where all are guilty, no one is; confessions of collective guilt are the best possible safeguard against the discovery of culprits, and the very magnitude of the crime the best excuse for doing nothing. – Hannah Arendt

The transition from the regimes of apartheid and communism followed rather different paths in their institutional choices to address the past. South Africa chose a mechanism of public hearings, giving voice to the victims of gross human rights violations as well as former perpetrators in televised sessions of the Truth and Reconciliation Commission (TRC), followed by less successful mechanisms of reparations for former victims and communities and an even less successful process of criminal justice for some of the perpetrators.[2] Central European countries have developed much more modest institutions for addressing the past, represented most visibly by the process of lustrations (with varying degrees of scope and success), and national memory institutes that serve mostly as archives for the communist and fascist past. Furthermore, the founding, state-forming narrative in South Africa revolves around the politically united Rainbow Nation, composed of a diversity of ethnicities, races, tribes, and languages, whereas Central European nations are founded on grounds of ethno-linguistic national ideas, leading to exclusivist, ethnicised notions of citizenship. Given these differences, it would be natural to expect that the outcomes of those transitional narratives, institutions, and processes would yield dramatically different results. The similarities are therefore all the more surprising.

Why are young people taking to the streets in droves, challenging their governments on corruption, links to organised crime, and social and economic inequality? Why is the generation now entering adulthood more radical than that of their parents?

---

1 This work was supported by the Slovak Research and Development Agency under the contract No. APVV-15-0682.

2 Villa-Vicencio, C. (2015). The South African Transition: Then and Now. In V. Tismaneanu, & B. C. Iacob, *Remembrance, History, and Justice: Coming to terms with traumatic pasts in democratic societies* (pp. 311-327). Budapest & New York: Central European University Press.

This paper links the answers to the political dimension of narrating the past and claims that the political use of the past has been captured in similar ways in both contexts. In public discourse, as well as in history lessons within the educational systems, the narratives were and still are subordinated to the political aims of the current administrations, and thus captured by the political power. The process of narrating then is not open to a diversity of actors and voices but tells a single story – and political power engages in the manipulation and commanding of memory.

Such a politicised approach to the past impacts the quality of democracy, leading to gaps in transitional justice which continue to impact the level of trust in democratic institutions. It also results in a severed intergenerational transmission of memory, resulting in a young generation that has grown up in a moral void, deprived of a meaningful relationship with the past that would inform their present collective identity and serve as a foundation for civic participation.

In the first sense, memory holes threaten the *democratic* project; in the latter, they pose challenges to the *national* project.

Do we *need* a narrative of cultural trauma?

In the transitional justice literature, it seems to be taken for granted that cultural trauma has to be addressed, discussed, and resolved. Alexander et al. define cultural trauma as a current narrative of a past event or era that is perceived as having caused significant damage to the social fabric of a society. This narrative is told by concrete actors and entrepreneurs for specific audiences and with current objectives.[3] But is there a direct link between cultural trauma and democracy? Does not dwelling on the past only contribute to reigniting conflicts?

Democracy, as understood by Amartya Sen,[4] Martha Nussbaum[5] and Ronald Ingehart[6] is founded on the ethic of social consequences of policies and institutions upon the well-being and fulfilment of potential of every individual, particularly the most vulnerable in the society. It is a *dignitarian* democracy,[7] the aim of which is to provide for a life in dignity for all its inhabitants.

Dignitarian democracy then also allows for cultural identities to flourish in safety, diversity, and interaction. 'Such a vision of a just society corresponds with Ricoeur's three layers of ethical life: personhood, sociality (interpersonal relations), and just

3 Alexander, J. (2012). *Trauma: A social theory. Cambridge*, UK – Malden, MA: Polity Press.
4 Sen, A. (2011). *The Idea of Justice*. Cambridge, MA: Belknap Press.
5 Nussbaum, M. (2011). *Creating Capabilities: The human development approach*. Cambridge, MA and London, England: The Belknap Press of the Harvard University Press.
6 Inglehart, R. (1997). *Modernization and postmodernization: Cultural, economic, and political change in 43 societies*. Princeton, NJ: Princeton University Press.
7 Fuller, R. (2006). *All rise: Somebodies, nobodies, and the politics of dignity*. San Francisco: Berrett-Koehler Publishers.

institutions.[8] For such a vision of democracy, it is quite clear that significant cultural trauma does indeed have to be addressed, lest some of the elements of the framework for the fulfilment of personal dignity were violated.

On a practical level, Jeffrey Alexander[9] maintains that a cultural trauma narrative opens the possibility for collectives to re-experience cultural trauma, which may lead to identity revision, becoming more inclusive and more empathic among various groups. 'By allowing the members of the wider audience to participate in the pain of others, cultural traumas broaden the realm of social understanding and sympathy, and they provide powerful avenues for new forms of social incorporation.'[10] When the wider audience is able to participate in the pain of the former victim, it allows for empathy to broaden the circle of 'we' and blurs the line between 'us' and 'them'.[11] Such a trauma narrative is able to provide grounds for greater social cohesion and interpersonal trust. This is especially important for societies in transition, which have to grapple with many emotions stemming from personal insecurities tied to rapidly changing social, economic, and political conditions.

That story matters. How it is able to include or exclude the various actors from a shared pool of empathy, how open it is to a multitude of voices, how controlling the storytellers are of its content, and even who can be a storyteller. It is here that South Africa and Central Europe share common patterns, trends, and consequences. The memory regimes – that is, the narrative frames, the institutions that were designed to address the past stemming from that narrative, and the legislation regulating both – were captured early on during the transition by the emerging political elite, initially to boost the potential for the success of the transition processes and build up the legitimacy of the first governments. But the grip on memory regimes has not loosened since. It is apparent in the political discourse, on the playing field of symbolic politics, and in the educational systems. Just as it was thirty years ago, and perhaps more in some instances, memory is used primarily to further the current political agenda.

Capture of memory regime

Governments everywhere set up the framework in which memory can flow through constitutions, legislation, institutions, and processes that address the past – the memory regime of a society. When a political establishment seeks to push forward a single story – a particular interpretation of the past in the pursuit of a political agenda – and blocks a diversity of voices from access to these channels of narration within the mainstream of the public discourse, we can refer to a captured memory

8 Ricoeur, P. (1992). *Oneself as another.* (K. Blamey, Trans.) Chicago and London: The University of Chicago Press.
9 Alexander, J. (2012).
10 Ibid. s. 24.
11 Ibid. p. 22.

regime. Collective memory is manipulated to justify and legitimise those in power, serving a specific cause or ideology, abusively commanded (such as the recitation of official histories, often in school history lessons) and commanded to forget (for example, amnesty granted to a specific individual or group of people).[12]

At this point, we turn to explore the memory regimes and their political underpinnings in South Africa and Central Europe to explore their openness and capture during the processes of transition in both areas.

Anatomy of the transitions

Narrative macro-structure

The broader geopolitical context of post-colonialism and post-socialism within which these two regions are embedded offers structural context that has significantly shaped the narratives of the past and their link to the current visions of democratic societies. A comparison of experiences across the two contexts is gaining currency in the social sciences. Post-colonialism and post-socialism both carry a legacy of the structures of oppression and dependency on external centres.[13] Furthermore, both influence the perceived status of being a periphery in relation to the power centres. There is also a shared deep mistrust in history as the narratives of the past are woven around victimhood, having always been on the wrong side of history. Collective identity narratives thus developed under similar constraints, in reaction to external narratives and power structures, and this heritage still shapes the perceptions of a political nation – a shared identity story, and a sense of who does and who does not belong to these communities today.

Naturally, the parallel is not to be overestimated. Post-socialism certainly does not carry with it the burden of slavery or racialism that further oppressed the colonised societies. Émigrés escaping the communist bloc had little trouble integrating into Western societies, whereas the 'pilgrims' from the former colonies, to use Benedict Anderson's terminology, would encounter the glass wall of the colonial mindset in the metropole.[14] But the impact of these grand structures of relations have left their marks on the narratives of the past and on the imaginations of political communities today.

Negotiated transitions

Another shared structural feature impacting the way the narratives of the past evolved and settled at the core of the political centres of the studied countries is the negotiated feature of transitions. The starting positions and the constellations

12 Ricoeur, P. (2004). *Memory, History, Forgetting*. (K. Blamey, & D. Pellauer, Trans.) Chicago: The University of Chicago Press.
13 Radstone, S., & Hodgkin, K. (2011). *Regimes of memory*. New York: Routledge.
14 Anderson, B. (2006). *Imagined communities*. London, New York: Verso.

of power could not be more different than those between South Africa and Central European sojourners at the starting line toward democracy. However, the nature of the journey, its negotiated character, and its consequences were shared across both regions.

Much of the outcome of the course of justice during the time of the transition depends on the dominant actors in the transition as well as on their social position and role during the previous regime. Raoul Hilberg has identified the triangle of social actors under the conditions of oppression: a perpetrator, a victim, and a bystander. Considering the social reality is more complex, Sharlene Swartz has broadened his triangle to include two more important social roles: a beneficiary of the regime (and an inheritor of the benefit) and a resister (then and now).[15] The nature of oppression and the constellation of actors at the time of transition determines how the narrative of the past will evolve – whether the primary focus will be on former victims and the healing of their traumas, on bringing the perpetrators to justice, or on downplaying the legacy of the past if the new elites come from the strata of former bystanders or beneficiaries.

Before the fall of the regimes, civil societies in the two regions had dramatically different positions. In South Africa, the sphere of the oppressed represented roughly 90% of the population, with movements, military branches, unions, and churches in the hundreds (the United Democratic Front alone, the coalition of civic organisations that formed in 1980s as the major organised anti-apartheid force, consisted of some 400 organisations). The transition was dominated by the charismatic personalities of that opposition, with Nelson Mandela at the forefront after his release from prison in 1990, surrounded by a team of capable and highly trained lawyers and experts, many returning from exile to assume leadership roles. The African National Congress (ANC), the leading force entering the negotiations on the side of the opposition, boasted nearly 80 years of existence, and was equipped with the Freedom Charter, drafted in the late 1980s in a ANC-led consultative process in exile and which later became the foundation for the current Constitution.[16] The ANC emerged as the dominant political player and assumed the role of heir to the anti-apartheid struggle, an assumption upon which its legacy and the mainstream narrative was developed and is still maintained.

Central European actors were positioned very differently. The grey zone of complicity with the former communist regime, in exchange for some modicum of comfort and 'bribes' by the system (allowing children to study, securing a system of promotions, rewarding with vacations or access to hard currency, and allowing to travel) led

15 Swartz, S. (2016). *Another Country: Everyday Social Restitution*. Cape Town, Western Cape, South Africa: HSRC Press.

16 Asmal, K. (2011). *Politics in my blood: A memoir*. Auckland Park, South Africa: Jacana Media (Pty) Ltd.

to the opposite constellation, so that there was no clear dividing line between the perpetrators, victims, resisters, and beneficiaries of the system. The bulk of the population would fall into the social category of bystanders and beneficiaries of the system.[17] Therefore, the narrative framework that emerged afterwards to address the past sought to downplay and relativise the crimes committed during communism, focusing on a kind of commanded amnesia instead. The period of 'normalisation', following the 1968 invasion of Czechoslovakia by the armies of the Warsaw Pact, served to silence the majority of the population. The former Czech prime minister and a historian by training, Petr Pithart, explained: 'We have kind of a minefield in between the present time and the past and that is the Normalization. When most of the nation kept mum and obeyed the marching orders. Nobody wants to reminisce about that, yet we cannot pass over this period entirely'.[18] The active citizens of resistance against the communist regimes (of whom Pithart once was) numbered in the hundreds (in Slovakia, for example) to a few thousands elsewhere. They were able to organise more after 1976, when the communist governments acceded to several international human rights treaties – a commitment that could be used to hold them accountable, and which gave rise to the Charter '77 movement, Solidarnośç, Helsinki committees, and other platforms formed around the human rights agenda. But, as the sociologist Ivo Možný explains, the dissidents in all four countries who spoke to the masses on the squares during the revolutions of 1989 and later sat at the roundtable negotiations with the former Communist Party leaders did not elicit massive popular support and trust.[19] There were exceptions, including charismatic personalities such as Václav Havel, Alexander Dubček and Lech Wałęsa, but the common people were somewhat suspicious of the intellectuals in these movements, asking what was in it for them.[20] Perhaps, due to their own feelings of discomfort related to their status of bystanders in the past, they were also reminded of the previous complicity of the few who spoke out.

Negotiated transitions had an impact on the types of narratives and how they were controlled thereafter. The nature of negotiation is compromise. Thus, the emphasis is more on reconciliation and healing rather than on achieving justice in relation to the former political leaders. Those were granted a generous amount of amnesty in both regions as the price for the peaceful transfer of power, both as a one-time gesture during the negotiations, as well as – and especially – later on, as a consequence of the narrative frames established during the transition. In both South Africa and in

17 Swartz, S. (2016).
18 Pásztor, D. (2018, Oct 29). *Pithart: Česi sa sekli, Slovensko je na tom lepšie, dokážete sa postaviť zlu [Pithart: Czechs made a mistake, Slovaks are doing better: you are able to stand against evil]*. Retrieved from Denník N: https://dennikn.sk/1276238/pithart-cesi-sa-sekli-slovensko-je-na-tom-lepsie-dokazete-sa-postavit-zlu/?ref=mpm
19 Možný, I. (1991). *Proč tak snadno?* Prague: SLON.
20 Ibid.

all of Central Europe, the vast majority of former leaders, who were responsible for political decisions leading to the deaths, torture, disappearances, and incarceration of countless citizens, never stood trial and were able to survive relatively untouched by the transition process.

The single stories

The narratives that interpret the past serve as the foundation stones for the regimes in transition. They name the key actors, distribute guilt and praise, emplot diverse episodes into an epic story which explains and gives meaning to the past, and provide a sense for identity.[21] Heidegger talks about the interpretation of the past as authentic and inauthentic historicity. Authentic interpretation is by nature introspective. It asks questions that seek answers to resolve dilemmas related to one's personal quest for meaning and integrity. Inauthentic historicity is steadily planted in the present. It is a public interpretation of the past driven by political motives, preserving and fortifying positions of power.[22] While there have certainly been actors in both regions searching for authenticity in relation to the past, the dominant narratives were captured for political legitimation of power. All regimes utilise historical narratives to a significant extent, and in the initial phases of transitions, such a narrative becomes a particularly useful tool in stabilising the power of new actors on the scene. However, during the process of democratisation, the memory regime should gradually open up to a variety of interpretations, decentralise and deconcentrate to allow breathing space and dialogue, providing nourishment for the ethos of democratic citizenship. This part of the process has not taken place in either region. If anything, in Poland and Hungary, we are witnessing a firmer grasp on control over the memory regime and, in South Africa, the struggle to transfer control over it to new leadership in a way that would be perceived as authentic. The political establishments in these regions are telling 'single stories'[23], which select and flatten meanings to one interpretation.

'Dismantling the Rainbow Nation' and rejection of 'reconciliation ideology'

In the literature on transitional justice, the South African journey through reconciliation and healing is predominantly lauded as largely successful. The country was able to transfer power without the massive bloodshed that most thought inevitable. Furthermore, it devised the ambitious scheme of the Truth and Reconciliation Commission (TRC), fostering public and personal healing for several thousand who were able to take part in the process or who were moved by these stories circulated weekly on SABC Special Report broadcasts on TV and radio for

21 Ricoeur, P. (2004).

22 Heidegger, M. (1996). *Being and time: A translation of Sein und Zeit*. (J. Stambaugh, Trans.) Albany, NY: State University of New York Press.

23 Term inspired by Chimamanda Ngozi Adichie's warning cry against the 'danger of a single story' (Adichie, C. N. (2009, July). *The danger of a single story*. Retrieved from TEDGlobal: https://www.ted.com/talks/chimamanda_adichie_the_danger_of_a_single_story).

several years. Within its mandate, this particular mechanism was decidedly impressive, meeting and surpassing the goals of healing, truth-telling, and reconciliation for those involved. Some twenty-one thousand victims of gross human rights violations have submitted their cases to the Commission, and over seven thousand have filed for amnesty.[24] Their cases have been extensively investigated, juggling carefully the goals of healing, truth-finding, and justice, and at the same time serving as a platform to facilitate the process of addressing the past for the public. It has spoken to the prevalent feelings of anger and has been able to transform part of that into constructive support for the reconstruction of society.

Tens of thousands of others, however, were not directly part of this process. Some could not be, and others did not want to be. Many of the former ANC activists interpreted the TRC's universal evaluation of human rights violation as being equated with the crimes perpetrated by the apartheid leaders and rejected the process on those grounds. They were also resentful of the fact that 53% of the amnesty applicants came from the ANC ranks, a further 15% were from the ranks of the Inkatha Freedom Party and other liberation movements, and only 23% from the ranks of the state security forces.[25] The ANC leadership, under the leadership of the new president, Thabo Mbeki, did not wish to circulate the final Report of the TRC process, and the Mbeki and Zuma administrations did little to follow up on its recommendations, particularly regarding the reparations for the victims and communities.[26] Even though the TRC has only granted 849 amnesties,[27] the vast majority of the remaining 5,392 cases were never followed up. The few trials being pursued today (for instance, the cases of Ahmed Timol and Ashley Kriel) were brought forth with the help of civil rights organisations by surviving family members seeking closure.[28]

The narrative of the memory regime crafted during and maintained after the negotiations of power transfer was a combination of a 'regime of criminals' narrative in which individual guilt is seen and acknowledged and a 'criminal regime' narrative (like those all-over Central Europe) puts the blame on the oppressive nature of the entire system. The ANC, carrying the legacy of the anti-apartheid struggle, crafted the memory regime's narrative often at the expense of other actors. There are palpable

24 Amnesty hearings and decisions. (2018). Retrieved from Truth and Reconciliation Commission: http://www.justice.gov.za/trc/amntrans/index.htm

25 Cited in Abrahamsen, T., & van der Merwe, H. (2005). *Reconciliation through Amnesty? Amnesty Applicants' Views of the South African Truth and Reconciliation Commission*. Retrieved from CSVR: http://www.csvr.org.za/docs/trc/reconciliationthroughamnesty.pdf.

26 Villa-Vicencio, C. (2015). The South African Transition: Then and Now. In V. Tismaneanu, & B. C. Iacob, *Remembrance, History, and Justice: Coming to terms with traumatic pasts in democratic societies* (pp. 311-327). Budapest & New York: Central European University Press.

27 Amnesty hearings and decisions. (2018). Retrieved from Truth and Reconciliation Commission: http://www.justice.gov.za/trc/amntrans/index.htm

28 IJR calls on prosecuting authorities to intensify their efforts in the Ashley Kriel case. (2018, July). Retrieved from Institute for Justice and Reconciliation: http://www.ijr.org.za/2018/07/31/ijr-calls-on-prosecuting-authorities-to-intensify-their-efforts-in-the-ashley-kriel-case/

tensions between the official narrative centrally featuring the ANC-led anti-apartheid struggle and the narrative of those who are left out or marginalised, such as those previously involved in the UDF, former combatants, and several other communities.[29] The capture of memory regime aids in the capture of the state, as it is used as a subliminal justification framework to occupy positions in the state administration. Gqubule, in her book of Public Protector Thuli Madonsela (herself from the UDF), explains the difference between the competing programmes of the UDF and the ANC. The UDF, she maintains, perceived democracy as a work in progress. 'Among the exiles, however, the dominant notion seemed to be that, once state power had been seized, those who had fought for freedom would be entitled to do with it as they wished.'[30] The differing cultural traditions between the UDF and the ANC are translated into political tensions, particularly around the questions of corruption in the top echelons of the state and of the ANC. Thokozani Mhlongo perceives this clash as a crossroads on South Africa's path to democracy. 'At one stop some former exiles live in glittering opulence, while at the other the true soldiers of our struggle have been left in bewildering proximity to unendurable poverty. It is antithetical that the former *amaqabane*, or comrades, who are the true (and sadly unsung) liberators of our country are now virtually pariahs in the land they forcibly liberated from the vices of apartheid.'[31] Being left out of or marginalised in the official narrative incites negative emotions for several additional groups, sometimes even from the ranks of the disgruntled ANC cadres who were left behind in the transition process, as former combatants often were. Many experienced humiliations during the process of the merger of their units with those of the South African Defence Force after the regime change, demoted in rank, with no recognition, and frequently battling depression and anxiety from untreated trauma, alongside homelessness and poverty.[32] The Robert Sobukwe Trust recently also complained of the South African media's silence over the reburials of the PAC/Poqo combatants who were hanged for activities related to their resistance against the apartheid regime. They maintain it is a sign of the silencing and erasure of critical voices and narratives in post-1994 South Africa.

The mainstream narrative is not necessarily untrue, but it does select events and their interpretation in a fashion when such omissions can be perceived as injuries. Due to the strong control over memory regime's narrative framework, some are referring to a 'reconciliation ideology' centred on the TRC, victims and healing, the Constitution, and the concept of the rainbow nation. The critics maintain that the social and

29 Gqubule, T. (2017). *No longer whispering to power: The story of Thuli Madonsela*. Jeppestown, South Africa: Jonathan Ball Publishers.

30 Ibid p.35.

31 Ibid p. 36.

32 Gcaza, P. M. (2018). Redefining self-identity as military ex-combatant in the post-apartheid era. In D. Kusá, (*Dis-)continuous identities: Globalization, trauma, and reconciliation* (pp. 107-114). Bratislava: Kritika & Kontext.

economic order built by the apartheid regime remains largely intact to the present day, but the official narrative leaves little room to address such lingering legacies, which it is now complicit in sustaining.[33] Molefe speaks of the 'the totalising effects of the transition period's concepts – of its reconciliation ideology, in other words – on the victims of apartheid ... on people classified as 'non-white'. Due to the single story circulated in public discourse, the media, and education, many people of colour are not even aware that apartheid touched their lives as well, that even if they were not first-hand victims of gross human right violations, they were victims of massive structural oppression, impacting their quality of life. The narrative's use of the labels 'victim', 'perpetrator', and 'crime of apartheid' has so narrowly defined their meaning that in order for an authentic interpretation of the past, they have to be taken out of that structure and completely rethought.[34]

The tragedy of the small Central European nations

In the 1990s, in the early years of the transition, US State Secretary Madeleine Albright called Slovakia 'the black hole of Europe'. This was the during the dark years of Mečiarism, rampant nationalism, and high levels of organised crime. Today, along with the remaining countries of the Visegrad Four, the region has received a new label: 'the memory hole' of Europe.[35] It earned it due to the fiercely negative reactions to the migrant crisis stemming from the ethno-linguistic, exclusivist conception of nation and citizenship, and its 'memory holes' – the inability and unwillingness to address the past of the totalitarian regimes of the twentieth century in a responsible way.

The exclusivist narrative has long historical roots. In 1984, Kundera,[36] echoing István Bibó's Miseries of the East European Small States[37] pondered the origins of the sentiments present in the national narratives:

> What is Central Europe? An uncertain zone of small nations between Russia and Germany. I underscore the words: small nation... the small nation... is one whose very existence may be put in question at any moment; a small nation can disappear, and it knows it... Central Europe as a family of small nations has its own vision of the world, a vision based on a deep distrust of history. History, that goddess of Hegel and Marx, that incarnation of reason that judges us and arbitrates our fate – that is the

33 Molefe, T. O. (2014, July 29). *Reconciliation ideology, or why I will not let Adran Vlok wash my feet.* Retrieved from The Reconciliation Barometer Blog: http://reconciliationbarometer.org

34 Ibid.

35 Čulík, J., & Mackinnon, A. (2015, October 2). Central Europe's Memory Hole. Foreign Policy. Retrieved from http://foreignpolicy.com/2015/10/02/central-europes-memory-hole-migrants-refugees/

36 Kundera, M. (2000/1983). Únos západu aneb tragédie střední Evropy (1983). In M. Havelka, & L. Cabada, *Západní, východní a střední Evropa jako kulturní a poitické pojmy* (pp. 101–114). Prague: Metropolitan University Prague.

37 Bibó, I. (2015/1946). The misery of small Eastern European states. In I. Bibó, *The art of peace-making* (P. Pásztor, Trans., pp. 130-180). New Haven, London: Yale University Press.

> history of conquerors. The people of Central Europe are not conquerors. They cannot be separated from European history; they cannot exist outside it; but they represent the wrong side of this history; they are its victims and outsiders.[38]

The events that are still perceived as traumatic in the Central European narratives are often connected with the feeling that the 'West' has abandoned the nations in peril and left them to fend for themselves. Still alive in collective memories around the region is the evidence of this abandonment: the 1848-1849 catastrophe, the 1920 Trianon Treaty that dissolved the Austro-Hungarian empire and relegated Great Hungary into a rather small republic, the Munich Agreement of 1938 that sacrificed Czechoslovakia to Germany in the hope of preserving peace, and the three partitions of Poland.

The mistrust in history and fear of the elimination of a political nation was also to blame for the shortcomings and eventual failure of the Central European democracies, Bibó maintains. Political hysteria stemming from that fear and unresolved traumas led to the rise of a particular type of political leader – the phony realist, shrewd manipulator, who rose within the ranks of a democratic framework on anti-democratic, nationalist sentiment. 'Thus, what genuine democracies know only in the actual hour of danger became the rule in the permanent anxiety and sense of danger – the curbing of public freedoms; censorship; a search for the "hirelings" of the enemy, the "traitors", excessively forcing order or its veneer at the expense of liberty.'[39] These sentiments and the corresponding style of political leadership are cemented in the specific type of ethno-linguistic nationalism that defines the nature of citizenship in Central Europe today. It is an exclusivist type of citizenship, where the vision of a state-forming identity coincides with the ethnic identity of the dominant nation. All others within the country are lower down in the imaginary hierarchy of 'who really belongs'. This type of national identity, Bibó claims, is a specific Central European phenomenon.

After the fall of the communist regimes, the distrust in the West and sense of vulnerability were underscored by the reiterations of the identity of Central Europe as such. Battling a sense of inferiority attached to the status of Eastern Europe, the newly freed countries declared the desire to 'return to Europe'. But the path was winding and non-linear. Péter Eszterházy, a Hungarian novelist and intellectual, summed up these peripeteias with a sigh:

> Once, I was an Eastern European; then I was promoted to the rank of Central European. Those were great times... there were Central European dreams, visions, and images of the future...Then a few months ago I became

38 Kundera, M. (2000/1983).
39 Bibó, I. (2015/1946).

> a New European. But before I had a chance to get used to this status, I became a non-core European.[40]

The continuing divide between Western and Eastern Europe was deepened by the recent crises in the European Union and have reignited some of the emotions woven into these narratives.

Exporting guilt: Memory holes of Central Europe

After the wave of the revolutions in 1989, the democratising societies of Central Europe chose some mechanisms to address the past that showed similarities across the borders. In the first years, they pursued the politics of lustrations (with the exception of Slovakia, which abolished the policy with its independence in 1993) and founded national memory institutes, which were tasked with investigating the crimes of the past and potentially indicting and bringing the former perpetrators to justice (although they rarely fulfilled the latter function). Another shared feature was criminalising the previous regime in legislation. Despite the official proclamations of 'drawing a thick line behind the past' (especially in relation to criminal justice) and focusing on the bright, economically prosperous future, anything but that was true in the area of mnemonic politics. As the West celebrated the 'end of History' and the defeat of communism, leaving liberal democracy the uncontested victor of the grand narratives of the twentieth century, many in the former communist countries were not so convinced of its passing and of the nature the post-socialist regimes would take.[41] There were radically different interpretations of the communist past and opinions on how it should be approached. These were utilised in political battles, both on the home front, as well as within the European arena.

At the time of the onset of the post-socialist regimes, European memory was not a field of joint political pursuit as it was to become a few years later. Leaders and institutions were careful not to meddle too much into the ways of addressing the past, unlike in the area of social and economic policies or the area of human rights and protection of national minorities. Central and Eastern European countries were pressured to place the Holocaust centre stage of their collective memories – this was either used by the local anti-Communist entrepreneurs or viewed as an imposition of Western colonialism.[42]

Yet the post-socialist states were mostly left to define their own approaches and en bloc criminalisation of the past. It was a combination of a good amount of amnesty and amnesia, however, that won out in the end. Liberal anti-Communist

---

40 Esterházy, P. (2005). How big is the European dwarf? In D. Levy, M. Pensky, & J. Torpey, *Old Europe, New Europe, Core Europe: Transatlantic relations after the Iraq War* (pp. 74-79). London and New York: Verso. s. 74.

41 Mark, J. (2010). *The unfinished revolution: Making sense of the communist past in Central-Eastern Europe*. New Haven and London: Yale University Press.

42 Ibid. s. xvi, xvii.

leaders that were at the foundation of the new regimes often sought compromise to enable a smooth and quick transition rather than search for individual perpetrators, something advocated by more radical anti-Communists. Instead, they wished to allow for social integration of a society which, in the past, had consisted of the majority in the grey zone of conformity. They were not interested in boasting a strong civil society of resistance. Ex-Communists, presenting themselves as reformed democrats, often took part in commemorations and boasted of their own opposition to the previous regimes. They tolerated the creation of the national memory institutes, as long as their fates were not touched by them. Criminalisation of the communist regime in Central Europe had a declaratory character rather than any criminal justice implication.[43] The prevailing narrative thus led to legislation of communist regimes as criminal in all of the Central European countries. While Hungary included the criminalisation of communism in its new 2010 constitution, Czechia, Slovakia, and Poland introduced acts on the criminality and immorality of their respective communist regimes. The acts lifted the statute of limitations on crimes which under the communist regimes of the past had been obstructed. They also prepared legal grounds for the judicial rehabilitation of former victims. However, the political leadership of Central European communist regimes enjoyed almost total impunity, or amnesty, as a result. Even in the Czech Republic, where the policies of decommunisation went the farthest, only the low-ranking Communist Party members suffered any consequences.[44] 'New dominant nationalist discourses on the "martyrdom of the nation" under Communism meant that bearing witness to one's victimization had the potential to align individual experiences with a right-wing analysis of the past they might not support.'[45] This also explains how the unreformed Communist Party was able to survive in the Czech Republic, not only without serious challenges to its existence, but even becoming a member of the current governing coalition and making Andrej Babiš's prime ministership possible.

Memory regime is shaped in a contest of memory entrepreneurs. Mark maintains that the narrative construction in Hungary and Poland was shaped by the struggles among the radical anti-Communists, moderate liberal anti-Communists, and former Communists. The negotiated form of transition of power favoured the pact among the moderate anti-Communists and the former Communists, a direction supported by some of the former dissident intellectuals like Adam Michnik.[46] Nonetheless, that form was overturned by the current political leadership of Orbán and Kaczynski,

43 Rupnik, J. (2002). *Coming to terms with the communist past: The Czech case from a comparative perspective.* (Tranzit, Ed.) Tr@nsit Online (22). Retrieved from *Tr@nsit Online:* http://monumenttotransformation.org/atlas-of-transformation/html/c/coming-to-terms-with-the-past/coming-to-terms-with-the-communist-past-the-czech-case-from-a-comparative-perspective-jacques-rupnik.html.

44 Ibid.

45 Mark, J. (2010), s. xxviii.

46 Ibid.

each in their respective states ascending to power on a counter-narrative – wrapped in nationalist creeds – of an 'unfinished revolution' with the need to oust the reformed Communists from power and advocating illiberal democracy and the rule of the strong hand. Thus, both garnitures proclaimed a break with the transitional era, announcing a new dawn which portrays itself as the direct continuation of the pre-communist past. There was no such dramatic elite change in Slovakia and Czech Republic, and thus the official narrative of the past towards the legacy of November 1989 remains lukewarm, continuing the narrative of a criminal regime while distancing itself from it and pushing it into the background.

The exclusivist sentiment, victimhood, and export of the guilt for the totalitarianisms of the twentieth century were embedded in the constitutions of the Central European countries (with the exception of The Czech Republic, although this does not mean the sentiments were absent in the political processes there at the time). These narratives were strengthened by harking back to a distant, idealised past, the mythical 'Golden Age'. The twentieth century was treated as a glitch in long heroic national histories. Reframing the past was cemented by introducing national holidays representing the distant past (for instance, Saint Stephen's Day in Hungary and Saints Cyril and Methodius Day in Slovakia) in lieu of several possible holidays commemorating important events of the recent past. The Slovak government of Robert Fico paid homage to the statues of the Great Moravian Empire era, and even commissioned a statue of a Great Moravian king at Bratislava Castle, unveiling it with all the pomp and circumstance of an official state celebration. The manipulation of the twentieth century past has been dealt with on a symbolic level as well. Hungary has been using museums, academia, and public spaces to solidify control over the narrative and etch the selected single story into stone. Orbán has, for example, unveiled a monument to the victims of the Second World War in Budapest, in which Hungary is depicted as an innocent victim (embodied in the statue of Archangel Gabriel) attacked by the German imperial eagle. It was, however, Hungary's Horthy government that had sent the Jewish population to the concentration camps during the war. Poland is recrafting its narrative through a new campaign to reopen the question of war reparations from Germany (which was closed in 1953), and also criminalising any intent implicating Polish citizens in the crimes committed during the Holocaust. While these mnemonic plays are staged, the ground is being prepared for a gradual curbing of the freedoms of association, of a free media, of independent courts and educational institutions.

Manipulated memory and education systems

Political culture theorists maintain that where democratic political culture is missing or lacking due to a past of oppression and denied freedom, education is the key tool to restore socialisation in families and communities.[47] It is the best bet of societies in

47 Almond, G., & Verba, S. (1963). *The Civic Culture: Political Attitudes in Five Western Democracies.* Princeton, New Jersey.

transition to prepare a generation of democratic citizens. But the educational systems in both regions' transitions are among their most problematic aspects. Underfunded and under-reformed, they underperform and suffer from developmental stagnation. Thus, it is difficult to imagine how they could be the engine pulling the political culture toward democratic citizenship through complex engagement of the past.

The South African educational system has also been 'captured' by the reconciliation narrative. Elnari Potgieter of the Institute for Justice and Reconciliation maintains that while it still holds benefits for many of the White South African community, many of whom learn about the oppressive nature of the apartheid regime for the first time, it fails to address persistent social and economic inequalities and to make connections between the present disparities and the past. It does not reach students at an emotional level, thus failing to deliver any morally and personally pertinent message.[48]

Research by Mackenzie and Steinberg[49] shows that the academic and political contexts of history curricula are at odds at times in the school environment. Schools should, on the one hand, teach dexterity in historical inquiry, asking questions, considering multiple perspectives, and establishing facts. However, political interference into curricula and textbooks themselves – in particular, into the teachers' manuals and there primarily through answers provided for question prompts – prevents such dexterity from developing and turns history lessons into rote learning. The tensions experienced within families are not addressed through encountering the past in a critical fashion, and teachers often not only lack training in addressing such issues but are those who themselves never experienced the regime changes. The political agenda instead pushes an 'over-arching promotion of "collective memory" thinking, even if some individual textbook tasks do assess multiperspectivity and therefore promote Wertsch's "historical" thinking.'[50]

The state of history and civics education in Central Europe is not much better. As in South Africa, educational systems are struggling to keep the quality of education from plummeting in international rankings. Although there has been some improvement in terms of opportunities and resources, history education is still largely based on rote learning. High school civics education curriculum and textbooks combine philosophy, law, economics and management, and human rights with a pace and style that leaves little space for creativity, exploration, and questioning. Students memorise the required knowledge in the time allotted, while there is little to no teacher training for the subject, leaving it up to the motivation and willingness of individual teachers

48 Personal interview, Jan. 2017.

49 Mackenzie, B., & Steinberg, C. (Dec. 2015). Recognising the academic and political purposes embedded in history textbook assessment tasks. *Yesterday and Today* (14), 125-150.

50 Ibid. p. 147.

to create a meaningful educational experience. If students are inspired during civics lessons, it is despite the curriculum and textbooks.

Furthermore, history textbooks are subject to centralised political control. As is the case with the memory regimes narrative, the single story is translated into history curricula as well. Aaron Waters points out that, save for a few exceptions, the events of the 'normalisation' era are skipped entirely in Slovak history textbooks, as is recent post-1989 history. Students know alarmingly little about the first years of the transitional regime and the circumstances of the formation of the new republic.[51] Governments maintain control over the content of the textbooks, subject to approval by the National Textbook Registry. The Registry is staffed by the governing administration. There have been instances when none of the staff were qualified in either history education or curriculum development. Textbooks are also often switched out when a new administration comes to power. In 2011, Samuel Jankovič, in charge of the national training programme at the time, complained that 'there has been a shift of focus – away from world history towards European history, meanwhile national history, especially recent events, appear to be of irrelevance. In Slovakia, the monumental events of 1989 are of a marginal nature. This is interesting when more than 60 to 70 percent of the curriculum is dictated by the Ministry of Education.'[52] Furthermore, the textbooks that are produced take years to make their way into classrooms. The narrative about the more distant past is marked by the exclusivist nature of the historical narratives. Again, Slovak history textbooks are a case in point. Students learn the history of the nation through the myth of 'a thousand years of suffering' (i.e., Hungarian oppression), pushing the trope of 'the thousand-year-old bee' (i.e., the hard-working Slovak nation), and perpetuating the notion of victimhood. Such generous historical interpretations are not only inaccurate, but they often also promote stereotypes of cultural superiority that have a lasting impact.

Meddling in history textbooks has been even more direct in Hungary in recent years. '[K]ey figures of the interwar period have been elected as national intellectuals worth studying in education curricula. Clearly, education is a key domain for memory, and the government can easily influence its policies through the Minister of Human Capacities.'[53] Teachers are restricted in terms of selection of textbooks, even when it comes to alternative textbooks, outside of the core curriculum.

---

51 Waters, A. (2018). *Coming of age in the 'lost' history of communism: Teaching the post-wall generations*. Retrieved from Academia.edu: https://www.academia.edu/7756806/Coming_of_Age_in_the_Lost_History_of_Communism_Teaching_the_Post-Wall_Generations

52 Ibid. p. 5.

53 Benazzo, S. (2017). Not all the past needs to be used: Features of Fidesz's politics of memory. *Journal of Nationalism, Memory, and Language Politics*, 11(2), 198-221.

Consequences of memory holes

Memory holes and captured memory regimes lead to several consequences on the quality of democracy. First and foremost, the single-story narratives and the outright manipulation of memory contribute towards a generation disconnected from the political vision of a nation, and growing up in a moral void, always searching for their own identity anchors in the world. At the institutional level, the lack of criminal justice – a consequence of the types of narrative frames that came to dominate the two regions after the negotiations of power transfer – led to a weakened rule of law, especially in Central Europe, and a perceived continuity of corruption. It has also translated into (as one of the factors rather than single-handedly) a low level of trust in political institutions, which are not seen as accountable and independent. It contributes to a slow improvement in interracial relations and to the escalation of distrust toward the 'Other' – minorities of all kinds, old and new in Central Europe.

Weakened quality of democracy

The nature of a negotiated transition has resulted in significant to almost complete impunity for the former political leaders responsible for decisions that led to many human rights violations and much suffering. Even though the full or partial confidence in the courts of law and the Constitutional Court are higher than trust in elected institutions and leaders in South Africa (over 50% in both cases (SARB)), it appears that the TRCs, as a mechanism, do not contribute towards trust in the judiciary. Since truth commissions are set up separately from the system of courts, they are a competing mechanism of justice.[54] The courts, and particularly the Constitutional Court, have much stronger backing in the South African Constitution than their counterparts in Central Europe, and have played a significant role in checking corruption. However, a growing number of South Africans feel always or often unequally treated under the law (63% in 2017, up by 20% since 2011) and 68% feel that public officials who commit crimes are not punished.[55] Those numbers are the highest in the countries of Southern Africa.

In Central Europe, trust in the legal system is low. Slovakia has sunk to the bottom of the EU rankings twice in recent years on the account of the perceived lack of independence of the courts. It is 93rd on the Judicial Independence index. By comparison, South Africa ranked 13th.[56] The quality of the judges plays a role in the lack of trust in the courts, and the perception of their dependence on the political echelons of power and their corrupt status. There was no accounting with the past

54 Ishiyama, J., & Laoye, O. (2014, Oct.). Do Truth Commissions promote trust in the judiciary in African states? *Journal of Asian and African Studies*, 1-17.

55 Chingwete, A. (2017, June 23). Crime and insecurity remain near the top of South Africans' agenda. *Afrobarometer Dispatch No. 154*. Retrieved from Afrobarometer.

56 Index of Public Integrity. (2017). *Judicial Independence*. Retrieved from Index of Public Integrity: https://integrity-index.org/?yr=2015

in the judiciary, and thus most judges survived the transitional period, keeping their places on the bench. Unlike in former East Germany where many judges were replaced by those from West Germany, in Central European countries, there were no replacements available. The independence and impunity thus acquired led to a culture of entitlement. Furthermore, judges became closely tied to political leaders who then interfered in the appointment and recalling of judges.[57]

The results of the yet-unpublished survey, *The Legacy of the Past and the Quality of Democracy*, show that people strongly perceive a direct link between the unresolved past and continuing corruption. Eighty per cent of respondents feel that former communist leaders should have been tried, and 56% believe they should not be forgiven even if they admit their guilt. Forty-five per cent disagree that corruption would be as widespread as it is without the totalitarian past and 75% perceive the continued impact of the legacy of the totalitarian past on the state of democracy today. Those who see a direct link between letting the former communist leaders off the hook and current corruption are also those who are critical of the current institutions yet most tolerant toward the 'Other'. When asked about the consequences of the unaddressed past, most respondents cited repetition of past mistakes, not learning any lessons, the inability to move forward, or passivity and a sense of lasting injustice. Some have also stated the state of the judiciary specifically, 'lacking rule of law – nepotism and connections gaining the upper hand' or 'turning to populist and authoritarian solutions.'[58]

The second impact of the captured memory regimes on the quality of democracy lies at the level of support toward the political community and feelings related to belonging. These are those state-formational ideas that embody how a nation and citizenship are understood. The exclusivist citizenship in Central Europe produces high levels of intolerance and social distance toward the 'Other' while in South Africa the captured narrative vis-à-vis the continued social and economic inequalities and lack of equal opportunities have resulted in a rejection of that narrative by a section of the young generation. However, it is tolerance towards otherness and the status of minorities in society, particularly women, that became the distinguishing measures of the quality of democracy among advanced democracies, stemming from modernisation and post-modernisation theories of human empowerment.[59]

57 Vagovič, M. (2017, Dec. 14). *Sudca Harabin rozdeľoal a panoval. Dobu temna vystriedala apatia [Judge Harabin divided and ruled. The dark era was replaced by apathy]*. Retrieved from Aktuality.sk: www.aktuality.sk/clanok/547661/sudca-harabin-rozzdeloval-a-panoval-dobu-temna-vystriedala-apatia

58 Kusá, D. (2018b, October). Legacy of the past and the quality of democracy. *Survey Report*. Bratislava International School of Liberal Arts.

59 Inglehart, R. (1997).

Dislike of the 'other'

South Africa and Slovakia are racially and ethnically diverse, whereas Poland, Hungary and Czech Republic are almost ethnically homogeneous. This homogeneity came as a result of ethnic cleansings of the post-Second World War era, primarily via transfers and 'exchanges' of population as states' borders were moved.

South African democracy, on the other hand, was built on the vision of the Rainbow Nation, united in diversity. Of such importance, it was significantly embedded into the Constitution along with the principle of non-racialism and individual (rather than group) human rights.[60] However, cultural rapprochement across racial lines is taking a long time and many are losing hope that it is getting better (although various polls produce rather divergent numbers on racial reconciliation). While intergroup contact has risen in South Africa, it has paradoxically led to heightened awareness of mutual stereotypes and presents a danger of greater rather than smaller tensions. However, in 2015, 52% of South Africans believed that race relations had got better or much better. For the young generation (i.e., the 18- to 25-year-old cohort), they have improved the most, with 58% saying as much (Afrobarometer R6 2014/2015 online analysis). The country is racially divided on perceptions of the legacies of apartheid. While 70-75% of Black South Africans feel that apartheid had lasting effects and led to the current spatial segregation, poverty among Black South Africans, lasting wealth among the white community, disproportionalities in land ownership, these proportions drop to around 55-62% among Coloured and Indian/Asian South Africans. Only around 40% of White South Africans subscribe to such legacies, excepting the first with 51% seeing spatial segregation as an outcome of the apartheid regime. However, there is a high level of distrust of foreigners, including those from other African countries. Only 14.5% of respondents trust foreigners not from African countries and slightly more, 15.8%, trust those from African countries. More than 50% openly distrust them.[61] 'This runs counter to the vision of the National Development Plan (NDP) that calls for an inclusive approach to nation-building' (as opposed to 'narrow nationalism').[62]

In Central Europe, the impact of exclusivist citizenship is directly translated into the interpersonal distrust toward the 'Other', and the great social distance from groups other than one's own. This relates not only to domestic ethnic minorities, but also foreigners, migrants, people of different religions, the LGBT community, and quite simply all that is perceived as 'Other'. Slovakia, Poland, Hungary, and Czechia repeatedly score at the bottom of the EU ranks on tolerance and social distance. In the 2015 Special Eurobarometer report on discrimination, respondents from these countries surprisingly placed great social distance against Muslims even though very few actually reside there. The same is true of migrants, often labelled

60 Asmal, K. (2011).
61 SARB 2017, p. 44.
62 Ibid. p. 43.

'Muslims' in the public discourse, who rarely remain in these countries.[63] For example, only 12% of Czechs and 16% of Slovaks would be comfortable with their children having a love relationship with a Muslim individual. Only 27% and 37% respectively would be comfortable having one as a colleague. These countries also score low on tolerance towards the LGBT community with only 12% of Slovaks saying they would be comfortable with an openly gay, lesbian, or bisexual person in the highest elected position and only 24% of Slovaks and 28% of Poles supporting gay marriage.[64]

The most recent research by the Pew Research Center confirms the divisions between West and East Europe in attitudes related to tolerance of diversity. Only 12% of Czechs, 22% of Hungarians, and 33% of Poles would accept a Muslim as a member of their family. The 47% result for Slovakia led to responses of incredulity among Slovak experts. The result may have been due to different data collection methods but also to political discourse that is much less anti-migrant than either in the Czech or Hungarian counterparts.[65] Previous research shows that in attitudes toward the 'Other', people closely mirror the political moods and statements of their political leaders, especially in younger populations. Central Europeans are also more likely than Western Europeans to think their own culture superior to others (44% and 46% respectively for Slovakia and Hungary and 55% in Czechia and in Poland).

Though it is certainly not the only factor, itself being a product of historical, geographical, political, and cultural interplays, exclusivist citizenship and its contribution to the capture of the memory regime shape the attitudes of Central Europeans toward minorities and foreigners. That, in turn, translates into, among other things, the implementation of human rights in this area, policies on immigration, family and same-sex rights, discrimination in the area of the right to adequate housing, and equal access to education.

One further note is due. Although the people in South Africa perceive their racial relations and relations towards foreigners as troublesome, South Africa fares comparatively better than the countries of Central Europe. The Social Progress Imperative, the index which measures societies' capacity to meet basic human needs and provide opportunities for fulfilment of human potential (and thus closely aligns with the dignitarian model of democracy) indicates that South Africans are more tolerant especially of other religions and of foreigners than Central Europeans. Central Europe provides better for other criteria found in the Social Progress

63 European Commission. (2015, October). *Special Eurobarometer 437 'Discrimination in the EU in 2015'*. Retrieved from Special Eurobarometer 437 'Discrimination in the EU in 2015': http://ec.europa.eu/public_opinion/index_en.htm

64 Ibid.

65 Pew Research Center. (2018, Oct. 29). *Eastern and Western Europeans Differ on Importance of Religion, Views of Minorities, and Key Social Issues*. Retrieved from Pew Research Center: http://www.pewforum.org/2018/10/29/eastern-and-western-europeans-differ-on-importance-of-religion-views-of-minorities-and-key-social-issues/

Imperative: basic human needs, and social and economic foundations for wellbeing such as healthcare, a healthy environment, and access to education. Given the economic disparities, the history of the apartheid, the multiracial and multilingual nature of South Africa, it seems apparent that the foundational narrative of a united nation, supported by strong constitutionally based institutions and their adherence to the rule of law in the most trying times are bearing some fruit. It is, therefore, all the more concerning that this foundational vision has been shaken among sections of the young generation.

The generational divide

The master narratives of the memory regimes and their institutional practice in the past significantly shape people's understanding of reconciliation. Whereas in South Africa reconciliation for most people signifies forgiveness (44.8% of people list it among their top three choices,[66] in Slovakia 56.6% of respondents understand coming to terms with the past as the uncovering and punishment of former crimes.[67] In both regions, moving on and focusing on the present problems and future challenges ranks second.

The generation now in middle age was asked for patience by the transitioning regimes. Justice, democratisation, living standards...all were to be ameliorated through policies such as fostering economic growth, investment from abroad, and attracting business. In fact, when pouring over the various public opinion polls related to reconciliation, trust, and interpretations of the past, it is clear that the 35- to 44-year-olds have been most affected, often showing slightly different results. This generation did not witness the regime turnover so has no direct loyalty to the promises of transition or its representatives. Their identity is related to the here and now and cannot be placated by the transition narrative any longer.

Dismantling the Rainbow Nation

In South Africa, inequality is perceived as the most severe divisive challenge to the society. Fifty-eight per cent of people list it as the first or second most divisive factor, more so than race, which amounts to 53% of combined choices.[68] Naturally, inequality is closely linked with race. As touched upon above, many South Africans do not normally make connections between the lasting inequalities and the previous regime. However, university studies provide an environment where many, especially first-time students from disadvantaged backgrounds, come to that realisation.

The student hashtag movements placed the interpretation of the past at the centre of their grievances. Students frequently echoed the sentiment that the 'Rainbow has to

66 SARB 2017. (2018, March), p. 44.
67 Kusá, D. (2018b, October).
68 SARB 2017. (2018, March), pp 44.

be dismantled' and that it is a myth. Regkogtsofetse Chikane, son of the well-known anti-apartheid activist Frank Chikane, summarised the sentiment:

> [W]e face a different type of discrimination. It can be difficult to describe or pinpoint, yet you can always feel it in the air. We might not be dealing with an enemy that manifests itself as "Europeans Only" benches; we face an enemy that has the same ideals as the apartheid system, only now it wears a very different mask... Our society since 1994 has maintained the endemic nature of all three of their wicked problems. That SA has genuinely advanced since the end of apartheid is a myth.[69]

Students claimed the legacy of the anti-apartheid student struggle, in particular, the legacy of the Black Consciousness movement. It is this heritage they put at the forefront, in contradiction to the reconciliation narrative. Especially at the universities, students politically align themselves with agendas that reject the reconciliation narrative. In recent elections to the Student Representative Councils, the Economic Freedom Fighters Student Command and the Pan Africanist Student Movement of Azania marked a series of successes, pushing aside the ANC's student branch, the South African Students Congress, and the Democratic Alliance Students Association (DASO),[70] even at some traditionally white universities, such as the University of Cape Town. Then ANC President Jacob Zuma's move to remove tuition fees for the vast majority of the students at the end of 2017, following two years of intermittent student protests, was not enough to win back the favour for the ANC among the students. On the other side, young people outside academia, especially from rural areas, do not feel represented by the student movements and the issues they promote. Their main concerns relate to day-to-day survival: employment, infrastructure, and service deliveries. But even if the student voices were not representative of the whole generation, they mobilised a movement and inspired other groups to join further protests such as #ZumaMustFall, #SaveSA, #UniteBehind against corruption and state capture.

Similarly, turbulent protests have been experienced in Central Europe, especially over the past year. The generational divide here coincides with and is strengthened by the globalisation crisis, breaking along the lines of the official memory narrative as well. In Slovakia, for example, we witnessed a student movement marching for transparency in government and protesting the gradual curbing of the freedoms of the press. The youth driving the protests are the educated youth of the urban centres,

---

69 Chikane, R. (2018, Nov. 6). *Why building a nation will take more than believing in rainbows?* Retrieved from BusinessDay: https://www.businesslive.co.za/bd/life/books/2018-11-06-why-building-a-nation-will-take-more-than-believing-in-rainbows/

70 Mabasa, N. (2018, Nov. 8). *Rise of the EFF youth: EFF Students Command brigades take university SRC elections by storm.* Retrieved from The Daily Maverick: http://firstthing.dailymaverick.co.za/article?id=127372#.W-SukHRKjOR

which believes democracy is the only suitable regime of governance but distrusts political institutions and their leaders. Altogether, such protests drew millions to the streets in the four Central European countries.

On the other hand, there is strong and significant support for the radical right. The Slovak People's Party Our Slovakia, which entered parliament in 2016 with 8% of the vote, was overwhelmingly supported by young voters. Sixty-three per cent of their voters were from the 18- to 39-year-old cohort, twice the proportion they represent in the overall population.[71] Organised youth involvement in the extreme right is also widespread in Poland and Hungary. In Poland, twenty-five thousand people, many of them youth, marched with torches at the 100th anniversary of independent Poland in November 2018. This march has become the largest extreme right gathering in Europe, in 2017 drawing 70,000 to march under the banner 'Poland for Poles.'[72] As extreme right-wing politicians were elected to parliaments, their rhetoric became a part of the mainstream. It appears this has emboldened right-wing youth movements, with a rise in violent attacks on minorities and the authorities passing by in silence.

Those 'left behind' by the process of globalisation, many of whom are young people seeking jobs but lacking higher education, skills, and languages, 'need an enemy to blame, and the far right gives them one. In Poland, a country that is nearly 98 percent ethnically Polish, that "enemy" has traditionally been Jews or Communists; occasionally it has been gay people. Now, overwhelmingly, it's Muslims.'[73]

Double divide among the Born Frees

There is a double divide related to the generation of the Born Frees in South Africa and Central Europe alike. Even if survey results of public opinion do not necessarily show a significant departure in value orientations from the generation of their parents (although those in Central Europe depart slightly more than their South African peers), the gap between generations is broadly perceived and pointed out in public discourse. The disenchanted groups among the youth, whether from the student groups or the more radical wings outside academia, may not be proportionally large within the whole of the generation, but narratives that form generational identities are not woven from the voices of the silent, but from those whose grievances rise above din and capture the public imagination. They may not be many in number, but they are loud and, thus, listened to. They can shape the discourse. Public opinion polls in the years of the protests did not indicate any significant shift in the opinions of young

71 Bútorová, Z. (2017, July 10). *Rozpustiť ĽSNS? Kto je za a kto proti*. Retrieved August 12, 2017, from Denník N: https://dennikn.sk/819428/rozpustit-ls-ns-kto-je-za-a-kto-proti/

72 Hume, T. (2017, May 9). *Poland's populist government lets far right extremism explode into mainstream*. Retrieved from Vice News: https://news.vice.com/en_us/article/nedyyb/poland-populist-government-far-right-extremism

73 Ibid.

adults compared to those of their parents and grandparents.[74] They were not any more likely to take part in protests or boycotts. Yet, when the opportunity presented itself, they have done so and have been leading the way since. The intergenerational transmission of collective memory is largely failing in both regions. The captured memory regimes, pushing single stories that manipulate and command memory to the extent that it is sanitised and inauthentic, do not provide an environment where any moral learning and interpreting the past in order to understand the present can take place. They fail to provide a sense of continuity, a guide for democratic citizenship, or a vision. This gap has been, for a part of this generation, filled by the protests. For another part, however, fast populist answers that operate on the basis of politics of fear are where they seek fulfilment. This is a generation that is increasingly polarised within, and whose collective memory is fractured. The young people are left to their own devices to craft their identity and they do so despite the moral vacuum and civic lessons they could take from their elders.

Conclusion

Narratives about cultural trauma stemming from previous oppressive regime(s) are an essential part of democratisation. The governments of the new regime play an essential role in setting up the institutional framework and shaping the master narrative, and the values and norms that are interwoven within it. This work with the past – addressing it and drawing responsibility and consequences out of it – must also be open to healing, providing space for multiple narratives, allowing a variety of actors take part in the process. The cultural trauma narratives are essential to shaping the vision and the trust in a political community, the pillar of political support and legitimacy. If trust, solidarity, and empathy on this level fail, the 'national project' will suffer and will have consequences for the 'democratic project', as a deep quality of democracy depends on such sentiments. The capture of trauma narratives by political power – the single-story narrative and manipulated memory – exclude segments of the population, lead to hierarchisation of citizenship, impacting the idea of 'who belongs' to the political nation, and who contributes to the intergenerational transmission of collective memory.

Memory holes, therefore, produce fractured memory in the young generation and a fractured political community, which have significant detrimental consequences on the quality of democracy. Consequently, when the idea of a political nation fails to materialise, the project of democratisation will necessarily be impeded and impoverished, applying different speeds and different measures for different categories of all those involved.

74 Mattes, R., & Richmond, S. (2015, Jan). Are South Africa's youth really a 'ticking time bomb'? (M. Bratton, Ed.) *Afro barometer*, p. 25.

8.
Transgenerational trauma transmission in Rwanda: Cases of children born out of rape during the genocide against Tutsi – the ARCT-Ruhuka Experience

Jane Abatoni

Background

During the 1994 genocide perpetrated against Tutsi, rape was used as a pervasive tool of genocide against Tutsi women. Women and girls were raped individually or in groups, by one man or a gang and multiple instances of rape. Some rape survivors received during counselling confess they cannot remember the number and how many times they were raped. Women were raped with objects such as sticks, matches, gun barrels, were sexually mutilated and they were subjected to other dehumanising actions. Many women were then left to die.

Some women were held as *kubohoza* (sex slaves). They were raped in privacy. Other women were raped publicly in front of their children, husbands, families and friends. They were often forced to kill their own husbands or children before or after having been raped.

In addition, some of the genocide rape survivors live with HIV/AIDS contracted from being raped. These women experience a number of traumatic memories, including of being raped, multiple times and humiliated in many ways, their families brutally murdered in front of them, giving birth and living with children born out of rape. The women live with these experiences that form the triggers for memories of these traumatic rape experiences on a daily basis. But then, they have a duty as parents to bring up their children. They invariably transmit their own trauma to their children.

According to Nowrojee, between 250,000 and 500,000 Tutsi women were systematically raped and forced into sexual servitude by members of extremist Hutu militia groups and some were left pregnant.[1] Consequently, rape survivors gave

1 Nowrojee, B. (1996). *Shattered lives: sexual violence during the Rwandan genocide and its aftermath* (Vol. 3169, No. 164). Human Rights Watch.

birth to children from the genocidal rape. The United Nations Special Rapporteur on Rwanda, René Degni-Segu, estimated that between 2,000 and 5,000 pregnancies resulted from genocidal rape (De Brouwer, 2005)[2]. Others estimate the number to be more than 10,000.[3] For Torgovnik, the number of children born from the genocidal rape could be as high as 20,000.[4]

As stated by Rohner the experiences of parents are known to have a significant impact on children's behaviours, attitudes, emotions, personalities, social competencies, academic performance and other aspects.[5] Trauma also affects the way in which children think and behave into adulthood. Parenting therefore plays an important role in the psychosocial development of children, and trauma symptoms are usually passed on to the next generation via learned behaviour.

Major problems presented in counselling sessions

Children often suffer severe psychological effects. Most cases that counsellors receive include lack of identity, who am I; most of them do not know their fathers, some mothers find it difficult to explain to their children and decide to show them those who would be grandfathers or uncles as their fathers (mother's father or brother); extreme anger towards sometimes their mothers and others, guilt, behaviour disorders, poor concentration, and lack of trust and suspicion. The children feel guilty because they see themselves as the source of their mothers' misery. They feel they are 'a mistake', that they are dirty, and in some instances even seen as 'evil'. Because they see themselves genetically connected to their rapist father, they also feel as if they are perpetrators of genocide themselves. Behaviour disorders present in patterns of hostility, and in aggressive or disruptive behaviours. Children born from genocidal rape often blame their mothers. They are often isolated because they are disowned by their parents' family and the community. The children are stigmatised because they are seen as 'unwanted' or they are labelled as 'children of bad memories', 'little killers', or Interahamwe and other nicknames. Rejected by family and friends and the community, these children feel disconnected from peers. These problems result in poor concentration at school, which affects their school performance. It can also lead to drug and alcohol abuse.

---

2 De Brouwer, Anne-Marie L.M. 2005. *Supranational criminal prosecution of sexual violence: The ICC and the practice of the ICTY and the ICTR*. Antwerp: Intersentia

3 Wax, E. (2004). Rwandans are struggling to love children of hate. *The Washington Post*, 28.

4 Torgovnik, J. (2008), Intended Consequences, available online at http://mediastorm.com /publication/intended-consequences.

5 Rohner, R. P. (1986). *The warmth dimension: Foundations of parental acceptance-rejection theory*. Sage Publications, Inc.

Challenges faced by children born out of rape during the 1994 genocide against Tutsi

The children feel they are not recognised in any category, such as survivors, or perpetrators, or bystanders. Except for a few organisations, there is no support for the children from government programmes in terms of education, social or medical needs. There is also no psychological support for their reintegration into families or communities. Because of a lack of bonds with extended family, the children often suffer poverty. Some children live with HIV from their parents and are in need of medication. They live in fear that their mothers may disclose their fathers' identities, leading to further isolation and stigma.

Conclusion

According to Smith rape shapes the future of victims, their families, communities, generations and nations, and has the potential to create a global impact.[6] Considering problems faced by children born out of rape committed during the genocide against Tutsi in 1994, more efforts need to be put into ensuring individual, family and group therapy.

A call for action

Considering these challenges, there is a need for mapping who and where these children are, so that they can be holistically supported. There is also a need to carry out more detailed research to identify the real needs of children born out of genocidal rape in order to plan and implement appropriate interventions.

Government and non-governmental organisations should make concerted efforts to ensure that all children born out of rape during the genocide benefit from psychosocial support to break the cycle of transgenerational trauma.

---

6 Smith, D. W., Letourneau, E. J., Saunders, B. E., Kilpatrick, D. G., Resnick, H. S., & Best, C. L. (2000). Delay in disclosure of childhood rape: Results from a national survey. *Child abuse & neglect*, 24(2), 273-287.

Part III: Reparative Practice

9. Spectres of reparation: The poetic justice of reparative citizenship and the discourse of the analyst in an irreparable world

Jaco Barnard-Naudé

> 'The ghost remains that which gives one the most to think about – and to do.' – Derrida *(Specters of Marx 98)*.

Introduction

In Volume 5 of the South African Truth and Reconciliation Commission's Report, in the 9th Chapter entitled Reconciliation, the Commission reports as follows:

> After a visit to Rwanda, Archbishop Tutu said: "We must break the spiral of reprisal and counter-reprisal ... I said to them in Kigali 'unless you move beyond justice in the form of a tribunal, there is no hope for Rwanda'. Confession, forgiveness and reconciliation in the lives of nations are not just airy-fairy religious and spiritual things, nebulous and unrealistic. They are the stuff of practical politics."

Over the past ten years, I have returned to the Archbishop's words many times in the context of a critical appraisal of the TRC's legacy in South Africa. In this work, I have had reason to focus and insist on a term that does not appear in the aforementioned quotation. That term is 'reparation'. Reparation is by no means absent from the discourse of the TRC as a whole, nor is it missing from the Archbishop's discourse as a whole. Yet, in these words in which the TRC reports the Archbishop's visit to Rwanda, reparation is not mentioned as one of the imperatives if there is to be hope. In this paper, I insist that the *reparative* – which I distinguish from reparation – can and must be an imperative for the generation of hope – for South Africa, for Rwanda, for post-conflict countries in general and, ultimately, as we shall see, for our continued planetary existence as such.

I am not here to dispute the Archbishop's words about the critical role of confession, forgiveness and reconciliation in the lives of (post-conflict) nations. I also do not dispute that there have been attempts and efforts to promote reparation in South Africa and, indeed, in Rwanda. The Fund for Neediest Survivors of Genocide in

Rwanda (FARG) is an admirable undertaking and I have no doubt that considerable reparation has been achieved through FARG and other measures such as the findings of the gaçaça courts.

On the other hand, nothing more than a quick internet search reveals the numerous media reports since at least 2014 in which the shortcomings of these measures in Rwanda are indicated, along with an increasingly prominent insistence in Rwanda and in South Africa that unity and reconciliation, or truth and reconciliation, cannot be expected to endure in the absence of meaningful reparation. This is a conclusion that the TRC itself reached in Volume 6 of its report when it wrote that its 'international legitimacy' (not to mention, presumably, its national legitimacy) depended on 'the provision of adequate reparations'.[1]

As for Rwanda, in April 2014, Jean Paul Mugiraneza published an opinion piece in *The Guardian* in which he argued that the government assistance to survivors – through FARG – is 'an obligation for any responsible nation' and that the availability of this form of assistance 'does not remove the right to financial reparations' from other sources. In March 2016, it was reported that 'at least 8,445 cases adjudicated by gaçaça courts have not been executed in terms of paying reparations to the victims'. A government report on which the reports relied, indicated that '854 court bailiffs have completely failed to execute compensation judgments; 1,016 cases involved genocide convicts who deliberately refused to pay damages, while 1, 277 cases have incomplete files'.

What these reports tell us is that the question of reparation continues to haunt Rwanda in ways that are similar to and different from the way in which the reparation question returns in various guises in post-apartheid South Africa. I am not going to dwell on the similarities and differences here – for my purposes it is enough to note the haunting quality of the question of reparation in both jurisdictions. In what follows, I will make a few remarks about the role that reparative citizenship and the discourse of the analyst can play in the generation of hope. I must immediately hasten to add that I do not see the generation of hope as hinging on the exorcism of the ghost of reparation. Rather, I think that hope, as a relationship to the future, can be generated when we change the ways in which we relate to the spectre. One cannot but recall here, Shakespeare's famous instruction to him who is faced with the spectre: 'Thou art a scholar, *speak* to it, Horatio'. Reparative citizenship and the discourse of the analyst are nothing more than ways in which we might change our relationship to the spectre of reparation, precisely by speaking to it.

1 Truth and Reconciliation Commission of South Africa 'Volume 6' in Truth and Reconciliation Commission of South Africa *Truth and Reconciliation Commission of South Africa Report* (6 volumes) (Pretoria: Government Printer, 1998), 110.

Irreparable

To say that reparation is a spectre is to say that it is always already never fully present, never simply 'here'. As a spectre, reparation is much like the justice that Jacques Derrida describes in his late work; justice as always already radically incomplete and thus deficient and absent. I have always thought that these descriptions – from the pen of the man who took responsibility for the much-maligned word and concept of deconstruction – are anything but fanciful. Is it not, on the contrary, very *realistic* to say that we are always already 'behind' on justice, always already lacking in reparation?

It is out of a similarly realistic appreciation of our world today, that Giorgio Agamben has proposed that the world is irreparable and that the irreparable is the world. Agamben writes:

> The Irreparable is that things are just as they are, in this or that mode, consigned without remedy to their way of being. States of things are irreparable, whatever they may be: sad or happy, atrocious or blessed. How you are, how the world is – this is the irreparable.[2]

This sounds like a highly resigned, dystopian and even nihilistic view of the world, yet it is difficult, almost twenty years into the new millennium, to disagree with Agamben. Every day, we receive more and more confirmations of the many ways in which our world has become irreparable: from unstoppable global warming, to annihilation in Syria, from famine in Yemen to the interminable conflict between Israel and Palestine, from widespread xenophobic hate crime to pernicious neo-colonial procedures of capture in Africa, from gun-related massacres and racialised police brutality in the United States, to the ongoing war on women everywhere; it seems that Agamben's view of the world as irreparable and 'without remedy', if somewhat nihilistic, is at least highly realistic.

Curiously enough, Agamben also writes – paradoxically, it seems – that 'we can have hope only in what is without remedy'. One of Agamben's commentators has interpreted this statement to mean that while '[we] can never go back on nihilism [...] it does not follow from this that the horizon of salvation is itself to be annulled' (Prozorov 167). Paolo Bartolini has pointed out that Agamben's thought on the relationship between the irreparable and hope is in fact inspired by none other than Paul's statement about hope in the letter to the Romans. That statement reads: 'We are saved by hope: but hope that is seen is not hope: for what a man seeth, why doth he yet hope for? But if we hope for that we see not, *then* do we with patience wait for *it*'. This means, Bartolini suggests, that 'what is left for us to do [in the face of the irreparable] is to patiently make hope, toil towards it, actively and incessantly.'[3] To put it somewhat differently, Agamben's philosophy holds that what is given to us as

2 Agamben, G. (1990). *The Coming Community* (6th ed.). Turin: University of Minnesota Press.
3 Bartoloni, P. (2008). Giorgio Agamben. Angelaki: *Journal of Theoretical Humanities*, 13(1), 51–63.

present, as here, is the irreparable world and what is not given to us is hope – we are responsible for 'making' hope.

In an effort to think through what the conditions of such a making of hope might be, I insist on a distinction between 'reparation' as the name of the spectre and the 'reparative' which is the first term of a political and ethical orientation to the irreparable that I have called 'reparative citizenship'. The etymology of the suffix of the word 'repar*ative*' indicates a tending to something, here, most obviously, a tending to reparation. But at the same time, the suffix indicates a 'relation with'. The way I see the reparative is as a term that relates itself to the 'irreparable' given and to the spectre of 'reparation' that haunts the irreparable. As such, the reparative is the name of an intervention. The reparative is what clears a space for negotiation between the irreparable and the spectre of reparation. And it is in this 'reparative' space as the space where the irreparable negotiates with the reparation that haunts it, it is in this reparative space that hope can be made out of that which is without remedy.

Reparative citizenship

To understand how citizenship becomes an indispensable part of this picture, it is necessary to consort with a few more spectres – ones that come not only from the past, but also from the future. As a starting point in this regard, it is worth noting that Agamben's views on the irreparable are articulated in a book entitled *The Coming Community*. As Van Riessen has argued, the title does not indicate a community that is 'drawing near in the future', but rather 'a community that is always in the process of coming' and as such, is always potentially present.

These references to 'community' and to 'potentiality' prompt the second term of my phrase, namely 'citizenship'. The 'citizenship' I focus on has a technical meaning: it designates the belonging to or membership of what the ancient Greeks called the *polis*, for which the closest modern English equivalent is 'political community'. This citizenship has always depended on making. It was Hannah Arendt who pointed to this aspect of it when she called it a 'sort of second life'. For Arendt, citizenship was constituted or made through the activities of action – 'deeds that are not brutal', as she called it – and speech – 'words that are not empty'.

At the very end of her book, *On Revolution*, Arendt quotes Theseus, 'the legendary founder of Athens and hence [its] spokesman', who, she says, let us know what it is that enables ordinary men, young and old, to bear life's burden: it is the *polis* which she describes as 'the space of men's free deeds and living words'. The *polis*, then, as that which can 'endow life with splendour' and citizenship as that which grants access to such a life.

Arendt was of course not blind to the ways in which this older form of citizenship is bound up with the modern, formal version of citizenship that simply designates belonging to a nation-state. Thus, in *The Origins of Totalitarianism*, Arendt writes painstakingly and hauntingly about the series of events that only became possible once the Jews were stripped of their formal citizenship and became 'stateless'. The Nazis, Arendt writes, only 'set the gas chambers into motion' once 'they had found out to their satisfaction that no country would claim these people'. The whole phenomenon of statelessness thus showed that 'The Rights of Man, supposedly inalienable, proved to be unenforceable [...] whenever people appeared who were no longer citizens of any sovereign state.[4] It is for this reason that Arendt stridently argues that 'the right to have rights, or the right of every individual to belong to humanity' cannot be guaranteed by humanity itself or in general. In all instances, the right to have rights is only meaningful when it is guaranteed by a specific, sovereign political community.

In the winter of 1970, the young Agamben wrote to Arendt that discovering her work was a 'decisive experience' for him. In no other area of his thought is Agamben's debt to Arendt more apparent than in his work on the 'potentiality' of the human being. This potentiality consists chiefly in the power of the human being to 'give itself a world'. There is for Agamben a certain 'poetic' dimension to this potentiality to give ourselves a world, in that, like poetry, it involves effort, a bringing forth, a making or actualization, even a giving birth to or an act of creation. It was Arendt, who, through her insights on natality, initiated Agamben's thought on potentiality.

Citizenship in the original sense is actualised or brought forth because of what Agamben calls man's poetic status, this power to give herself a world of life, as opposed to a sphere of mere existence. Agamben refers to this distinction between mere existence and life by relying, as Arendt does, on the Ancient Greek distinction between zōe and bios; and it is out of this distinction that he will draw, in the book that made him famous, *Homo sacer: sovereign power and bare life*, the notion of bare life which he believes to be politically at stake for all of us in the modern world today.

The figure of *homo sacer* as bare life points us back to the irreparable world and especially to the role that the neoliberal State's right to 'make live and let die', as Foucault put it, has played in this state of affairs. Here it is worth mentioning that the mere formal fact of citizenship, or a status akin to it, has not been enough to prevent the rendering by the State of parts of its own people as nothing more than bare life. The factual state of human existence in increasingly growing spaces in our cities, towns and townships shows the irreparable extent and power of the neoliberal State's right to abandonment – its right to 'let die'.

Yet it is here where the two terms of my phrase come together, precisely because it is in the very absence of hope, reparation and meaningful citizenship that the notion of 'reparative citizenship' must be patiently made, toiled towards, 'actively and incessantly' created. Slavoj Žižek has recently asserted, relying on Agamben, that

4 Arendt, Hannah. 1973. *The Origins of Totalitarianism*. New York: Harcourt, Brace, p. 293.

today we need to gather the strength to fully assume the hopeless. Žižek continues to quote Göran Therborn who, he writes, succinctly characterises our predicament: 'Never before have the possibilities of a good world for the human species as a whole been greater. At the same time, the gap between human potential and the existing conditions of humankind in its totality has probably never been wider.'

It is precisely in this gap between human potential and the existing conditions of humankind that we must make reparative citizenship if there is to be any hope for a future that will not amount to yet another recurrence of the past. It is in this gap between the actual and the potential that it is necessary to negotiate with the spectre of reparation. The 'reparative' aspect of reparative citizenship indicates that reparation is 'in the making', as they say, without ever being fully repaired. Reparative citizenship, as such, thus hints at the coming community, the community that never arrives but is always already potentially here. It is in the name of that coming community, then, that we are required to act now.

Poetic justice

It is not only because of the aspect of 'making' involved in reparative citizenship that I have referred to the justice to which it gives rise as 'poetic justice'. Jean-Luc Nancy defines poetry as the 'technique productive of presence'. I cannot go into a long explanation of what Nancy means with presence, except for saying that reparative citizenship's concern with an irreparable present out of which it has the potential to produce justice, means that that justice will always be poetic, because it produces a new present.

Reparative citizenship thus knows that justice 'finds its place neither in the romanticism of the past nor in the yearning for a utopian future but, rather, in a profound presentness, in the realization that within the present lies the possibility/potentiality of change and transformation. Radical change must begin with the time of the present and in this world'.

As Jelica Šumič Riha writes: 'What restores the human being as "a potential being", or, to be more precise, what restores the poetic status of man in the world, the potentiality that we are, is not the world, which confronts us in its unfathomable givenness, but a perspective which opens us to the transformation of the world that is presented to us precisely as given and immutable into a space in which the possibility of the world being otherwise than it is, indeed, the possibility of another world, can be brought to presence.'

I am a lawyer by training and therefore find myself compelled to emphasise that the poetic justice of reparative citizenship cannot be made without the law. I hope the short reference to Arendt's right to have rights and statelessness has shown that we are still desperately in need of a juridical order that would guarantee and protect the *bios politikos* of us all in a concrete and practical way and for no other reason than that we are singular beings-in-common. In other words, it is necessary to call on the juridical order to guarantee, protect and promote a 'citizenship' – a belonging to the political community – that can serve as the basis upon which the reparative can be made. In this way, law can co-create both the minimum conditions on which the space of reparative citizenship depends as well as reinforce and enforce reparative measures. The judgments of the gaçaça courts are of course relevant here as are the multiple ongoing efforts to make the law responsive to the reparative in other parts of the world.

The phrase 'poetic justice' thus encapsulates a point of contact between the argumentative order of law and politics as it exists and the creative order of the poetic that is always in the making. Poetic justice occurs in a moment in which law is not found but founded in 'exceptional situations where the themes and terms of the discussion are themselves open to debate.'[5] In such moments, 'creators form new languages enabling common experience to be described differently or invent new metaphors that are later called on to enter the arenas of common linguistic tools [such as law] and of consensual reality [such as the political]'. To put it quite frankly, what I have in mind with the notion of the poetic justice of reparative citizenship is nothing less than what Julia Kristeva has called a 're-foundation as survival' – a creative re-foundation of law and politics as the very condition of our common survival.

Discourse of the analyst

These references to the role of poetry, language, discussion and argument in reparative citizenship point us to the order of discourse. In conclusion, I will rely on the thought of Jacques Lacan to argue that reparative citizenship necessarily works towards a profound shift in the *discourse* of the political community. With 'discourse', I do not simply or merely refer to specific forms of speech. Rather, discourse, as Lacan used it, is the proper name of the structure of the social link that underlies all forms of speech and is expressed in these forms of speech. To advocate a shift in discourse is thus not simply to advocate a shift in the ways in which we address one another in language. It is, rather, to advocate a shift in the dominant configuration of the social link. The dialectical expression of this point is thus that language both changes the world for us *and* that the world for us is changed by language.

For Lacan, there are essentially four forms of discourse, four forms of the social link, in contemporary society: the master's discourse – which is the discourse of patriarchal authority and unquestioning obedience; the hysteric's discourse – which is the discourse of demand and protest; the university discourse – which is the techno-

5 Ranciere, J. 1999. *Disagreement: Politics and Philosophy*, trans, Rose, J. Minneapolis: University of Minnesota Press.

scientific discourse of the all-knowing subject; and the analyst's discourse – which is the discourse of care and love. It is this discourse of the analyst that concerns me with respect to reparative citizenship.

Already when he was giving his seminars on the discourses in the late 1960s, Lacan thought that our societies today are dominated by what he called the Discourse of the University, that is, the discourse of knowledge as techno-scientific rationality. In the later part of the twentieth century and now in the new millennium, we have experienced just how accurate Lacan's impression has proven to be. We refer to the Information Age as dominated by a 'knowledge economy' and as a recent article by Robert Samuels argues, society today 'suffers from an over-abundance of knowledge and information, and, in the knowledge economy, capitalism and science are inter-mixed.'[6] The primary effect of this inter-mixing is that knowledge has become thoroughly commodified. As Samuels goes on to suggest, the ultimate target of Lacan's critique of the discourse of the university is the neoliberalism of the biopolitical state which turns human beings into 'human resources' and 'consumable objects' – Agamben's bare life.

Dominated as the global order undoubtedly is by the discourse of the university, I am not one of those Lacanians who believe that Lacan was so naïve as to argue that the other forms of discourse have faded into insignificance. Neither is it likely that a thinker as nuanced and complex as Lacan would have yielded to the temptation to homogenise and simplify the complexity of the Earth into a single ultimate discourse that totalises the sphere of our existence. I believe that the discourse of the Master is still very much part of our world, and that we have also seen all over the world, including in Africa, a profound resurgence in the discourse of the Hysteric. But it is Lacan's fourth discourse, the discourse of analysis, which he called the *inverse* of the discourse of the master, which I believe has not yet come into its own in the world.

I do not want to be misunderstood as advocating a panacea, an ultimate discourse of salvation and redemption here. It is thus necessary to say that the discourses of the master, the university and the hysteric have served their purposes over the years. I am not sure, though, that the discourse of the analyst has yet been allowed to serve its purpose. That purpose, as those who are analysts would know, is radical emancipation.

As I have indicated, the discourse of the analyst is by turns described as the discourse of care, of love, of transformation and of revolutionising. It is called the discourse of the analyst in order to call to mind the psychoanalytic setting and the psychoanalytic relation and this tells us quite a bit about the qualities of the social link involved here. First, the psychoanalytic setting requires by definition from the analyst a certain openness, because free association means that the patient must be allowed to say

6 Samuels, R. From the discourse of the university to the discourse of analysis. *Psychoanalysis Culture Society* 23, 68–76 (2018). https://doi.org/10.1057/s41282-018-0071-6

whatever. Second, the patient comes to the analyst not for anything other than for help. Typically, the patient seeks out an analyst when her life as she knows it has become, for her, in a word, hopeless. For the analysis to work, the patient must come to believe that the analyst can help her with this hopelessness. From the imperative of openness thus flows an ethic of listening and of care and from the belief that the analyst can help flows not only the trust necessary to practise the free association of saying whatever but also, I would suggest, an ethics of hope.

The unbearable aspect of life always relates invariably, in one way or another, to something the patient lacks. *This* is the fundamental reason why it is the analyst's discourse that must concern those interested in making reparative citizenship. In the context of this paper, it should be quite clear that the lack I am referring to can only be the lack of reparation. Here it is necessary to refer to Nicolas Abraham's statement that dealing with transgenerational haunting in psychoanalysis requires what he calls a 'genuine partnership between patient and analyst'[7] because the lack in transgenerational haunting is not simply the specific lack of the particular analysand, but also the lack of someone else that has transgenerationally been transmitted to the analysand.

The analysand thus lacks at least doubly. It is in the continuous confrontation with this redoubled lack, that is, in talking about it and through it, that the analysand produces her own master signifier, which is Lacan's name for the subject's new primary identification. This master signifier or primary identification is, however, *of a different style* to the master signifier that has hitherto been imposed on the subject from outside. This is, as Mark Bracher writes, 'a style which, we might surmise, is less absolute, exclusive, and rigid in its establishment of the subject's identity, and more open, fluid, processual, constituted, in a word, by relativity and textuality'. To this Dany Nobus adds the following: 'psychoanalysis is geared towards making discoveries, towards the creation of wonder and surprise at the revelation of the unexpected, in short towards the crystallization of new signifiers that *reduce the painful necessity of repetition* and are therefore *able to change the analysand's life*'.[8] My wager here is that 'reparative citizenship' can be just such a life changing signifier for the polis.

I want to be clear that my reference to the realisation by a patient in analysis, that she already has what she is imagining the other to have, in no way constitutes an argument that those in need of reparation must simply come to terms with its lack, must simply accept their fate. To adopt a master signifier of reparative citizenship by definition means that one has not accepted or resigned oneself to the irreparable. What it means is that one has changed one's relationship with the irreparable. For instance, instead of being traumatised and thus rendered speechless by the twists and

7 Abraham, N. *Critical Inquiry, Winter, 1987*, Vol. 13, No. 2, The Trial(s) of Psychoanalysis (Winter, 1987), pp. 287-292. The University of Chicago Press. https://www.jstor.org/stable/134349

8 Nobus, D. (2000). *Jacques Lacan and the Freudian Practice of Psychoanalysis*. London: Routledge.

turns of the spectre, one is speaking about it and with it; in other words, one is *making something* out of its visitations. That something may very well be hope.

It follows, then, that the analyst's discourse is integral to reparative citizenship. Lacan famously stated that taking up the position of analyst in relation to society can 'accomplish what truly merits the title of revolution in relation to the discourse of the Master'. Revolution, therefore, is not made by anarchists but by *analysts*. As Bracher also writes, analysts, by exposing the lack 'which the system of signifiers, and particularly the master signifiers, fail to grasp' can 'interpellate the subjects of society to an activation of their alienated condition, their non-identity with their master signifiers, and thus create an impetus for the production of new master signifiers'.

What will become of our world?

A spectre is haunting our societies and that spectre is reparation. The new millennium is already proving to us once more what happens when we refuse to face the spectre, when we pretend that it is not there, in other words, when we repress it: it does only one thing – it returns. To conclude with an answer to a question that Pumla Gobodo-Madikizela posed in the form of the title of her recent book: 'Dare we hope?' Yes, if we are prepared to *make hope* out of the hopelessness of our irreparable world. That, indeed, requires the courage of daring to act in what Jacques Derrida called 'the night of non-knowledge and non-rule'. I leave you, however, ultimately with the words of Jean-Luc Nancy:

> What will become of our world is something we cannot know, and we can no longer believe in being able to predict or command it. But we can act in such a way that this world is a world able to open itself up to its own uncertainty [..] Invention is always without a model and without warranty. But indeed, that implies facing up to turmoil, anxiety, even disarray. Where certainties come apart, there too gathers the strength that no certainty can match.[9]

9 Jean-Luc Nancy, *The Sense of the World, trans*. by Jeffrey S. Librett (Minneapolis: University of Minnesota Press, 1997).

10.
On hurting, wanting to hurt, and giving up the right to hurt those who hurt you

Kopano Ratele

'I am the one who killed the parents of this girl.'

So says Emmanuel in a scene towards the end of the film *Kinyarwanda*. The girl in question is Jeanne, Emmanuel's former employer's daughter.

Shot on location a decade and half after 1994 Rwandan genocide, *Kinyarwanda* was the directorial debut of African American filmmaker Alrick Brown. Released in 2011 the film won a clutch of awards, including the World Cinema Audience Award at the 2011 Sundance Film Festival and the World Cinema Audience Award at the 25th American Film Institute Fest. Weaving together several stories, reportedly based on true accounts of survivors, the filmmaker seeks to tell the story of this horrific and historically momentous event. One of the stories the film portrays is indeed that of the character of Emmanuel (played by Edouard Bamporiki) and Jeanne (Hadidja Zaninka). Among other things that I found striking about the film is its suggestion that a subjective reason Emmanuel ended up killing the parents is that he had feelings for Jeanne, who is in a relationship with another young Hutu man. In one scene the film shows Emmanuel, watching Jeanne arriving at her home with her parents, change from a lustful toothy expression to a serious face on realising that the boyfriend was with them. In one of the chapters of the film called 'Guns and Cockroaches' the film shows Emmanuel with two other young men with machetes. One of the young men asks Emmanuel if he has a girlfriend. Emmanuel lies, and so exhibits a common characteristic of hegemonic heterosexual masculinity in most western and westernised cultures of some men's propensity to inflate their sexual virility. He says he had a girlfriend, but he got rid of her because she was half-cockroach (meaning part Tutsi and part Hutu). He is talking about Jeanne. It is at this moment, with Jeanne having been brought into his mind by his fellow would-be genocidaires, that Emmanuel says perhaps they should go pay her a visit one last time so that he can give her one last kiss. One of his companions then asks if Emmanuel would really kiss a cockroach because one does not kiss a cockroach but rapes it/her, a sentiment with which Emmanuel agrees.

It might seem that I am offering a reading of *Kinyarwanda*, but that is not what I wish to do. However, the film comes into view as a re-presentation of the event and one of the readily available memory-texts that seek to draw, not always convincingly, our attention to think about traumatisation at such a scale of society and, at the same at time, at such an everyday personal level. The movie, like other cultural and memory texts that seek to re-present historical trauma and preserve memory, like the Kigali Genocide Memorial we visited on Wednesday, like the Apartheid Museum in South Africa, like the National Museum of African American History and Culture in Washington DC, left me with numerous questions. One of these is precisely what is a person doing when he – I am talking of men as men, not in any way as representative of humans – asks for forgiveness in such cases? But I am also very keen on the offering of forgiveness.

What is the nature of both these acts, what are their limits, their futures and possibility for the self, or a sub-national group, or society, and how best to represent them? The question is not whether asking for forgiveness for such acts or forgiving is necessary or desirable, but rather, on one hand, why perpetrators would expect to be forgiven for such acts, and, on the other, why would survivors forgo their *right* (if that is the word) to vengeance against those responsible for their injuries or the death of loved ones. It is not too hard to appreciate why those who have been hurt would want vengeance, yet we must always want to understand why they do not seek vengeance when they have a right to it. And it is due to a certain idea about humans – for instance that *ubuntu* is inherent in *bantu* – that we come to expect that individuals who have violated us will, if they are *abantu*, ask pardon: yet we cannot permanently close searching to understand why and under what conditions perpetrators ask for forgiveness and whether we can know if it is genuine.

In the scene in question, here is what Emmanuel says: 'From my heart I ask for forgiveness.' It is worth quoting all the words Emmanuel is given to speak in this scene within which his plea for forgiveness is embedded. He says:

> I stand before you, accepting accusations of all the wrong I did. Because I actually did them. I don't remember the number of people I killed. This is the right time to condemn myself, because during that period I made a bad decision and betrayed Rwanda. I ask for forgiveness. [At this point the film cuts back to the moment when Emmanuel and his companions burst into his former employer's house and, among other things, he says to Jeanne's father, "I want your cockroach daughter"]. I am the one who killed the parents of this girl, looted all of their property. From my heart I ask for forgiveness. And if you pardon me, I will use my strength to repay all that I destroyed. And will use my strength to work for my country. And

> if you forgive me, I wish to be your neighbour again. I wish to be a good neighbour to you again. From my heart, I ask for your forgiveness. Please.

I have replayed this scene several times and I am interested in the character and words of Emmanuel – in what drives him, in what he is asking for when he asks for forgiveness from Jeanne. However, I am also interested in the response by Jeanne, who all this time is in fact standing in front of him. This is what she says to him in answer to his plea: 'From the bottom of my heart I am giving him pardon. And you will be a friend to me as you once were to my mother and father. And I will respect you.'

Although I have read about, and since being here have heard a little more on the gaçaça courts, and I want to believe this is possible and desirable, I found both Emmanuel and Jeanne at this point of the movie hard to believe, their words too contrived. His plea for forgiveness, with its reference to Rwanda, sounds as false as her words that she will 'respect' him. Why is there a need to befriend and respect the killer of her parents, besides pardoning him? More broadly, what makes it possible for some women and men who have a right to hurt their violators to end up giving up on wanting to hurt those who have hurt their people, their parents and them? How are these women and men able to integrate trauma in their present lives and live well with and beyond the memory of a hurtful past?

It may be a failure of the character or the movie and not gaçaça themselves that tests my suspicion of this plea and granting of forgiveness. However, it may also be due to an incredulity on my part with not only violence and forgiveness represented and flattened out in this way, but also with what I see as a lack of empathy with the rage of those who hurt and those who have been hurt, with the lack of creative space to allow us to stay in the tension. Of course, violence and not wanting to forgive some things can be destructive. Of course, rage can wreck not only those at whom it is directed but can also burn the one in whose chest it blazes. But it is also the case, as far as I can see in my work, to comprehend the historical and ongoing wounds and brokenness in many men, especially those who are young, the men in whom I observe the ongoing humiliations and invisible shame that turn into anger and erupt as violence, with how long it took to battle the physical but most crucially the emotional and mental injuries that wanted to and did erupt into uncontrolled rage, that the haste with which some talk about nonviolence and forgiveness has not brought peace and self-forgiveness to many of these men.

What I am doing here is somewhat unusual. I am not in a hurry to offer any answer to the main problem with which I am grappling: the productivity in allowing a space for some men (that is, those who violate from the position of being violated, after bell hooks) to fully work through the tension of wanting to hurt others but not hurting them; similarly, the productivity of a space for entertaining giving up the right to hurt those who hurt you without rushing to forgiveness. The answers to the question of what to do when hurt, some of which I have offered so many times, now seem too easy and overly reasonable, and I will offer them again in contexts and platforms other than this. But it is not the answers, not the snap explanations, not the theoretical formulations, that I have been thinking of, since March 2015 when some young men and women during the UCT #RhodesMustFall really challenged me. What I am doing is staying with the troubling questions and the troubling emotions. How should I understand that some men (having been violated or suffered themselves, whether due to colonialism, or apartheid racism, or rape, or parental maltreatment, or abandonment) want to hurt others, when they want to avenge their hurt, whether this is this good, under what circumstances? I am interested then in a certain set of feelings connected to being hurt and wanting to hurt back, wanting to understand what enables me to quickly integrate some memories of hurt but take longer to deal with others. Because such feelings are hard to measure, difficult to fix in place, to know once and for all times when and by whom and why they will be caused to bubble up.

Even when I keep saying say 'I', I am not always talking about myself. I am also trying to put myself in the place of the young man on a street in Addis Ababa who jumps on another and starts punching him. Or the young men in an H&M store who apparently go mad and pull down the clothes racks in protest against the racist clothing by the store. Or the policeman who kills his lover and children. Or the man who rapes the student. Or the husband who pushes and kicks the wife. But even if I am trying to be this man and place myself in his feelings of hurt or shame or humiliation, which turn to anger and rage and aggression in search of better seeing this trouble when one is feeling hurt, it is an emergent pre-social truth that I am trying to track, to perform a kind of inward-looking psychological ethnography. But as embodied truth, when the self speaks to the self, this subjective knowledge never seems to stay in one place forever.

It is true that there are times, which do not seem to have a very clear pattern and which I can put into any shape, when I have wanted to hurt someone who has hurt me, when I have barely contained my aggression against those who I feel have wanted to humiliate and shame me, or wounded those with whom I identify. Sometimes it is a stranger who is the object of this barely held back rage. But at other times, I am ashamed to say, it is a close one I want to hurt because they have hurt me. Are these not similar feelings that have impelled Emmanuel? Are these not similar feelings many man have? Are these not what men in South Africa who inflict harm on their partners and strangers feel; similar feelings to those that lie below the aggression and violence of men in the United States, in Pakistan, in France, in the Democratic Republic of Congo, in Rwanda? How precisely does one give up what we can call 'the right to revenge', or palatably, the right to justice? How does one learn to integrate these feelings of being hurt, perhaps even live with those who have hurt oneself or those for whom one cares?

The notion of giving up one's right to payback was best articulated by the former Archbishop of Cape Town, Mpilo Desmond Tutu. For those who may not be familiar with him, Tutu was the chairperson of the South African Truth and Reconciliation Commission (TRC). He is closely connected to the concept of forgiving and reconciliation in democratic South Africa. In an interview on PBS in the United States, he was once asked, 'What do you actually do when you forgive someone?' This was part of his answer:

> Well, basically you're saying, "I am abandoning my right to revenge, to pay back. I mean, I have, I, by the fact that you have abused me, you have hurt me or whatever it is that you have done, you've wronged me, by that you have given me a certain right, as it were, over you that I could refuse to forgive you, I could say I have the right to retribution. When I forgive, I say I jettison that right and I open the door of opportunity to you to make a new beginning. That is what I do when I forgive you".

Why would one give up the right to retribution? Tutu's words are powerful, and even make considerable sense at some level of consciousness, and perhaps, furthermore, to imagine the kind of human being that Tutu is seeking to hail. But I would like to contrast this powerful sentiment and the heights that Tutu wants us to reach with what Winnie Madikizela Mandela, who passed away on Monday, said about the TRC. Madikizela Mandela had been angry, I suspect, about being subjected to the TRC for her role in the torture and murder of 14-year-old activist James 'Stompie' Seipei in 1989 by members of the Mandela United Football Club, which was associated with Madikizela Mandela. Speaking later to a television news channel about the apartheid security agents who testified that they murdered her driver and blew up his body, she said:

> We were expected to listen to this, listen to this TRC confessions and then forgive. We were expected to forgive, forgive this type of thing, forgive this type of situation where you don't even have a grave, where a man proudly says in the hearing, "there was a toe left, and that toe was blown with a hand-grenade". You can imagine the glee with which they are doing that. And what type of human being is expected to forgive that?

To understand forgiveness is a very difficult thing. Equally or more so, one can imagine, when you bring to mind a moment when you were badly hurt, such as a close one being blown up, the intense psychical and moral energy that one calls up to forgive. In one moment, then, forgiveness is an ordinary human occurrence, but for some wounds, especially when no reprieve has been forthcoming, it feels that it is too high a mountain to climb. We are told that we have to let go of our anger and hurt in order to be free, but pay back against those who have injured one is celebrated in films and television series. We know it is a virtuous thing to forgive, but vengeance can assuage some of the pain. Against all this, the question that I am troubling here, which I want to stay with for the duration of this symposium, and which has given me pause in how I think of men, is to find ways to better appreciate the circumstances under which – in the context of the kind of historical transgenerational, multiple and on-going traumas that have and continue to challenge men and women in a place like South Africa – some might want to and do hurt others, while others manage not to.

11. 'Gukurahundi' and transgenerational trauma: Reburials, memory and the politics of 'reconciliation' in Matabeleland, Zimbabwe

Shari Eppel

Peace is a product of truth – nothing must be done in darkness and shadows[1]

Zimbabwe is a nation with a long and tragic history of state organised violence, in which the ordinary citizen has repeatedly been targeted for political reasons. British colonial rule was brutal: dating back to the 1890s, a white minority established and maintained its power over the nation, then called Rhodesia, by racist laws and oppression. Laws deprived the majority black population of their land, through the Land Apportionment Act of 1931 and the Land Tenure Act of 1969, which restricted access to land on the basis of race. Movement in and out of the towns was policed and restricted to work forces needed for white-owned factories and businesses, and access to health and education was similarly controlled. From the late 1950s, organised resistance to the colonial state grew, and led to the formation of the Zimbabwe African Peoples Union (ZAPU), led by Joshua Nkomo. In 1963, the party split as a result of personal and ideological struggles. The breakaway party called itself the Zimbabwe African National Union (ZANU) and marked the beginning of a long and uncompromising split in the nationalist movement. Both ZAPU and ZANU created armed wings, known as the Zimbabwe People's Revolutionary Army (ZIPRA) in the case of ZAPU, and as the Zimbabwe African National Liberation Army (ZANLA) in the case of ZANU. ZIPRA was trained mainly with support from the Russians, and ZANLA with support from the Chinese, marking further divisions in the two.

The liberation war

A protracted struggle for freedom lasted throughout the 1970s and cost over 30,000 lives. A further 750,000 were internally displaced, often forcibly by the Rhodesians. The colonials deliberately practised a 'divide and rule' policy between the Ndebeles,

1 Comment made to the first outreach session of the National Peace and Reconciliation Commission in Gwanda, Zimbabwe, in February 2018, by a second-generation trauma survivor.

the minority comprising around 15-20% who resided in the western part of the country, and the Shonas who comprised the rest of the black population. In fact, there are at least 10 ethnicities in Zimbabwe, who were conflated into these two broader groupings. Over time, ZANU and ZANLA drew more support from Shona-speaking regions, and ZAPU and ZIPRA from Ndebele-speaking regions. Whenever the two guerrilla armies met in the bush, they fought one another fiercely, and the antagonism remained throughout the war of liberation.

The Lancaster House Agreement of 1979 led to the first democratic election in April 1980: ZANU won most of the country, while ZAPU won all the seats in Matabeleland and parts of the Midlands, the provinces where the Ndebele resided.

Failed combatant integration – and 'Gukurahundi'

Robert Mugabe became the first nationalist Prime Minister in Zimbabwe, and the integration of three armies into one began – ZANLA, ZIPRA and the Rhodesian National Army. Almost immediately, ZIPRA cadres began reporting enforced disappearances, punishments and name-calling, which led to defections as they fled, ostensibly fearing for their lives. Banditry and caching of arms happened throughout the country, as nervous guerrillas on both sides hedged their bets. Rhetoric targeted only ZIPRA, however, as Mugabe began to implement what had clearly been a long-cherished ambition to crush ZAPU/ZIPRA and create a one-party state. In August 1980, Mugabe flew to North Korea and commissioned them to train him a special army Brigade: this brigade was to remain outside of the National Army and was answerable directly to Mugabe himself. The date is significant, as August 1980 preceded various disturbances that occurred later, between ZANLA and ZIPRA, and points to a longstanding plan to eliminate ZAPU. The 5 Brigade passed out at the end of 1982, and Mugabe himself called them the 'Gukurahundi' Brigade, a Shona phrase meaning the 'first rain of spring that washes away the chaff from the last season'.

The 5 Brigade was deployed in Matabeleland North on 29 January 1983, and there was immediately epidemic violence: rural villagers were rounded up and mercilessly beaten. They were accused of being Ndebele, and therefore of being dissidents who supported ZAPU. Men and sometimes women were massacred throughout the province, in well witnessed community-based murders: wives and mothers were forced at gunpoint to bury their newly dead, and in other instances, bodies were left to rot and be scavenged. In spite of curfews and problems in information about these atrocities leaking, by April 1983, the outcry was sufficient to cause 5 Brigade to be withdrawn and retrained. They were redeployed in Matabeleland South in 1984, with new modus operandi that involved rural civilians being moved to 5 Brigade bases, such as the notorious Bhalagwe Camp, where they were tortured, often to death. Burials were now often clandestine and anonymous. By 1985, 5 Brigade had moved to the more sinister policy of enforced disappearances: wanted individuals were taken in the dead of night and never seen alive again.

The 5 Brigade era, and the associated policies of repression of ZAPU, continued until the signing of the Unity Accord in December 1987. This led to the absorption of ZAPU into ZANU, and effectively a one-party state. However, the damage done by the 'Gukurahundi Era', was immeasurable and remains so today. There was scarcely a family in Matabeleland and parts of the Midlands who were not directly affected by the killings, beatings, property loss and disappearances of the 1980s.

The aftermath: the angry dead

As the perpetrators remain effectively in power in Zimbabwe, this time of atrocities has remained cloaked in silence. There has been no truth allowed to surface about what happened – no recognition, no reparation, no reconciliation. As a health practitioner and part of a team working in rural Matabeleland with victims of Gukurahundi, it became apparent to us in the late 1990s that wounds were still raw, and fear blanketed these rural villages. Beneath the fear was terrible grief over the fate of those who had been killed or disappeared. In terms of local belief systems, the angry spirits of the dishonoured dead are the most serious legacy of the massacres. Ancestral spirits play a daily role in the lives of the living, and if you have not buried your dead loved one in the right place in the right way, with the right traditional rituals, in front of the right people, then they have been dishonoured and will punish you, with droughts, failed marriages, failed development projects, infertility and illnesses. While the official government position was that the past must be forgotten, families found themselves unable to forget their aggrieved loved ones, unable to move on with their lives. According to traditional leaders, we were told that:

> Culturally it is not right for someone's bones to be exposed. It brings bad luck which denies people rain [2014 interview].
>
> Human bones are in the bush and some are exposed – I don't think God is happy with that [2014 interview].

We realised that the bones were key and active players in the well-being of their communities, and began a project that we called 'healing the dead'. We realised that in order to heal the living, we had first to heal their dead – by exhuming and reburying the murdered, we could release the suppressed processes of mourning. While 'healing' is not a simple event, allowing the living and the dead to speak to each other, and to allow the dead to be acknowledged, witnessed, listened to and reburied in the right place with the right rituals could unlock the beginnings of healing. It was also apparent that the correct way to work with communities was to engage them on their perceived needs, rather than imposing a western medical model, that assumed Post-traumatic Stress Disorder or Mixed Anxiety-Depression Disorder. Families needed to be listened to and believed, and they needed their dead back for decent reburial, to ensure continuity and succession of roles in the family and community.

Exhumations and reburials – 1999-2001 and post-2014

The Argentine Forensic Anthropology Team (EAAF) agreed to come to Matabeleland and conduct training exhumations, to develop capacity to exhume in Zimbabwe. For four years, our team of Amani Trust exhumed together with them, developing a skill base in forensic anthropology and forensic archaeology. When a new political crisis led to a wave of state-led violence in the wake of the 2000 elections and the rise of a new political opposition, exhumations stopped for some years. However, the process of skill building continued, and in 2014, exhumations resumed on an ad hoc basis. Our team may be unique in that it offers detailed emotional support to families and communities, before, during and after exhumations, as we are deeply committed to ensuring that the process is as useful and restorative to families as possible and are interested in tracking the advantages and pitfalls of this.

Forensics expertise can help to fulfil the humanitarian objective of the 'right to know' what happened to family members in a time of killings – which is linked to the 'right to truth', both recognised rights in terms of the UNCHR, 2005. With the help of professionals, bones can speak, and can restore historical memory. In every case that we have exhumed, the bones have played a role in revealing what happened to the murdered individual in the hours leading to the death: peri-mortem trauma can be distinguished from pre-mortem and post-mortem trauma, and can clarify what took place. Clothing and the way in which skeletons are revealed to be lying are part of the recovery of truth. In one instance, eyewitnesses reported that 'Max' had been badly beaten by soldiers while being forced down the dirt road with others. His jaw was so painful that a neighbour had offered a cloth to tie up his jaw. Max was nonetheless marched into the hills and beaten to death. He was not buried, but relatives had returned to search for him a few days later and had hurriedly buried him against a rock in a clandestine site, to prevent scavenging. When Max was exhumed, the cloth was there, tied around his skull, still protecting the jaw after 34 years in the grave. This vindicated the memories of the witnesses and gave credibility to all that they had said, in the face of a government that was still resistant to such truths.

Another family witness reported that:

> Daniel could not walk, he had blood coming out of his ears – we were forced to push him on the wheelbarrow for a long distance, then the soldiers took him into the hills. We heard gunshots, and never saw him alive again...

> We exhumed Daniel, and his cranium was in 64 pieces. On reconstruction it was possible to identify a minimum of two bullets to the skull, also one to the right humerus, again proving in death what had been reported.

It is apparent that families, driven by intense fear and emotional inability to talk about the past, often effectively 'disappear' relatives and all evidence of them from the family tree and the lexicon. In almost every case, as an exhumation looms, the 'missing', unmentioned family member gradually eases back into view and into conversation among siblings and children. A long hidden and almost forgotten photographic image of the person may one day be produced, in a context where it is becoming safer to refer to that person. Daniel's brother suddenly produced two beautiful portraits of him, a few days before the exhumation. Another relative reported to us:

> Yesterday, when one of his daughters saw the photos for the first time, she said that she had never seen her father before – although she used to dream about her father a lot, he had no face in her dreams....

The exhumations thus become catalysts for a broader reclaiming of the dead for the family. Exhumation and identification restores the personhood of the dead. This same uncle reported that:

> I could not talk to Daniel's sons then because it was painful. But now we have got proof of how it ended and so I feel free to fill in the gaps of their father's history and the type of man he was.

In another village, a young man, Edwell Ndlovu, was tied upside down to a tree and beaten and bayonetted to death, before being buried in an antbear hole on the side of the local primary school field. When, in 1998, this site was first pointed out by his mother to our team, the current headmaster at the school had no idea that there were human remains on the school premises, having arrived at the school in the 1990s.

The silences around the past have left entire regions ill at ease and the partial knowledge and hints of terrible events strands newcomers into a strange world where the angry dead haunt the landscape, but without precise details being known of what transpired.

Repression of truth – impact on the next generation

At the national level, the Gukurahundi history has been largely repressed, silenced and denied. For 35 years it has been effectively impossible to mourn the dead of that era: mourning, anger, truth – all have been suppressed for decades. There is no national day to commemorate victims of Gukurahundi, and no memorials or monuments, apart from one that we have erected on the site of Edwell's exhumation.

There is also a yearly soccer tournament in Edwell's name on the field where he was buried. There have been a few brave attempts to record the atrocities of the era in the public domain. In 2010, a young artist, Owen Maseko, dedicated an entire art exhibition to Gukurahundi – and was arrested and charged with 'undermining the authority of the President' as well as 'offending an ethnic group', even though his work simply portrayed the atrocities. The fact that it was Owen – a man too young to have been directly affected by the massacres, is significant. It is clear that in Matabeleland it is the next generations, the children and grandchildren of those who suffered and died, who have taken up the struggle for this history to be heard. It is my observation that the direct victims remain mostly too intimidated to break through their silences and to confront the state. But within the family, it is clear that the descendants of victims have absorbed the subliminal message that they should give voice to anger and pain. They have picked up the burden of the past in a way that their parents cannot, and are determined to carry it into the future.

In the meantime, the broader context has shifted. Robert Mugabe, in power from 1980, was ousted by a military coup in November 2017. His replacement, Emmersen Mnangagwa, is almost as implicated as Mugabe in the massacres, having been deeply involved in managing the secret police at the time. However, he is eager to portray a more democratic state and spaces have begun to open up, if uncertainly. The new constitution, adopted in 2013, also makes a National Peace and Reconciliation Commission (NPRC) a legal necessity. The commission, with seven Shona commissioners and only one from Matabeleland, rolled out in February 2018.

The first meetings were telling indeed. In Gwanda, a small centre in Matabeleland South, the NPRC meeting was mostly attended by second-generation survivors. One after another, they stood up and confronted the commission. Below are some comments made:

> How can you say let bygones be bygones if we have not had the truth? How can I forgive you? We think there is something behind this commission.
>
> There is only one Ndebele and three Shonas here today. This commission is the face of marginalisation. How can someone go to address murders committed by his siblings?
>
> You cannot deny marginalisation and segregation – don't lie to us.

The speakers told of a deep perception of ongoing structural violence, of cultural and economic oppression and domination. A young father challenged the commission with the fact that his six-year-old child was being taught in IsiShona, the language of the oppressor, instead of in IsiNdebele, which is his constitutional right in Zimbabwe. A young woman stood up and asked why all senior government officials in Gwanda are Shona-speaking – is the entire of Matabeleland not capable of producing one person who can be a district commissioner, in this district where most rural people can only speak IsiNdebele? The cultural dominance of Shonas over Ndebeles was referred to as a continuation of 'Gukurahundi', which was said to have never ended. The commission was referred to as a 'commission of perpetrators'. Practical examples of current hardships perceived to be ethnically driven were mixed with family accounts of the violence of Gukurahundi:

> We have been denied permission to bury our loved ones decently. We have our parents that disappeared during that genocide. How do they get death certificates? Our sisters who were raped and left pregnant during Gukurahundi – whose burden was it to make sure those children went to school? If you need rituals for the dead, how do you facilitate this?
>
> We know one reason people were killed is they failed to speak Shona. Deep in our hearts we hate one another to the core. We see tribalism because of inner feelings dating back to this genocide, when people came from outside [Matabeleland]. Allow people from this region [Matabeleland] to head their own institutions.
>
> We have come from genocide and are heading to another one. In Matabeleland you don't count – if you don't speak Shona you are not recognised.

In Bulawayo the following day, the NPRC meeting was entirely disrupted by second-generation survivors, who, in recent years, have formed various angry pressure groups in response to Gukurahundi. These young men and women toyi-toyi'd and prevented the commissioners from standing up and speaking, although a few victims were chosen by the activists to tell their stories of horror. There are several Mthwakazi separatist groups, who among their angry demands call for a separate Ndebele nation. However, in discussions with them, it is clear this is more of an angry position than a real demand for a separate Mthwakazi nation. It is attention-seeking by a lost generation who are striving to draw national attention to the suffering in their region, and who justifiably have little faith in the current government. The alienation of this generation from the body-politick has left them with a regional rather than a national identity. Members often wear a headband made from animal hide to emulate the Ndebele/Zulu warrior tradition of their forefathers. Young people in Matabeleland have headed en masse to South Africa, where they feel more accepted among other Nguni ethnic groups, rather than looking for work in other parts of Zimbabwe.

During 2018, this second-generation Gukurahundi survivor has leapt to the fore and is driving the Matabeleland agenda. They are angry, they are in deep pain – and they carry an uninformed version of the Gukurahundi history, because there is almost no route to an informed version of the history. The primary victims, their parents and grandparents, remain most often too afraid to talk to their descendants about what happened, which was often humiliating and degrading. Where events are talked about, it is in hushed tones and in corners, and in confusion as to why such bad things happened. Such family histories also do not shed light on the broader spread and context of events.

For several years, pressure groups such as Ibhetshu LikaZulu, a traditionalist group headed by a young man aged barely forty, have attempted to hold commemorations at Bhalagwe camp in Matabeleland South. Hundreds died here in 1984, when it was a torture base. It is a remote venue, in a valley. It is easy to prevent access, and every time Ibhetshu has attempted to get to the site, they have been stopped by police. However, in February this year, for the first time, they were allowed to proceed. What resulted was a group of slightly bewildered youngsters driving around what is now simply an overgrown valley: all evidence of the torture camp has fallen into disarray over the last nearly four decades. They were without landmarks, and whatever they had expected to see at the site, it was not there. This is symbolic of the broader history around Gukurahundi. It is difficult now, with so many eye-witnesses already dead, to reconstruct the events in any historically accurate detail. This in turn has created a conundrum both for the state and for those who have tracked and recorded what they can about the era over the decades. Is it now too late to verify the scale of what happened and to provide some semblance of a real history?

Another second-generation survivor, Zenzele Ndebele, recently produced a documentary called *Gukurahundi Genocide*. In this, he interviews several eye-witnesses who provide a partial picture of events. He also claims that 40,000 died, which is double the number usually associated with the massacres. But who is to contradict him? His response when challenged is simply to say: 'Let the state come forward with evidence of how many it was that died, let them prove my figure wrong, let them say how many they killed.'

It is clear that many of the older generation are grateful and feel indebted to this younger, braver generation.

Far from feeling that their exaggerated versions of what happened and their rage at government should be curbed, they are relieved to see this generation has picked up the baton, and they do not see them as extremist at all. Discussions with senior church leadership in Bulawayo had them openly declaring gratitude to Mthwakazi for raising so powerfully the pain and anger in the region, in a way the older generation would be too afraid/respectful to do. These pressure groups are seen as necessary and as a to-be-expected outcome after 35 years of suppression.... A bishop said: 'the trouble with we Ndebeles is we remain silent and in pain for a long time, and then explode in anger. These youths offer us all catharsis.'

Where the issue of Gukurahundi and the need for recognition, reparation and reconciliation is heading remains to be seen. Zimbabwe's political space remains highly unstable. While the NPRC is determined to move forward and claim some legitimacy, they are seriously under resourced and have a limited staff and skill base. The task will fall back to civics and the churches to facilitate trust for the NPRC in the Matabeleland region – and the NPRC will have to convince civics and the churches they deserve this. Civics may identify ways in which the NPRC can, in a mutually beneficial way, open political space for those with resources and experience to move in and work with victims. What is clear is that if this does not happen, there is a risk that subsequent generations, far from forgetting, will increasingly build an identity in which pain and anger at the continued denial of the past is central. This could become explosive in decades ahead.

12. Historic trauma as a site of cultural creativity and social negotiation: A reflection on aesthetic and political challenges

Andrea Bieler

Introduction

This essay reflects on the phenomenon that the aftermath of atrocious violence frequently becomes a site of cultural and religious creativity insofar as artists experience the freedom to develop, publish, perform or display their works publicly. Accordingly, we can observe in many cases that historic trauma does not only entail silence, loss and disorientation but rather holds the potential for creativity and aesthetic response to the experience of shattered worlds. This creativity is embedded in an aesthetic 'memory boom' that has been unfolding in recent decades in the arts as well as in the world of museums and public memorials. It reflects a transnational and transcultural response to the memory imperative 'never again' first powerfully articulated in the aftermath of the Shoah. We can identify a huge number of novels, autobiographic writings, musical compositions and works of visual art that were created in different proximity to the originating atrocities. Some of these artworks grapple with religious questions or imply a spiritual dimension; others do not. These artistic responses follow a different logic than political and legal interventions. They might however share some sort of overlap.

In what follows I will focus on a few selected memorials and sculptures that reframe the public spaces residents dwell in, tourists visit or survivors, families and friends approach.

We can distinguish between two groups:

The first cluster consists of official memorials and museums that commemorate state-sponsored violence. Examples hereof have been chosen from Argentina, the United States, Germany and Cambodia. These sites are frequently placed at historic locations marked by previous violence. The second set of samples is made up of artistic interventions in the public square that do not carry the weight of official governmental approval. These examples have either an ephemeral gestalt in the form of temporary installations or are sculptures designed to be displayed throughout time.

In what follows I do not intend to do a close interpretation of individual sites. Instead, I want to highlight shared challenges that come to the fore in very different contexts. By doing so I do not aim at making substantial comparisons regarding the political and historic nature of these events and circumstances. I rather seek to draw lines of connection with regard to aesthetic, pedagogical and performative questions that are relevant to the discussed examples.

Three interrelated sets of issues can be identified:

a) Many artworks and memorials reflect the fact that remembering violence is a contested terrain. This terrain is affected by conflicting political interests, the politics of voice (who is allowed to speak, whose perspectives are depicted) and the aspect of time in the intergenerational transmission of memories. The latter also includes changing patterns of interpretation that dominate public discourse in relation to a violent past. Besides political interests and transgenerational issues aesthetic questions are debated that are related to ethical issues.

b) In addition, memorials promote the ambiguous dimensions of how historic events are remembered. On the one hand this ambiguity arises from the event itself. For instance, in many wars individual soldiers have been perpetrators and victims. When the wars that were supposed to turn them into heroes are lost they came home as part of a defeated army. On the other hand, in most cases war memorials attempt to erase ambiguity; war memorials are deliberately one-sided with regard to who and what is supposed to be remembered. This erasure however holds the potential for new conflicts to emerge.

c) Finally, many memorials need to grapple with the absence of dead or identifiable bodies and with the erasure of the singularity of human lives in mass killings. This challenge is entangled in the impossibility of remembering each victim respectfully with attention to his or her individual life story. This unresolvable dilemma is a challenge to the aesthetic, cultural and religious collective memory.

The necessary discussion around contested, ambiguous as well as dilemma-filled aspects of public memorials and artworks is confronted with a set of questions that arise in different contexts. These pertain to the degree of open-endedness of the aesthetic expression and artistic freedom of the artist. One might just recall the provocative line of Peter Eisenman, the architect who designed the *Memorial to the Murdered Jews of Europe*: 'Now handing over the memorial to the German people and the population of Berlin. They will decide what to do with it. If they want to dance or have a picnic on the stelae, that's fine with me.'[1]

Especially with regard to museums and memorial sites, another debated issue concerns the targeted visitors and how they are supposed to interact with these places of commemoration. Who is actively invited, who actually visits and who is not interested or refuses to visit? Here, the motivating intention and the museum concepts need to be differentiated from the actual reception by the public and by visitors. The expected as well as the actual interaction of visitors can be recognised as the performative dimension of a memorial or a museum. It exists not only as the product of artists, designers and architects but rather comes alive through the engagement of visitors who interact with these places and objects.

A third linked question is the connection between educational and affective aspects. Regarding museums and memorials, the question arises as to what visitors are expected to learn and if there exists an undergirding core message that shapes particular exhibitions. This relates to the approach chosen with regard to how artefacts and visuals are displayed, how mnemonic devices are introduced and how historical narratives are formed. If there is a focus on documentation you will likely find a narrative presented that visitors are supposed to receive, e.g., through texts, photos, videos or artefacts that seek to create a consistent story line or message. If there is an emphasis on the creation of affective impulses such as empathy with victims, particular aesthetic means are employed. Documenting, for instance, the timeline of how a genocide has been painstakingly planned and purposefully exercised might evoke a sense of shock in the one who studies it for the first time. In this case the cognitive dimension of conveying facts is emphasised in the display, yet emotional responses are expected to be released too. However, if a visitor enters a room filled with bones and skulls a different kind of evidence is produced. The display of human remains is limited in its ability to explain complex historical events. It rather points to the gruesome gravity of atrocious killing. In that vein, remains are supposed to create an affective validation. Consequently, learning processes occur on the cognitive and the affective level and are constantly intertwined. Displays in memorial museums shift their focus intentionally in a single exhibition in order to provide a multi-layered experience.

Another layer within the affective dimension is the interrelation of public grief messages and private mourning. For instance, the *Kigali Genocide Memorial* in Rwanda seeks to attend to both dimensions. The website of the memorial introduces their intention to provide a space for grieving and learning:

---

1 See Brigitte Sion, Absent Bodies, Uncertain Memorials. Performing Memory in Berlin and Buenos Aires, Ann Arbor, MI: Proquest LLC, 2008, 22.

> The centre was officially opened on 7 April 2004 to mark the tenth commemoration of the 1994 genocide against the Tutsi in Rwanda. The memorial is the final resting place for up to 259,000 victims of the genocide and serves as a place where people can grieve for their lost loved ones and remember them. It also serves as a museum where both local and international visitors can learn about the history, implementation and consequences of the genocide.[2]

The structure of the memorial consists of two distinct spaces, namely a documentation centre and the grave site, which consists of terraced, concrete surfaces placed in a park and leading down the hill. The graveyard has three purposes: a) Public commemoration ceremonies are held here; b) it is considered to be a resting place for the dead; c) it is designed to also be a place for intimate mourning and expressions of grief. One can observe from time to time a few individuals remaining in silence at this site and flowers are put down on the concrete surfaces.[3] Particularly tourists who have not have lost loved ones are instructed by museum guides to dwell in the place in a silent and respectful manner and to respect the calm of the dead.

The educational framework of the documentation centre has a clear, yet constrained focus. It is geared towards an international as well as a local visitorship. It focuses on the genocide against the Tutsi by explaining it historically, introducing the colonial legacies involved and the various waves of 'ethnic cleansing' that happened beginning in the fifties. It offers a detailed documentation of the massive atrocities that occurred in 1994. It is also clear about the failure of the United Nations, its troops and political entities, since these did not help prevent or stop the unleashing of violence during the genocide.

It focuses on the genocide against the Tutsis, which also includes the victims on the side of the Hutus who resisted the political developments. The exhibition, however, does not also document and explain the counter aggression against the Hutus that finally stopped the genocide and simultaneously unleashed an enormous amount of revengeful killing. Since the public message of the museum does not leave room for this complicated part of Rwanda's history, it does not offer a space for the current youth, or other remaining relatives, who come from Hutu families and whose fathers – who might have been perpetrators – were also killed.

These dimensions – namely the aesthetic, the performative, the educational and the affective – need to be explored not as discrete entities but also in their synergetic interdependence.

---

2 http://www.genocidearchiverwanda.org.rw/index.php/Kigali_Genocide_Memorial (accessed on November 5th, 2018).

3 More ethnographic work is needed in order to assess if this site is vital for many survivors and family members who have to deal with the loss of loved ones due to the genocide.

In what follows I can only highlight a few of the dynamics I have briefly described while giving selected examples of the aspects introduced here: the terrain of contestation, the aspect of ambiguity and the negotiation of dilemma.

Memorials, museums and art works as contested terrain

Frequently, official memorials as well as artworks are steeped in deep controversies from their very beginning. These controversies reflect the fact that commemoration practices in general are a contested terrain. The question of how stories of violent conflicts, genocide and enduring structural violence are depicted and interpreted is an open debate. For instance, conflicts arose in Argentina about the erection of official memorials that were sponsored by governments that followed totalitarian regimes. In Argentina, ten human rights organisations took the initiative to make a proposal to local officials of the city of Buenos Aires for the allocation of a site and a public memorial park that would include the names of the 'disappeared ones'.[4] In 1998, a law was passed by the local officials that included plans for the realisation of the proposed space of commemoration. This plan, however, was opposed by some human rights groups that represented the families and friends of the *desaparecidos*. They were concerned that an official memorial site would create a closure or a kind of institutionalisation of memory that would brush over the open wounds and the still unresolved murder cases. These organisations raised a political and an aesthetic issue that became pertinent in many other countries as well.

In therapeutic settings of trauma therapy, the goal is to calm down and disempower haunting memories that are out of control and hurting those who are overwhelmed by them in order to create a safe environment for the patient.[5] Human rights activists and artists, however, who are aware of the unresolved truth and justice issues in the aftermath of state-sponsored violence are keener on reflecting on haunting memories not only as a destructive but also as a productive force that provides a necessary, vital and unsettling energy for dealing with the past. They express a suspicion that if you give these haunting spirits a place, by erecting memorials set in stone or by building a memorial museum, you might paradoxically create more oblivion or apathetic rest that silences the quest for truth and justice.[6]

4 See Sion, Absent Bodies, 25f.

5 This is at least true for therapeutic approaches that seek to activate resources in patients rather than go for exposure therapy. An example hereof can be found in the work of Luise Reddemann, Psychodynamisch imaginative Traumatherapie PITT – Das Manual. Ein resilienzorientierter Ansatz in der Psychotraumatologie, Stuttgart: Klett Cotta 2011.

6 See for an interpretation of haunting spirits from the perspective of postcolonial theology Mayra Rivera, 'Ghostly Encounters: Spirits, Memory and the Holy Ghost.' In Planetary Loves: Spivak, Postcoloniality and Theology, eds. Stephen Moore and Mayra Rivera. New York: Fordham University Press, 2011, 118–135.

On a related note, the philosopher Jacques Derrida calls for a hauntology that rejects a clear cut, linear understanding of past, present and future and rather calls for an attentiveness to the 'non-contemporaneity of the living present'.[7]

In *Specters of Marx*, Derrida proceeds from the assumption that the possibility of a just future depends on our readiness 'to learn to live *with* ghosts'. He insists on an obligation to live not solely in the present but 'beyond all living present', aware of and attentive to those already dead or not yet born. According to Derrida, being neither fully present nor fully absent, ghosts belong to a liminal *hauntological* domain.[8] This domain opens up the possibility for practices of commemoration that do not offer false consolation but rather provide a sense of an unsettling awareness that closure is not possible, and that the cultivation of hate-filled memories is not an option either.

In the discussed example, however, we can argue that those who were in favour of the proposal for the *Parque de la Memoria* are issuing a mission statement that includes a hauntological perspective:

> The monument to the Victims of State terrorism is going to be erected on the riverbanks because it is in its waters that many of the victims were thrown. It is not the intention of this memorial to close any wounds that cannot be closed or replace truth and justice. Nothing will restore real peace to the relatives that have not been able to know the final fate of their loved ones, savagely tortured and murdered, and nothing will ever replace the social emptiness created by their absence.[9]

The *Parque de La Memoria* that was finally built was dedicated to victims of state-sponsored terrorism during the military dictatorship between 1976 and 1983. It was placed along the Rio de la Plata in the Belgrano neighbourhood in Buenos Aires. The park was also deliberately placed in close proximity to a detention centre where inmates who had been accused of being enemies of the state were tortured. Part of the torture occurred from the airport where prisoners were deported, taken up into the air and then dropped into the river or the ocean. Hundreds of civilians were killed this way and 'disappeared' under governmental terrorism.

The memorial was designed to cut into the landscape like an open wound. The architect who conceptualised this design was inspired by the work of Maya Lin who created a similar representation.[10] A wall was erected as the centrepiece that preserves the names of 9,000 murdered victims as well as empty plaques for the *desaparecidos*. It is surrounded by eighteen different sculptures that have been installed in the park.

---

7 Jacques Derrida, *Specters of Marx* (Routledge Classics) New York: Routledge 2006, XIX.
8 Derrida, Specters, XVIII.
9 Sion, Absent Bodies, 26.
10 See further the discussion of Lin's work in this essay.

Many of the conflicts around aesthetic issues grapple with the question of how artworks and museum designs relate to a violent past that has powerful repercussions in the present.

In order to answer this question more satisfactorily a theoretical approach is needed that moves beyond the alternative of a presentist approach and an essentialist approach. A presentist approach comprehends works of art as mere constructions that serve certain purposes in the present while an essentialist approach understands memorials or artworks as straightforward representations of a past that can be 'reproduced' by those who remember it. The sociologist Jeffrey K. Olick suggests as an alternative a process-relational approach for the analysis of commemorative practices that is also useful within the realm of the arts.[11] Olick's theory focuses on collective remembering as a thoroughly interactive phenomenon in which the connections between the present and the past are constantly negotiated: In this vein, collective memory can be understood as a field of contestation that exists in constant flux.

In this field, official and vernacular memory is navigated. Diverging narratives of a violent past might all exist at once while also being shaped and contradicted by the arts. These narratives are shaped by different groups within a society, such as politicians, human rights organisations that represent victims and survivors or educators. In this vein, controversies around memorials and artworks can also impact public discourse.

This contested commemorative field is also in constant flux due to the transmission of narratives from one generation to the next. These changes pertain particularly to the experiences of younger visitors at memorial sites who were born after particular atrocities occurred. Accordingly, understanding collective memory as a field that is in constant flux takes the factor of time and intergenerational transmission of collective memory into account. Narratives of a violent past that were perceived as the common-sense paradigm in one generation might change in the following generation.

For example, for many decades after World War II it was very difficult to talk about the victimhood of German civilians in a nuanced way in public; since those who brought up the subject were often right-wing politicians who meant to downplay the devastating role of Nazi Germany during the war. In the mid-nineties things changed and it became possible to also talk about the destruction of German cities by

11 See Jeffrey K. Olick, The Politics of Regret: On Collective Memory and Historical Responsibility. New York: Routledge, 2007. According to Olick an essentialist approach assumes mimetic directness which means that 'collective memory in one way or another represents or mirrors a pre-representational past, rather than being from the very first moment embodied in representational form.' (89). In contrast a presentist approach would stress that remembering our individual and our collective past is a highly subjective endeavour. In this subjectivist and functionalist view, acts of remembering become mainly an instrument to navigate diverging interests of various groups or individuals. Both approaches are too one-dimensional.

the Allied Forces that caused the death of thousands of inhabitants, mainly in urban centres. This change was also reflected in the work of artists.

Benita Joswig's installation *altäre* serves as an example of this shift of interpretative patterns. She designed an artwork in the mid-nineties for the Messeplatz in Kassel, Germany that had been bombed in 1943 by British Allied Forces. On October 23, 1943 the inner city was entirely destroyed. Approximately 10,000 inhabitants died during the fire storm over two nights.

Joswig's installation was part of a larger project with the title *Archeology of the Present*. Through archival research and with the help of historic maps and photo material she reconstructed where the houses at the Messeplatz once stood and where the streets were located. She invited 100 inhabitants of Kassel to participate in the installation by asking them if they would be willing to give away a table that was in active use as a kitchen or dining room table and if it could be placed where people once met over common meals.[12]

This installation was by its very nature only temporary. Joswig's work had the character of an ephemeral intervention. It brought traces of a past into the present through an alienation effect. By asking inhabitants to give away a table they were using in their ordinary lives, participants had to put themselves into the scene. The installation, which was up for three days, created a space for conversation between inhabitants who had survived the fire storm and those who had no clue that the parking space they used for shopping trips was built on the rubble of the inner city.

Ten years earlier such an art project would have probably fallen under suspicion of being a right-wing activity of revanchists denying German aggression during World War II and emphasising only German victimhood. Yet in the mid-nineties we can observe that the topic gained greater credibility in the wider society. A possibility opened up to talk about victimhood in times of war in more nuanced ways, especially in regard to the entanglement of aggressive foreign policy and warfare and the simultaneous suffering of civilians in Germany. In this environment it was possible for Joswig to attend with her work to the destruction of a German city during World War II in a way that helped to enrich the conversation about commemorative practices. She opened a space for citizens of different generations to share their experiences and knowledge of that time period. And those who experienced the bombing had the opportunity to share how these two nights shaped their lives in the decades that followed. There was, however, another layer to this work. It can be understood as an embodied practice of hauntology. By placing tables where houses once stood, the void that the destruction created became visible. People mingled and walked through this void, filling it for a few days with conversations, walking in silence and with a

12 See for a description of the project Benita Joswig, altäre. Theologie und Kunst im urbanen Raum. Ein Tischprojekt, Gütersloh: Gütersloher Verlagshaus 2003.

jazz trumpeter who played sounds reminiscent of the bomb alarms that had once alerted residents of the incoming threats. This intervention had a temporal character, it offered a window for unexpected conversations and an aesthetic experience of a place that had once been the vivid centre of a medieval town.

And finally, it touched upon a deeply human experience: what does it mean to enjoy a meal together or to lose fellowship around a table? By posing the question: Could you imagine your table as an altar? Joswig also hinted at the religious connotations that sharing a meal around a table implies. The term altar refers also to the sacralisation of the object. This reference has multiple ambiguous layers. It hints at the altar as the object and the place where people commune not only with each other yet also with God. Thus, the notion of the altar potentially denotes redemptive communion or community. Yet it also implies the contested subject of sacrifice, which is in civic religious discourse around the globe. This discourse interprets the death of soldiers as a sacrifice given for the sake of a nation's freedom.

Joswig's approach to installations as aesthetic interventions in public spaces resonates with Joseph Beuys's concept of the social sculpture (Soziale Plastik) in that it reflects the ability of ordinary citizens to engage in highly relevant social and cultural issues by means of collective aesthetic practice. The social sculpture blurs the distinction between artists and visitors as a space of shared participation opens up. Besides the chosen space and the chosen tables, the installation altäre created multilayered interactions that unfolded in a limited time span. These particular aesthetic means created an ephemeral commemorative space.

Aesthetic and political negotiation of ambiguity

The second aspect I want to explore and that arises in conflicts around memorials is the issue of ambiguity. Ambiguity comes especially to the fore in relation to war memorials that remember soldiers exclusively of one's own nation.

In order to discuss this topic, I chose the *Vietnam Veterans Memorial* in Washington DC, which is the official national war memorial dedicated to the US-American soldiers who died in the Vietnam War. The American War, as it is called in the view of the Vietnamese people, resulted in an enormous death toll. The US-American involvement in this war lasted from the mid-fifties until 1975. Approximately five million Vietnamese people were killed or wounded, another twelve million were displaced and had to flee from their homes. An estimated 58,000 US-American soldiers were killed or missing in action. Most died at the average age of 21 due to the compulsory draft that the US-government exercised at that time. The returning soldiers became highly ambiguous figures in the US society; many protesters of the war saw them as agents of merciless killing. The senseless devastation of the Vietnamese village of May Lai where 400 civilians were killed became a gruesome point of reference. For the promoters of the war these soldiers had failed since the US-American army had not been able to win. Many of the returning veterans perceived themselves as walking dead, as living shadows in a society that did not receive them back in respectful ways. Probably about one-third of the returning veterans were diagnosed with Post Traumatic Stress Disorder, many of them experienced a profound disorientation as they were not able to continue with the lives they had before Vietnam. There are various layers of ambiguity related to the memory of this war.

One layer is the complicated perception of the returning soldiers. On a political level, the majority of the US-American population severely opposed this war in the end although many had embraced it in the beginning. The way this war ended smashed the myth of American invincibility. Conflicts arose around these ambiguities as the question was posed about what it would take to publicly remember the Vietnam War and the human beings that died in it.

The US government at that time was not willing to create a public space of remembering and learning that would embrace these complexities. It was determined to push for a memorial that would entirely leave out the atrocities that were done to the Vietnamese people.

During the early eighties it was still controversial to publicly discuss the causes of why the war had been waged in the first place and what kind of interests it had supposedly protected.

Finally, the political decision was made to create a war memorial, thus a space that would exclusively remember the American soldiers who had died in the Vietnam War. For one of the initiators of the memorial project, Jan Scruggs, this space of commemoration was supposed to help veterans gain social recognition and offer them the opportunity to connect and build networks of support amongst themselves. The involvement of the veterans hints at another layer of ambiguity in this process. Many soldiers had to suffer from the consequences of the war psychologically and physically. They were however not only victims but perpetrators as well, since they killed other civilians and soldiers or participated in war crimes. Many suffered not only from post-traumatic stress disorder but also from moral injury that included a profound shattering of their value system. These soldiers who had to live with severe ambiguities were seeking a place where they could gather and leave their social isolation behind – at least for a moment.

In 1981, in the midst of these controversies, a design competition for an official national war memorial took place. Maya Ying Lin's proposal was chosen out of a pool of 1,421 submissions. She designed a black stonework with the names of 57,661 soldiers who died in Vietnam. Their names were etched in the surface of the masonry. Over time, more than three hundred additional names were supplemented. The stonework consisted of a dark grey granite wall shaped in a V, with one side pointing to the

Lincoln Memorial and the other to the Washington Memorial, placing it amidst the historic narrative of the founding fathers of the United States of America.

Lin's intent was to symbolically create a wound-like opening in the earth as a gesture towards the enormous loss of soldiers. From a bird's-eye perspective, the design looks like a huge scar cut in a zig-zag shape into the earth. This design was an inspiration for further memorials and museums to come. The wall of names situated in the Memorial Parque in Buenos Aires, Argentina, has a similar V-shape. Also, the Jewish Museum in Berlin has as its main structure a smashed Star of David whose V-shaped ends are cut loose, perforating the surrounding Topography of Terror.

As visitors enter the *Vietnam Veterans Memorial*, they walk a pathway that goes slightly down into the 'wound'. The material Lin used for the wall of names has a reflective quality. Those who are reading or searching for the names can recognise the reflection of their own face in it. This way they also become a visible part of the commemorative scene. In some spots the sky with its moving clouds is also reflected.

This memorial grapples with the tragedy of young lives lost, but it does not turn them into heroes or sacrifices for the nation. Lin deliberately wanted to move away from the sculptural tradition of war monuments depicting military generals on rushing horses surrounded by a group of unified and determined soldiers. No figurative allegories should appear in the form of angel-like figures that would symbolise peace or justice.[13] Lin's memorial explicitly breaks away from this European and North American tradition of heroic war monuments. It rather displays a stunning simplicity that gestures towards deep sorrow, grief and tragedy since it distances itself from any victorious symbols.

The memorial has since become a location where family members, friends and veterans go in order to commemorate the US-American soldiers who died in Vietnam. One can see visitors searching for names, touching names on the wall, laying down personal items or flowers. In the midst of the vast number of names carved into the wall, moments of intimacy are created. People stand in silence, sometimes they cry.

Since its inception there have been lots of controversies around this memorial. Its abstraction was disapproved of. Critics complained that it does not honour the surviving soldiers by not conveying that the death of these young men was a worthwhile sacrifice given to the nation and for the glory of America. Some opponents expressed the opinion that Lin's proposal resembled mainly disgust towards the Vietnam war.

These accusations were taken up by reinserting the traditional war monument aesthetics into the scene – a move Maya Lin certainly was not fond of. A 50-foot-high

13 See the Khan academy video on Maya Lin's concept: https://www.youtube.com/watch?v=wuxjTxxQUTs (accessed on November 4th, 2018).

flagpole with the American flag accompanied by an 8-foot-high statue entitled *The Three Soldiers* were added to the Vietnam Veterans Memorial landscape to soothe fierce critics. The statue depicts three warriors in uniform, a White Anglo-American soldier standing slightly in the leading position, accompanied by an African-American and a Latino soldier. The sculptor Frederick Hart intended to depict a sense of togetherness of comrades as well as individual strength and determination.

These additions need to be understood as the result of the political as well as the aesthetic conflicts that Maya Lin's memorial provoked. They stand in contrast to and certainly damaged the consistency of her design. *The Three Soldiers* put next to Maya Lin's memorial reflect the contestations of the time period. The tensions produced aesthetic inconsistencies and new ambiguities. They reflect a very ambiguous past of atrocious warfare and its challenges for the present in a country that is divided, up to this very day, around the question of how to commemorate the devastation brought forth by the Vietnam War.

Negotiating dilemmas: The erasure of singularity and the captivity of spirits

Many artworks and memorials need to negotiate unresolvable dilemmas. One example hereof is the problem of how to respond to the horrifying fact that the remains of the dead are unidentifiable, or that the bodies of victims cannot be found. In various contexts, the logics of annihilation and genocidal erasure have created deep psychological and spiritual damage for family members, friends and survivors since they amplify issues of unresolved grief that often remain unaddressed.

The absence of bodies is deeply complicated in many cultures and religious traditions. Without a body the human need to find some form of consolation by accompanying the deceased on a journey from the land of the living into the realm of the dead becomes impossible. Consequently, a problem arises if those who have to continue living are denied this journey which ritually and symbolically is supposed to help them to return to their own lives in a transformed way. The deceased as well as the mourners dwell in an in-between place in which they are stuck since performing the necessary rites is not an attainable option.

In the aftermath of massive collective violence, relatives oftentimes claim that the remains of their loved ones ought to be found and that that they should be buried properly. These claims are understood as a crucial form of symbolic reparation. These claims point to the significance of a basic human need.

This urgent desire to find a place of rest for the deceased has a religious or spiritual dimension as well. Burial rites in Judaism, Christianity, Islam and Buddhism normally necessitate individual remains, either in the form of corpses or ashes, in order for the symbolic soul release, hope for resurrection or peaceful rest for the dead to be acted out properly in the respective burial rites.

A striking example of how the absence of identifiable bodily remains can be highly problematic can be found in Cambodia at the memorial in Choeng Ek, which is in close proximity to one of the infamous killing fields of the Khmer Rouge regime. At Choeng Ek 9,000 bodies were mercilessly thrown into mass graves.

Performing studies scholar Brigitte Sion, who researched this site thoroughly, writes:

> Between 1975 and 1979, the Khmer Rouge regime, under the leadership of Pol Pot, caused the death of about 1.5 million people, or a quarter of the population. Thirty years later, memorialization of the genocide stands at the center of conflicted interests – the government's politics of reconciliation, Buddhist beliefs in Karma, economic development, mass tourism opportunities, international law, and national historical narratives.
>
> Located ten miles southeast of Phnom-Penh, Choeung Ek is described, on the official flyer, as "hell on earth in the 20th century". A former orchard and Chinese cemetery, it was the main killing field where prisoners from Tuol Sleng prison were transported to be murdered between 1977 and 1978. When Vietnamese troops discovered the site, they found about 9,000 bodies in mass graves; many were headless, their hands tied and naked; the separated heads were blindfolded. The skulls and bones showed traces of bullets, knives, and other forms of violence inflicted upon men, women, and children. Babies were thrown against trees and instantly killed.[14]

At the memorial site, a monumental stupa was erected as a centrepiece: a translucent tower that preserves about 8,000 skulls and further remaining bones. These are displayed for the visitors who are almost exclusively tourists. In Khmer Buddhist belief a stupa is a sacred object that contains the remains of revered individuals. Remembering the dead as respected persons who have a name and are thus identifiable serves to increase the merit of those who remember.

Sion points to the fact that the erected stupa is a rather frightening object for the local population. It opposes the conviction that human beings who died a violent death have to be cremated or buried as quickly as possible, otherwise the spirits of these victims will haunt the surviving community. A speedy cremation also helps the spirit of the deceased move successfully into the next karmic realm. This stupa, however, is a desacralised and senseless object for the locals, since a stupa is not meant to keep unidentifiable remains of ordinary people.[15]

---

14 Brigitte Sion, Missing Bodies, Conflicted Rituals: Performing Memory in Germany, Argentina, and Cambodia, Leipzig: Evangelische Verlagsanstalt 2011, 71f.

15 Sion, Missing Bodies 76f.

This particular commemorative praxis seems to be inadequate if not even harmful for the local population. It points to the larger spiritual issue for Khmer Buddhists who feel they have to live with restless spirits since the mass killings of the Khmer Rouge dictatorship left millions of bodily remains that have to this day not been identified.

13. Intergenerational genocide legacies and peacebuilding from below: The case of Rwanda in comparative perspective[1]

Annemiek Richters

> *They (children) experience the consequences, it is incorporated somewhere, it sticks in their mind and heart, it will remain across generations. Constance – genocide survivor with experiences of genocidal rape.*
>
> *My child born during the genocide has more symptoms than I have. Berthilde – genocide survivor with experiences of genocidal rape.*
>
> *I can suddenly have fear, but I do not know where it comes from. Eric – child of genocide survivor parents.*
>
> *Some children today are poisoned by their parents. Look at me. I used to show my daughter the only photo I have of my children who were killed, telling her 'these are your sisters and brothers who were killed by Hutu people'. Don't you see that I behaved bad? Charles – genocide survivor who lost almost all family members during the genocide.*
>
> *They (survivors) are suffering the loss of their relatives, but also, we are suffering the loss of our human dignity. We all need to heal and reconcile. ... The effects of the genocide will extend to the next generations. Imagine how heavy it is for a young person to be called a son or a daughter of interahamwe (the militia who killed during the genocide). One of them said to me: 'sin to them, shame to us'. Henri – génocidaire who took part in the killing of Charles' relatives.*
>
> *I hated both my family and everyone else. Jean – descendant of a family of genocide perpetrators, confronted with memories community members have of the genocide crimes committed by his father and uncle.*

1 This is a working paper. Please do not quote.

Introduction

The above quotes[2] are extracted from interviews and focus group discussions conducted in Rwanda in the context of community-based sociotherapy. Sociotherapy was introduced in Rwanda in 2005 as a psychosocial programme facilitating Rwandans to take charge of their lives again in the aftermath of a period of war and genocide that had inflicted deep psychological and social wounds on them. Over the years, community-based sociotherapy developed into a programme that more explicitly than in its start-up phase integrates an element of peacebuilding in its psychosocial support approach.[3,4,5] This development was set in motion by what sociotherapy group participants shared with each other and with sociotherapy staff, including researchers, about their daily life problems. As the stories like the ones from which I quoted rose in number and intensity, the urgency increased to respond to what we in sociotherapy started to name 'intergenerational legacies' covered by these stories through psychosocial peacebuilding facilitation. In this paper I will not address the details of the way the sociotherapy programme in actual practice did respond.[6] I will mainly explore from a theoretical perspective some elements of the transmission of traumatic memories as well as some other genocide legacies from the first generation (the generation that consciously lived through the genocide) to the second generation (the generation that did not live consciously through the genocide or was born after), linking these elements to what we hear and observe in the field. While doing so, I will bring in a comparative element; comparing responses of descendants of survivors and perpetrators of mass violence committed in different parts of the world in different periods of time to the legacies of the respective mass violences.

The term second generation was introduced in Holocaust literature with reference solely to the children (descendants) of survivors of the Second World War. Over time, the meaning of the term was broadened to also include children of perpetrators. Various authors identified similarly damaging effects of belonging to the second generation among both groups of descendants, descendants of survivors and of

2 All names of respondents used are pseudonyms.
3 See e.g. Richters, A., Rutayisire, T., Sewimfura, T. & Ngendahayo, E. (2010) Psychotrauma, healing and reconciliation in Rwanda. *African Journal of Traumatic Stress* 1(2):55-63.
4 See e.g. Ingabire, M.C., Kagoyire, M.G., Karangwa, D., Ingabire, I., Habarugira, N., Jansen, A. & Richters, A. (2017) Trauma informed restorative justice through community based sociotherapy in Rwanda. Intervention: *Journal of Mental Health and Psychosocial Support in Conflict Affected Areas* 15(3):241-253.
5 See e.g. Sarabwe, E., Richters, A. & Vysma, M. (2018) Marital conflict in the aftermath of genocide in Rwanda: An explorative study within the context of community based sociotherapy. *Intervention: Journal of Mental Health and Psychosocial Support in Conflict Affected Areas* 16(1):14-21.
6 This response so far has been mainly described in a policy brief and leaflets. See, however, for a brief note Richters (2015).

perpetrators, while also finding radical differences.[7,8] As McGlothlin observed, while 'the legacy transmitted to the children [is] quite different for the two groups, the general positions of the children to their parents' pasts are quite similar: both groups feel marked by the Holocaust, an event that is ever present in their lives but not personally experienced, and both struggle to understand their own place in the world in light of their link to the traumatic past.'[9,10] In our exploratory sociotherapy research we also find differences as well as similarities between both groups of descendants in Rwanda. Because of the specific cultural and socio-political context of post-genocide Rwanda, however, the genocidal marking of the second generation of Rwandans is not in every detail similar to this marking of second-generation Holocaust survivors and perpetrators or for that matter the marking of the second generation in other post-conflict settings.[11,12] In that respect, 'the Holocaust can no longer serve simply as a conceptual limit case.'[13,14]

My focus in this paper will be mostly on parent-child transmission of the legacies of genocide, in particular the genocide against the Tutsi in Rwanda, to the neglect of a detailed exposé of the transmission of genocide legacies through a child's socio-ecological environment as included in the focus of the study presented in Berckmoes et al.[15] and Eichelsheim et al.[16] My exploration is work in progress. It is only in its early stages but has already proven to be helpful to me as well as sociotherapy staff in explaining what we hear and observe in the field. It also justifies the choices we have made in paying more attention to a range of intergenerational legacies in including more young people as participants in sociotherapy groups. Repairing society's wounds occurs in dialogue with the past, and youth are or should be at the centre of this dialogue. The book 'Troublemakers or peacemakers? Youth and post accord

---

7 cf. e.g., Berger, A.I. & Berger, N. eds. (2001) Second generational voices: Reflections by children of Holocaust survivors & perpetrators. Syracuse University Press.

8 McGlothlin, E. (ed.) (2006) Second-generation Holocaust literature: Legacies of survival and perpetration. Rochester, NY: Camden House.

9 Ibid. p. 14.

10 Rosenthal, G. (2002) Veiling and denying the past. The History of the Family 7(2):225-238.

11 See e.g., Argenti & Schramm 2010; Gobodo-Madikizela 2016; Grand & Salberg 2017

12 The empirical study of these details in post-genocide Rwanda is still in its infancy (see e.g., Kagoyire & Richters 2018; Kagoyire et al. 2018). I expect that in its advanced stage this study will certainly enrich the global body of empirical as well as theoretical literature on the topic of the imprints of genocide legacies on the body, mind, heart and soul of second and third generation Rwandans.

13 Hirsch, M. (2012) The generation of postmemory: Writing and visual culture after the Holocaust. Columbia University Press, p. 18.

14 See for research that underlines this point, the research by the anthropologist Carol Kidron (e.g., Kidron 2012).

15 Berckmoes, L., Eichelsheim, V., Rutayisire, T., Richters, A. & Hola, B. (2017) How legacies of genocide are transmitted in the family environment: A qualitative study of two generations in Rwanda, *Societies* 7, 24. Open access.

16 Eichelsheim, V., Berckmoes, L., Hola, B., Rutayisire, T. & Richters, A. (2018) Before my time? Addressing the intergenerational legacies of the genocide against the Tutsi in Rwanda. Intervention: *Journal of Mental Health and Psychosocial Support in Conflict Affected Areas 00:1-9.*

peacebuilding'[17] illustrates well that the way history is passed on to them matters, for it may aggravate current divisions and sow the seeds of future conflict or promote healing and reconciliation. Hence, youth are not just carriers of past trauma, but also agents of future conflict or builders of sustainable peace.[18] All this is what this paper aims to address.

In this one paper I cannot do justice to all complexities of the themes I have chosen to address in this paper. I also find it difficult to present all in a detailed and well-balanced way. For instance, the theoretical concepts I present need more unpacking, and more empirical data would give more evidence of what is proposed in theories to be the case. The paper is therefore no more than a working document with many loose ends. The idea is to make better connections between the subthemes addressed together with sociotherapy staff as we go along in our work, continuously trying to link theory and practice, generate new empirical data, and contribute to the literature through our writings.

Traumatic memories[19]

Trauma can be understood as a memory affliction dominated by ghosts from the past.[20] Traumatic memories are a form of implicit memories. Implicit memories are relatively unconscious memories; 'hot' and powerfully compelling. They arise as a collage of sensations, emotions and behaviours. They are to be distinguished from so-called ordinary, explicit memories, which are conscious memories (see figure 1). Explicit memories can be differentiated in declarative memories ('cold' factual information) and episodic ('warm' textured). One form of episodic memory is autobiographic memory.

An event becomes a trauma when overwhelming stress, threat or injury interferes with proper memory processing and the tremendous energy generated by our survival responses remain fixed in the body.

Traumatic memories consist of recurring sensations and movements (bodily memories) that are accompanied by intense negative emotions such as fear, shame, rage and collapse (emotional memories). They are the result of a breakdown of the brain systems that are responsible for creating 'autobiographical memories'. The brain and body, however, have an amazing capacity to regenerate and implicit memories

17 McEvoy-Levy, S. (2006) *Troublemakers or peacemakers? Youth and post accord peacebuilding*. Notre Dame: University of Notre Dame Press.
18 cf. Münyas 2008; Nou 2013.
19 This paragraph draws heavily from Van der Kolk (2014) and Levine (2015).
20 Prager, J. (2016) Disrupting the intergenerational transmission of trauma: Recovering humanity, repairing generations. In P. Gobodo-Madikizela (ed.) *Breaking intergenerational cycles of repetition: A global dialogue on historical trauma and memory*, pp. 12-26. Opladen: Barbara Budrich Publishers, p. 17.

Figure 1

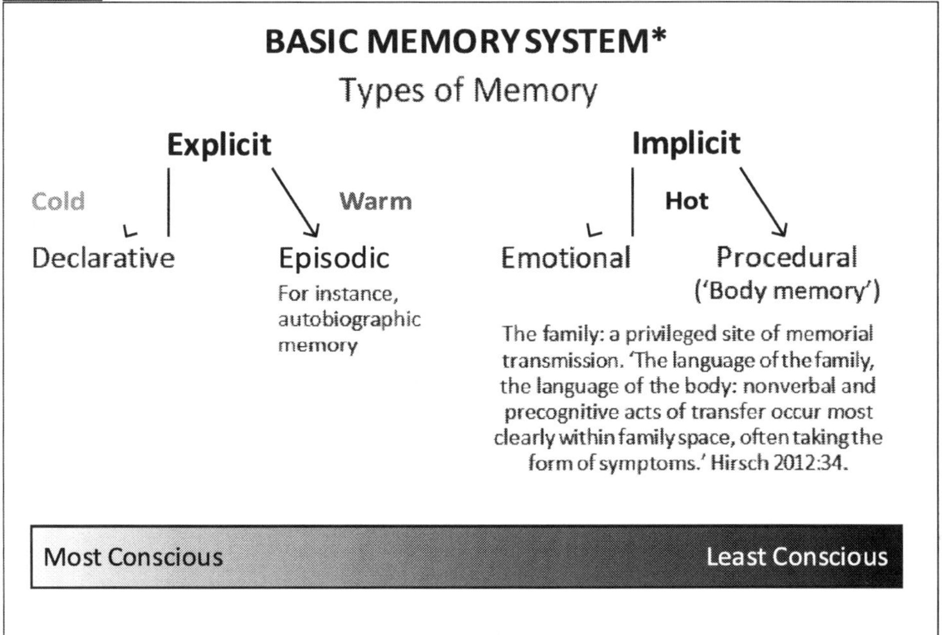

* P.A. Levine (2015) Trauma and memory: brain and body in search for a living past.

Figure 2

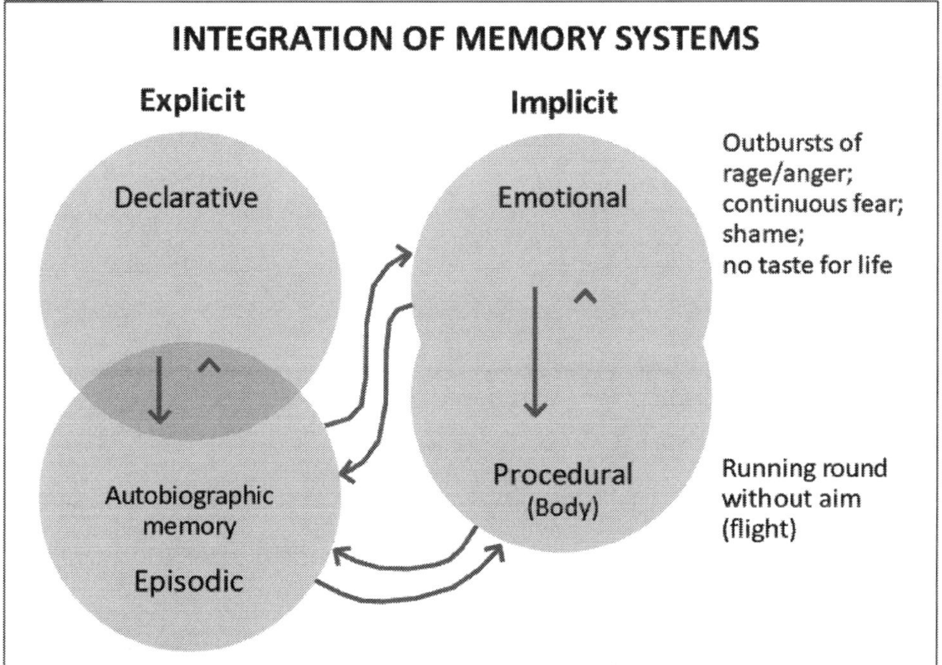

Adapted from P.A. Levine (2015) Trauma and memory: brain and body in search for a living past.

can be transformed into autobiographical memories (see figure 2), to be shared with other people.

Traumatised people though are stuck in the past. Many never get a chance to develop a narrative that allows them and those around them to know what happened. The safe relational space created in a sociotherapy group and the trust gradually built between participants gives people this chance. In this space, traumatic memories may be transformed into autobiographical memories, which, in addition to other new experiences, helps people to again take charge of their lives, restore social relationships and look into the future, which Brewer (2016) calls remembering forwards. However, as Levine[21] and van der Kolk[22] argue, to begin to integrate the implicit experience into a conscious narrative, the frozen energy in the body that is at the core of people's trauma needs to be released. I am not sure if and how this is accomplished in sociotherapy. Most probably at least the games and dancing as part of the repertoire of sociotherapy play a role in this release.[23]

Intergenerational transmission of trauma

Clinical investigations of children of Holocaust survivors have shown a reduced psychological wellbeing and more psychopathology in their later life, in particular feelings of depression and problems with the regulation of aggression.[24] However, the possible traumatisation of these children, as is assumed in the concept of intergenerational traumatisation,[25] is not undisputed. Van IJzendoorn et al. established in a meta-analysis that 'no evidence of the influence of parents' traumatic Holocaust experiences on their children could be found in a set of adequately

21 Levine P. Trauma and Memory: Brain and Body in a Search for the Living Past: A Practical Guide for Understanding and Working With Traumatic Memory. Berkeley, CA: North Atlantic Books; 2015.

22 Van der Kolk, B.A. 2014. The body keeps score: Brain, mind and body in the healing of trauma. New York: Viking Penguin.

23 What is important to take notice of is that sociotherapy is not meant to be a trauma therapy. Sociotherapy recruits all kinds of people with all sorts of daily life problems. Among its participants one does find severely traumatised people. It is our experience that at least part, if not most, of their symptoms disappear due to sociotherapy. For those who remain troubled by trauma symptoms, one would wish them to have access to more specialised care, including bodily therapy. Sociotherapy has a referral system to specialised care in place.

24 cf. Kleber 2014.

25 Kleber (2014) uses here the concept of transgenerational traumatisation. I have replaced his transgenerational by intergenerational. Both terms are often used as interchangeable for the transmission/transfer of trauma within families. Following Hirsch (2008, 2012), I distinguish between the two. Familial transfer of embodied and affective experience to the next generation is intergenerational, while 'political' and 'cultural' memory is transgenerational; in the latter case the transfer from one generation to the next is not mediated by embodied practice but solely through symbolic systems. However, distinctions and specificities between the two are difficult to maintain. 'Even the most intimate familial transmission of the past is, it seems, mediated by public images and narratives' (Hirsch 2012:30), while both 'embodied communicative memory and institutionalised cultural/archival memory would be severely impaired by traumatic experience' (Hirsch 2008:111).

designed nonclinical studies.'[26] Kleber concludes from this latter study and his own studies that the concept of intergenerational traumatisation is rather inappropriate.[27] Previously, a shift in terminology in clinical studies had already taken place from 'transmission of trauma' or 'secondary traumatization' to 'intergenerational effects of trauma' and 'intergenerational aspects of trauma.'[28,29] The idea behind this shift is that trauma is not transmitted from parents to children but that due to their traumatic experiences parents' child rearing capacities are compromised. Traumatisation can cause limitations in parenthood and these limitations can disrupt the development of children. Growing up in an unsafe and unpredictable environment where chronic basic emotions of fear, sadness and anger surround and pervade the child results in disorganised and disturbed parent-child attachment relationships.[30] Children growing up in such environment start to struggle with their own identity with respect to the genocide experiences of their parents. How do I relate to my parents? How to I develop my own individuality? Where do I belong? What is my attitude towards violence and peace? How do I solve being different from the rest of society? These and similar questions we find descendants of genocide survivors as well as genocide perpetrators struggle with.[31] Nonetheless, we also find an amazing resilience among parents affected in one way or another by genocide legacies and among their children. The resilience among the children may have been transmitted from their parents or it may have developed in reaction to the situation their parents are in.

What I like to take issue with is the explanation of mental health and psychosocial problems of the second generation in terms of mainly or solely attachment problems due to parental trauma. We as sociotherapy staff also find phenomena described by our respondents that do point to direct transmission of trauma. This is illustrated, it seems to me, in the quotes above of Berthilde and Eric. And what to think of the statement of another female genocide survivor who experienced genocide rape: 'My child who was two months old during the genocide has all symptoms genocide

26 See van IJzendoorn, M.H., Bakermans-Kranenburg M.J., Sagi-Schwartz A.J. 2003, p. 49.

27 Kleber, R.J. (2014) Transfer of psychotrauma to the next generation? Inside insights from scientific literature and empirical research, in E. Captain & T. Mooren (eds.) Family, generations and war: Historical, psychological and artistic views, pp. 118-141. Amsterdam: Nationaal Comité 4 en 5 mei.

28 Kellermann, N.P.F. (2001) Transmission of Holocaust trauma: An integrative view. Psychiatry 64(3), p. 257.

29 Kidron, C.A. (2009) Toward an ethnography of silence: The lived presence of the past in the everyday life of Holocaust trauma survivors and their descendants in Israel. Current Anthropology 50(1):5-27. Includes comments by other scholars and reply by author, p. 7.

30 Kleber, R.J. (2014) Transfer of psychotrauma to the next generation? Inside insights from scientific literature and empirical research, in E. Captain & T. Mooren (eds.) Family, generations and war: Historical, psychological and artistic views, pp. 118-141. Amsterdam: Nationaal Comité 4 en 5 mei.

31 Sociotherapy is not a clinical intervention, which raises the question whether or not the group of young people we reach through our research should be considered as a clinical sample. Most of these young people are recruited through either sociotherapists or their parents who graduated from sociotherapy. The latter implies that many of their parents are mentally and/or psychosocially affected by genocidal legacies.

survivors have.' And, why is it that over the years more and more young people, lately even more than adults, have a so-called 'trauma crisis' during the annual genocide commemoration week in Rwanda? I found the approach taken by scholars like Kellermann[32,33] and Wolynn,[34] in addition to that of others who elaborated similar approaches, helpful in this respect.

Despite the controversies regarding the concept of trauma transmission, Kellermann retains the concept as useful and adequate.[35] For him, it includes the 'direct and specific' transmission of a mental health syndrome from parent to child as well as a more 'indirect and general' transmission.[36] In the latter case, it is the inability to function as a parent that indirectly lead to 'a general sense deprivation in the child.'[37] To limit ambiguity in transmission terminology, Kellerman differentiates between the process of transmission (how the trauma was carried over from one generation to the next) and the content of transmission (what was in fact transmitted).[38] Below I will follow Kellerman in this respect.

It is not easy, however, to differentiate throughout in what follows in the how and what of intergenerational transmission of trauma between genocide survivor parents and their children and between genocide perpetrators and their children. Research by Heide Rieder and colleagues in Rwanda shows that, despite differences, post-traumatic stress disorder and other mental health problems as well as poor psychosocial conditions are high among genocide survivors as well as perpetrators, impacting on the wellbeing of the next generation. Descendants of genocide survivors though presented with more symptoms than descendants of former prisoners regarding all assessed mental disorders.[39]

One of the differences between the two groups of parents is the nature of traumatic stressors and, between descendants of both groups, the problems they have with their identity. While, for instance, the children of survivors may struggle with over-identification with parents' 'victim/survivor' status, children of perpetrators may struggle with their often self- and community-imposed identity as child of a killer,

32 Kellermann, N.P.F. (2001) Transmission of Holocaust trauma: An integrative view. Psychiatry 64(3):256-267.
33 Kellermann, N.P.F. (2013) Epigenetic transmission of Holocaust trauma: Can nightmares be inherited? The Israel Journal of Psychiatry and Related Sciences 50(1):33-39.
34 Wolynn, M. (2016) It didn't start with you: How inherited family trauma shapes how we are and how to end the cycle. Penguin Books.
35 See Kellermann 2001.
36 Kellermann's use of the concept of indirect transmission is different from the way Berckmoes et al. (2017) and Eichelsheim et al. (2018) use it, which may be a bit confusing.
37 Kellermann, N.P.F. (2001) Transmission of Holocaust trauma: An integrative view. Psychiatry 64(3), p. 257.
38 Ibid.
39 Rieder, H. (2014) Legacies of the 1994 Rwandan genocide: Organised violence, family violence, mental health and post-conflict related attitudes examined among families of genocide survivors and former prisoners. PhD Dissertation Universität Konstanz.

and they may want to disconnect from that parent in an emotional, personal sense. Both groups, in different ways, struggle with a sense of belonging. As Schwab writes with reference to descendants of Holocaust perpetrators, '... a history of perpetration can instill identity trouble in children of perpetrators, including a pervasive self-hatred and concomitant sense of not wanting to belong.'[40] This seems to be the case with Jean, quoted above, when he said, I hated both my family and everyone else. What both groups of descendants may have in common though is the experience of a disconnection from their parents in terms of intelligibility;[41] in the case of descendants of survivors in terms of the violence that was exerted on one or both of their parents and in case of descendants of perpetrators in terms of the atrocities committed by one or both of their parents.

Models of transmission

Kellerman[42] distinguishes between psychoanalytic and relational, sociocultural and socialisation, family systems and communication, and biological or genetic models of intergenerational trauma transmission, while Wolynn points to recent developments in the field of cellular biology, neuroscience, epigenetics and developmental psychology regarding trauma transmission.[43] What we see in the field as a result of trauma transmission among the second generation in the context of sociotherapy is most likely best explained by an addition of elements of these different theories available for explanation. Let me focus briefly on only epigenetics.

Epigenetic marking of children of parents who are traumatised refers to a chemical coating upon their chromosomes transmitted from their parents. This marking would represent a kind of biological (implicit) memory of what the parents experienced. Perroud et al.[44] and Rudahindwa et al.[45] conducted a study in Rwanda among a sample of 25 genocide survivor widows who were pregnant (second and third terms of pregnancy) during the genocide period, and their 25 offspring born from those pregnancies who were diagnosed with Post-Traumatic Stress Disorder (PTSD) symptoms similar to those of their mothers. It was concluded that from not only a clinical point of view but also from a biological one the intergenerational impact of trauma is a reality and that epigenetic modifications in stress-related genes found

40 Schwab, G. (2010) *Haunting legacies: Violent histories and transgenerational trauma.* New York: Columbia University Press, p. 36.

41 cf. Parens 2009, Schwab 2004, Van Alphen 2006

42 See Kellermann 2001/2013

43 See Wolynn 2016.

44 Perroud, N., Rutembesa, E., Paoloni-Giacobino, A. et al. (2014) The Tutsi genocide and transgenerational transmission of maternal stress: Epigenetics and biology of the HPA axis. *The World Journal of Biological Psychiatry* 15(4):334-345.

45 Rudahindwa, S., Mutesa, L. Rutembesa, E. et al. (2018) 'Transgenerational effects of the genocide against the Tutsi in Rwanda: A post-traumatic stress disorder symptom domain analysis', *African Academy of Sciences Open Research* 1:10.

in their study among mothers and their children may have played a key role in the transmission of PTSD from these mothers to their children. The authors, however, do not exclude the role of impaired parenting in this transmission and promote further research for the sake of prevention of the development of PTSD in subjects exposed to traumatic events and thus of the transmission of trauma to their offspring.

Content of transmission

What is transmitted is a long list, too long to reproduce here. According to Kellerman problems usually centre on the following areas: 1. Self (for instance, impaired self-esteem with persistent identity problems), 2. Cognition (for instance, catastrophic expectancy, pre-occupation with death) 3.[46] Affectivity (for instance, nightmares, frequent dysphoric moods, inability to feel happy), and 4. Interpersonal functioning (exaggerated family attachments and dependency or exaggerated independence, difficulties in intimate relationships, aggression towards others). These contents have been primarily described in clinical studies among descendants of survivors of the Holocaust. We identify them also in our research in Rwanda, among descendants of survivors and well as perpetrators. So far, however, we have not conducted any rigorous study of them but only some qualitative studies with small samples of respondents. The question for me is whether these problems among descendants of perpetrators identified by us are the result of parental transmission or the result of at a certain age being confronted with parental crimes. Some of the following quotes may illustrate the latter.

> It was as if the soil under my feet was taken away, I left the library, I stretched out on a bench. The five years that followed were going to be years of severe depression.
>
> Granddaughter of a famous German mass murderer, who only by chance discovered in adult life who her grandfather was.[47]
>
> To discover that you are the son of a murderer is worse than having been a murderer yourself. The murderer has his justifications, he can hide behind language, he can deny, he can brag, he can take responsibility for his crime and proudly face the gallows, he can claim he was only following orders, he can run away, change his identity, find new justifications, can mend his ways, he can do anything. What can the son do but enumerate his father's crimes and drag the millstone with him all through life?
>
> Son of a Nazi criminal. (quoted from Sansal 2011).

46 See Kellermann 2001.
47 Quoted from Teege, J. (2015) *My grandfather would have shot me: A black woman discovers her family's Nazi past*. London: Hodder & Stoughton.

> The fact that he took part in the genocide is so difficult for me to imagine. I try to think of the reasons he did it, but I cannot find any. Today when I think about it, it is beyond my understanding! I cry when I think of how genocide was a time of pain and sadness!
>
> Daughter of a convicted génocidaire in Rwanda. This quote, it seems to me, can be considered as an example of disconnection from her father in terms of intelligibility.
>
> After learning what my parents went through, I felt like I hated them. They did not love me. If they did, they would not have been involved in genocide and leave a legacy of poverty to me/us. The fact that they [parents] were involved in genocide has put me in a position that affects my life, my relations, and even my future. I live in poverty. Thinking all the time what my life will be, I can spend a whole night without sleeping. I don't feel comfortable with peers. I feel like I want to be alone.
>
> Young Rwandan woman whose both parents were convicted of genocide crimes.

A difference between the majority of descendants of perpetrators of the genocide in Rwanda and those of the Holocaust is that the latter mostly later in life come to know about the deeds of their father or grandfather, while descendants in Rwanda know mostly at a relatively early age about their fathers' or mothers' crimes through neighbours or the community justice courts that took place in their neighbourhood where their fathers or mothers were judged.[48] While descendants of Holocaust perpetrators usually do not live in an environment where they are in daily contact with descendants of Holocaust survivors, this is different in Rwanda. There, one finds descendants of both groups living in the same neighbourhood and attending the same school. That is why peacebuilding from below needs attention. As Eramian[49] with reference to Doughty[50] writes, 'the sources of post-genocide hardship are often not the *absence* of relationships, but rather all the ways in which victims, perpetrators, and bystanders are *already* enmeshed in relationships.'[51] Based on the empirical evidence we have, the same is the case for descendants of these three categories of people. This implies, as Eramian argues, that reconciliation in practice is about re-establishing relations in which people are already entangled, and not always by choice.[52]

48 We occasionally found among children of perpetrators a disbelief of what their fathers were accused of, but overall, there was less chance for these children in Rwanda to deny the evil in their father's past than for children of Nazi criminals (cf. Lebert & Lebert 2000).

49 Eramian L. (2018) Peaceful selves: Personhood, nationhood, and the post-conflict moment in Rwanda. New York: Berghahn.

50 Doughty, K. (2015) 'Law and the architecture of social repair: Gaçaça days in post-genocide Rwanda', *Journal of the Royal Anthropological Institute* 21(2):419-437.

51 See Eramian 2018, p. 15, italic in original.

52 Ibid.

Emotional inheritance of trauma across multiple generations

Depression, anxiety, chronic pain, phobias, obsessive thought, the roots of these issues may reside in the traumas of our parents, grandparents, and even great-grandparents.[53] The unfinished business in terms of processing traumatic memories and silencing them to cover up traumatic events or history only leads to its being unconsciously handed down from one generation to the next; the haunting by the traumatic memories in question spans generations.[54,55] In this respect certain authors refer to the bible, where it is stated (Numbers 14:18) that the sins of the parents can affect the children up to the third or fourth generations, and conclude, as Wolynn does, that the claims of modern science corroborate this statement or vice versa.[56] Similarly, trauma can also affect children up to the third or fourth generation.[57] It can travel through the generations for a period of at least a hundred years. The latter is illustrated vividly in the documentary *Trois Journées d'Août* (Three Days in August).

100 Years of intergenerational trauma transmission – An example and lessons learned

This documentary was made 100 years after a mass execution by German soldiers of civilians of a Belgian village in 1914, at the start of the First World War. In the documentary a small sample of descendants – children, grandchildren and greatgrandchildren of those who were killed during the massacre or survived it – testify about their being haunted by the family ghosts of the past. Alain, the son of a father who as a 15-year-old child survived the massacre, under a pile of dead bodies, as the only one of his extended family and neighbours narrates passionately about the trauma his father transmitted to him, his sisters and nieces.[58] The quotes below summarise well, it seems to me, what the impact of the haunting can be on the quality of life of 'the generations after'.

> I missed a lot with my father. ... On top of that, my father wasn't a great communicator and didn't tell us about our roots. We know nothing about his childhood, our grandparents, how they lived. ... The only thing we know for sure are the scars, the pain that was passed to the next generation. We do have that. Fear, guilt, insomnia. And bizarrely, we can't overcome our phobias. My fear stops me from overcoming my phobias.

53 See Wolynn 2016.
54 Abraham, N. & Torok, M. (1994) The shell and the kernel. Chicago: University of Chicago Press. Edited, translated, and with an Introduction by N.T. Rand, p. 167.
55 Schwab, G. (2010) Haunting legacies: Violent histories and transgenerational trauma. New York: Columbia University Press, p. 79.
56 See Wolynn 2016, p. 39.
57 cf. e.g., Jilovsky et. al 2016.
58 Ramaut (2014), transgenerational psychoanalyst, analyses the 'ghost' that haunts the descendants who testify in the documentary, including Alain, mainly from a psychoanalytic perspective but also highlights epigenetics as most likely playing a role in the transmission.

> I am convinced that he never stopped feeling guilty. Those images never left him. His insomnia, which I inherited, was the result of the fact that he kept reliving everything. Constantly. ... He never complained. ... He was never interested in revenge.
>
> My claustrophobia, my fear of fire ... When I wake up at night, I feel like a tectonic plate has crashed. As if the concrete I put there is breaking. And sparks fly, memories that aren't necessarily mine. [Reviewer: 'Do you think it's the terror that your father passed on to you?'] It is terror. That's the word. I was afraid to call it that. That word 'terror' expresses everything. ... The town was overcome with terror ... That's handed down from generation to generation. Unfortunately, we couldn't prevent my nieces, my sister's daughters, from struggling with the same problems, this anxiety.

When growing older, Alain has started to understand where the fear he suffers from comes from. Eric, quoted above, is probably too young yet to understand.

After a long struggle with himself, Alain developed a conciliatory attitude towards the Germans. As he narrated, *to close the chapter*. This is different for his sister Danièle. Like Alain she stressed that their father raised his children to be tolerant; no revenge, openness. She narrates, *my father always said: 'You can't live with hatred'. ... I can't forgive and forget yet. It's impossible. I can't forgive the people who did this. No. But I can't hate innocent Germans.*

After watching this documentary together, the staff of sociotherapy were shaken. What, they wondered, will become of Rwandan society when even the fourth generation (at the end of the documentary a fourth-generation young woman testifies) remains affected by the pain and horror. Fortunately, in Rwanda, perhaps more than in any other post-conflict society, many programmes are in place to break the intergenerational cycles of pain, horror and attitudes of revenge. As Alain cynically said: *Now, even after a minor bus accident there's a small army of psychologists to offer support to those who didn't get injured. In his case* (Alain's father, Dr. Felix Bourbon), *they just said he was lucky. He went on to become a good doctor.* We have met many parents who, like Dr. Bourbon, do everything possible to transmit a conciliatory attitude towards their children. But we also heard children speak about their parents as not being conciliatory at all. Charles and Henri (quoted above) admitted indirectly having transmitted different kinds of pain to their children and a non-conciliatory attitude towards 'the others'. Due to participation in sociotherapy they became aware of this. Their relationship with their children took a positive turn and by restoring their relationship they demonstrated to their children that hatred can turn into friendship.

As I referred to above, the traumas one inherits or experiences first-hand 'cannot only create a legacy of distress, but also forge a legacy of strength and resilience that can be felt for generations to come.'[59] We find this resilience illustrated in the life of Dr. Felix Bourbon. However, his resilience was not enough to prevent distress among his descendants. In Rwanda, in contrast, we found that inherited emotional pain among descendants can be accompanied by an amazing strength and resilience. As, for instance, one young man said: 'There is someone who thought of revenging, but I reasoned with him and asked him to fight hatred with love. I ask myself if my parents transmit hatred to me, and if I do the same to my children, what may be the end of that hatred?'

Intergenerational legacies of genocide in Rwanda

As stated before, well designed studies about intergenerational transmission of trauma among large samples of people focusing on the how and what of this transmission and the prevalence of problems resulting from this transmission are not available yet. However, that this transmission can be a problem does not go unnoticed. Based on interviews with experts in the field, Stéphanie Agliette wrote in an article published in *The Sun Daily* (April 12, 2015) entitled *Ghosts of Rwanda genocide haunt new generation*: 'Many young people born after 1994 experience the same symptoms of posttraumatic stress as those who witnessed and survived the brutality. The young Rwandans report feelings of intense anxiety and obsessive visions similar to the horrors that occurred before they were even born.' The quotes used by Agliette to make her point are the following: 'Survivors unknowingly transmit what they experienced to successive generations' (Francoise Murekatete, coordinator of the mental health program of Avega). 'It is a phenomenon that was expected ... all that is not said, is transmitted' (the recently deceased psychiatrist Naasson Munyandamutsa). 'Even children whose families were unscathed by the violence are similarly affected by a "contagion in the collective unconscious"' (psychiatrist Rutakayile Bizoza).[60]

Sociotherapy researchers conducted a few exploratory studies among small samples of parents and young people between 18 and 25 years old focusing in particular on parent-child communication and self-representation among the young adults. It was found that due to the impact of traumatic experiences, parents run the risk of becoming less attentive to or less available for their children, which can subsequently affect developmental outcomes, such as unfavourable effects on children's well-being, educational achievements and social interactions. Young people, encouraged by government programmes, such as 'We are all Rwandans', want to do things differently than the previous generation and feel a collective responsibility for protecting the peace in Rwanda. However, they seemed to experience a contradiction between their collective identity as a new generation to protect the peace and their relational identity, which was aligned with personal emotions of anger, fear, shame

59 See Wolynn 2016, p. 24.
60 http://www.thesundaily.my/news/1381966

and mistrust. While they did refer to physical or emotional absence of parents, they also referred to positive elements transmitted to them, such as resilience and the process of 'unbelievable forgiveness' that some parents, specifically genocide survivors, demonstrated; a process that can be perceived as post-traumatic growth.[61]

In a recent community-based sociotherapy project of grassroots advocacy, community members were asked, through 'the problem tree approach', to identify legacies of genocide in their community. They presented mainly daily life problems such as early pregnancies, school drop-outs, drugs and alcohol abuse, and negative sentiments towards 'others' in the community. Sometimes, one had the impression, these and other problems were too easily attributed to the genocide. What remained underexposed were problems in the area of self, affectivity and cognition as an effect of direct trauma transmission or in case of descendants of perpetrators of their struggle to come to terms with having a parent found guilty of genocide crimes. Looking specifically for cases of direct transmission, one case drew my attention.

A poor genocide widow offered her teenage son, who spent his days idle at home, one of the monthly allowances she receives from the government to meet her daily survival needs, so that he could start up a small business to keep him busy and earn some money. The son refused the offer, saying 'why should I start a business, youngsters of my age died during the genocide'; in other words, why would I make the effort while being at risk of not living much longer. Another case that stayed with me is the one shared by a woman participating in ongoing research among female genocide survivor with the experience of genocide rape. She said, *my daughter* [20-years old] *born in the swamp* [while hiding during the genocide] *does not want to be far away from me; she always sleeps in my bed, she then frequently licks my back.* These to me are examples of direct trauma transmission, which were seldom shared by community members in the grassroots advocacy project. In that project mostly genocide legacies transmitted through the socio-ecological environment,[62] such as absent fathers and the socio-economic situation of the family, were mentioned. In conclusion, there is still a long way to go to understand all the hows and whats of intergenerational trauma transmission in Rwanda.

Peacebuilding from below

The above has shown that there is a common agreement that the transmission of trauma in whatever way may severely affect the mental health and psychosocial wellbeing of the second and following generations. What may also be transmitted or may be a consequence of what has been transmitted are feelings of revenge and a propensity to violence, which are both potential risk factors for another cycle of

61 Grayson, H. (2018) 'Articulating growth in Rwandan terms: Adapting the post-traumatic growth inventory', Studies in Testimony 1:4-30.

62 cf. Berckmoes et al. 2017.

violence. However, the next generation is not necessarily caught in a continuous line of sorrow and evil. Posterity can soften the effect of suffering and mistakes of the previous generation or even lift them. Some succeed out of their own initiative, building on their own strength, while others need some encouragement or help.

Research in the field of the neurodynamics of attachment and caregiving (which is embedded in the growing field of interpersonal neurobiology) shows 1) 'how early exposure to poor care tunes the child's brain for living defensively', and 2) 'that later in life, "enriched" social experiences can retune the brain and support a biobehavioural shift from mistrust to trust, reawakening and strengthening the child's capacity for social engagement.'[63,64] These research findings among others justify programmes that facilitate the gaining of these 'enriched' social experiences. Sociotherapy is one of these programmes that has the potential to make a difference. Adults' participation often results in a lifting of their social isolation and a renewed social engagement with people in their living environment.

Memorising is a reconstructive and relational process. People memorising in interaction with each other in a sociotherapy group proves to be not only a remembering backwards but also remembering forwards, as Brewer calls it.[65] The latter releases them from the hold that oppressive and haunting memories had over them. Brewer (ibid.) suggests 'that it is through remembering forwards with truth, tolerance, togetherness and trajectory that people in post-conflict societies can inherit the future despite their divided pasts and live in tolerance in the midst of contested memories'. Charles and Henri (quoted above) testified that this is indeed possible. It resulted in a reduction of a harmful transmission of feelings and attitudes to their children.

The parents' lifting of their social isolation can be experienced by their children as a great release of the burden they felt of having to be there for their parents all the time. The change in parents' social behaviour usually results in healthier parent-child attachment and parental care. One wonders, however, how much damage has already been done to the child in terms of interpersonal functioning. We notice that even though the parent-child relationship may have improved significantly, children are still happy to interact with peers in a sociotherapy group. Parents also repeatedly ask sociotherapy staff to organise groups for their children.

63 Baylin, J. & Hughes, D.A. (2016) The neurobiology of attachment-focused therapy: Enhancing connection and trust in the treatment of children and adolescents. New York: Norton & Company, p. 1.

64 cf. also Cozolino 2014.

65 Brewer, J.D. (2016) Remembering forwards: Or how to live together in the future with divided memories. Lecture, Dublin 17 May 2016. Retrieved from https://pure.qub.ac.uk/portal/files/38572205/Remembering_forwards.pdf

Jean, quoted at the start of this paper, ended up participating in a sociotherapy group for youth, which included descendants of both survivors and perpetrators. In this group, one of his school mates who is the child of a survivor also participated. Jean had always looked at her as a child of parents who pretended to suffer from trauma to get government support. Through sharing their life stories in sociotherapy he came to understand that he had been wrong. He concluded the interview with one of our researchers by saying, *I wish that what happened to me would happen to everyone in the community. Young people have many things in their heart that prevent them from developing.* Our experience is that many young people benefitted similarly from participation in a sociotherapy group.

Silencing or disclosure of the familial past with respect to peace across the generations

What we have no response to (yet) is the request often posed to us: 'Please tell us what to do in communication with our children; should we tell them the whole truth about the family history or better not disclose it (all)?' Parents want to protect their children from knowing about the atrocities they had suffered from or the atrocities they committed, being afraid that that knowledge will affect them emotionally too much, which they cannot handle, or that it will incite in them an attitude of revenge and propensity to violence. The son of the Nazi criminal quoted above was shocked when he found out about his father's history. After struggling a lot with it, he eventually committed suicide.

While silencing the past in family and community settings is often understood as a form of denial and inherently detrimental to processes of reconciliation, contest this.[66] In post-war social processes and everyday life among people of different ethnic groups, they argue, silence may also help to create a sense of 'normality' and facilitate encounters between former foes. The authors refer to their research in post-war Bosnia and Herzegovina. Silence, according to them, can be used to protect close relationships and family continuity. This may be so in certain circumstances for a particular time period, as is for instance the case in families of refugee women who experienced sexual violence in the context of war where women for good reason silence their rape experience.[67] The other side of the coin is that silencing traumatic memories by parents to their children may have negative effects in terms of wellbeing of the following generations (as is illustrated in the documentary *Three days in August* referred to above). Second-generation memory work, Fischer explains with reference

66 Eastmond, M. & Mannergren Selimovic, J. (2012) 'Silence as possibility in postwar everyday life', *The International Journal of Transitional Justice* 6:502–524.

67 Tankink, M. & Richters, A. (2017) Silence as a coping strategy: The case of refugee women in the Netherlands from South-Sudan who experienced sexual violence in the context of war, in P. Wilson & B. Drozdek (eds.) *Voices of trauma: Treating survivors across cultures*, pp. 191-210. New York: Springer.

to second-generation Holocaust survivors, results in connecting with one family's pre-genocide life, a 'usable past,' in spite of horrific loss.[68]

An African folk wisdom is that atrocities refuse to be buried; 'ghosts refuse to rest in their graves until their stories are told'. The silence of the parents regarding their past can be highly suggestive to the child. She does not dare to ask questions but attempts to fill the gaps with her own imagination, which may lead to the trauma crises among young people, which are on the increase in Rwanda. Whether transfer takes place in the mother's womb, in early relationship with the mother, through unconscious loyalty or epigenetic changes, it usually leaves something unresolved from the past up to the third or fourth generation. Remaining silent about the past does little to immunise the next generation.[69] As the Dutch child psychiatrist Sita Sommers, argues, 'the ghosts that haunt the child's life, should not be chased away, but identified and be negotiated with, re-humanised.'[70] Through sharing one's life history with descendants, ghosts can go from haunting the next generation to becoming simply part of their history.

Some parents with whom we discussed the issue very wisely promoted a kind of 'modulated disclosure' of traumatic memories and perpetration of genocide. The term modulated disclosure refers to a 'style of intrafamily communication in which the timing and manner of disclosure are emphasised and in which parental sensitivity to the child's cognitive and emotional needs is seen as more important than the content of what is disclosed.'[71] Pushing disclosure, they argue, may actually be harmful. Parents do not want to fuel hatred in their children of 'the other'. Also, some children do not want too much disclosure, being afraid that it may affect them negatively. As one descendant of *a génocidaire in Rwanda shared, I do not like to deepen those things, because I think it can create in me another personality. I am curious, but I am afraid.*

In our research we aim to continue addressing the issue of silencing and disclosure and hope to come up with some well-founded responses to the request for developing guidelines for parental communication about the past that will contribute to peace of mind as well as to interpersonal peace across the generations.[72]

68 Fischer, N. (2015) *Memory work: The second generation.* Palgrave Macmillan.

69 See Wolynn 2016, p. 61.

70 Sommers, S. (2017) Getraumatiseerde gezinnen: Temmen van draken en monsters (Traumatised families: Taming dragons and monsters). Presentation study-day on Ethnopsychiatry of the Section Transcultural Psychiatry of the Dutch Society for Psychiatry. Amsterdam 15 December 2017.

71 Dalgaard, N.T. & Montgomery, E. (2015) 'Disclosure and silencing: A systematic review of the literature on patterns of trauma communication in refugee families', Transcultural Psychiatry 52(5), p. 581.

72 See also Ingabire 2018.

Conclusion

As way of conclusion a few bullet points only:

- Almost 25 years after the genocide against the Tutsi in Rwanda, the need to pay more attention in research and practice to intergenerational trauma is more and more recognised.
- There is a need for research focused on what and how of trauma transmission among all categories of people in Rwandan society.
- The Holocaust can no longer serve as a conceptual limit case in this research.
- There is a need for psychosocial support of parents and children for the sake of their wellbeing and as a contribution to the prevention of another cycle of violence.
- In Rwanda, the need is expressed for the development of a model to guide parents in disclosure of the family past.
- Care providers need to be better informed about the processes of healthy as well as disturbed and disorganised parent-child attachment relationships for the sake of mitigating parenting impairment.
- In the rebuilding of societies after genocide and war, peacebuilding should be integrated in mental health and psychosocial support and the other way around for the sake of durable peace.

Acknowledgements

Thanks are due to Chantal Ingabire and Emmanuel Sarabwe for a close reading of this paper and their comments, to sociotherapy staff for generating information from the field, and to research respondents for generously sharing their life experiences with us.

Part IV: Empathic Encounters

14. Encountering the suffering of the other – experiences from Palestinians and South Africans visiting concentration camps in Germany and Poland

Martin Leiner

Introduction

The following presentation focuses on three visits of Palestinian groups to concentration camps in Poland and Germany that have been researched by qualitative and quantitative methods. The project was funded by the German national funding organisation DFG and included additional elements such as 'encountering experiments' with Israelis through courses, personal encounters and site visits. It also included 15 PhD and post-doctoral studies related to the main topic, social-psychological laboratory experiments conducted in Tel Aviv and Jena, and articles and a book.[1]

In my presentation I will focus on the results concerning empathy, trauma and national identity. As the final evaluation has not yet taken place, I will submit preliminary results for discussion. Please be aware that after translating all the data and doing the one-year-later tests for the last two trips, we might come to different results. The main question of our research was, 'Can encountering of the suffering of the 'other' foster empathy and, if yes, will this lead to increased willingness to reconcile?'

The terms encountering the suffering of the other (ESO); empathy (E); and willingness to reconcile (WTR) are used here.

When we designed the project in 2013, several scholars had very high expectations regarding empathy as a tool to overcome conflict. Meanwhile, several studies and books went in the opposite direction claiming that empathy might have many forms

1 The project 'Hearts of Flesh – not Stone' (LE-1620) was organised by the four leaders Prof. Dr. Martin Leiner (main leader), Prof. Dr. Shifra Sagy (Beer Sheba), Prof. Dr. Mohammed Dajani (Al Quds University/Wasatia) and Prof. Dr. Arie Nadler (Tel Aviv University).

and several not very positive effects on peace-making and ethical behaviour.[2,3] The purpose of the research project was to find out whether encountering the suffering if the other and empathy can be key for reconciliation. In the first trip, as we had no direct survivor of a concentration camp, but only two children of survivors, we could mainly find empathy 'only' as perspective taking, as putting oneself in the shoes of people you do not encounter directly, but only through documentaries and other indirect means.

Reconciliation on the other hand was also difficult to measure, because no political reconciliation had taken place in Israel and Palestine. On the contrary, after the first trip, war in Gaza started and during the entire period many human rights violations, especially against Palestinians but also attacks against Israelis, took place. We only could measure WTR according to a questionnaire developed jointly and based on a questionnaire Shifra Sagy and her team had already worked with at Beer Sheba University.

What we did

In April 2014 and in June and October 2017 we travelled with 30 Palestinians, mixed according to gender, age and local region in Palestine, to the concentration camps.

In April 2014 we travelled with Israelis, and in 2017 both trips were with only Palestinian travellers. The trip in June was under the condition of learning German history and separating to the maximum the suffering of the Jews from the State of Israel today. No victim of the Holocaust was an Israeli citizen at the time when it occurred was one message, we pointed out that the memorial in Buchenwald indicated that there were Albanians, Algerians, Egyptians, Moroccans, Syrians and Tunisians among the victims of Holocaust. On the third trip, we allowed much more comparison with Israel today.

The first trip was, against our will, publicised and had a very positive response in the press, first in Haaretz, then in newspapers around the world from the New York Times and the Washington Post to Le Monde, La Republica, Die Zeit and small newspapers in Uruguay and Japan. It was framed as the first trip of Palestinians from the West Bank to Auschwitz. Even Mahmoud Abbas made a declaration, acknowledging the Holocaust three weeks later, though it is difficult to say whether there was a link with our travels or not.

However, even during the trip very negative reactions started in Palestine. Al Quds News published an alleged translation of the Haaretz article replacing the two witnesses of the Holocaust with two Zionist organisations who would have funded the trip. Professor Dajani, the leader of the Palestinian team, was accused of collaboration

2 Breithaupt, F. (2017) Die dunklen Seiten der Empathie. Frankfurt/M.: Suhrkamp.
3 Bloom, P. (2018) Against Empathy. The case for Rational compassion. New York: Vintage.

with Zionists and even lost his position at Al Quds University. He received personal threats. Some months later his car was burned. Fortunately, none of the Palestinian participants in the trip was attacked. But at the end of the trip, participants received critical phone calls from their families telling them to come home as soon as possible.

The second and the third trip were much quieter. We planned them after a break of more than three years, we did not go to Auschwitz the emblematic place, but to Berlin and Buchenwald and we framed the trips as a German history experience. In Berlin we also visited the wall and gave them hope that walls can fall. One of the most touching moments was when, during the second trip, Palestinians were dancing on the former death strip at the memorial Bernauer Straße.

Some results concerning empathy

Before describing the results, the numbers of the sample must be clarified. They were relatively similar: N (ESO 1) = 27 (one participant was denied passage by Israel)

N (ESO 2) = 27 (one participant was excluded from the analysis, since he did not answer the questionnaire at T2)

N (ESO 3) = 30

In total: Males: 42, Females: 39

Mean age = 27 (Min. =17, Max. = 52)

The first correlation ESO – Empathy functioned more or less as expected during the second and the third trip:

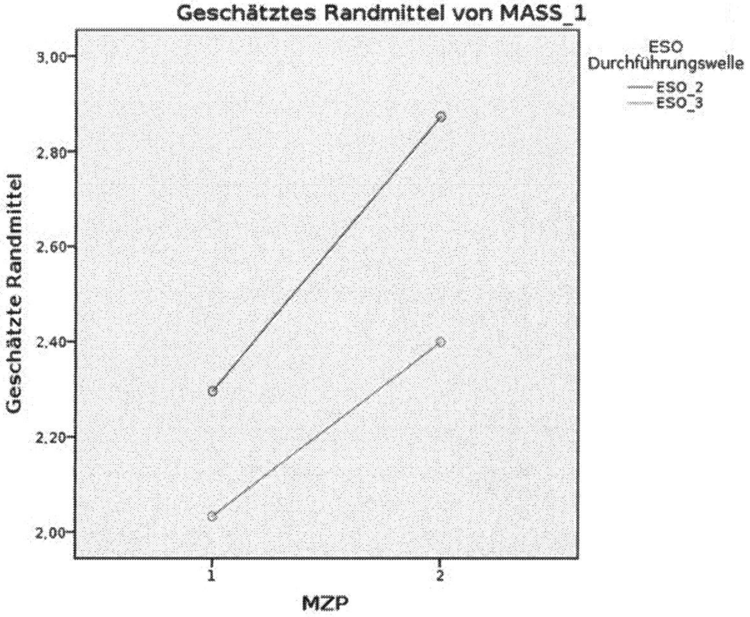

With a significant main effect: $F(1,55) = 6.74$, $p = .012$, the effects were less strong than we hoped, but nevertheless interviews, texts the students wrote, and observations of participants shocked and crying during the visits, would it make difficult to downplay those effects.

One problem was certainly that the lack of recognition of the Palestinian suffering led to a lesser willingness to encounter the suffering of Jews.

The most surprising result we found was the first trip:

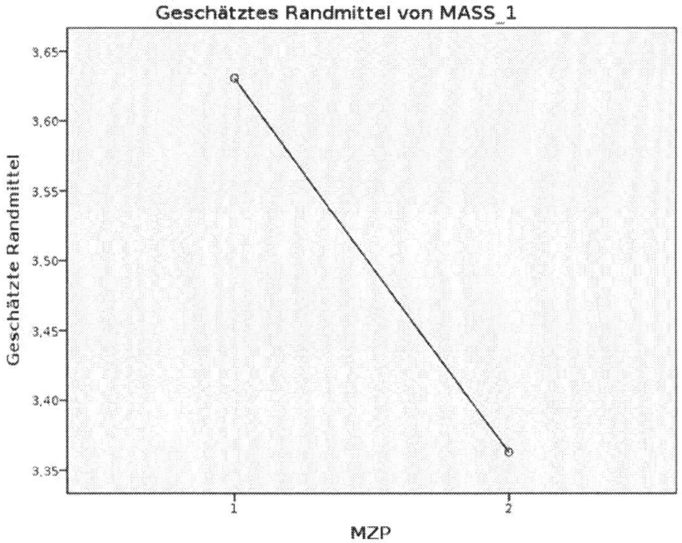

From a high level of empathy, which was an effect of the preparing workshops before the trip, empathy decreased during the trip.

As in all the trips, the questionnaires were filled in when participants arrived in Europe and again before they left; the result already reflects the negative reaction on the trip by relatives who read the Al Quds News. Feelings of being betrayed evidently played a role for some of the participants.

However, there were also other effects. One was that we could observe reactance against the Israelis present during the trip. They provoked Palestinian participants by making claims such as, when you have seen this you should acknowledge that we had no other choice than to go to Israel.

Another effect we could observe on the trip is that the concentration camp triggered experiences of trauma some had experienced in Israeli prisons. For example, one female participant had been in an Israeli prison over several years. She agreed to write an article about her experience in a book we published after the trip.[4]

4 Dajani, M., Leiner, M., Nadler, A., Sagy, S., Barakat, Z. (2015) *Teaching Empathy in the midst of Conflict. Jerusalem:* Wasatia publications.

One participant in the second trip revealed that her brother had been tortured and burned by radical Israeli soldiers in an act of revenge murder only a bit more than one year before the trip. She also spoke in front of the group about her experience and said that she left everything to Allah, not wishing to take revenge, but wondering why, when Jews went through such atrocities, they are inflicting atrocities on Palestinians.

This picture shows an Israeli prison, which has some similarities with prison cells in concentration camps, at least for Palestinians (thanks to Dr. Zeina Barakat who showed me that photo).

Some results concerning willingness to reconcile

More disturbingly than those results, we found that willingness to reconcile did not increase but decreased during all three trips.

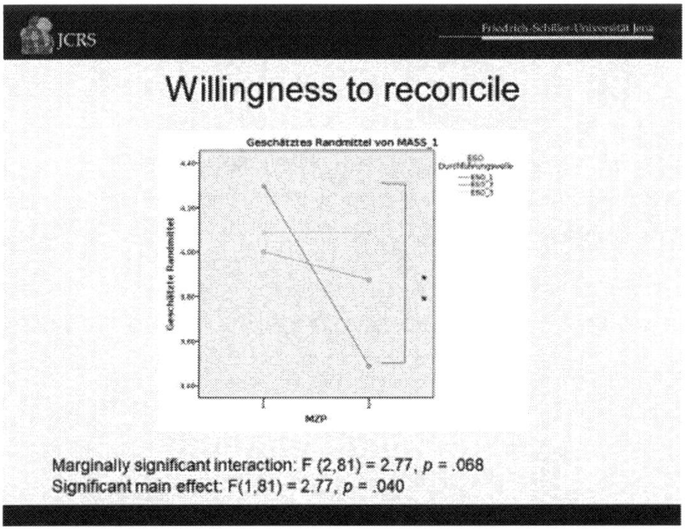

During trips 2 and 3 the decrease was so insignificant that we can start from the idea that the empathy had no effect on willingness to reconcile. Our interviews showed that many of the Palestinians answered that there is no one on the Israeli side who wants to reconcile with Palestinians, and it is a political question that must be separated from the empathy with the victims.

This result is also consistent with studies that show that empathy without hope for peace does not lead to more willingness to reconcile.[5]

During the first trip, however, the willingness to reconcile decreased significantly. How can we explain that effect? Certainly, what already has been mentioned is true: reactance against the Israelis, triggering of trauma and feeling betrayed played a role.

However, it seems that there is still another factor. The sense of national coherence increased during all three trips.

This could mean that the danger to be called a traitor led to a more nationalist counter-reaction. WE are good Palestinians, even better ones when we saw concentration camps.

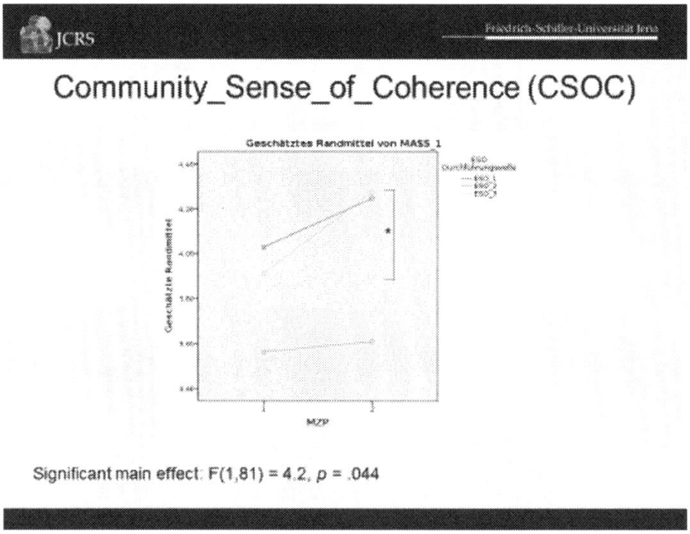

Other effects and conclusion

Those results seem to be quite sobering for those who want to find keys for reconciliation through encountering the suffering of others. Nevertheless, we could find other results that give a different sense of the just-presented data.

5 Halperin, E. (2017). *Emotions in Conflict. Inhibitors and Facilitators of Peace Making*. New York /London: Routledge.

One is that after the second and third trip participants felt more sympathy, less fear and less hatred against Israelis. Paradoxically, that was mostly the case during the second trip.

Another impressive result was that almost all said that they now are convinced that the Holocaust happened with the numbers science today is using. Many wrote that they will talk about the reality of the Holocaust, and a group of Palestinians even started to make the trip again with friends and to visit concentration camps with them in December and January 2017/18.

The presence of Germans played an important role in overcoming denial of the Holocaust.

Altogether, the research project showed that reconciliation is a multidimensional process. There is, at least as far as we can see, not only one key and tool to open the hearts for willingness to reconcile. We need a combination of different keys.

15. Walking in another's shoes: Empathy and perspective taking in second-generation South African students

Melike Fourie

Introduction

South Africa provides an important opportunity to study intergroup processes and the transgenerational impact of historical trauma, given its racially divided past. While much attention has been paid to righting the wrongs of the past at a socio-political level, the long-term implications of gross human rights violations at a more interpersonal level, and how this plays out in the day-to-day lives of descendants of this violence have not been considered adequately. Notably, it is important to understand how the legacies of historical trauma affects outgroup perspective taking a n imperative ingredient for national unity. Perspective taking has been described as a 'sensitive understanding' of the other the process whereby we actively try to imagine how another person thinks and feels given their situation, and is a powerful means to elicit empathy and concern for others. Here we investigated cross-racial perspective taking in Black and White university students using multiracial social scenarios to examine how outgroup behaviour and motivation is construed in the born-free generation. We hypothesised that perspective taking will be diminished for members of racial outgroups, but that the presence of perspective taking will translate to enhanced empathy for those portrayed in the scenarios.

Background

Empathy is fundamental to all human interaction and can be described as the capacity to think and feel oneself into the inner reality of another person, while recognising that their emotional experience is separate from our own.[1] Scholars have

1 Decety, J., & Lamm, C. (2006). Human empathy through the lens of social neuroscience. *The Scientific World Journal, 6, 1146-1163.*

parsed empathy into three dissociable but interacting neurocognitive components: emotional sharing, perspective taking and empathic concern.[2,3]

Emotional sharing constitutes the affective component of empathy and is also commonly referred to as *emotion contagion or affective resonance*. It refers to the automatic capacity to become aroused by another's emotions, and relies on subcortical emotion circuits.[4] For example, seeing an angered individual may lead the empathic observer to vicariously experience similar feelings.

Perspective taking constitutes the cognitive component of empathy and refers to the capacity to view a situation from another's point of view, or to put oneself in their shoes, as it were. Doing this allows one to better recognise and understand another person's affective experience. It therefore partly overlaps with the theory of mind-like processing and relies on the mentalising network.[5] Because perspective taking begins with the perception of affective signals from another individual, low-level processes involved in face perception and emotion recognition are integral to understanding another individual's internal state.[6]

Finally, empathic concern constitutes the motivational component of empathy, and refers to other-oriented feelings of care and compassion when perceiving an individual in distress. The experience of empathic concern may stimulate prosocial helping or caring behaviours in the observer.[7,8] Empathising with others in distress is thus particularly important because it motivates behaviour aimed at alleviating those others' suffering, and this, in turn, promotes social cohesion and resource-sharing amongst members of society.[9,10]

Unfortunately, empathy is also a very malleable phenomenon, in that its elicitation is not automatic, but modulated by multiple factors, including personal and interpersonal factors, but also the social group membership of the person in distress (e.g., race or political affiliation). Whereas greater empathy toward one's ingroup

---

2 Decety, J. (2015). The neural pathways, development and functions of empathy. Current Opinion in Behavioural Sciences, 3, 1-6.

3 Zaki, J., & Ochsner, K. N. (2012). The neuroscience of empathy: Progress, pitfalls and promise. *Nature Neuroscience*, 15, 675-680.

4 Decety, J. (2011). Dissecting the neural mechanisms mediating empathy. *Emotion Review*, 3, 92-108.

5 Morelli, S. A., Rameson, L. T., & Lieberman, M. D. (2014). The neural components of empathy: Predicting daily prosocial behaviour. *Social Cognitive and Affective Neuroscience*, 9, 39-47.

6 Echols, S., & Correll, J. (2012). It's more than skin deep: Empathy and helping behaviour across social groups. In J. Decety (Ed.), Empathy. *From bench to bedside* (pp. 55-71). London: MIT Press.

7 Batson, C. D., Fultz, J., & Schoenrade, P. A. (1987). Distress and empathy: two qualitatively distinct vicarious emotions with different motivational consequences. *Journal of Personality*, 55, 19-39.

8 Eisenberg, N., & Miller, P. A. (1987). The relation of empathy to prosocial and related behaviours. *Psychological Bulletin*, 101, 91-119.

9 Batson, C. D., Lishner, D. A., & Stocks, E. L. (2015). *The empathy-altruism hypothesis*. In D. A. Schroeder & W. G. Graziano (Eds.), The Oxford Handbook of Prosocial Behavior (pp. 259-281). New York, NY: Oxford University Press.

10 Eisenberg, N., & Miller, P. A. (1987).

makes sense from an evolutionary perspective,[11] empathic failures toward outgroup members may lie at the heart of most intergroup conflict, including political violence, xenophobia, and genocide.[12]

Of significance is that recent research suggests that outgroup empathy failures do not depend on a person's trait empathic concern in interpersonal contexts.[13] That, is, even the most deeply empathic person can mute their empathic response toward a perceived enemy under the right circumstances. Whereas empathic concern (compassion) is related to greater helping in interpersonal contexts.[14,15] Bruneau and colleagues have argued that in intergroup contexts, outgroup behaviour might be predicted best by the parochial distribution of empathy towards the ingroup versus the outgroup.[16,17] Thus, very high ingroup empathy in the absence of equally strong outgroup empathy might lead to worse treatment of or violence towards the outgroup. Research within three different intergroup contexts (Hungarians regarding refugees, Americans regarding Arabs, and Greeks regarding Germans) showed that parochial empathy is a much stronger predictor of passive harm and intergroup helping behaviour than trait empathic concern.[18] In intergroup contexts, what seems to be important then, is how empathy is distributed between the ingroup and outgroup.

In a previous fMRI study of intergroup empathy conducted in the South African context, we investigated Black and White South Africans' empathic reactions to each other's emotional distress.[19] Because we wanted to study empathy in a more ecologically valid experimental context than is usually done in neuroimaging paradigms, we made use of video clips from the South African Truth and Reconciliation Commission portraying Black and White individuals in poignant emotional distress. Data from this research suggested that outgroup perspective taking (rather than affective sharing mechanisms) is particularly affected with regard to outgroup suffering: activation in areas associated with mental state representation (including the right

11 de Waal, F. B. (2012). *The antiquity of empathy*. Science, 336, 874-876.
12 Cohen, T. R., & Insko, C. A. (2008). War and peace: Possible approaches to reducing intergroup conflict. *Perspectives on Psychological Science*, 3, 87-93.
13 Bruneau, E. G., Cikara, M., & Saxe, R. (2017). Parochial empathy predicts reduced altruism and the endorsement of passive harm. *Social Psychological and Personality Science*, 8, 934-942.
14 Batson, C. D., Ahmad, N., Lishner, D. A., & Tsang, J. A. (2002). Empathy and altruism. In C. R. Snyder & S. J. Lopez (Eds.), *Handbook of positive psychology* (pp. 485-498). New York, NY, US: Oxford University Press.
15 Davis, M. H., Mitchell, K. V., Hall, J. A., Lothert, J., Snapp, T., & Meyer, M. (1999). Empathy, expectations, and situational preferences: personality influences on the decision to participate in volunteer helping behaviours. *Journal of Personality*, 67, 469-503.
16 Bruneau, E. G., Cikara, M., & Saxe, R. (2017).
17 Cikara, M., Bruneau, E. G., & Saxe, R. R. (2011). Us and them: Intergroup failures of empathy. *Current Directions in Psychological Science*, 20, 149-153.
18 Bruneau, E. G., Cikara, M., & Saxe, R. (2017).
19 Fourie, M. M., Stein, D. J., Solms, M., Gobodo-Madikizela, P., & Decety, J. (2017). Empathy and moral emotions in post-apartheid South-Africa: An fMRI investigation. *Social Cognitive and Affectice Neuroscience*.

temporoparietal junction and precuneus) were significantly reduced for outgroup compared to ingroup members' emotional distress. These results suggested that we are not as good, or perhaps that we do not try as hard, to perceive an outgroup member's pain and distinct reality as that of an ingroup member.

In the present study, we wanted to extend these findings by examining perspective taking more explicitly. Specifically, we wanted to examine Black and White participants' responses to complex social scenarios typical to the South African context, to see whether responses were also characterised by reduced perspective taking and therefore empathy, for racial outgroup members in these situations.

Before considering the research questions of the present study, it is necessary to have a closer look at perspective taking and how we operationalised it in the present study. The construct of perspective taking largely overlaps with that of theory of mind (ToM), the ability to explain, predict, and interpret behaviour by attributing mental states such as desires, beliefs, intentions and emotions to oneself and to other people.[20] During the course of our daily routines (e.g., reading a book, conversing with someone), we seamlessly and continually attribute invisible internal states to others (real or fictitious), as such inferences underpin all social interaction.[21] Perspective taking, however, represents a more effortful, extended process whereby we actively try to imagine how another person thinks and feels given his/her situation (i.e., an imagine-other perspective), without self-other confusion.[22] In this sense, perspective taking involves more than simply making mental inferences, it involves an 'empathic attentional set'[23], whereby one is simultaneously sensitive to the thoughts and feelings of another person and conscious of how this conception affects the self.[24] A fully developed capacity to reason about other minds is thus critical for negotiating the complexities of social life.

With regard to previous research, a substantial body of evidence documents the effectiveness of perspective taking as a powerful means to elicit empathy and concern for others.[25,26] Moreover, in intergroup contexts, perspective taking has been shown to

20 Decety, J., & Svetlova, M. (2012). Putting together phylogenetic and ontogenetic perspectives on empathy. *Developmental Cognitive Neuroscience*, 2, 1-24.

21 Saxe, R. (2006). Why and how to study Theory of Mind with fMRI. *Brain Research*, 1079, 57-65.

22 van der Heiden, L., Scherpiet, S., Konicar, L., Birbaumer, N., & Veit, R. (2013). Inter-individual differences in successful perspective taking during pain perception mediates emotional responsiveness in self and others: An fMRI study. *Neuroimage*, 65, 387-394.

23 Barrett-Lennard, G. T. (1981). The empathy cycle: Refinement of a nuclear concept. Journal of Counselling Psychology, 28, 91-100, pp. 92.

24 Batson, C. D., & Ahmad, N. Y. (2009). Using empathy to improve intergroup attitudes and relations. *Social Issues and Policy Review*, 3, 141-177.

25 Ibid.

26 Todd, A. R., & Galinsky, A. D. (2014). Perspective-taking as a strategy for improving intergroup relations: Evidence, mechanisms, and qualifications. *Social and Personality Psychology Compass*, 8, 374-387.

combat intergroup biases (both overt and covert) and to reduce outgroup stereotypes, which is critical to foster positive intergroup relations.

Present study: Perspective taking in complex social scenarios

In the present study, the following research questions were posed:

1. Do White and Black South Africans display diminished perspective taking of the other's behaviour/ motivation/intent in real-life situations?
2. Does diminished perspective taking translate to a breakdown of empathy (compassion)?

Hypotheses

1. Empathic responding (as measured by self-reported emotion scales) will be less for racial outgroup compared to racial ingroup members (i.e., parochial empathy).
2. Perspective taking (as measured by participants' qualitative written responses) will be diminished for racial outgroup versus ingroup members and might be displayed by diminished insight into outgroup members' behavioural motivations and/or a reduced tendency to explicitly view the situation from the other's point of view.
3. Perspective taking will predict empathy: Individuals who adopt a perspective taking response to the reflective scenarios will be more likely to understand and respond with empathy to those portrayed in the scenarios.
4. Parochial empathy (difference between ingroup and outgroup empathy) will be predictive of more negative intergroup outcomes (e.g., interest in participating in a cross-racial dialogue event).

Methods

The final sample of participants who met criteria for taking part in the study consisted of 29 Black African and 138 White South Africans, recruited in lecture halls at Stellenbosch University. We employed a mixed-methods study design, incorporating both qualitative and quantitative measures to explore participants' responses.

The qualitative section consisted of three ecological reflective scenarios concerning both a Black and White individual(s), and related questions designed to probe spontaneous perspective taking in relation to ingroup and outgroup targets. These questions were framed in an open-ended manner so that participants were not primed to imagine each party's motivation or intentions. Furthermore, each scenario was roughly modelled on a real event (but with fictitious names) to ensure that they appeared authentic and elicited strong emotional responses.

Because of space constraints, and because the data for scenarios 2 and 3 were very similar, I will focus only on responses to the first two scenarios, which are presented below:

> *Scenario 1*: Last year the following incident was reported to the Transformation Office at Stellenbosch University: During a protest by the university's outsourced workers, workers threw mud on the J.H. Marais statue (considered a heritage treasure). A group of White students subsequently decided to do something about the situation. They went to the statue with cleaning materials and started to clean up the mess. The cleaning of the statue by the students angered the workers, however. Soon a cycle started where workers threw more and more mud on the statue and the students kept cleaning it without backing off.

> *Scenario 2*: Nomusa is a domestic worker who has worked at the Eksteen household for the past 2 years. Recently Nomusa suffered a great loss: her house burned down as a result of an accident involving tile glue and she lost most of her possessions. She was devastated. Two months after the incident she asked her employers, Mr and Mrs Eksteen, whether they would sponsor an expensive dress for her daughter's matric farewell. The dress cost R800. While Mr and Mrs Eksteen have been very supportive following the accident, they decided not to give her the money for the dress.

Each participant's responses to the reflective scenarios was analysed using qualitative thematic analysis. In general, the analysis was approached in an inductive fashion, but the themes *empathy and impaired empathy* were approached in a deductive fashion. Because of the study's particular focus on perspective taking, responses to each scenario were also coded in absolute terms as either having *perspective taking (perspective taking* = *1*) or not (*perspective taking* = *0*) with regard to each target. Specifically, a response that suggested 'responsively knowing' or a 'sensitive understanding' of a target's internal state was taken to confirm the presence of perspective taking. Responses that were unclear or ambiguous in terms of perspective taking were omitted from data analysis (i.e., they were coded as missing data).

The quantitative section was comprised of several self-reported emotional scales to measure participants' reactions to each target in the reflective scenarios. Emotion items here included frustration, compassion, anger, pride, shame, and anxiety, measured on 9-point Likert-type scales ranging from 1 (*not at all*) to 9 (*very much*). In addition, an intergroup contact measure was included to assess the effect of intergroup contact on participants' responses to the reflective scenarios (Hewstone et al., 2011). Finally, a real-world intergroup outcome measure (interest in participating in a cross-racial dialogue event) was included to assess whether parochial empathy predicted negative intergroup outcomes. Responses here also ranged from 1 (*not interested at all*) to 9 (*very much interested*).

Results

Thematic Analysis

Although the scenarios were characterised by different themes, six overarching themes were identified from the thematic analysis of the qualitative data (displayed below).

Table 1

Summary of Themes and Subthemes

	Theme	Subthemes
1.	Impaired Empathy	Poor understanding; distancing/indifference; patronising/belittling; high negative emotion
2.	Ingroup Identification	White pride; Black pride; White identity threat; White shame; Outgroup fear
3.	Political Ideologies	Black oppression; inferred racism; democratic ideals
4.	Empathy	Imagine-other perspective; imagine self-perspective; empathetic concern
5.	Moral Judgements	Morally right, morally wrong; lack of responsibility
6.	Inequality	White priviledge; Luxury versus necessity

Briefly, the results suggested that a history of trauma and oppression impacted the emotional responses of individuals significantly: The theme political ideologies (particularly Black oppression) was more prevalent among Black participants for scenario 1, as they were the oppressed group historically. By comparison, prevalent among White participants for scenario 1 were themes of Ingroup identification (particularly White pride and White identity threat) in response to the *White students* and Impaired Empathy (particularly Patronising/Belittling responses) in reaction to the *Outsourced workers*. These responses may be the result of self-preservation and resistance in the face of social change.

With regard to scenario 2, common themes among Black and White participants included lack of social responsibility and White privilege with regard to *The Eksteens*, and empathic concern with regard to *Nomusa*. It should be noted that White participants' expression of empathic concern towards *Nomusa* may also be confounded by her being a 'pitied target' and was observed as such (i.e., responses suggestive of pity rather than care and concern) in some of the qualitative data. This observation is consistent with research suggesting that people feel worse about negative events when they affect pitied targets compared to admired ingroup targets, despite pity targets belonging to social outgroups.[27]

Ingroup Empathy Bias (Hypothesis 1)

With regard to scenario 1, paired t-tests indicated significant ingroup empathy biases for both White and Black participants: White participants responded with significantly more compassion towards the *White students than the Outsourced workers*, $t(124) = 7.79$, $p < .001$, and Black participants responded with significantly more compassion towards the *Outsourced workers* than the *White students*, $t(22) = -2.36$, $p < .05$. Furthermore, White participants felt predominantly compassion and pride with regard to the White students, but frustration and anger with regard to the *Outsourced workers*. By contrast, Black participants felt predominantly compassion and pride with regard to the *Outsourced workers*, but frustration and anger with regard to the *White students*.

With regard to scenario 2, paired t-tests indicated significantly higher compassion for *Nomusa* than *The Eksteens* for both Black and White participants ($ps < .001$). Whereas Black participants thus continued to respond with an ingroup empathy bias, White participants' responses reflected an outgroup empathy bias. In terms of other emotions, both groups reported experiencing predominantly compassion with regard to *Nomusa*, but frustration and anger with regard to *The Eksteens*.

Perspective taking (Hypothesis 2)

Qualitative analysis of participant responses suggested that hypothesis 2 (i.e., diminished outgroup perspective taking) was confirmed for Scenario 1 for both participant groups: Both Black and White participants displayed significant perspective taking in response to own-race targets in the scenarios, but significantly impaired ability to take the perspective of outgroup targets. By contrast, for scenario 2, both Black and White participants displayed greater frequency of imagine-other perspectives for *Nomusa* than *The Eksteens*. These results suggested that White participants' responses were more egalitarian for scenario 2, whereas Black participants also displayed diminished outgroup perspective taking for scenario 2.

27 Cikara, M., & Fiske, S. T. (2011). Bounded empathy: Neural responses to outgroup targets' (mis) fortunes. *Journal of Cognitive Neuroscience*, 23, 3791-3803.

It should be stressed that beyond these general trends, there were also powerful instances of participants taking the perspective of an outgroup member in scenario 1. Two examples are presented below:

> 0037 (Black female, in response to the *White students*):
>
> I think that's what they think is right, but I feel they are being ignorant to the reason why the workers are throwing mud – it's not just to destroy property for no reason. Frustration because they continue to be ignorant of the issues. I feel they should be using their privilege for more good.
>
> 0080 (White female, in response to the *Outsourced workers*)
>
> I think they were angered because they are trying to get a certain message across and the students cleaning it is telling the workers that their problems and beliefs are unimportant. People are allowed to voice their frustrations in any way they seem fit as long as they aren't causing harm to people.

Perspective taking and empathy (Hypothesis 3)

To investigate the predictive value of perspective taking on empathic responding, four linear regressions were conducted, one for each target individual or group in each scenario. In addition, each linear regression included participant race as an independent variable in the analysis.

These analyses indicated that, across scenarios and targets, perspective taking significantly predicted empathy (compassion) scores ($ps < .01$). Of significance, however, was that for scenario 1, race in addition to perspective taking significantly predicted empathy ($ps < .01$), whereas race played no significant role in predicting perspective taking for scenario 2. For scenario 1 only, participant race thus played a significant role in whether or not participants reported compassion for the target individuals.

Parochial empathy (Hypothesis 4)

On average, Black participants (*Mode: 9*) were significantly more interested in attending the cross-racial dialogue event than White participants *(Mode: 5)*, $p < .001$.

With regard to the exploratory hypothesis, the present data confirmed that for White participants, parochial empathy (i.e., the difference in empathy for ingroup compared to outgroup members) significantly predicted the real-world intergroup outcome: greater parochial empathy was associated with reduced interest in attending the cross-racial dialogue event. No significant associations were observed for the Black participant group. Finally, greater cross-racial contact among White participants was associated with greater interest in attending the cross-racial dialogue event.

Discussion

The results presented above confirmed the anticipated association between diminished perspective taking and empathic breakdown, both within and across racial groups. Of significance, however, is that perspective taking and empathic concern were not always aligned with the ingroup. Rather, the social context significantly modulated perspective taking responses: events set in the public discourse around race (scenario 1) had a strong ingroup polarising effect on responses, whereas politically neutral events (scenario 2) had the effect of enhancing empathy and perspective taking toward Black individuals across participants. The context therefore impacted participants' responses in significant ways, particularly those of White participants, who as a group changed from outgroup derogation to outgroup compassion. This phenomenon of 'contextual empathy failures' becomes even more glaring when one considers the responses of the same White individual in response to the *Outsourced workers* (scenario 1) and Nomusa (scenario 2):

> 0077 (White female)
>
> Outsourced Workers: It is a barbaric way to try to "say your say." Nomusa: Where else could she go? It must've taken her courage to ask.
>
> 0084 (White female)
>
> Outsourced Workers: Indicates a level of immaturity. Their continued actions are of little significance.
>
> Nomusa: It is brave and by no means unreasonable. The task would not have been easy for her.

If we can begin to understand what underlies or triggers these empathic failures (in some cases even instances of dehumanisation), we can begin to design interventions to try to address or prevent them. In what follows, the discussion will focus on potential explanations for White participants' responses.

It can be argued that there are at least two, and potentially more, possible explanations for the diverging reactions of White participants in response to scenarios 1 and 2. These are a) the fact that scenario 1 presented an intergroup context whereas scenario 2 presented and interpersonal context, and b) the fact that the stakes were personal for scenario 1 (i.e., the participants' *own* university were involved) whereas the stakes were impersonal for scenario 2 (i.e., the participants were not affected in any way by the Eksteens' decision). Let's take a closer look at each of these possibilities.

From research we know that intergroup contexts tend to exacerbate people's motivation not to empathise or care about someone else's misfortune, in that groups may provoke significantly more competition and aggression than interpersonal interactions.[28,29] Even in the absence of overt competition, differences in power and resources between groups have been shown to predict perceptions of competitiveness and conflict.[30] And when explicit competition is present, this has the effect of increasing the salience of social identity, and generally strengthens the positive relationship between ingroup identification and intergroup bias and hostility.[31,32] It is interesting to note that the mediating process between perceived competitive threat (whether its status threat, being outnumbered, or violence/physical danger) and hostility, is not negative attitudes (prejudice), but rather reduced empathy for the threatening outgroup.[33]

In the second instance, the events of scenario 1 may have posed a *social identity threat* to White students from Stellenbosch University. The threat value was, of course, augmented by the nature of the interaction (i.e., conflict), and was also evident in White participants' high negative emotional responses of anger and frustration that emerged. More specifically, it may be described as an 'identity' threat because White identity is construed around tenets of superiority and a denial of racism in order to maintain power and privileges. Furthermore, White identity resists disruption, in that assumptions about Whiteness and privilege have been able to be carried forward into post-apartheid South Africa.[34] One could therefore argue that Stellenbosch University became part of this White identity, namely as a place of heritage, a place of attaining power and privilege. Black people can 'assimilate' into this space, but they must not 'change' or 'rupture' or 'deplete' anything. In this vein, the Outsourced workers' behaviour could have been perceived as a threat to the university, and to White privilege itself, by the White participants. Indeed, instances of heightened ingroup identification and/or ingroup threat were readily observed in White participants' responses:

> I experienced pride that the students would look after our campus.
>
> I think it is good as it shows pride in heritage and Stellenbosch as well as resilience. It's good that they feel so strongly about their institution of study.

---

28 Cikara, M., Bruneau, E. G., & Saxe, R. R. (2011).

29 Meier, B. P., & Hinsz, V. B. (2004). A comparison of human aggression committed by groups and individuals: An interindividual–intergroup discontinuity. *Journal of Experimental Social Psychology*, 40, 551-559.

30 Fiske, S. T., Cuddy, A. J., Glick, P., & Xu, J. (2002). A model of (often mixed) stereotype content: competence and warmth respectively follow from perceived status and competition. *Journal of Personality and Social Psychology*, 82, 878-902.

31 Hewstone, M., Rubin, M., & Willis, H. (2002). Intergroup bias. *Annual Review of Psychology*, 53, 575-604.

32 Hogg, M. A. (1993). Hogg MA. Group cohesiveness: A critical review and some new directions. *European Review of Social Psychology*, 4, 85-111.

33 Bruneau, E. G., Cikara, M., & Saxe, R. (2017).

34 Steyn, M. (2012). The ignorance contract: Recollections of apartheid childhoods and the construction of epistemologies of ignorance. *Identities*, 19, 8-25.

> The white students are right. They are educating the workers to not destroy property and have a peaceful protest. I would've done the same.
>
> I think it was a good decision seeing that the statue is a heritage treasure and they tried to 'protect' it. I felt proud that people from my race stood up for what was right.
>
> I think they had the right to clean it, they were cleaning the statue because the workers made the statue look ugly, not because they're white. Pride for looking after our campus.
>
> They felt that it was their place to respect our heritage no matter what form it is in.

Relatedly, it is interesting to note that another feature of White identity is a carefully constructed ignorance around the realities of apartheid, which has strategic value in that it warrants avoidance or neglect of one's social responsibility to right the wrongs of the past. Melissa Steyn has aptly termed this the 'Ignorance Contract.'[35] It can be regarded as a social accomplishment in that it keeps systemic racial hierarchies in place in racialised societies. Importantly, these ignorances are perpetuated in the present context by the older apartheid generation, who impart this amended reality of apartheid to their children. When we look at White participants' responses to the question of attending cross-racial events, we see very clearly how these ignorances manifest. At closer look, they appear to present in three different flavours.

First, it is not desirable to attend cross-racial dialogue events, because these experiences are too painful or uncomfortable to endure. Moreover, they might elicit significant shame, which is undesirable. Responses of this nature might therefore be described as instances of '*I don't want to know*' (in each case, the number in brackets represents participants' quantitative response from 1 (*not interested at all*) to 9 (*very much interested*) in attending the cross-racial dialogue event):

> I don't want to be overwhelmed by negative emotions. (1)
>
> Because I am white, even if I didn't live then, NOR agree with the Apartheid regime AT ALL, I will feel like it's still my fault, that so many people have suffered. (1)
>
> I believe in creating awareness is important but personally hearing horrific tales first angers me and makes me feel somewhat uncomfortable to be my race. (2)
>
> It is uncomfortable discussing these things, and some people may be able to talk more than others (white people cannot necessarily have a say). (3)

35 Steyn, M. (2012).

The second kind of ignorance is exemplified in a more active type of denial, i.e., '*Nothing is really wrong*':

> I think apartheid experience talks are necessary, yet I feel that those directly affected should attend. And the rest of the nation must not dwell on the past but instead move on into an equal future. (2)

> I was not alive in apartheid, I have not discriminated or been discriminated against, and thus would have nothing to contribute. I should not have to be argued on behalf of my race. (1)

Finally, the third kind of ignorance is reflected in responses of utter indifference, i.e., 'I don't care':

> I know apartheid is an important part of our history, however, personally hearing about it every day of my life is more than enough. Thus, I would not attend an event. (1)

> Apartheid is over. Constantly reminding people of it, won't solve a situation or take it away. (1)

In contrast to these responses of White participants, Black participants typically expressed a desire to know more and to set things right, and an eagerness to attend the cross-racial dialogue event:

> I like hearing all opinions and experiences. (9)

> We need to understand and listen to each other. (9)

> I would strongly like to know other people's experiences and learn from them. (9) I want to hear all sides and experiences. (9)

> In order for society to progress, individuals ought to engage in such conversations. (9)

One detects no counter ignorances in these statements by Black participants, which stands in contrast to the ignorances Black people developed during apartheid in order to maintain their mental health and manage their social condition within unequal power relations. There thus appears to be differences in how far the different racial groups have come in terms of reaching into the spaces of not-knowing created during apartheid. In particular, the 'Ignorance Contract' of apartheid seemingly continues to be recycled for White second-generation students (especially around issues of privilege).

A third potential explanation for the polarising effects observed in response to scenario 1, is that the events were set in the public discourse around race, and as such highlighted ideological differences between the different racial groups. This explanation is of course also connected to the previous two (i.e., group versus individual context and social identity threat) but may more specifically involve discrepancies around the different racial groups' perceptions of discriminatory or racist behaviour. For example, scenario 1 may represent an instance of institutional racism against Black people, which White people may actively resist (perhaps for the reasons presented above on privilege). When such a scenario presents itself, White people might therefore actively contest this narrative, resulting in aggressive or discriminatory behaviour. By comparison, scenario 2 might better be described as an instance of interpersonal racism, something that both racial groups recognise and perceive to be bad/wrong. These provocative explanations are speculative, however, and will need to be teased apart and tested by future research.

Final comments

The results of the present study confirmed the anticipated link between perspective taking and outgroup empathy. However, the social context (e.g., intergroup or interpersonal) and the nature of the outgroup (e.g., threatening or pitied) played a significant role in perspective taking and compassion responses. Notably, the results pointed to significant discrepancies in the social perspectives of Black and White participants, with potentially far-reaching consequences. Hence, understanding the circumstances under which people have high levels of ingroup identification (or experience salient ideological differences), is fundamentally important, because these circumstances influence their emotional responses (such as lack of empathy), which in turn predicts behaviour, including hostility and discrimination as well as prosocial behaviour.

16.
The Limits of Remorse: Internal and External Dynamics

Pumla Gobodo-Madikizela

Introduction

My interest in this discussion is two-fold. First, it is in trying to understand the dynamics of remorse: how it emerges, how it becomes manifest, what purpose it serves for the perpetrator, and what it means for the victim. I am interested in remorse when expressed in the context of major crimes that have led to destruction of lives. By showing remorse, the perpetrator is communicating acknowledgment of the crime and moral accountability to the victim. At the same time, however, because these crimes disturb the moral fabric of the communities within which they occur, a perpetrator's remorse also serves as an appeal to the wider community for the perpetrator to be readmitted into the world of moral humanity. The expression of remorse shows that the perpetrator acknowledges something they did not want to see when they were committing the crime, and they are facing and feeling the guilt and shame for their actions.[1]

My second interest, umbilically linked to the first question around remorse discussed above, is in two parts: (i) understanding the broader ramifications of the meaning of a perpetrator's remorse at the social and public level, and (ii) the question of what happens when, despite the victim's embrace of the remorse, it is rejected by others and hence its ratification at the wider societal level does not happen. The moral reflection that occurs with remorseful feeling can be quite painful, and because a perpetrator has to face the damage done and the fact of its irreparability daily, they need the affirmation of the wider community to "confirm" and validate their belonging and worthiness to be part of a moral community. The absence (or perception of absence) of such confirmation by the community which the perpetrator has joined may lead to an "undoing" – a shattering of the perpetrator's self-conception, a disintegration of the self. The risk of disintegration may be greater when the rejecting community benefited from the perpetrator's crimes, and at the time, participated in promoting the values and ideology that supported the crimes.

In this paper, I explore the dynamics of remorse and reflect on the broader ramifications of significant and notable expressions of remorse by perpetrators who

1 For elaboration of this point see Gobodo-Madikizela, P. *A human being died that night: A South African Story of forgiveness*. Houghton Mifflin, 2003.

appeared before the Truth and Reconciliation Commission (TRC) in the course of South Africa's coming to terms with its apartheid past. Eugene de Kock, the former commander of covert and death squad operations of the apartheid security police will be a central figure in this discussion, but other stories will also be used to illuminate specific points and dynamics of remorse. Before addressing this theme of remorse, I would like to clarify the perspective and assumptions that inform my analysis. The perspective I take is based on understanding remorse as a relational intersubjective phenomenon that opens up the possibility of transformative moments and a space for the production of ethical subjects in societies emerging from mass trauma and violence. Looking at remorse in the context of punishment and sentencing processes, where the question of the avoidance of the remedies of the law may be relevant, takes it out of its relational context and confines the debate to the role it serves for individual perpetrators. This often leads to a search for evidence of remorseful feeling in a way that shines the spotlight too narrowly on physical manifestations of a perpetrator's distress.

Characteristics of remorse

It is often assumed that when perpetrators exhibit overt and excessive dramatic bodily expressions when confronted with their crimes they are showing signs of remorse. An example of how the perception of an offender's physical distress as remorse influenced sentencing is the shooting murder of South African model Reeva Steenkamp by the much-celebrated former "Blade Runner" Olympian Oscar Pistorius. When a pathologist described the gunshot wounds on Steenkamp's body during Pistorius' trial in the High Court of South Africa, Gauteng Division, Pretoria, Pistorius broke down into sobs, retching and vomiting while seemingly trying to shut out the pathologist's voice by pressing his fingers into his ears. Justice Masipa, the presiding judge on this case, found that Pistorius was genuinely remorseful and that his remorse was a mitigating factor with regard to her sentencing decision.[2]

A similarly striking example is from Joshua Oppenheimer's film, *The Act of Killing* in which a group of elderly men who, when younger, operated as death squads during the 1965-1966 Indonesian "communist purge" re-enact murders that they committed with exceptional brutality. In a scene that has been interpreted as a show of remorse in some scholarly analyses of the film, one of the perpetrators, the self-confessed executioner Anwar Congo, is filmed on a rooftop at the site where he killed many of his victims by choking them with wire nooses. In the film, his body suddenly breaks into spasms. He is seen in the film bending over a trough dry heaving and making

2 Pistorius was convicted of culpable homicide and sentenced to five years imprisonment by Judge Mapisa (see her judgment in *State v Oscar Pistorius* [2014] CC113/2013). The conviction and sentence were appealed (see *Director of Public Prosecutions, Gauteng v Pistorius* [2015] 96/2015). The appeal was heard by the Supreme Court of Appeal, which overturned Mapisa's finding to murder, and replaced the sentence handed down with 13 years and five months.

seemingly uncontrollable retching sounds. Although questions have been raised about the authenticity of this scene, with some authors suggesting "the remorse might be … scripted"[3] and "seems staged,"[4] others have interpreted this performative act of revulsion as a sign of the death-squad leader's remorse. In the words of Janet Walker: "If we are not satisfied with Anwar's verbal expression of remorse, here is the somatic evidence."[5]

My own view on this is that it would be misleading to think that bodily reactions alone are a sign of remorse. It may well be that a perpetrator's remorse is made visible through embodied wrenching pain. But I wonder: is the experience depicted in Oppenheimer's film the perpetrator's remorseful confrontation with guilt for the murderous callousness of the crimes he committed? Or is it a case of the explosive eruption of shame in memory, the return of the perpetrator's voice of conscience – previously silenced – exploding into a feeling of self-disgust and a self-focused revulsion? In other words, rather than empathic resonance evoked in the perpetrator by the recognition of the human suffering caused by his murderous legacy, could this be a self-focused reaction that reflects a feeling of disgrace and a diminished sense of worth as a human being, rather than the concern for the suffering of his victims usually associated with remorse?

In my view, remorse emerges from a deep sense of guilt, recognition and acknowledgment that the perpetrator's actions led to the harm and suffering of the victim. In order to be meaningful, remorse should evoke feelings of concern for the victim enough to wish to make amends for the suffering that the perpetrator's actions caused. I call this "true" remorse (although there are different levels of "true-ness" in expressions of this kind of remorse, which I will not go into in this paper). Remorse occurs at an internal (intrapsychic and cognitive) level and it requires the following three characteristics.

First, an admission of wrongdoing without any excuse or justification. The perpetrator should not only face their guilt, but they should also *feel* their guilt. This is an important distinction, because a perpetrator can simply "face up" to what they have done but deny personal responsibility by rationalising their actions with justifications – "it was a war", or "I was obeying orders". It is as if the person were saying, "I give you what you want, full disclosure. Here is the list of evil deeds in which I participated under orders."

Second, acknowledgment of personal responsibility of the perpetrator's actions and recognition of the pain and suffering that these actions caused. I consider

3 Wijaya, E. "To see die, again: The Act of Filming and the The Act of Killing," *Parallax* 22, no. 1 (2016), pp. 91.

4 Cribb, R. "The act of killing." *Critical Asian Studies* 46, no. 1 (2014) pp. 148.

5 Walker, J. "Referred pain: The Act of Killing and the production of a crime scene." *Film Quarterly* 67, no. 2 (2013), p. 16.

acknowledgment – the knowledge that answers the question "what happened, who is responsible?" in a way that goes beyond simply dishing out facts – the most critical aspect of remorse.[6] Albie Sachs, retired Justice of the Constitutional Court of South Africa has emphasised this point about acknowledgement. Reflecting on perpetrator testimonies presented at South Africa's Truth and Reconciliation Commission, he argues that acknowledgement "presupposes a sense of responsibility for the occurrence, an understanding of the meaning that it has for the persons involved and for society as a whole."[7] An acknowledgement of wrongdoing that conveys a preparedness to take responsibility involves responding in a manner that implies care. This meaning of responsibility is clearly conveyed in the Xhosa phrase for "to take responsibility". The expression "*ukuthatha uxanduva*" or "*ukuthwala uxanduva*" (*to bear* responsibility for an act), both in its onomatopoetic sound and its actual meaning points to an obligation to "carry the burden" of moral responsibility and being obliged to respond to another's suffering. Used in this context, it denotes the capacity *to see* the other's pain and to care enough to *carry* the responsibility for the burden of the harm that the perpetrator's actions have imposed on the victim.[8] The repeated calls for acknowledgment by different groups of indigenous people and descendants of enslaved and oppressed people are a crying out for those implicated in violent histories to carry this burden of transgenerational pain and hurt inherited by the descendants of victims.

An important dimension of acknowledgement that should be made more explicit is the acknowledgement of the debt that perpetrators owe to their conscience – at least those who have a working conscience – which they repeatedly suppressed to a point that enabled them to commit gross human rights violations. The problem is not only the suppression of perpetrators' conscience. The circle of accountability extends to include communities that shared and supported the enabling ideology that made perpetrators' actions morally acceptable. Therefore, the acknowledgement of complicity by members of a society that benefited from perpetrators' crimes is as important as the community's validation of the perpetrator's remorse.

A third aspect of remorse that should be present is the *sense* – from the victim's standpoint – that the remorse signals a change of perspective in the perpetrator. When the victim experiences remorse as genuine, there is an expectation – a "promise" – that the deeds for which the perpetrator is remorseful will not occur again. Arendt has argued that this promise serves "to undo" historical crimes.[9] This is not to suggest that these crimes should become "undone" or obliterated from memory. Rather,

6 Gobodo-Madikizela, P. "Remorse, forgiveness, and rehumisation: Stories from South Africa." *Journal of humanistic psychology* 42, no. 1 (2002): 7-32.
7 Sachs, A. *The strange alchemy of life and law.* Oxford University Press, 2011, p. 79.
8 The image evoked by the word "*ukuthwala*" in the second Xhosa phrase is that of the subject sorrowfully and publicly carrying a heavy load on their head.
9 Arendt, H. *The human condition.* University of Chicago Press, 1998.

Arendt recognises that because of the irreparability of these crimes, the promise that they will not happen again is crucial and serves as a corrective that enables people to continue living and working together to build a new future. Ultimately, what makes remorse possible is the perpetrators' subject position of facing their guilt, being accountable and acknowledging personal responsibility for the crimes they committed – rather than the position of innocence "until proven guilty." The TRC's invitational stance and its promise of amnesty in the absence of a threat of punishment was facilitative and made it possible for some perpetrators to face and to admit guilt.

We found out, too, that not all perpetrators rose to the challenge of truth telling. For example, the apartheid-era politician Clive Derby-Lewis, who was responsible for the assassination of Chris Hani, the former head of the ANC military wing, invoked his Christian faith at his TRC public hearing as justification for the killing: "we as Christians are told that it is our duty to fight the anti-Christ in whichever way we can."[10] Derby-Lewis was using a Christian moral framework to recast murderous actions as "good" and legitimate. This justification of wrongdoing is common among perpetrators who avoid facing the truth about their past by hiding behind rationalisation. Accountability is inverted by simultaneously shifting blame away from the self in order to project it externally, often onto the victim or survivor: victims were killed because they were the anti-Christ. The strategy is deployed to efface the feeling of personal responsibility. Although this avoidance of guilt may occur consciously, underlying this narrative strategy is sometimes an unconscious failure to integrate aspects of the self that the person finds difficult to incorporate into consciousness. This compartmentalisation, expunging the "bad" aspects of the self while identifying with the "good" – for instance, as a Christian and eschewing the identity of murderer – is a manifestation of "splitting," a psychological state of mind mostly associated with the "object relations" psychoanalyst Melanie Klein[11] which seeks to conceal unwanted parts of the self from awareness. From a Kleinian perspective, this strategy is designed to protect the self from crushing under the weight of the darkness of the perpetrator's murderous past. Even when a window opens to acknowledge the crime, another may close, shutting out the rising tide of shame and guilt that threatens to engulf the subject. Remorse follows confrontation with the kind of guilt that seeks to repair the damage done, and it is unlikely to emerge under these conditions of splitting.

How can one tell when remorse is not "witness stand" remorse because, with no way out, the perpetrator wants and needs moral leniency? One set of questions – the how-can-we-know questions – has to do with verifiability. A second set has to do with the moral possibility itself – the psychological and epistemological possibility –

10 As cited in *TRC Final Report* 1998, 294.

11 Klein, M. *Love, Guilt and Reparation and Other Works 1921-1945*. Free Press, 2002.

of achieving authentic remorse in the wake of having performed "indescribable and undiscussable" crimes, to paraphrase Dan Bar-On.[12] Both sets of questions are real and both are legitimate. Yet it remains equally legitimate that when perpetrators do in fact express regret or guilt or contrition, however it may be ascertained, what seems to lie "beyond the purview of apology", as Nicholas Tavuchis[13] has put it, can in fact be transformed from an unforgivable deed, into a forgivable one. In this sense then, remorse transforms a perpetrator into a moral agent, because, in the first place, it lays bare the fact that the perpetrator transgressed accepted moral codes. In the second place, an expression of remorse demonstrates that the perpetrator is ready to embrace the values shared by the wider community and that they reaffirm acceptance of these values and show willingness to contribute to the rebuilding of a moral community. This demonstration by the perpetrator of acceptance of society's values is critical; it lays the ground for the wider community's validation of the perpetrator's remorse. The following section explores the dynamics of remorse and examines the interplay between internal (intrapsychic) and external (social context) factors. Using the South African TRC context as backdrop, I consider some of the factors that created an enabling environment for the emergence of remorse.

Dynamics of Remorse

In the preceding section, I discussed characteristic features of remorse and some of the strategies that may be used by perpetrators to eschew remorse. The following section of the paper deals with what is involved when remorse becomes manifest in victim-perpetrator encounters, in other words, the psychological (and intrapsychic) interacting factors between victim and perpetrator that lead to the expression of remorse. Before delving into these dynamics, however, I will discuss factors external to these dynamics – the social and political context that provided an enabling environment for the language of remorse to emerge. In this regard, I consider the values established through the TRC process and South Africa's interim Constitution to have played an important role in setting the tone for expressions of remorse.

External Dynamics: Ubuntu as Inspiration for Expression of Remorse

The TRC was founded on values and principles of respect for human dignity, values enshrined in the African ethic of *Ubuntu*, which I will describe in detail below. The post-amble of South Africa's Interim Constitution of 1993 was imbued with the conciliatory tone of the values of *Ubuntu*. In the section entitled "National Unity and Reconciliation", the Interim Constitution lays strong emphasis on the importance of *Ubuntu* as a framework for dealing with past violations of human rights. It implores South Africans to approach the past on the basis that there is a need for understanding

12 Bar-On, Dan. *The indescribable and the undiscussable: Reconstructing human discourse after trauma.* Central European University Press, 1999.

13 Tavuchis, N. *Mea culpa: A sociology of apology and reconciliation*. Stanford University Press, 1991, p. 21.

but not for vengeance, a need for reparation but not for retaliation, a need for *Ubuntu* but not for victimisation. To advance such reconciliation and reconstruction, amnesty shall be granted in respect of acts, omissions and offenses associated with political objectives and committed during the conflicts of the past.[14]

It is worth noting that the reference to the need to pursue the goals of the TRC with "understanding" and "*ubuntu*" suggests a particular orientation to the work of the TRC, one that is specific to the South African cultural context. The concept of *ubuntu* is an ethic based on the understanding that one's subjectivity is inextricably intertwined with that of others in one's community. From the perspective of *ubuntu*, all people are valued as part of the human community and worthy of being so recognised. This does not entail blind acceptance of others, no matter what they do. Rather, it is an orientation of openness to others and a reciprocal caring that fosters a sense of solidarity with one's community.

Evoking the ethic of *ubuntu* in the post-amble of the Interim Constitution pointed toward building a society in which people could come together and be fellow human beings sharing in the vision of a more humane society. Since its appearance in the post-amble of the Constitution, the application of *ubuntu* has gone beyond the function it served in the work of the TRC and influenced constitutional reasoning by South African judges with profound consequences. For instance, the decision to declare the death penalty unconstitutional in South Africa in a landmark Constitutional Court judgement was based on the elaboration by judges of the meaning of *ubuntu* as a constitutional value.[15] Among the judges who attribute to *ubuntu* a fundamental role in constitutional reasoning is Justice Albie Sachs. Justice Sachs has argued that *ubuntu* should not be invoked just "to add a gracious and affirmative gloss to a legal finding already arrived at":

It [*ubuntu*] is intrinsic to and constitutive of our constitutional culture. Historically it was foundational to the spirit of reconciliation and bridge building that enabled our deeply traumatised society to overcome and transcend the divisions of the past. In present day terms, it has an enduring and creative character, representing the element of human solidarity that binds together liberty and equality to create an affirmative and mutually supportive triad of central constitutional values.[16]

Justice Sachs argues further, rightly in my view, that an important value of *ubuntu* is its emphasis on repair, reconnection and a shift "from reparations taking the form of monetary compensation toward restoring the connection between people."[17] The TRC was an effort to imbue the realms of law, justice and politics with a relational cultural

14 South African Interim Constitution, 1993
15 S v Makwanyane and Mchunu, CCT/3/94. South Africa: Constitutional Court, 6 June 1995.
16 J Dikoko v Mokhatla CCT/62/05 para 113. South Africa: Constitutional Court, 3 August 2006 (see also Sachs 2011, 100)
17 Personal communication, May 2020.

ethics of *ubuntu*, which places emphasis on the value of a reparative process rather than one that may deepen divisions of the past and perpetuate the victimisation that characterised South African society under apartheid rule. There is a tendency for international legal institutions and among scholars of human rights to rely too narrowly on retribution as the only legitimate response to state-orchestrated violence to help countries transition to democratic rule. This approach has been inherited from the post-Nazi Germany Nuremberg trial model. One of the problems with trying individuals who have committed crimes under the explicit or implicit orders of their governments is that the law focuses strictly on the question of individual responsibility. All law does and must focus on individual responsibility because it is not possible to hold anything else responsible. Individuals must take the stand and be accused. But where the law fails in trying human rights violations is that it pays little or no attention to the question of structural and systemic crimes – the surrounding ideology/political philosophy, the setting up of enabling structures for perpetrators, and an administrative-executive system that protect their murderous operations.

Aligned with the prosecutorial values of the Nuremberg trials, the International Criminal Court and the United Nations Tribunals have been important judicial processes and a global accountability framework for countries that have not dealt effectively with past human rights abuses. However, their tendency to focus only on perpetrators from one side of past political conflict may disrupt the fragile unity that might be forged by two sides that were at war with each other. This could fuel the anger of one side, and of people who may feel that the law is "biased" against one group in the conflict, the oppressor group, when in fact, for whatever reasons it happened, there is often a record of human rights crimes committed by the oppressed group as well. The issue is not a simple one, for in recognising that both sides produced victims, one stands on shaky ground by seemingly applying the same moral standard to judge the actions of the oppressor and those of the group that was fighting to end such oppression.[18]

It is worth noting that it is not easy for perpetrators to rise to the level of extending a spirit of *ubuntu* to victims, despite the benefits of remorse that may facilitate their readmission into the community. Neither apology nor remorse were required for the granting of amnesty. Some perpetrators took this as a licence not to make any effort to reflect on, and fully to appreciate the consequences of their actions. Instead,

18 This problem played out in South Africa when Thabo Mbeki, the former president of South Africa, and at the time the deputy president, rejected the final report of the TRC when it was handed to Nelson Mandela in 1999 for the perception that the report equated the anti-apartheid struggle with the actions of apartheid operatives. The TRC made the finding that in its fight against apartheid, the ANC committed gross violations of human rights. The effect of this finding, Mbeki argued, was to "deligitimise (*sic*) or criminalise a significant part of the struggle of our people for liberation" and to detract from the TRC's mandate "to honour those who suffered for justice and freedom" (cited in Fullard and Rousseau 2008, 236)

they were more inclined to repudiate whatever feelings of guilt that listening to victims' testimonies may have evoked. In some cases, their lawyers were to blame for this, perhaps because they were more familiar with the adversarial approach than a conciliatory stance that required meaningful (rather than superficial) expressions of apology. Thus, there were moments when some of us on the TRC, frustrated by the lack of signs of even the slightest show of regret and aware of the potential dangers that such attitudes posed for retraumatisation of victims, broke the rules (so to speak), and appealed directly to perpetrators to show better versions of themselves.

We challenged them in different ways to respond to the generosity shown by the TRC process and by victims and to demonstrate a spirit of *ubuntu*. This is what Archbishop Tutu's message to Winnie Madikizela-Mandela conveyed when he famously asked her during her testimony to admit that "things went wrong" and to apologise for the actions of the men who acted as her bodyguards, the Mandela United Football Club.[19] A less-known example will suffice to illustrate this kind of intervention to appeal to perpetrators to respond according to the values that the TRC process represented. The example is from a Special Hearing of the "Bisho Massacre". Bisho was the capital of one of the apartheid-era nominally independent homelands, the Ciskei, which at the time of the massacre was under the rule of Brigadier Oupa Gqozo. The massacre occurred in September 1992 when the Ciskei army opened fire on an estimated 80,000 ANC supporters who had marched into Bisho to demand free democratic action in the Ciskei during the political transition period. The example that follows is an excerpt from the testimony of Brigadier Gqozo:[20]

> **DR RAMASHALA** (TRC Commissioner): Brigadier may I ask you to just cast your eyes to the second, third and fourth rows, just scan ... second, third and fourth rows. These are either victims, survivors or their families, do you recognise any of them?
>
> **BRIGADIER GQOZO:** No.
>
> **DR RAMASHALA:** I asked you to scan the second, third and fourth row because that is just a small sample of the after-effects, the after-effects of the massacre. This document [copy of his amnesty application] presents some political positions – I asked you to scan because what you see as a sample of the aftermath cannot in any way be represented in this document. I ask you again Brigadier ... is there anything you want to tell this small sample population of people sitting on the second, third and fourth row? You don't have to because you see, I ask you to speak from the

19 See the transcript of the TRC Special Hearing of the "Mandela United Football Club" on their violent actions and their role especially in the murder of 14-year-old anti-apartheid activist Moeketsi "Stompie" Seipei in 1989: https://sabctrc.saha.org.za/documents/special/mandela/56342.htm

20 TRC Special Hearing of the "Bisho Massacre", Day 2, 1996.

> heart and that is why I asked counsel not to interfere because this is not a legal question. I ask you again because this is your opportunity Brigadier. Reconciliation with your people does not depend on how articulate you are today... And so, I appeal to you to speak from the heart and look at the people sitting on the second, third and fourth row. Thank you, Chairperson. Asking perpetrators to "speak from the heart" gives them permission, in effect, to abandon the protective barriers usually associated with adversarial court proceedings. It is asking them to speak from a position of emotional responsiveness and to face their responsibility as a reparative act of "moral repair."[21] Inviting perpetrators to engage with the "heart truth" allows them to thaw out what moral sensibilities they have buried under a seared conscience, and to face what they have done in public in the presence of the families whose lives they shattered. We knew that if victims saw signs of a change of heart in perpetrators, this would go a long way to address their psychological need for acknowledgment. Victims appeared before the TRC not only to experience the facticity of perpetrators' accounts. "Truth" can only go so far in providing some measure of repair of victims' deep emotional scars. What victims want, in addition to the facts about what happened to their loved ones, is to witness in the testimonies of perpetrators what Nichols and Connolly in their elaboration of the meaning of the concept of reparation refer to as "reparative morality."[22]

The public also had to be prepared for a new ethos that the TRC was introducing into South Africa's post-apartheid public discourse. To this end, I organised a "Public Dialogue on Reconciliation" on the sidelines of the TRC to extend the broader goals of the TRC, and to try to bring into public awareness the articulation of the values and principles that guided the TRC's work. The main speaker at this event was Cynthia Ngewu, one of the mothers whose sons were lured into a trap and ambushed by apartheid security police. Following her encounter with one of the black police officers involved in the killing at a TRC public hearing, Mrs. Ngewu had reached out with forgiveness to him. At the public dialogue event, she spoke about the importance of giving perpetrators an opportunity to be rehabilitated. All South Africans should be committed to "re-accepting" perpetrators back to their communities as part of nation-building, she said, and perpetrators should be shown compassion "so that they

---

21 Walker, M. U. *Moral Repair: Reconstructing Moral Relations after Wrongdoing*. Cambridge University, 2006.

22 Nichols, B. K. and Connolly, M.L. 2019. "Transforming Ghosts into Ancestors: Unsilencing the Psychological Case for Reparations to Descendants of American Slavery," htt://static1.squarespace.com/static/50ff32e1e4b06718f08016a/t/5d262a2beb582b00011b00af7/1562782252202/Reparations+-+Nichols+and+Connolly.pdf

in turn may restore their own humanity."[23] This expectation of reciprocal mutual recognition, acting in a way that does not foreclose the human flourishing of the other, is consistent with the African value of *ubuntu*.

Internal Dynamics of Remorse

Remorse has been associated with feelings of guilt; both guilt and shame affect the remorseful subject. With few exceptions[24] very rarely do these discussions explain the psychological and intrapsychic dynamics of remorse. Earlier in the paper, I explained how the psychological defence mechanism of splitting comes into play to aid perpetrators in their denial of guilt and efforts to justify wrongdoing. Splitting is an intrapsychic mechanism by which contradictory aspects of the self (and the other), thoughts, or feelings are kept apart. The defence mechanism is mobilised to protect the individual from internal destructiveness, threats of annihilation and disintegration. Splitting is more than simply rendering separate the disparate parts of self and other. It is holding on to – and through introjection strongly identifying with – the good features of the narrative about the self while splitting off and projecting the unwanted anxiety-provoking parts of the self into an "Other": a person (or object). This Other is in turn felt to be "dangerous and especially threatening" to the good aspects of the self.[25]

Perpetrators' actions are imbued with elements that diminish their moral and ethical obligations toward the victims. Splitting makes this possible by diminishing the victim's standing as a human being in the mind of the perpetrator. This allows perpetrators to perform their murderous deeds without flinching. Robert Lifton made a similar observation in his study of Nazi doctors and advanced the concept of "doubling," which he described as a mechanism by which one part of the self "disavows" the other.[26] "What is repudiated is not reality," he argued, "but the meaning of that reality"[27] Nazi doctors knew that they were participating in the policy of "selections" of Jews for the gas chambers. But they did not interpret selections as murder. In order for the Nazi "medical" experiment to be successful, doctors in Auschwitz had to relate to their environment as if it were some kind of fantasy and not part of the real world. Eugene de Kock, who became infamous as the apartheid government's chief assassin captured this sense of construction of the surreal in one of the interviews, I had with him thus:

---

23 Ngewu, C. *Truth and Reconciliation Commission Final Report*, Volume 5, 1998. Cape Town: The Commission, p. 366.
24 See for example Brooks and Reddon 2003
25 Bateman, A and Holmes, J. *Introduction to psychoanalysis: Contemporary theory and practice*. Psychology Press, 1995, p. 39.
26 Lifton, R.J. *The Nazi Doctors: Medical Killing and the Psychology of Genocide*. Basic Books, 1986.
27 Ibid. p. 422.

> In that second or two seconds, you sometimes see the other person's face. I can see some of the faces today still, the shock, the fear, the desperation, the look of: this is it! ... no, you see the people. It's real. I mean, this person is alive, you can see the fear – but you are on automatic because your training takes over. You don't allow yourself to think of the faces you see.[28]

The question of whether splitting operates to an extent that allows perpetrators not to *see* the faces of victims has been remarked upon by other scholars who have interviewed perpetrators. Both Dan Bar-On[29] and Gitta Sereny[30] give us to understand that in cases of absolute dehumanisation of victims, perpetrators do not recognise the victims' subjectivity and fail to see them as human others. Consequently, they often do not remember any of the faces of their victims in their human form. For example, when Sereny interviewed Franz Stangl, an SS Nazi commander in Auschwitz, he could not remember any of the faces of his victims. The following account from Eugene de Kock's encounter with the daughter of one of his victims provides a striking contrast with Sereny's findings.

Marcia Khoza was five years old when her mother, Portia Shabangu was murdered by de Kock in 1985. On the 23rd anniversary of her mother's death, she decided to visit de Kock in prison to ask him questions about the killing and about her mother's final moments. She related a moment in her encounter with de Kock when he was overcome by the recognition of her likeness with her mother. Khoza explained that when she waited for de Kock to be brought out from the prison cells to the visitors' area, she sat at a strategic position that would allow her to watch de Kock when he walked in to meet her. When their eyes met, de Kock tripped and had to catch his balance as he walked toward Khoza. "You look so much like your mother", de Kock said as he greeted her. He could still see some of the faces of the victims of his murderous operations and the faces haunt him "day and night" – he had told me when I interviewed him more than twenty years before this incident with the daughter of one of his victims. He was not able completely to obliterate the human face of his victims who are now a living memory of human beings whose lives were snuffed out by his actions.

De Kock's experiences recounted here offer a marked difference from Sereny's findings and raise the question whether there are "degrees" of splitting and dehumanisation of victims. What seems clear – and according to Kleinian psychoanalytic thought – is that confrontation with guilt in a way that evokes concern for the victim is the first step on the path toward feelings of remorse. Acknowledgement and remorseful

---

28 Interview with Eugene de Kock, February 1998. Also see Pumla Gobodo-Madikizela, (2003). *A Human Being Died that Night: A South African Story of Forgiveness.*

29 Bar-On, Dan 1999.

30 Sereny, G. *Into the darkness: An examination of conscience.* Vintage. 2011.

apology stem from this "reparative guilt", a wish for the "repair" of the pain and suffering for which the perpetrator is responsible.

Concern for the victim's pain and suffering, I wish to argue, is made possible by a combination of the following factors: a working (but suppressed) conscience; a degree of critical moral reflection during the perpetration of murderous acts; and/or the fact that the disavowed parts of the self, though split off and projected outward, still remain unconsciously connected to the self. In the latter case, the unconscious link that connects the self to the very material that it is trying to rid itself of becomes the source of what Klein refers to as "persecutory anxiety"[31] – a "persecutory" fear of attack by the object which now carries the projected bad aspects of the self. Klein argued that the process of undoing this labyrinth of conflicting emotions of anxieties, phantasies of persecution and defences requires "making reparations" in order to repair – to "make good" – the damage inflicted on the object. Thus, as scholars whose work seeks to illuminate the relevance of Kleinian theory in social-political life have argued, the Kleinian notion of reparations is a template for the development of moral sensibilities. It offers a useful framework for understanding the capacity for the production of ethical subjects, a process that Fred Alford has referred to as the transformation of the "ugly passions"[32] of human nature into love and concern for the human dignity of others. In this sense then, reparative guilt is a manifestation of a mature type of guilt where the individual faces and at once acknowledges that actions that in the past were a source of pride have now become "sources of shame and loathing."[33]

My understanding of the drama that plays out in "persecutory anxiety" is that when splitting does not hold steady, when the attempt to obliterate the humanness of victims falters, to make it work requires constant internal justification and reinforcement through one's behaviour and other external forces, such as encouragement by one's community, which help to sustain the disavowal of reality. However, sometimes the intersectionality of the "bite of conscience" – to appropriate a Freudian expression – and the simultaneous unconscious confrontation with guilt, the disavowal of this guilt through projection, rationalisations and justification of the violence may overwhelm and create chaos in the perpetrator's internal world, leading to a breakdown of the mechanism of splitting. Evidence that splitting may not have been successful can be found in a range of symbolic expressions. The example of Eugene de Kock taking several showers after one of his killing operations to cleanse himself of the "smell of blood" that refused to be washed off is a single, but striking example of this

31 Klein, M. Notes on Some Schizoid Mechanisms. *Journal of Psychotherapy Practice and Research*, 5, no. 2 (1996), p. 167.
32 Alford, F. "Reason and reparation." *Theory and Society* 19, no. 1 (1990), p. 42.
33 Weisman, R. *Showing Remorse: Law and the Social Control of Emotion*. Ashgate, (2014), p. 127.

phenomenon of persecutory anxiety or the return of the bite of conscience.[34] It does not always lead to remorse, and as I will show later, the aggressive confrontation with the perpetrator's own projections may lead to disintegration of the self. The fact that the unfolding of this state of mind (and heart) leads to remorse may be attributed to an enabling environment already discussed earlier. This includes the invitational, rather than adversarial, stance of the TRC, the acceptance of the remorse by the victim, the presence of a "holding" community that validates the perpetrator's remorse, granting the perpetrator's re-entry and a chance to be rehabilitated.

Splitting prevents perpetrators from acknowledging their crimes, foreclosing the possibility of reparative guilt. From a Kleinian psychoanalytic perspective, the reparative or restorative drive is fundamental to understanding the development of empathy, care and concern for the other in human relationships. It seems to me therefore, that the intrapsychic dramas that lead to remorse extend beyond the perpetrator's unconscious to engage intersubjectively with the victim. For in order for empathy to take root, the subject must *be inspired* to step into the shoes of the other, in this case, the dehumanised Other, and to identify with them and to respond to their expression of pain. The conflicting emotions associated with splitting in the perpetrator are therefore "in conversation" with the victim's own emotions and other dynamics at both an unconscious level and at the level of the visible and external aspects of the intersubjective communication. Evidence for this "communication" between victim and perpetrator is borne out by the cumulative, subtle and ever so imperceptible transformational moments that move the perpetrator to remorse and the victim to respond with acceptance and forgiveness. This complex intersubjective process finds resonance with psychoanalyst Alfred Bion's views that expand the Kleinian notion of projection.[35,36] Bion saw projection not simply as a question of splitting off unwanted aspects of the self to an Other. Rather, he understood it to be a process that involves a kind of communication between two internal worlds in the intersubjective relationship – and I think this includes nuances of responses and the external aspects of the communication (for example tearfulness, a look of sadness), some of which may be so subtle as to be unremarkable. These dynamics enable a reflexive capacity on both sides – the enactment of remorse by the perpetrator, and a response of receiving and holding the remorse by the victim, which sometimes manifests in forgiveness. As I understand it, the remark by the daughter of one of de Kock's victims cited at the beginning of this paper – "you can't understand ... I can't explain it" – captures the consequences of this underlying subtlety of

34 See Gobodo-Madikizela, 2003
35 Bion, W. R. *Learning from Experience*. Routledge, 1984.
36 Bion, W.R. *Brazilian Lectures: 1973, Sao Paulo; 1974, Rio de Janeiro/Sao Paulo*. Routledge, 2018.

the communication between victim and perpetrator.[37] At the same time, this also suggests some congruence between the perpetrator's remorseful feelings as a sign of "atonement" and emotions that this evokes in the victim – the remorse *resonates* in a way that speaks to the victim's pain.

The Rupture of Remorse and the Impossibility of Repair

As I pointed out earlier, when perpetrators commit atrocities, they do not only dehumanise the victim; they first have to dehumanise the self, that is, they have to silence the voice of conscience in order to break the human bond between themselves and their victims, a point cogently made by Pogany-Wnendt in his discussion of the perpetrator's "self-dehumanisation."[38] Sometimes the dehumanisation was so extreme and the acts committed by the perpetrator were simply beyond what any human being could imagine. When it came down to it, some of the acts described by perpetrators at the TRC were beyond what they themselves could understand, at least for those who were able to take a step back and reflect on the destruction that they caused, standing at a critical distance from the demands of the destructive life they had led. When perpetrators have gone "too far" to the depths of depravity, coming up to rejoin the human community is challenging for them because when in their experience of remorse, they are no longer protected by the psychological defence of splitting, they have to face what they did. I think that perpetrators' need for the embrace of their remorse by the victims and others in the broader community is stronger when the crimes they committed are so cruel, so egregious that they are crimes that are not only against direct victims, but crimes that, according to Justice Richard Goldstone's characterisation, are "against all humanity."[39] Without this "holding" response by victims and the community, perpetrators can be thrown back into a cage of loneliness where they have to face the bodies and blood and the destruction that they caused alone.

I want to suggest that the going too far by a perpetrator who has dehumanised the self in their murderous deeds begins with such a perversion of morality that the perpetrator loses all barriers that serve to shield human beings from the shame of descending into a vortex of cruelty. When a perpetrator plunges into these depths of

37 A dramatic example from a United States courtroom illustrates this point. Delivering his victim impact statement in an American court, the brother of Botham Jean, an African American man shot and killed by a white police officer who thought he was an intruder in her apartment, expressed forgiveness for the police officer. He asked the court's permission to embrace her: "I don't know if this is possible, but can I give her a hug, please?" This gesture was highly criticised and sparked an acrimonious debate about forgiveness. (https://www.washingtonpost.com/nation/2019/10/03/judge-botham-jeans-brother-hugged-amber-guyger-igniting-debate-about-forgiveness-race/)

38 Pogany-Wnendt, P. 2019. Der Wert der menschlichkeit: Psychologische perspektiven für eine humanisierung der Gesellschaft. Psychosozial.

39 Quoted in King Jr, H.T. "*The legacy of Nuremberg,*" Case W. Res. J. Int'l L. 34 (2002), p. 349.

depravity, they may have reached a point of no return, a fundamental limit on the capacity of the self to be fully restored as the perpetrator tries to come out of this abysmal pit. For instance, a perpetrator may express remorse, but because remorse requires confronting the evildoer self, the remorse may force the perpetrator to face, and to own the aspects of the self that were denied and projected outward. But this may be too much to bear; a limit beyond which one is unable to face the self and to identify with these previously expunged bad elements has been reached, and the perpetrator cannot reconcile with that darkness. The consequence is not being able to connect to any sense of oneself as a human being among others. This tragedy confronted Eugene de Kock.

What I want to do here, albeit schematically for the sake of brevity, is to try to explain what I mean about this notion of "the rupture of remorse." If we understand that the dehumanisation of the other and of the self are situated within the Kleinian position of splitting, we can understand how the opposite position of the integration of the split off parts unfolds and develops into remorse when the perpetrator confronts their guilt and shame for the harm they caused. In this case, there is a deeper awareness of the wounds the perpetrator has caused; this enables the perpetrator to face the reality that their actions are responsible for the victim's pain and loss (the acknowledgement to the self). It is an acknowledgment that potentially bears responsibility and the capacity to enter the pain of the other and face the consequences of one's destructive actions – the perpetrator's reparative quest, which communicates compassion and care. As pointed out in earlier sections of this paper, the paradox of remorse[40] is that in order for remorse to be sustained, it requires "holding" by both the victim and the perpetrator's wider community to help with the transition toward the work of repair. The work of reparation that seeks to make amends for the damage done to the object (the victim), however, requires deep identification not just with the object upon whom pain and suffering was inflicted. It also requires reconnection with all the emotions and actions associated with the deed, which were split off, expunged, projected outward and disowned. This involves reclaiming the destructive part of the self – yes, the murderous "evil" history of one's actions – and integration of this into the core of the perpetrator's identity. The dismembered bodies, the violent actions that destroyed countless lives, the screams of tortured victims – all these are hauntings from real events that the perpetrator has to face, the gruesome trail of their past that has to be integrated into the self. But when the perpetrator's remorse does not have the support of the community on whose behalf the murderous crimes were committed, the self crumbles precisely because of an inescapable reality: the perpetrator *is* the split off parts of the self. No longer in the heady climate of the period of mayhem but in the sobering atmosphere of facing shattered human lives, the perpetrator is now alone without the community's support. The reference point

40 See Gobodo-Madikizela 2002.

for defining the self as part of the community that shared the belief in the moral appropriateness of the crimes crumbles. It is a reality too much to bear.

More than the victim's embrace of the remorse, perpetrators need the affirmation of the wider community to validate their worthiness to be part of the wider human community (their crimes were "against all humanity"). The same process by which the perpetrator is accepted as a member of a moral community, however, "is also the process by which membership is barred."[41] In this section, I am interested in the rejection of the perpetrator's remorse by the community that previously encouraged, supported, and benefitted from the perpetrator's actions. I return therefore to the story of Eugene de Kock and the rejection of his remorse by white South Africans. De Kock, and many other apartheid's henchmen who appeared at the TRC have said repeatedly that what kept them going – what sustained their zeal and conviction in the moral rightness of their murderous actions – was the tacit but powerful support they felt they were receiving from the beneficiaries of apartheid privilege: the polite churchgoers, the cultured suburbanites, the voters. It is at their feet that the moral responsibility for apartheid, ultimately, can be laid. When Eugene de Kock attended one of South Africa's premier book events in the Western Cape, the Franchhoek Literary Book Fair, shortly after he was released from prison on parole, he was barred from participating in this event by the mostly white audience and was thrown out of the venue. The incident evoked a public debate that was divided between those who expressed moral indignation at de Kock's presence at the book event, and those who scoffed at this reaction.[42] This incident had a major impact on de Kock, and he was hospitalised a few weeks later, spending several months in psychiatric care.

De Kock's experience and the experiences of other perpetrators I have interviewed led me to think about remorse as a blessing and a curse. For without the embrace by the wider community, remorseful perpetrators are likely to suffer disintegration and may be thrown back into the darkness of the abyss they had fallen into with a trail of their murderous actions. This is not because the perpetrator cannot face the guilt, but rather that the remorse is felt too deeply, and facing their shame alone may be too much to bear without the acknowledgement and support of their community. Let me share two examples of perpetrators' stories to show different responses with similar underlying dynamics of perpetrators' struggle with the magnitude of their deeds. The first story concerns the experience of one of the men who was granted amnesty

41 See Weisman, R. 2014, p. 127.

42 Among those critical of this public expression of outrage is an opinion piece by Palesa Morudu, whose family was assisted by de Kock with information about how her anti-apartheid activist brother "disappeared": "He was their [white South Africans'] foot soldier," wrote Morudu in the *Daily Maverick*. "He took the proverbial bullet. Apartheid was prime evil; De Kock was simply its loyal servant. You can't be morally outraged by De Kock and not be morally outraged by De Klerk [apartheid government's last president], or the devastation apartheid brought to black South Africans". Morudu P., *Daily Maverick*, 16 May 2016.

by the TRC for the 1993 murder in Cape Town of the Stanford University Fulbright Scholar Amy Biehl.[43] Peter and Linda Biehl, Amy Biehl's parents, fully supported the TRC's granting of amnesty to their daughter's killers. When the men were released from prison after their successful amnesty applications, two of them were offered employment at the Amy Biehl Foundation, which the Biehls had established in Cape Town. One of the men left the Foundation for a brief period and joined his former comrades who were involved in cash heists and car hijacking. He returned to the Foundation after Linda Biehl sought him out and encouraged him to rejoin the Foundation.[44] Interviewing him as a guest in my Masters class at the University of Cape Town, he explained that he left the Foundation because he could no longer cope with the kindness of Amy Biehl's mother. But why would he return to a life of violence, I asked? His reply was that in joining his former comrades and the life of their collective involvement in crime, "I did not have to think."

The second example, which I will present briefly to highlight some of the key points of my argument, is from a report of the failure of a restorative justice process in the American criminal justice system.[45] The report tells the story of a family that participated in a victim-offender dialogue process in search of healing and "closure" following the murder in 2017 of a 62-year-old woman, Deborah Liles of Jacksonville, Florida. Her killer, 24-year-old Adam Lawson Jr. was due to meet the Liles family for the restorative justice process, apparently, until a letter from one of the Liles' sons offering him forgiveness was read to him. As the family waited in a separate room for the process to begin, the prosecutor on the case told them that the young man was refusing to meet with them. His response is described in the report thus: "Lawson's head was in his hands, his legs shaking. Then he started murmuring. 'I can't, I can't, I can't. After what I've taken from them? I can't ...'"[46]

It would hardly be an exaggeration to say that forgiveness by victims is what remorseful perpetrators desire the most. Yet in this case, forgiveness evoked an "unimaginable" amount of guilt for Adam Lawson Jr., and listening to the forgiving words of the son of his victim transformed him into a "pitiful" state that rendered him "completely nonverbal ... like he's still a little child," according to the prosecutor in Hager's paper.[47] If we understand the reparative quest that leads to remorse to involve facing one's deeds and the horror of their destructive consequences in the lives of victims and their descendants and reintegrating what was projected outward

43 For a comprehensive background on the story of Amy Biehl in South Africa see Gish, S.D. *Amy Biehl's Last Home: Bright Life, a Tragic Death, and a Journey of Reconciliation in South Africa*. Ohio University Press, 2018.

44 In my book, *A Human Being Died that Night*, I explore forgiveness and consider what it means for victims' families actively to support the rehabilitation of perpetrators who were responsible for their loss.

45 Hager, E. (July 21, 2020) The Limits of Restorative Justice in Jacksonville. *The Atlantic*, July 21, 2020.

46 Ibid.

47 Ibid.

back into the self, reestablishing one's identity as belonging to a moral community is a crucial phase in this process. Forgiveness by the victim also has an important role to play in helping the perpetrator's feeling of acceptance and belonging to one's community. In the two stories above, however, neither community acceptance nor forgiveness served their universally acknowledged respective purposes.

In the first story, the man who could not cope with the kindness he encountered from Linda Biehl whose daughter he murdered seems to have needed something more than forgiveness. By seeking out her daughter's killer and encouraging him to return, Linda Biehl went out of her way to demonstrate her preparedness to carry some of the burden of his anxiety about what was coming back at him to haunt him. I believe it can be argued that in both examples the reparative quest was under threat of being doomed precisely because of the anxiety brought about by confrontation with the consequences of the perpetrator's deeds. Facing daily the realisation of the impossibility of repair – repair of the rupture of the self, the violence done to the Other and to the relationship with one's community – is another layer of experience that may evoke debilitating anxiety. This convergence of factors inhibits not only the possibility of meaningful reflection, but also of constructive interaction with the victim. This is manifested, for example, by the avoidance of a face-to-face-encounter with the family members of the victim in both stories, further articulated as an escape from "thinking" in the first example. Thoughtlessness is a problem that has been observed repeatedly in systematic crimes against humanity.[48] It is another form of defence, a way of shutting out the voice of conscience. As I have argued elsewhere[49,50] ironically, ultimately the burden may fall on the victim to absorb these impossible consequences, and this, in my view, is what the response by Linda Biehl demonstrates. Far from being an unnerving proposition and a burdensome act of moral sacrifice, this may be deeply therapeutic and restorative for some victims. The psychological compulsion that makes us identify with and want to "rescue" others in severe psychic pain – even someone who has denied us humanity – and responding to their wish for affirmation and to be rehumanised, are two powerful sets of emotional dynamics that drive many victims toward sowing seeds of hope for the sake of the rehabilitation of offenders. Victims' motivation is to enter into constructive encounters with perpetrators, even when their internal moral compass points toward its inappropriateness and the offender seems morally undeserving.

48 This calls to mind the argument put forward by Hannah Arendt concerning the Nazi perpetrator Adolf Eichmann: "It was sheer thoughtlessness ... that predisposed him to become one of the greatest criminals of that period. ... That such ... thoughtlessness can wreak more havoc than all the evil instincts taken together ... was the lesson one could learn in Jerusalem. (Arendt, H. 1994. *Eichmann in Jerusalem: A report on the banality of evil.*)

49 See Gobodo-Madikizela 2002.

50 See Gobodo-Madikizela 2003.

Conclusion

Bringing victims and perpetrators to a space of dialogue, as truth commissions and other restorative justice processes do, creates the possibility of setting the perpetrator's actions, through testimony and witnessing, in the broader framework of the political-ideological context that may have supported and even directed their deeds. It is this component of the crime, the one that resides at the systemic, institutional, and policy levels rather than at a personal level, that is notoriously difficult to substantiate within the strict evidentiary rules of a purely legal process. All this goes to show that the politics of abuse that were enshrined in the policies of an oppressive system can be acknowledged and confirmed in ways that the more rigid, adversarial relationship of courtroom exchanges cannot. Remorse is more likely to emerge in this kind of environment. Facing the past – acknowledgement of past wrongs by perpetrators, bystanders, and beneficiaries alike – is the touchstone of reconciliation. A problem that is often debated nowadays, but which has not received adequate scholarly attention, is the denial of accountability by groups that have supported and benefitted from oppressive regimes. This issue is of crucial relevance in our discussion of remorse and its significance for reconciliation if we accept the importance of the role that communities play in the rehabilitation of remorseful offenders. Some people see remorse as a masquerade for impunity. When remorse emerges as part of reckoning with a violent and oppressive past, it is an important outcome of the shift from an exclusive focus on prosecutions and allows the flourishing of a profoundly new politics of engagement with the past, not to rekindle old hatreds, but rather to face the past and to learn from it.

Part V:
Perspectives from Rwanda Community Researchers

17. Round Table: Perspectives from Rwanda Community Researchers

Three community researchers affiliated with the organization Community-based Sociotherapy, share a wide range of insights from the field in their work in Rwanda. The discussion was framed around three questions that sought to illuminate what living together means for Rwandans. The diverse group of Round Table panelists Angela Jansen, Grace Kagoyire, and Samantha Lakin are from the Netherlands, Rwanda, and the United States respectively. Each of their responses reflects this diversity in the encounters they have had in the Rwanda communities.

1. As a researcher working with communities in Rwanda, what has been your experience of how communities in Rwanda deal with the ever-present difficult issues of the memory of the genocide, and the reality of victims and perpetrator families living together as neighbours?

Angela Jansen

Some months ago, there was a representative of the Dutch Ministry of Foreign Affairs asking me: 'Angela, you work here in Rwanda now for a couple of years, if you have to rate the level of reconciliation between 1 to 10, what rating would you give it?' I think this question reflects a fundamental error that is often made. What I observed from my research and work in sociotherapy, is that the process of reconciliation and forgiveness is being facilitated by the national/policy level, but it is experienced at individual/family and community level. And it is at these latter levels where the experiences greatly differ. So, rating reconciliation will be impossible. What is obvious to me is that still many Rwandans are struggling with the process of living together again. If this would not have been the case, it would be quite difficult to understand from my point of view, because the cruelties people experienced and committed in 1994 are beyond what one can imagine. However, Rwanda has a quite unique trait, which is the willingness to continue to build and maintain a peaceful society. This desire seems to be so powerful that many people have been able to find a way to deal with the struggle.

Grace Kagoyire

As a local researcher, my response will address how communities in Rwanda deal with the ever-present difficult issues of the memory of the genocide. I will try to compare four categories of people: those (people) who went through the sociotherapy programme and those who did not and the current situation among adults versus young generation with the focus on the youth who did not go through the traumatic events.

As you all know, we shall start the genocide commemoration period tomorrow. The government offers one week of mourning, but genocide survivors still have 100 days to go through because the genocide lasted one hundred days. It was stopped at the end of July. So, when you enter communities during this period (the commemoration) you may observe different kind of behaviours among different categories of Rwandans because this is a time of mourning and commemorating. Giving some examples, one may find genocide survivors being ready and happy to join commemoration activities though some may face trauma crisis.

When you look at the genocide perpetrators some isolate themselves. However, this isolation can happen to genocide perpetrators' families too. They may lock themselves inside their rooms, isolate and cry being alone. But these experiences are observed most of the time at the individual level. It depends on which kind of support people benefitted from since after the traumatic event. For instance, genocide perpetrators who testified and repented about their wrongdoings during gaçaça courts are not like those who did not yet, because those who did not yet repent are still suspected by their communities as perpetrators. Genocide survivors who buried theirs killed during the genocide are not like their counterparts who did not bury the bodies of their loved ones. It is somehow challenging, but it is also good for some to face the event. Out of the commemoration period, you may think nothing happened. Community life seems to be normal. People may talk to each other. They can dare to meet, while in the commemoration periods some perpetrators may hide themselves and survivors isolate.

The life outside the commemoration, such as relationships between people, depends on who wronged who, how things went during the genocide and how relationships have been re-established or not. This means that though you may find many trauma cases during the mourning and commemoration period, it is difficult to say these people are traumatised or not or they are not still having those historical scars especially during other months of the year. People keep those experiences and try to show that they want to move on, that they don't have to cry.

While looking at graduates of sociotherapy intervention, one may observe other differences. We do qualitative and quantitative research. When you meet people for instance during the pre-intervention study which is conducted before people start their socio-sessions or during their first weeks of joining the programme, you can notice that some people are not free to talk. Some cry when you start asking questions listed in the questionnaire. But it is also difficult for them at that stage, to open up and go deeper and explain why they are showing such emotions. Throughout or after going through the programme, we start observing that people distance themselves from their own individual experiences and history. Most of them keep being strong when they are talking about their past experiences, something that you cannot hope for before they enter sociotherapy. When they graduate, you can find that they are no longer guided by their strong emotions, but they are able to manage those emotions.

Regarding age, in the local communities, it is perceived as if adults are allowed to deal with the past, to show their suffering and they are allowed to be supported while this is not the case for the young people. It seems adults who were in Rwanda, especially genocide survivors, are the only category allowed to revive or experience their trauma of the past. The communities seem not to understand why young children should. This can be explained by the next example: It happens that during the commemoration some young adults may also experience trauma crisis. But it seems they are not allowed to experience that. In the past few years, some young adults born after the genocide, and descending from our respondents composed of women survivors of genocidal rape, showed trauma symptoms. These were similar to the common symptoms adults are likely to show while suffering from trauma crisis (post-traumatic stress disorders) such as numbing, reviving the traumatic events, etc; and these symptoms among the youth resulted (mainly) from what those youths imagined after observing their mothers' suffering during the commemoration. Instead of assisting their children then, their mothers beat them saying 'you should not play such games because you don't know what it is about, you don't know what it is. Why are you imitating things you don't know?' To me this shows that these women feel that these youths don't have that right of suffering due to the past history. From my point of view, there is a lack of understanding how youths who did not go through the traumatic events connect to the past of their country. This issue of withdrawing the youth from the past history can also be observed between families of survivors and non-survivors.

Some people think survivors are the only parts of the population allowed to show suffering as if ex-perpetrators and their family members are not, as we shared above.

Samantha Lakin

As a PhD candidate researching memory and transitional justice in the aftermath of genocide in Rwanda, my experience understanding how communities in Rwanda deal with difficult issues of genocide memory and living together in its aftermath present a number of key debates and conclusions. My research is primarily based on 100 interviews with genocide survivors, former perpetrators, ordinary citizens, and key informants, or elites, who lived through the genocide and have participated in memory efforts. These interviews are coupled with research in four archives in

Rwanda, and direct observation of commemoration and memorialisation processes from 2013-2018.

First, memory affects each Rwandan differently. Even within seemingly monolithic groups there are nuances of what types and what factors of memory and memorialisation efforts are meaningful, for who, and why. For example, not all genocide survivors feel the same about memorialisation in Rwanda. In some cases, genocide survivors are at the forefront of the planning and preparation of *Kwibuka*, or commemoration, each year, from April 7-13. They are instrumental in planning the commemoration events, selecting individuals to give testimonies, and even organising the flow and protocol around the events. Other genocide survivors, however, do not attend *kwibuka* because of retraumatisation. They get physically sick, weak, and feel both physical and psychological symptoms of utter illness.

Second, my research has shown that there are some silences around who is remembered at official commemorations. These silences are often imposed or perceived to promote peace and social cohesion, yet they sometimes come at the expense of achieving justice. For example, certain groups feel that commemoration does not represent their experiences during genocide. These groups include survivors who have instances of trauma, children of mixed parents (one Hutu and one Tutsi), some Hutus who did not participate in genocide yet who lost their families not during genocide, but through war crimes and even crimes against humanity that took place during the war between the Rwandan Patriotic Front (RPF) and the Rwandan Governmental Forces (RGF) in 1994 and immediately after. At present, commemoration and other official or public memory practices are aimed at remembering Tutsi victims of genocide. Other forms of memory have emerged, like holding a mass at a church for family members killed but not during the genocide, and who might not have been considered purely Tutsi, or praying in a private home to remember a loved one who perished in a different way.

Social obligation is also a huge factor to understand in the Rwandan context. Many Rwandans comply with social obligations, which can include attending commemorations, coexisting with perpetrators in society, accepting a false accusation and prison sentence, or confessing to wrongdoings when individuals did not commit the crimes they were accused of. Social obligation affects all groups of people who lived through the genocide, and every Rwandan interviewed felt the pressure of adhering to a social obligation at one point or another after the genocide.

In conclusion, Rwanda must consider some factors that might complicate the process toward successful reconciliation. First, some genocide survivors are still marginalised and impoverished based on their experiences during the genocide. They often feel their needs have been put aside in favour of the rhetoric of recovery, specifically that the Rwandan government has favoured stability over privileging survivors' needs.

While some genocide survivors have been successful in business and education, many remain poor based on economic standards. They are elderly widows without family; others suffer from HIV/AIDS or other physical diseases that were contracted during or because of the genocide. Children born of rape are stigmatised, and others suffer from post-traumatic stress or other psychological ailments, making it difficult to maintain a job or family. These practical issues often resurface in local communities, and can hinder feelings of justice or reconciliation, especially when basic economic, social, and medical needs are not met.

In Rwanda, as in many post-atrocity and post-genocide societies, transitional justice can be viewed along a spectrum. On one end, scholars argue that transitional justice in Rwanda can promote positive psychosocial healing, can validate survivors' experiences, can help them rebuild trust in the new society and faith that the new state will protect them from future violations. On the other end of the spectrum, other scholars argue that transitional justice in Rwanda has been a means for the Rwandan state to gain control over the society and to maintain its legitimacy amongst a diverse and traumatised population. The truth contains elements of both positions. Rwanda was an experimental site of justice after 1994, and the efforts to provide justice have had the challenge of meeting the needs of various stakeholders with different views of the genocide and experiences of violence. As Rwanda is a relatively young post-genocide nation, and as every individual living in Rwanda at the time was affected by the genocide in some way, the potential for reconciliation remains positive based on the attention paid to justice-seeking mechanisms, and the diverse approach to restorative and retributive justice that the country has adopted.

2. How do you balance your role of conducting research as an exercise of knowledge production on the one hand, and on the other, the impact on you personally of your daily encounters with people who have directly experienced the tragic events of 1994 and their aftermath?

Angela Jansen

I do not share the same history and the same culture with the people who went through the genocide. But as a foreigner I have another identity, the identity of being an outsider. And before you study the situation of others, they are first studying you. I have noticed that in practice this can mean different things/ identities in the eyes of research respondents:

1. As a European I represent the colonial period (e.g., representing the Belgians who introduced the ethnic ID cards in Rwanda).
2. I also represent the international community who failed or actually neglected Rwanda in 1994 – therefore I can never be fully trusted.

3. I can potentially be seen as a spy of a foreign government who tries to get information from the respondents.
4. I can be the neutral person; someone you can really trust with your story and who listens to you.
5. I can be seen as a person who can potentially give support to get someone out of prison or give access to a life in Europe.
6. I can be seen as someone who will never be able to understand them, because I have never experienced something like the genocide.

I realise that the type of identity a respondent assigns to you (and there are many more in addition to the list above), has an influence on the stories that respondents are willing to share with you and the way they narrate them.

However, though the 1994 genocide against the Tutsi is not my personal story, hearing the different stories of people has an impact on you every time. But at the same time, you feel that you are not entitled to, for example, show your emotions. This is a kind of struggle sometimes, but moreover I feel very privileged to be able to work in this country and talk with so many people and build connections. The people we are working with in the communities are so rich in terms of knowledge and experience. This is very inspiring for someone like me who grew up in a simple farmer's family in the Netherlands.

In the domain of international development, we often refer to 'the most vulnerable people', but in my eyes the people we are working with are the strongest people, they have much more wisdom to share with us/ me, than what I have to share with them. It also makes you wonder what vulnerability actually means. Would I, for example, be able to cope with a traumatic experience?

Grace Kagoyire

From my experience, before leaving my home or office, I try to reflect and think about 'who' are/is my respondent(s) today? We have different topics we research, and we also have people having different backgrounds. So, before leaving, I keep in my mind that I have to be neutral towards my respondents' suffering. In addition, due to my former profession of being a trauma counsellor, I try to listen to them and assist them especially when they show strong emotions – and this may happen depending on the topic of discussion. So, that background also plays a big a role. It happens that I shift my role from being an interviewer towards becoming a counsellor who is there to listen to people or the other way around. It is frustrating to look at a person who is crying because of the topic you are exploring, raising, asking about and fail to do anything. When you don't show a kind of empathy, you then risk getting nothing, or getting data that are out of your topic of discussion. In addition, there are some challenges. I may plan to collect three interviews but end up with one only at the end of the day. It happens that I also feel frustrated due to the emotional responses my respondents show during an interview. Sometimes, I go back home feeling weak, asking myself why we ask such questions that hurt people. It may happen that I spend much time thinking on what I can do so I protect people from suffering during the interviews. However, when I hear from them narrating how strong they are or how they are resilient I feel happy; I get much energy and feel more committed to continuing my work of research.

Samantha Lakin

Professionally, I have trained myself how to engage in meaningful interviews on difficult subjects. For any interview, oral history, or testimony I conduct, I aim to make sure that the interview is also a worthwhile experience for the person who has agreed to be interviewed. This means preparing for the interview, to aim to show the person that you respect them by having a baseline of knowledge about their history, that can allow them to go deeper in the interview and the information they give. I dislike the concept of 'data mining', which puts the production of data at the forefront of the interview. Instead, I take the perspective that the interviewee should be comfortable speaking, which involves establishing elements of trust between the researcher and the interviewee, and also making sure that the interviewee does not experience any unnecessary retraumatisation at the expense of getting information. Trust can be established in many ways, from deciding on an appropriate translator for the situation, to building rapport by speaking the same language, for example learning to give informed consent and other information about the research in Kinyarwanda, the local language, before shifting to speaking English or French again. These small signs of respect will go a long way.

Of course, there will always be respondents who will view a Western researcher, often of a different skin colour, educational level, economic situation, family situation, and might only say what he or she thinks that this foreign person wants to hear. This could be an overly positive or an overly negative version of the truth. However, according to scholar Lee Ann Fujii, such interviews can be best interpreted by focusing on 'meaning-making rather than differentiating between factual and non-factual statements, overlapping with the constructivist stance that meaning is socially produced and reproduced'. This reduces the pressure to try and get candid information from every interviewee.

Personally, after working in Rwanda since 2013 and most recently spending 11 months in the country as a Fulbright Scholar for dissertation research, I have become uniquely embedded in Rwandan society and daily life. Social and personal involvement has included becoming friends and even family with many Rwandans, especially genocide survivors. As such, I have attended commemorations, funerals, family meetings, weddings, births, baptisms, and other events with genocide survivors, not always as a researcher but also as a friend. I have been particularly privileged and thankful to have been invited to enter these spaces and share these intimate moments with Rwandans. I have also been the recipient of secrets, including very challenging contradictions that accompany the negative consequences of surviving genocide – desires to leave Rwanda, to commit suicide, alcoholism, financial issues, and other barriers that have existed for many Rwandans. Even though these are personally challenging experiences, they have served to deepen my relationship to Rwanda and Rwandans, and even to improve my research by helping me understand some of the realities, both positive and negative, about life in post-genocide Rwanda.

3. Could you share with us what has surprised you the most in your work – about how people live together after so much tragedy, and the strategies they use daily to cope with what happened in Rwanda?

Angela Jansen

Maybe I can start with the story that triggered me to go to Rwanda in the first place. In 2004 I saw a documentary about Jean Marie. He was a Hutu married to a Tutsi woman. During the genocide, the *interahamwe* came to his house. They wanted to kill his wife, but he was able to buy them off with some money. This happened a few times, but at some point, he was no longer able to pay them. They said: 'Today we are going to kill your wife.' She heard this and she started hiding in the bush around this house. Then the *interahamwe* said: 'If you don't find your wife now, we are going to kill you and your children instead.' At that point, his wife came out of the bush and she said: 'Please don't kill my husband and children, just kill me.' Then the *interahamwe* forced Jean Marie to take the machete and kill his wife. At first, he couldn't, but later she put her head down and begged him to do it. After the genocide Jean Marie was imprisoned for 8 years for killing his wife. In the documentary they also interviewed his daughter, she was 9 at the time when she witnessed her father killing her mother. I was also 9 during the genocide, but I was just watching the news about the genocide safely in the Netherlands.

This documentary triggered me to go to Rwanda and what surprised me the most is that there are numerous stories like this one, which implies that there is not only a kind of dichotomy between survivors and perpetrators, but there are so many stories representing the complexity of what happened during the genocide. What I learned, for example, is that during the post-genocide period there were not just tensions between the survivors and perpetrators' families, but also within families the genocide led to many tensions. For example, in gaçaça, it was often the wives, brothers and sisters of the killers who had witnessed what happened in the communities. They had to choose between remaining loyal to their family member who participated in the genocide or justice for the victims and society. This often led to conflicts in the family. So, this living together again as perpetrators and survivors cannot be separated from other family and community dynamics which ask a lot from people. But again, the vision towards a peaceful society seems to be stronger than being led by a violent past.

Grace Kagoyire

In terms of coping, some people are committed to strive for surviving. Survivors used to say: yes, I have to survive because the killers tried to finish me, but they failed. There are some other strategies that people try to use. For instance, perpetrators have their own ways of negotiating reconciliation. In this respect, some may start by saying 'hi' to neighbours they victimised in the past, or they invite them for a special event at their homes or they visit the victim slowly by slowly or they seek a part-time job. For me, this is like finding their own way of re-starting relationships, laying the foundation for their future relationship re-establishment. There is one example of an ex-prisoner, who testified while in a sociotherapy group how he negotiated forgiveness and this inspired me: After 15 weeks of sociotherapy, he apologised to the victim, but he did not feel himself forgiven though he did that publicly when he was still attending the sociotherapy programme. He had been in front of gaçaça courts, never repented. Through sociotherapy, he found that courage of apologising. He did so while in the group, but he was not himself convinced that he was forgiven by the victim since he had not given any offer as a sign of a true apology, which is widely known in Rwanda as *icyiru* (offering or paying something a symbol of recognising own wrongdoings). So, what he did, is that he invited the woman whose husband he had killed (his colleague in the same group) and showed her where he had thrown the remained bones of her husband. After doing that, it was that time, the perpetrator expressed he feels he deserve to be forgiven, he feels his heart is relieved. He testified, if the justice would come to pick me and put me in jail, I will not complain, that is something someone like me deserves. So, this surprised me, because it happened after 23 years. I was surprised by that heart and the ways he undertook so he feels he is truly forgiven. If all the people could truly repent as this man did, then the process of reconciliation will be easy, and we can hope for a high level of social cohesion among Rwandans and ensure sustainable future peace is possible.

Samantha Lakin

One thing that has surprised me in my work is the level of resilience among Rwandans. Having worked in Rwanda since 2013, I have heard many stories that explain the unthinkable horror that took place during the months of genocide. Friends and interviewees alike have shown me physical scars on their bodies – machete cuts strewn across their stomachs, on their heads or above their eyes, bullet wounds in their backs – and the physical scars are often even harder to see than the emotional ones. I have witnessed the great moments in Rwandans' lives, the birth of a first child born from two genocide survivors, and also hard moments, like disputes over land ownership between children of survivors and perpetrators, or revenge killings on both sides. As an outsider, I can listen and empathise, but I can never understand what truly happened to Rwandans during the period of the genocide. What surprises me the most is that many Rwandans have the mentality that things will be fine, even if they are not fine in the immediate moment. While they may struggle in their private communities, families, with friends, or even alone, they choose to portray a positive image to the world, especially through their culture of respecting and welcoming guests and visitors. Imagining that Rwandans would be this resilient after an atrocity such as genocide can be a challenge, but it is the reality that I have experienced.

Brief Response

Diogene Karangwa

I am reminded of an interview in Nyamagabe district in which the woman I was interviewing was sharing her painful story seemingly in a relaxed manner during which she smiled at times while telling the story while at the same time she had tears streaming down her cheeks. This *painting the suffering with a smile* is also culturally constructed like hiding the suffering through silence. As Robert Clair said, silence is socially and culturally constructed.[1] In some cultures, silence is seen as acceptable behaviour while in others it is interpreted as a symbol of distress. He argues that there are moments and situations when silence is demanded during social interactions but Von Buchholtz argues that there are painful and punitive aspects of silence in relationships.[2]

Jutte compares silence to a cancer of the soul. As it grows, it does damage to the self, yet speaking can also cause harm to others. The problem then is how to avoid harm to ourselves and others.

In Rwanda, the culture of silence is encouraged. This can be observed in Rwandan proverbs like *Amarira y'umugabo atemba ajya munda*, which means, the tears of a man flow inside. A strong person should not show her/his feelings or emotions. Another proverb says that *a man with integrity should know to hide his suffering [Imfura ishinjagira ishira]*. Some scholars say that the culture-specific idioms have been found to shape trauma survivors' phenomenological experience of suffering, and that the idioms

1 Clair, R. N. S. (2003). *The social and cultural construction of silence*. Festschrift for Masanori Higa. San Antonio, Texas: Trinity University.

2 Von Buchholtz, J. (2014). *A Collage of Thoughts and Images on Silence*. from www.jungatlanta.com

influence how the difficult past is articulated.[3] Here is how one woman in the village of Muhanga spoke about the need for silence:

> My grief was that I buried these who died, and I am burying those who are alive. I just keep quiet. The eldest warned me to not tell anyone about our problems.

In Rwandan culture, sometimes people say a person can die when s/he is still alive [*gupfa uhagaze*]. This is referred to a person demonstrating unacceptable behaviours within their community. In other words, being 'socially dead' although the person is still 'physically alive'. The quote above of a mother talking about burying her children who are still alive suggests this notion of being 'socially dead'. These pattern of how people deal with pain and suffering in the aftermath of the genocide are transmitted from generation to generation, and children have been found to suffer the most from silences about the past through the cultural transmission of silences.[4]

3 Hinton, D.E. & R, Lewis-Fernández. (2010). Idioms of distress among trauma survivors: subtypes and clinical utility. *Culture Medical Psychiatry*, 34(2): 209–18.

4 Lentin 2000 as cited by Kidron, C. A. (2009). Silent legacies of trauma: a comparative study of Cambodian Canadian and Israeli holocaust trauma descendant memory work. *Remembering violence: anthropological perspectives on intergenerational transmission*, 185-220.

Part VI: Coming to Terms with the Past: Film-based Interventions

21.
No More Fairy Tales

Sue Williamson

In this session artist Sue Williamson's film, It's a pleasure to meet you *was screened. The film is part of a series entitled* No More Fairy Tales, *commissioned for the project the project Trauma, Memory and Representations of the Past, an initiative of Studies in Historical Trauma and Transformation at Stellenbosch University. The project was funded by the Andrew Mellon Foundation.* It's a pleasure to meet you *is a conversation between Siyah Ndawela Mgoduka and Candice Mama, whose fathers were killed at the height of the apartheid government's covert operations. They were both toddlers when their fathers were murdered. In the film, they share stories about how they found out about the killing of their fathers, how they have dealt with growing up with this tragic story in their lives, and how growing up without a father has affected them. They also share their feelings about Eugene de Kock, the man who was responsible for the killing of Candice Mama's father and was implicated in the murder of Siyah's father.*

It's a pleasure to meet you (2016)[1]

A conversation between Candice Mama and Siyah Ndawela Mgoduka

It's a pleasure to meet you, Siyah Ndawela Mgoduka and Candice Mama *(Film still 2016)*

Film Transcript:

CANDICE: My father was murdered by an apartheid assassin called Eugene de Kock. As they were approaching the Nelspruit bridge, Eugene de Kock and his team had been waiting for them. And they started shooting at the

1 *It's a pleasure to meet you* is a dual channel video by Sue Williamson (playing time 25 minutes). It has been exhibited at the Johannes Stegmann Gallery, Bloemfontein, the Goodman Gallery Johannesburg and London, the Apartheid Museum, Johannesburg, the University of Stellenbosch, the Louis Vuitton Foundation, Paris, MAXXI Museum, Rome, the Zeitz MOCCA Museum, Cape Town, Shrine Empire, New Delhi, Birkbeck College, University of London and Gertrude Contemporary, Melbourne, Australia.

vehicle. So, the vehicle started losing control and as it got under the bridge, De Kock realised that the vehicle wasn't coming to a halt, so he decided to run down the bridge, and he emptied his gun magazine on my father. Afterwards, he continued to douse the vehicle in fuel, he set them alight, they further doused it in fuel, and then they set it alight again, and they went on about their day, and the news read my dad and his team were basically against the government and they were killed. Ja.

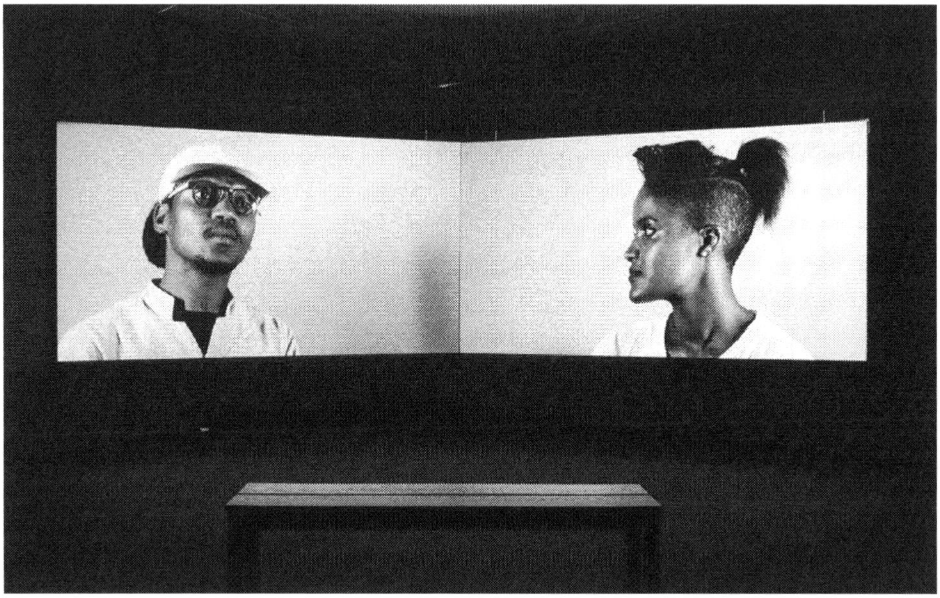

It's pleasure to meet you, Siyah Ndawela Mgoduka and Candice Mama *(Film Still 2016)*

SIYAH: My father was bombed by de Kock and Nieuwoudt and I say it, the rest of them, because they were all involved in it. My father was a policeman. There was a lot of claims of why my father was killed. One was because they were going to go forward about certain people's deaths, or killings.

From what I've heard, they, they were called into a meeting, and they had to go into a car in Motherwell, so then they got into that car, the car was bombed. So, it was a trap, basically. So that's how my father was murdered.

CONVERSATION BETWEEN CANDICE AND SIYAH ABOUT THEIR LIVES

CANDICE: I'm Candice Mama, I'm 24 years old and I'm from Jo'burg. Ja.

SIYAH: I am Siyah Mgoduka and I am from Port Elizabeth.

SIYAH: I can't remember how I found out exactly, I grew up not having a father, so when we moved from one township to a suburb, there was remnants of that there was a father figure in this house. You know, so I would play in the garage, and I would find his handcuffs somewhere in the garage. Or I will find his boots, you know, somewhere. Or his uniform here and there. So, there was remnants of there was a male figure, there was a father figure somewhere. In the back of my mind, I knew I had a father, but I didn't find out in a certain way.

CANDICE: It's, it's funny, because I didn't actually hear the story, I found out the story and it was a complete coincidence. I went and my mom always used to host people and when people would come to the house, she would send me for this book. And she told them some sort of a story about how my dad had died, and I thought to myself, but I want to see, I want to see what's in this book that I'm not allowed, you know, to see. So, I went the one day, my mom was gone, and I took the book. And when I saw the page, it was just my dad's burnt body clutching the steering wheel. And I closed the book very quickly and I just threw it into the cupboard, and I never spoke of it.

It's a pleasure to meet you, Candice with a photograph of her parents *(Film still 2016)*

I was just scared, because I thought to myself well if my dad was a good person, then how could he die in such a brutal way? And since I was only nine, and I couldn't tell anyone, I just kept it to myself, and further on in life, as I grew older, I started discovering more details about more or less what had happened, but I didn't ask too many questions.

I still have that book to this day, you know. I keep it with me, and I think it's become a story of more, for me personally at least, that just every time I look at that, you know, I think to myself I can't waste my life.

SIYAH: What difference would a sit down have made? If there was more dialogue maybe, but it makes no difference to me whether there was a sit down or not. I think me finding out the way that I found out influenced me in certain things my father used to, when he was not being a policeman, he used to take a lot of pictures and videos and do gardening and so forth, so artistic sort of things. So, it influenced me to look at things in a similar way on how to connect certain dots.

It's a pleasure to meet you, Siyah with his father's photo of him as a baby *(Film still 2016)*

CANDICE: I knew that of course at a certain point I had to acknowledge and tell my mom that this is what I did. I read the book. And because my mom herself wasn't really sure of the details of how it happened and why it happened, you know, so she was really clueless and her way of dealing with it was like shouting, like hey! Don't, don't speak to me about that, you know.

SIYAH: How did my mother deal with the loss of my father? Books, she has a lot of books, she had to protect herself,

SIYAH: The last conversation I had with my mother about my father was probably about 15 years ago, I think.

SIYAH: I can't remember. I remember her crying, it was the first time me seeing her crying. I was, I remember the feeling I had was this sort of feeling of, I was in primary school and I think, I think it was because there was this kid in primary whose father had passed away, and then a year later, the mother remarried you know. So, I was like it must be nice, you know. So, I think that kind of sparked some emotion with me and I went home and I, I can't remember what I was saying to my mother about, but I mentioned father, it was my first-time saying father, why don't I have a father? I wish I had a father. Or something like that. And then that's when she got into it, she started crying, but she said it was probably God's will you know, if he would have, if he would have been alive, we don't know how, what a man he would have turned out to be maybe, you know. Maybe he wouldn't have been the good man that we knew him at that stage you know. So that was her kind of trying to put me at ease like you know, it's bad happens for the good, good happens for the bad, you know, nothing exists without its opposite type of thing.

CANDICE: You know it's, it's ironic, because I was very hard on my mom, mentally at least. I'm growing up. You know? I thought this is what you should have done, and this and this and this is how you should have raised me, blah, blah, blah. But then it got to a point, when I reached womanhood, and I looked back on my mom's decisions, and I realised she did the best she could under the situation, you know, and the cards she was dealt. And I mean she was very young. When all of this happened to her, she was the age that I am now, which is 24. And she had to deal with losing her husband, having two children, both under the age of four and really do not knowing what she's going to do with her life.

SIYAH: I think during the TRC hearings, that's when things were more clear to me that okay, well my father was killed in this manner by these people. So, I think that's how I officially found out, but there was never a sit down to say hey...

I remember very clearly how it felt like. Well, I remember being, leaving the TRC and they went to court, and I remember having a sense of hate and anger and wanting to kill this man that did that. Because of his actions towards me, this Nieuwoudt, Gideon Nieuwoudt, because of his actions to me, that's, that was the first time I've ever felt a sense of retaliation, anger and bitterness. And those actions being during the court sessions, there was a break and then everyone had a break outside, and then we were moving back inside, Nieuwoudt looked at me, he stuck his tongue out and he did that to me, you know. So that was my first encounter, with oh, okay, well these are the feelings that I have to have towards these people.

SIYAH: Yes, I was about six or seven at the time.

CANDICE: So, one day I walked into the house, and my mom says I got a call from the National Prosecuting Authority. And she says they want to know if we want to meet Eugene de Kock, but it's not a must. You can or you don't have to, or you know? And I, immediately I just said yes, I want to meet him. And she looked at me and she said okay, well if you're going to go, then I'll come with you.

And we, we got to the prison, and they took us to a board room, and then they give us tea and they brief us, and they say okay, you know this is what this meeting is about, don't be afraid of asking questions, you know. Just be yourself and it will be over and if at any point you don't feel comfortable, please let us know. So, my family being very light-hearted and jokey about everything, we just started teasing each other and we were like haha, you know, this is what's happening, can you believe it? And we were laughing, and it was okay.

And I was speaking to my younger brother who was sitting next to me, and I turned around, and as I turned around, the empty chair that had been assigned to Eugene, he was there.

We didn't know what to say, we just looked. And the pastor said okay, I'm going to introduce everyone at the table, and he started with my mom who was the farthest and he said that's Sandra Mama, the widow of the deceased, Glenack Masilo Mama, and Eugene leaned forward, and he said it's a pleasure to meet you. And we looked at him. And he introduced my grandfather and then he introduced my older brother, and then he introduced my younger brother, myself, and with each one of us, Eugene would lean forward and say it's a pleasure to meet you, it's a pleasure to meet you, it's a pleasure to meet you, it's a pleasure to meet you, it's a pleasure to meet you.

And my mom, thank goodness, she took the lead and she said all I want to know is why? Why my husband, and what happened? And not even a moment's hesitation, Eugene just launched into the entire story of how my dad had been killed, how he ran down the bridge, how he did everything, and he remembered it as if it had happened yesterday.

He gave us details until I was sitting back in my chair and just, at one point I thought I wanted to just say to him stop. Stop, it's enough, it's okay, we know. And we did. My mom just said okay, I think that that's all I needed to know And, she said to him okay Eugene, I just want you to know I forgive you.

It's a pleasure to meet you, Candice with a photograph of her family and Eugene de Kock *(Film still 2016)*

CANDICE: And then it got to me and I took a pause, and we looked at each other, and I was about to say I forgive you, but there were so many things I still wanted to say, and he actually stopped me. And he basically went on to tell me about his family, and how his life had gone and what had led him to those events. And I said you know, thank you for sharing that with me, I, I want to know something. I, I do want to say I forgive you, which I do, but I want to know do you forgive yourself? And at that moment, he avoided eye contact and he, he kind of just shifted around the room, and I think out of the whole encounter, that was the first time I saw him uncomfortable. That was the first time I saw him flinch. So, I looked at him in the eyes and I said I'm sorry, but you didn't answer my question. Do you forgive yourself? And he looked at me and he said when you've done the things I've done; how can you forgive yourself? And I think at that moment I sat back, and I saw the sincerity that just, was just in the room, I just saw it and I saw him like look away to dab the side of his eye. I just couldn't stop crying, and afterwards, I think my mom followed suit, crying and after a while, we just thought you know, this is pretty much it; you know?

I stood up first because of course I was the closest to him, and I walked up to him and I said would you mind if I gave you a hug? And he looked at me, and he shifted in his seat, and he stood up and he gave me a hug, and as he gave me a hug, he said your father would have been so proud of the woman you have become, and I am so sorry for what I've put you through.

And all of a sudden, I thought did I embrace the person who killed my father? You know, was, is he a master manipulator and he like fooled me? Is... you know you start, I started asking myself all these questions and then I, I discussed it with my family, and I was, like how did you feel? I didn't want to give them ideas or notions on how to feel – I said how did you experience his sincerity? Do you think it was genuine and you know, was it sincere in your opinion? And everyone in my family, without a shadow of a doubt, said that's how I felt it. So, it's been an incredibly intense rollercoaster.

SIYAH: When I hear, when I hear the stories about de Kock, how do I feel? To me it's just one of the few men who were involved in killing my dad and killing other people's parents.

CANDICE: I think the one thing that stood out was, exactly how do you become that person? How, how does life navigate you on that route to being able to kill without any conscience, and conscience, and he told, he just told us a story that you know, at the end of the day, he, all he wanted to do was be a soldier, and he saw his father being a soldier and that was what was revered in his world, and how he was raised.

In his opinion, he wasn't fighting black people, he was fighting people that were against his government, and that were against his people. I think the one point I asked was but surely it stems from a place of racism. You must be a racist? And he said I don't consider myself racist. And I thought out of all this you're going to start lying to me now? He says that in his time, he never looked at a black person and thought I hate you because you're black. He said he always came from a standpoint that you're trying to destabilise and destroy my country. But I mean that again, can't be, you know it's kind of saying I'm not racist because I've got a black friend.

SIYAH: My question would be what if I were to kill your, your kid right now? Because I would probably do it. How would you feel now? And then I come back to you later, and I'm sorry, because you must understand this is how I grew up after what you did.

So, I respect though, forgiving and having the opportunity to, to sit with him and kind of hear things from his side, and in some way getting into his mind, I think. But I don't know what will stem from that you know, bigger branch you know. I, I'm, you know, I don't... So, I feel, I feel, I feel interested, I am interested in all these things, why did he, who, who, who, who coordinated this, these meetings? Why? After how long while he was serving his sentence? Why was there a priest there? You know, why? You know, so I, I [indistinct] you know, of this whole situation. You know. Saying it's a pleasure to meet you. Why? Why is it pleasurable for you? You know.

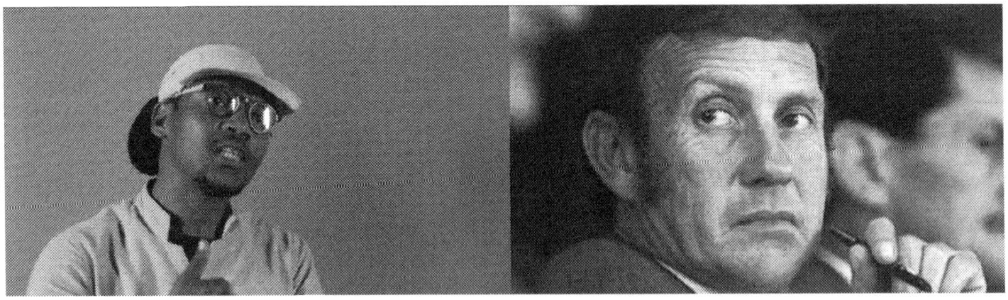

It's a pleasure to meet you, Siyah with an image of Gideon Nieuwoudt (*Film still 2016*)

I have no ambitions of forgiving. Maybe I will grow older and wiser, but I have none of those ambitions of forgiving these men, because I was never approached, the only time I was approached, like I told you when Nieuwoudt gave me the finger. That is my interaction with them.

CANDICE: Like I said before I even got into the prison and looked at Eugene in the eye, I had forgiven him. Only because I thought to myself you robbed me of my father, you robbed me of a life I could have had and I will not let you rob me of my tomorrow, and I will not let you have the power to rob me of my happiness and joy and experiencing life.

SIYAH: Is my anger a burden?

SIYAH: It becomes, it has become normal for me the anger, and the bitterness, the so-called bitterness. If, if at some point if I see white kids and they have you know a mother and a father, I know what that is able to do for you when you have a mother and a father, because I see it from the white kids. You know, because most of my friends who are black, they don't have fathers. And also, I can immediately make out the difference, you know. Or previously when I was at tertiary, or college, you can see the difference on how they live and how we live directly from not having two parents.

SIYAH: I mean my dad was killed when I was 18 months and the only way that I knew that he was around, was through a picture that, because he always used to be behind a camera, was through a picture that he had taken. He would never be in any shots that he's taken, you know – in any photo albums you would never see my dad, so he was the only one that's taking photos. So, the only way that I knew that okay, there was a dad, was when I see, saw a picture of myself when I was, probably a couple of months before he was killed. I'm looking into the camera and, me and my sister and he's behind the camera. You know, so in a way I'm looking at him and so forth. So, that's, that's how I know you know, I just came into this world, boom! No dad kind of thing.

I mean my father passed away when my mother was 30 years old. Ja, so at this age, she has to raise 4 kids and she has to make sure that she takes care of, so I think there was none of that time or that, or that ability to, to, to focus on let's talk this out for, for, until you're okay and what not, and at the same time trying to make sure that there's a proper house and food and that you guys go to school, and I'm still dealing with this, with this man's death you know, you know so there was a lot of these things that she literally handled on her own, you know.

Not to take anything away from anyone who forgives, you definitely forgive if you can, but I'm always a bit cautious of forgiving too quickly and then actually having to deal with that on your own now when the person you said you've forgiven, they have walked away feeling okay, I've been forgiven. Then you will have to, on your own, carry this oh, I thought I had forgiven this person, but I... Because I have no reason to forgive him anyway, whatsoever. So... Ja. That's from my part.

SIYAH: Ja, I mean it might be. A question for you.

CANDICE: Please.

SIYAH: If you were to see or meet de Kock, or Gideon Nieuwoudt's kids, how would you react to them, how would you?

CANDICE: I don't know. I think, I, I can't tell you, but I know it wouldn't be anger.

So, I think pre, pre this age of forgiveness and living free and lighter for me, I think my response would have probably been a rather aggressive one, because I dealt with a lot of aggression. But now I, it would just, I don't know how it would impact me. I think I'd want to know if, how, how their experiences were. I, I'd want to find out from them if them lacking a father, whether the father deserved it or not regardless, was similar to my experience,

What feeling would you have?

SIYAH: Like for me, I'm here, I'm still in this country, I carry it, and then you have the ability just to run away and go to England or Australia and live out your life there. And not even, actually know what, this is what happens, this is what my dad did, I would love to engage with them and hey, so how is your day? How is your life? How is England, Lad?

I'm pretty sure those kids go to therapy – oh yes, my dad killed people and you know. Black people, 90, 89%, they never went to therapy, you know.

And something's going to happen if you keep on being overlooked. The things are already happening you know, if you keep on acting as if...

CANDICE: Ja ...

SIYAH: There's something it's really going to happen, so...

CANDICE: But do you think on that, do you think that the sins of our parents should be our own?

SIYAH: But should, should we pay for the sins of our fathers or mothers? No. Of course not. But if you know that, you know it's like a friend. If a friend of yours hurts somebody else that you know, what, you will at some point say hey man, I'm sorry for what my friend did, he didn't mean it that way, or yes, they were being an idiot, or, and so forth.

CANDICE: So, the collective voice, I think?

SIYA: It's a collective, ja.

CANDICE: I think the biggest problem is when people don't understand what apartheid actually did, – and it goes so much deeper, and so much, so much more scarring than the fact that you were poor. It is the fact that you weren't even recognised as a human being, and I think when people can start to acknowledge that, we would hear less of the "get over it". Apartheid...

SIYAH: But TRC had a chance to do that.

CANDICE: It did have a chance and unfortunately, they failed. They did fail. And I think that's why it's now the 20 year reunion of the TRC, and I tuned on and I saw a very famous journalist at the time who was covering the story, and he was being interviewed, and he said you know the biggest problem with the TRC, was that it failed to address the fact that it needed to enlighten the white, the white demographic of the fact that what you are being given is a gift. And you are being gifted this opportunity to restart and readdress what has been done.

SIYA: Ja, ja. I don't know, I don't. because you, you, you can't be the one who is arrogant when I am forgiving arrogance is BS. Because our folks, and we are the ones who had to do this whole forgiveness thing, you know, but your arrogance doesn't show any humility, any of ja, we are equal. It shows it's an arrogance of ja, well we're here, you're here, get over it.

You know, so and then other situations where socially you know, you still have to, you can't voice this being a black person out, because ag come on, don't come with that, we're trying to have a drink type of thing, you know?

SIYAH: You know. I go to work, and no one knows any you know, African language. How, how? How is it that no one knows any African language? I have to, as a black person always adapt to these places, always adapt, always, always, always, and it's tiring. It's tiring. That's the thing.

You talk my language; I'll talk your language. You know, we can't always be giving, giving, giving, giving, giving forgiveness, giving our culture, our language away just to adopt being forced to.

CANDICE: Well, I think everything you said, the only word that really comes to mind is respect. But just saying I respect you as a human being and I respect your identity and I think that is the biggest step we can take forward. Teaching people to actually respect other people.

SIYAH: And acknowledgement as well.

CANDICE: Acknowledging and respect.

SIYAH: It's literally about let's recognize that we are all in this country, and if you really, really, really mean this thing, then let's put it down the middle and all, standing in one line and just be there, you know.

That Particular Morning (2018)[2]

A conversation between Siyah Ndawela Mgoduka and Doreen Mgoduka

In the first film, It's a pleasure to meet you, we hear that Siyah Mgoduka has not discussed his father with his mother for 15 years. Following the conference, second film, That particular morning, *co-authored by Sue Williamson and Siyah Ndawela Mgoduka was made. This sequel brings mother and son together for a first time ever open conversation. Siyah asks his mother if he reminds her of his father in any way, and hears how Doreen was informed of her husband's death. Later, he learns for the first time that Eugene de Kock, whom he has hated all his life, was in fact responsible for the imprisonment of the policeman involved in the death of his father.*

Film Transcript:

That particular morning, Doreen and Siyah *(Film still 2018)*

SIYAH: Out of interest, just out of interest ... er ... is there anything about me that reminds you of my father?

DOREEN: Yes, I think so, because he was a loving person, to begin with. He loved his family. Loved the children. He loved everybody around him. He was an outgoing person. Like, he would organise the neighbours, the friends, to come to our house and do those braais, you know.

DOREEN: (laughs) He was a kind person. Ja ... he was a kind person. He loved helping people, and that's always something that I relate to people.

SIYAH: Umm ... it might get me in trouble, but I'm very much like that. (Doreen laughs)

SIYAH: I mean I've never heard that before, so ... but um .. I relate to that.

2 'That particular morning' is a dual channel video (playing time 29 minutes) by Sue Williamson and Siyah Ndawela Mgoduka. It has been exhibited at the University of Stellenbosch, the Goodman Galleries in Johannesburg and London, and at the Zeitz MOCCA Museum, Cape Town.

SIYAH: I think he liked clothing. I used to see... there are very few pictures of my father ... because he's always behind the camera ... and I hate being in front of the camera, and I prefer being behind the camera, but ...

DOREEN: I remember, last December, during his engagement, you know, ja, Siyah's engagement, he was wearing a jacket ... then I looked ...this is beautiful, but it looks familiar ... I was looking, this jacket looks familiar. And it was ... smart. Then after the function, a few days after, I said, the jacket you were wearing was smart.

He said, I saw you, you were looking at this jacket, and I could see what was in your mind. It's my Dad's. I said, Ja, man, (laughs) You can imagine, you know, he was a year old when he died, but even today he can wear a piece of his clothing, so ... he was a fashionable person. He loved beautiful clothes.

That particular morning, Doreen, and Siyah at his engagement party wearing his father's jacket *(Film Still 2018)*

SIYAH: Every time when I do visit my father I either sit on the grave or I lie on the grave, and stuff like that. I think that's just like the child in me, you know. Like when you're lying on your father's arms or sitting on your father. I think maybe that's where it comes from. But I'm very relaxed when I'm there. At his graveside. And I guess I've never spoken to him face to face, touch, in the physical realm, you know, it's kind of like a play, like it's a bit fun, as well, when you talk out loud like that, it feels a bit funny, you know, because it's just like imagining how it would be like, you know.

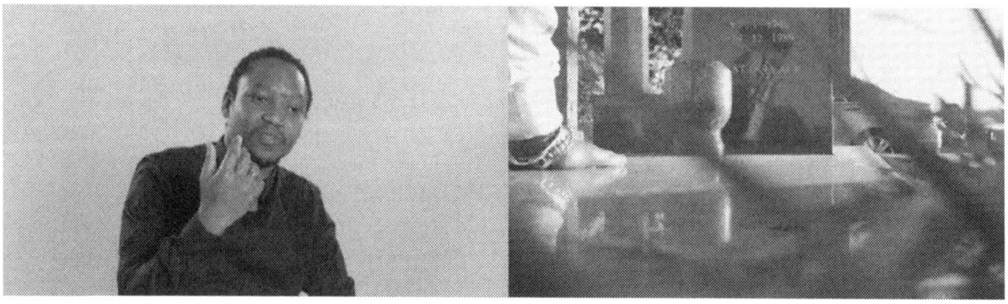

That particular morning, Siyah and his photo of his father's grave *(Film still 2018)*

SIYAH: When you say these things out loud, when you speak to your ancestors out loud ... it, it feels good, it feels like you can touch it, it has some texture to it, it feels like he can hear you.

I remember being in a bus back from PE while we were in talks regarding my engagement and the ceremony. All the way back, on the bus, I was talking to my father. At the back of a bus, I was just talking to my father. You know ...

As I normally would, talk to someone who can make something happen for me Listen, please help me, I need this. Can you please make sure this, and this happens ... can you please make sure that things go well?

This is why I want this, can you please, if not please make sure there is something else that can happen. At least give me a sign that you are going to do this or that. So, I talk just normally like that no matter where.

Um ... since I've been ... since I've been engaged, the one thing I always think about, almost every day is, and I ... literally, almost every day, think about it is, don't die. So ... which means, where I walk, which area I move to, which transportation I take ... if I'm cycling, which route I'm going to take... I think about that every day.

Don't die. And I think it's because I'm about to get married and enter a point in my life at the age where my mother ended it off. I'm thirty, I think she was around my age... my age?

There's always this thing in the back of my mind, don't die. Don't die. Don't die. And I think it has a lot to do with, like my mum, you know, like, if I die, I drop? Just like that, like my father died, then my wife is going to go through the same thing... that my mother went through.

SIYAH: So, it's actually very difficult to ask actually. (isiXHosa translation) How did you find out that uTata passed away?

DOREEN: I remember very well ... umm ... there was a special duty, she, he had to attend to...was not supposed to be at work that night. So, he had to obey the instructions. Didn't come back. He didn't come back and er ... hours ... I don't know what, because I used to wake up early in the morning,

There was a programme, *Morning Live.* Then, I think it was called *Good Morning News.* I would wake up go to the lounge and watch Good Morning News every morning. But that particular morning I didn't wake up. I think I was pondering in my mind as to why he didn't come back, that night.

There was a knock at the door in the morning and I was told our neighbour was there. It was the neighbour together with umm ... security police. The neighbour said, these people asked me to accompany them to the house and they said, Glen was killed in a bomb. In a bomb blast.

That particular morning, Doreen and an image of the bombed car *(Film Still 2018)*

That's how I got to know. And from ... from ... from other people, they said, it was already in *Good Morning News*, you know, but that morning, I didn't watch Good Morning News. That particular morning.

SIYAH: Mm, hmmm

DOREEN: This whole thing was very suspicious, from the onset was very suspicious, and they couldn't provide us with answers.

And the ... the ... the other thing was without, I mean ... er er ... we are still in shock, as a family, they were already busy with funeral arrangements. Why was the limpet mine not detected when it was leaving the police station? There were those metal detectors there. Why this specific one?

After exchanging the vehicle, within a short distance, the limpet mine goes off. They hear the sound. They drive back as if somebody was anticipating this is going to happen.

We even rejected that we said 'No. No military police funeral. Because you did not provide us with answers'.

And you look at the circumstances and how surrounding his death, it was caused by a human being not a natural death. That creates in you that element of mistrust. You don't trust a human being. You become vulnerable when there is no Father, no husband in the home.

If one becomes a lawyer, people are scared of lawyers, no one will come in that gate. That was one way of protecting my family. I believe as soon as I started studying law, that's when we got peace.

DOREEN: I also lost my parents at a tender age. Both parents. Then, also at a tender age when I have said, Please God, now, I have got somebody to confide to, somebody to talk to, after coming from work, you know, I mean, telling about the day's experiences. If there's something that you feel, this is confidential, you have this person to confide to. But all of a sudden, within a short space of time, he's also gone.

You're grieving at the same time. You're going through these emotions. Children are very small ... small children ... you ... you ... now, what do you do? Yes, going by the growing with you having these emotions that are being suppressed. You are keeping a face; you are playing a happy person when you are not.

Let me tell you something ... regarding my ... My mother died first. It was ... my father thereafter. In a short space of time. We were very young. There was no-one to look after us. The family had to come together to see who is going to take responsibility for these children. We're minors, all minors.

My father was to be buried on Saturday. The government of the day came to our house on Friday. They said,' You bury on Saturday, on Sunday, we want the house.'

We're still renting then. There was no ownership in the township. They said Fri ... 'Sunday, move out of the house'. So, these little children must move out of the house. Imagine. The double blow, you are a child, the double blow then comes. The government officials to say, we want this house, move out. Where are you going to go to?

So, I'm happy that he realizes now why was it so, so if I was hard on them, you remember when you are a parent, a single parent, I think it's better if you are a single parent and a man. But if you are a woman, there are so many challenges, raising up boys, you know. Actually, I've been voicing that out that ... 'You know what, there is no father here. I don't want to see police vans coming here looking for you. I don't want if there is something wrong happening in the neighbourhood, people point at this home. They say, 'It's those children', you know. 'So, I want you to be good children' You know. And indeed, I managed to do that.

SIYAH: I'm not sure if I am elaborating properly, the things that I didn't have by virtue of not having a father are the reasons why I want to have, or to be those, to become a father to become a husband, to become softer you know, to become loving, to become ... you know.

I mean even, and also I feel like I am raised by women, you know me, so I don't have the problems of being the alpha male or trying to prove myself as a man you know, 'cause my mother proved that she is more of a man than I will ever be anyway, so there's those things I'm fortunate to have, you know, so, ... ya, I don't know.

DOREEN: It was difficult, especially four children, small and two babies because the one before Siyah was four at the time, so almost a baby, so it's two babies and two small ones. To an extent you had to bury your grief.

SIYAH: I never saw that she's grieving now, she's going through pain. I always saw strong, providing, protection. And so up until the one day when I spoke about me wishing I had a father and then she cried for the first time, that's when I realized that she must have been grieving for a long time, but she has to hide it.

I mean, since a young age I always...I've always was aware of what a partnership provides. I've always been aware that a partnership provides, its companionship. A partnership provides mpani a sense of security. There's help, you know, one party helps the other party...

So, I have always been aware of that, so it's been one of the reasons why I have always longed for partnership, and marriage and a family, because I understood the importance...

SIYAH: cries

SIYAH: These ... the things that me and my mother are talking about now, for the first time are things that ... under normal circumstances, the dinner table is for. You know.

She comes back from work, he comes back from work, being the husband., the kids are picked up from school, they make dinner together, we do our little children thing, you know, we fight, we watch TV or whatever we do, they call us to have dinner and then you play catch up during the day, How was your day, how was your day ...

I never realised up until I turned. I think, nineteen, why other families, they have dinner tables. They eat at a dinner table. Together. So, these things we are talking about is playing catch-up because ... some sacrifice had to be made you know ...

Like dysfunctionality becomes normal, you know ... just to cope. Like my mother has the biggest room in the house but she doesn't share it with anybody. That's not normal. And you are aware of those things as a kid.

But you don't know how to articulate that. You should be sharing this room with somebody ... I mean, what does she think about., what is she thinking about .... I've watched my mother my whole life sleeping alone. What is she thinking about? Who is she talking to every night for thirty years that I've been alive?

DOREEN: When there was the TRC hearing, followed by the criminal case, I felt it necessary and important for all of them, including you, to attend those hearings.

Attending those hearings led to a greater understanding, bearing in mind that at the time of your father's death, it was enough for me and the family to say that your father had been killed in a bomb blast, without giving details, because we felt you were still very young at the time and were also grappling with the details.

SIYAH: I think it was, it was. I would say, a very good decision. Because from then on, that's when I started becoming conscious of what's going on, what's really happening, and where my position lies when it comes to what happened, you know, like seeing Niewoudt, or Snyman or de Kock, you know.

DOREEN: I'm not sure whether you know why Niewoudt, and the others got conviction. It was er... when they lost the case. When the State was about to close its case, and they could see they could not prove it beyond a reasonable doubt, as is required, there was a call that was made to the ... it was then, the Attorney General, by Eugene de Kock, who said he wanted to come and testify, he has crucial information as to what happened. So, he came down to PE. And he detailed everything that happened. Where the decision was taken to, they were using the term to eliminate them. So, I thought, let me make you aware of what happened and the reason they got conviction. So much that that made me to be at peace with De Kock. Only De Kock, not Niewoudt.

SIYAH: I didn't, I didn't, I didn't, I didn't know De Kock ... I didn't know that he was a critical part in their conviction ... so now, I don't know if that changes things regarding me and how I feel towards De Kock you know ... how I've always felt towards De Kock. I mean, it can't be denied that what he did was a good thing, you know ... by going forward ... that can't be denied.

So that alone changes things a bit ...

DOREEN: To me, it does not necessarily mean you must change your position ...

SIYAH: The whole TRC period ... the TRC ... was for me ... one of my other positions is the TRC, I don't feel it did much for. ... specially for yam, my generation. But ... for wena ... did it ... did it ... what did it achieve?

DOREEN: I think that ... that ... the TRC hearings, followed by amnesty were a platform for people like me to be able now to talk about what you've been suppressing.

DOREEN: But during the TRC process followed by amnesty, it was then that it came out that it was indeed the police who did this. So, it unearthed the truth.

SIYAH: So ...

SIYAH: Okay. So, it was immediate resolution in TRC which was for the victims as opposed to long term effect ...

But regarding TRC, I further understand now, the intentions of it. It was just the intention stopped there. If it would have gone further, then maybe, most of my generation would not respond so harshly to it. If I make any sense, I'm not sure.

I feel I've learned way more than I thought, I feel it is my time to listen more than to speak you know ... that's how much more I am learning about everything. I can't even speak, because if I speak, I might lose out on information. I'd rather just listen ... you know. There are some things that ... I don't want to say changed, but ... definitely more softened than the last time, and er ... definitely I'm better than the last time that I spoke about my father. That's the first time ever in my life speaking about my father without being angry or bitter.

DOREEN: And I think he is going to be the husband and the father he wants to be. He knows what will be expected of him as a man, a husband, a father and a grandfather.

SIYAH: Do I feel forgiveness or ... um ... before my mother revealed what De Kock had done, because I have been harbouring hate for my whole life. I have a lot of anger and hate. Violence in me reflects violence that surrounds me, you know, so I've been surrounded by that violent act. I do have some violent tendencies when I'm triggered by people who remind me of Gideon Niewoudt or De Kock, and what not, you know ... Or situations that make light of what happened.

And then the forgiving part. I mean, I had no ambitions or thoughts or of forgiving you know. But up until my mom now revealed that actually the person who came forward with certain information was De Kock, I became softer, I think ya, the word is I'm softer.

'Cause there was times in my life when I was looking for their families and what not, you know. So now I don't, I mean, I don't care for that. I'm more softer, and I'm looking forward to other things, I haven't forgiven anyone, I agree with my mother, it's not on me to forgive, but I'm completely softer and accepting, more accepting of what is and what happened ... Ja ... (leans forward, smiling).

Bibliography

Abel, Olivier et al. (eds.) 2006. *La juste mémoire: lectures autour de Paul Ricœur*, Geneva.

Abraham, N. & Torok, M. 1994 *The shell and the kernel*. Chicago: University of Chicago Press. Edited, translated, and with an Introduction by N.T. Rand.

Abraham, N. and Torok, M. 1994. *The Wolf Man's Magic Word: A Cryptonomy. Trans. Nicholas Rand. Foreword: Jacques Derrida*. Minneapolis: University of Minnesota Press.

Abraham, N. *Critical Inquiry, Winter, 1987*, Vol. 13, No. 2, The Trial(s) of Psychoanalysis (Winter, 1987), pp. 287-292. The University of Chicago Press. https://www.jstor.org/stable/134349

Abrahamsen, T., & van der Merwe, H. 2005. *Reconciliation through Amnesty? Amnesty Applicants' Views of the South African Truth and Reconciliation Commission*. Retrieved from CSVR: http://www.csvr.org.za/docs/trc/reconciliationthroughamnesty.pdf

Adichie, C. N. 2009, July. *The danger of a single story*. Retrieved from TEDGlobal: https://www.ted.com/talks/chimamanda_adichie_the_danger_of_a_single_story

Adorno, T., W. 1963. Kulturkritik und Gesellschaft. Prismen. *Kulturkritik und Gesellschaft*, 7–26.

Agamben, G. 1990. *The Coming Community* (6th ed.). Turin: University of Minnesota Press.

Agamben, G. 1990. *The Coming Community* (6th ed.). Turin: University of Minnesota Press.

Alexander, J. (2012). *Trauma: A social theory*. Cambridge, UK – Malden, MA: Polity Press.

Alford, Fred. "Reason and reparation." *Theory and Society* 19, no. 1 (1990): 37-61. https://doi.org/10.1007/BF00148453

Almond, G & Verba, S. 1963. *The Civic Culture: Political Attitudes in Five Western Democracies*. Princeton, New Jersey. https://doi.org/10.1515/9781400874569

Alphen, van E. (2006) Second-generation testimony, transmission of trauma, and post memory. *Poetics Today* 27(2): 473-488. https://doi.org/10.1215/03335372-2005-015

Amnesty hearings and decisions. 2018. Retrieved from Truth and Reconciliation Commission: http://www.justice.gov.za/trc/amntrans/index.htm

Anderson, B. 2006. *Imagined communities*. London, New York: Verso.

Arendt, H, 1998. *The human condition*. University of Chicago Press. https://doi.org/10.7208/chicago/9780226924571.001.0001

Arendt, Hannah. 1973. *The Origins of Totalitarianism*. New York: Harcourt, Brace.

Argenti, N. & Schramm, K. 2010. (eds.) *Remembering violence: Anthropological perspectives on intergenerational transmission*. New York: Berghahn Books.

Argenti, N. 2007. The intestines of the state: Youth, violence, and belated histories in the Cameroon Grassfields. Chicago. https://doi.org/10.7208/chicago/9780226026138.001.0001

Asmal, K. 2011. *Politics in my blood: A memoir*. Auckland Park, South Africa: Jacana Media (Pty) Ltd.

Assmann, A. 2008. The Religious roots of cultural memory, in: *Norsk Teologisk Tidsskrift*, 109, 270-292. https://doi.org/10.18261/ISSN1504-2979-2008-04-02

Assmann, J. 2006. Das kulturelle Gedächtnis, in: Jan Assmann (ed.), *Thomas Mann und Ägypten. Mythos und Monotheismus in den Josephsromanen*, München, 67–75.

Bar-On, D. 1999. *The indescribable and the undiscussable: Reconstructing human discourse after trauma*. Central European University Press.

Barrett-Lennard, G. T. 1981. The empathy cycle: Refinement of a nuclear concept. *Journal of Counseling Psychology*, 28, 91-100. https://doi.org/10.1037/0022-0167.28.2.91

Bartoloni, P. (2008). Giorgio Agamben. Angelaki: *Journal of Theoretical Humanities*, 13(1), 51–63. https://doi.org/10.1080/09697250802156067

Bataille, G. 1986 *Writings on Laughter, Sacrifice, Nietzsche, Un-Knowing*, trans. Michelson, A. Cambridge, M.A. https://doi.org/10.2307/778551

Bateman, A, & Holmes, J. 1995. Introduction to psychoanalysis: Contemporary theory and practice. *Psychology Press*. https://doi.org/10.4324/9780203298398

Batson, C. D. & Ahmad, N. Y. 2009. Using empathy to improve intergroup attitudes and relations. *Social Issues and Policy Review*, 3, 141-177. https://doi.org/10.1111/j.1751-2409.2009.01013.x

Batson, C. D., Ahmad, N., Lishner, D. A., & Tsang, J. A. 2002. Empathy and altruism. In C. R. Snyder & S. J. Lopez (Eds.), *Handbook of positive psychology*, 485-498. New York, NY, US: Oxford University Press.

Batson, C. D., Fultz, J., & Schoenrade, P. A. 1987. Distress and empathy: two qualitatively distinct vicarious emotions with different motivational consequences. *Journal of Personality*, 55, 19-39. https://doi.org/10.1111/j.1467-6494.1987.tb00426.x

Batson, C. D., Lishner, D. A., & Stocks, E. L. 2015. The empathy-altruism hypothesis. In D. A. Schroeder & W. G. Graziano (Eds.), *The Oxford Handbook of Prosocial Behavior*, 259-281. New York, NY: Oxford University Press.

Baylin, J. & Hughes, D.A. 2016. *The neurobiology of attachment-focused therapy: Enhancing connection and trust in the treatment of children and adolescents*. New York: Norton & Company.

Berckmoes, L., Eichelsheim, V., Rutayisire, T., Richters, A. & Hola, B. 2017. How legacies of genocide are transmitted in the family environment: A qualitative study of two generations in Rwanda, *Societies* 7, 24. https://doi.org/10.3390/soc7030024

Berger, A.I. & Berger, N. eds. 2001. *Second generational voices: Reflections by children of Holocaust survivors & perpetrators*. Syracuse University Press.

Bhabha, H. 2010. *The Location of Culture*. New York: Routledge.

Biko, S. 2012. *I Write What I Like.* Johannesburg: Picador.

Bion, W.R. 1984. *Learning from Experience.* Routledge.

Bion, Wilfred R. 2018. *Lectures: 1973 Brazilian, Sao Paulo; 1974, Rio de Janeiro/Sao Paulo.* Routledge.

Blanchot, M. 1986. *The Writing of the Disaster.* Lincoln: University of Nebraska Press.

Bloom, P. 2018. *Against Empathy. The case for Rational compassion.* New York: Vintage.

Boesak, A. 1984. *Black and Reformed: Apartheid, Liberation and the Calvinist Tradition.* Johannesburg: Skotaville.

Boym, S. 2001. *The Future of Nostalgia.* New York: Basic Books.

Breithaupt, F. 2017. *Die dunklen Seiten der Empathie.* Frankfurt/M.: Suhrkamp.

Brewer, J.D. 2016. *Remembering forwards: Or how to live together in the future with divided memories.* Lecture, Dublin 17 May 2016. Retrieved from https://pure.qub.ac.uk/portal/files/38572205/Remembering_forwards.pdf

Brock, M., & Truscott, R. B. 2012. Nostalgia, melancholia, and working-through. *Peace & Conflict,* 18, 318–328. https://doi.org/10.1037/a0029073

Brooks P, 1993. *Body work: Objects of desire in modern narrative,* Cambridge.

Brooks, John H., and John R. Reddon, 2003. "The two-dimensional nature of remorse: An empirical inquiry into internal and external aspects." *Journal of Offender Rehabilitation* 38: (2): 1-15. https://doi.org/10.1300/J076v38n02_01

Bruneau, E. G., Cikara, M., & Saxe, R. 2017. Parochial empathy predicts reduced altruism and the endorsement of passive harm. *Social Psychological and Personality Science,* 8, 934-942. https://doi.org/10.1177/1948550617693064

Chikane, R. 2018. *Why building a nation will take more than believing in rainbows.* Retrieved from BusinessDay: https://www.businesslive.co.za/bd/life/books/2018-11-06-why-building-a-nation-will-take-more-than-believing-in-rainbows/

Chingwete, A. 2017. Crime and insecurity remain near the top of South Africans' agenda. *Afrobarometer Dispatch* No. 154. Retrieved from Afrobarometer.

Church, C., Johnson, L.S. & Visser, A. 2004. A path to peace or persistence? The single identity approach to conflict resolution in Northern Ireland. *Conflict Resolution Quarterly* Vol 21, (3) Spring 2004. https://doi.org/10.1002/crq.63

Church, C., Visser, A. & Johnson, L-S. 2004. 'A path to peace or persistence? The "single identity" approach to conflict resolution in Northern Ireland', Conflict Resolution Quarterly, 21(3): 273-291. https://doi.org/10.1002/crq.63

Cikara, M., & Fiske, S. T. 2011. Bounded empathy: Neural responses to outgroup targets' (mis)fortunes. *Journal of Cognitive Neuroscience,* 23, 3791-3803. https://doi.org/10.1162/jocn_a_00069

Cikara, M., Bruneau, E. G., & Saxe, R. R. 2011. Us and them: Intergroup failures of empathy. *Current Directions in Psychological Science,* 20, 149-153. https://doi.org/10.1177/0963721411408713

Clair, R. N. S. 2003. *The social and cultural construction of silence*. Festschrift for Masanori Higa. San Antonio, Texas: Trinity University.

Cohen, T. R., & Insko, C. A. 2008. War and peace: Possible approaches to reducing intergroup conflict. Perspectives on Psychological Science, 3, 87-93. https://doi.org/10.1111/j.1745-6916.2008.00066.x

Cole. E, 2014. *Theorizing the disfigured body: Mutilation, amputation, and disability in post-conflict Sierra Leone*. Trenton, NJ.

Council on Higher Education. 2016. *2013 Higher education data: Participation*. Retrieved Aug 30, 2017, from Council on Higher Education South Africa: http://www.che.ac.za/focus_areas/higher_education_data/2013/participation

Cozolino, L. 2014. The neuroscience of human relationships: Attachment and the developing social brain. 2nd Edition. New York: Norton & Company.

Crapanzano, V. 2011. *The Harkis: The Wound That Never Heals*. Chicago: Chicago University Press. https://doi.org/10.7208/chicago/9780226118789.001.0001

Cribb, R. 2014. "The act of killing." *Critical Asian Studies*, 46: 147-149. https://doi.org/10.1080/14672715.2014.867621

Čulík, J., & Mackinnon, A. 2015. *Central Europe's Memory Hole. Foreign Policy*. Retrieved from http://foreignpolicy.com/2015/10/02/central-europes-memory-hole-migrants-refugees/

Dajani, M., Leiner, M., Nadler, A., Sagy, S. & Barakat, Z. 2015. *Teaching Empathy in the midst of Conflict*. Jerusalem: Wasatia publications.

Dalgaard, N.T. & Montgomery, E. 2015. 'Disclosure and silencing: A systematic review of the literature on patterns of trauma communication in refugee families', *Transcultural Psychiatry* 52(5): 579–593. https://doi.org/10.1177/1363461514568442

Danieli, Y. 1998. Introduction: History and conceptual foundations. In Y. Danieli (ed.), *International Handbook of Multigenerational Legacies of Trauma*, 1–20. New York, NY: Plenum Press. https://doi.org/10.1007/978-1-4757-5567-1_1

Davenport, T. R. H. 1986. *South Africa: A Modern History*. Johannesburg: Macmillan.

Davis, M. H., Mitchell, K. V., Hall, J. A., Lothert, J., Snapp, T., & Meyer, M. 1999. Empathy, expectations, and situational preferences: personality influences on the decision to participate in volunteer helping behaviours. *Journal of Personality*, 67, 469-503. https://doi.org/10.1111/1467-6494.00062

Davoine, F & Gaudillière, J.M. 2004. *History beyond Trauma*. New York: Other Press.

De Gruchy, J. 2009. *John Calvin: Christian Humanist and Evangelical Reformer*. Wellington: Lux Verbi.

de Waal, F. B. 2012. The antiquity of empathy. *Science*, 336, 874-876. https://doi.org/10.1126/science.1220999

Decety, J. 2011. Dissecting the neural mechanisms mediating empathy. *Emotion Review*, 3, 92-108. https://doi.org/10.1177/1754073910374662

Decety, J. 2015. The neural pathways, development and functions of empathy. *Current Opinion in Behavioral Sciences*, 3, 1-6. https://doi.org/10.1016/j.cobeha.2014.12.001

Decety, J., & Lamm, C. 2006. Human empathy through the lens of social neuroscience. The *Scientific World Journal*, 6, 1146-1163. https://doi.org/10.1100/tsw.2006.221

Decety, J., & Svetlova, M. 2012. Putting together phylogenetic and ontogenetic perspectives on empathy. *Developmental Cognitive Neuroscience*, 2, 1-24. https://doi.org/10.1016/j.dcn.2011.05.003

Derrida, J. 1994. *Specters of Marx: The State of Debt, the Work of Mourning and The New International*, trans. Kamuf. P. New York.

Derrida, J. 2004. 'A time for farewells: Heidegger (read by) Hegel (read by) Malabou', preface to Malabou, C. The Future of Hegel: Plasticity, Temporality, and Dialectics, trans. L. During. New York.

Dikoko J. v Mokhatla CCT/62/05 para 113. 2006. South Africa: Constitutional Court, 3 August.

Dlamini, J. 2009. *Native Nostalgia*. Auckland Park, South Africa: Jacana.

Doughty, K. 2015. 'Law and the architecture of social repair: Gaçaça days in post-genocide Rwanda', *Journal of the Royal Anthropological Institute* 21(2): 419-437. https://doi.org/10.1111/1467-9655.12213

Eastmond, M. & Mannergren Selimovic, J. 2012. 'Silence as possibility in postwar everyday life', *The International Journal of Transitional Justice* 6: 502–524. https://doi.org/10.1093/ijtj/ijs026

Ebach, Jürgen. Erinnern und Vergessen 2009. Biblisch-exegetische und hermeneutische Anmerkungen, in: Ökumenische Rundschau 58, 275-294.

Echols, S., & Correll, J. 2012. It's more than skin deep: Empathy and helping behaviour across social groups. In J. Decety (ed.), *Empathy. From bench to bedside*, 55-71. London: MIT Press. https://doi.org/10.7551/mitpress/9780262016612.003.0004

Ee, E. van 2013. *A new generation: How refugee trauma affects parenting and child development*. PhD Dissertation. Universiteit Utrecht.

Eichelsheim, V., Berckmoes, L., Hola, B., Rutayisire, T. & Richters, A. 2018. Before my time? Addressing the intergenerational legacies of the genocide against the Tutsi in Rwanda. Intervention: *Journal of Mental Health and Psychosocial Support in Conflict Affected Areas* 00: 1-9. https://doi.org/10.4103/1571-8883.239711

Eisenberg, N., & Miller, P. A. 1987. The relation of empathy to prosocial and related behaviours. *Psychological Bulletin*, 101, 91-119. https://doi.org/10.1037/0033-2909.101.1.91

Enns, F. 2013. Transformative Gerechtigkeit als Möglichkeitsraum zur Versöhnung, in: Kirchliche Zeitgeschichte, 26, 23-35. https://doi.org/10.13109/kize.2013.26.1.23

Eramian L. 2018. *Peaceful selves: Personhood, nationhood, and the post-conflict moment in Rwanda*. New York: Berghahn. https://doi.org/10.2307/j.ctvw048sj

Esterházy, P. 2005. How big is the European dwarf? In D. Levy, M. Pensky, & J. Torpey, *Old Europe, New Europe, Core Europe: Transatlantic relations after the Iraq War*, 74-79. London and New York: Verso.

European Commission, 2015. Special Eurobarometer 437 'Discrimination in the EU in 2015'. Retrieved from Special Eurobarometer 437 'Discrimination in the EU in 2015': http://ec.europa.eu/public_opinion/index_en.htm

Eyerman, R. 2018. 'Perpetrator trauma and collective guilt: My Lai' in Boynton E, & Capretto, P, (eds), *Trauma and Transcendence: Suffering and the Limits of Theory*, New York: Fordham University Press. https://doi.org/10.5422/fordham/9780823280261.003.0009

Falconer, A. 1996. Erinnerungen zur Versöhnung führen, in: Ökumenische Rundschau, 45, 468-478.

Fanon, F. 2008. *Black skin, white masks*. Grove Press.

Fassin, D. & Rectman, R. 2009. *Empire of Trauma: An Inquiry into the Condition of Victimhood*. Princeton: Princeton University Press.

Fischer, J. 2009. Zum narrativen Fundament der sittlichen Erkenntnis. Metaethische Überlegungen zur Eigenart theologischer Ethik, in: Friederike Nüssel (ed.), Theologische Ethik der Gegenwart, Tübingen, 75-100.

Fischer, J. 2011. Ethik als rationale Begründung der Moral?, in: Zeitschrift für evangelische. *Ethik* 55, 192-204. https://doi.org/10.14315/zee-2011-55-3-192

Fischer, N. 2015. *Memory work: The second generation*. Palgrave Macmillan. https://doi.org/10.1057/9781137557629

Fiske, S. T., Cuddy, A. J., Glick, P., & Xu, J. 2002. A model of (often mixed) stereotype content: competence and warmth respectively follow from perceived status and competition. *Journal of Personality and Social Psychology*, 82, 878-902. https://doi.org/10.1037/0022-3514.82.6.878

Flynn, J. E. 2015. 'White Fatigue: Naming the Challenge in Moving from an Individual to a Systemic Understanding of Racism', *Multicultural Perspectives*, 17(3): 115–124. https://doi.org/10.1080/15210960.2015.1048341

Fourie, M. M., Stein, D. J., Solms, M., Gobodo-Madikizela, P., & Decety, J. 2017. Empathy and moral emotions in post-apartheid South-Africa: An fMRI investigation. *Social Cognitive and Affectice Neuroscience. https://doi.org/10.1093/scan/nsx019*

Frankish, T., & Bradbury, J. 2012. Telling stories for the next generation. *Peace & Conflict*, 18, 294–306. https://doi.org/10.1037/a0029070

Fresco, N. 1984. Remembering the unknown. In *International Review of Psychoanalysis* 11: 417-27.

Friese, S. 2010. Politik der gesellschaftlichen Versöhnung. Eine theologisch-ethische Untersuchung am Beispiel der Gaçaça – Gerichte in Ruanda, Stuttgart.

Frontisi-Ducroix F & Vernant J.P, 1997. *Dans l'œil du miroir*. Paris.

Fullard, M., & Rousseau, N. 2008. Uncertain borders: the TRC and the (un) making of public myths. *Kronos*, 34(1): 215-239.

Fuller, R. 2006. *All rise: Somebodies, nobodies, and the politics of dignity*. San Francisco: Berrett-Koehler Publishers.

Gallagher, H. L., & Frith, C. D. 2003. Functional imaging of 'theory of mind'. *Trends in Cognitive Sciences*, 7, 77-83. https://doi.org/10.1016/S1364-6613(02)00025-6

Garland-Thomson, R. 1997. *Extraordinary bodies: figuring physical disability in American culture and literature*, New York.

Gcaza, P. M. 2018. Redefining self-identity as military ex-combatant in the post-apartheid era. In *D. Kusá, (Dis-)continuous identities: Globalization, trauma, and reconciliation*, 107-114. Bratislava: Kritika & Kontext.

Gilliomee, H. 2004. *The Afrikaners – A Biography*. Cape Town: Tafelberg.

Gish, S.D. 2018. *Amy Biehl's Last Home: A Bright Life, a Tragic Death, and a Journey of Reconciliation in South Africa*. Ohio University Press.

Gobodo-Madikizela, P. (ed.) 2016. *Breaking intergenerational cycles of repetition: A global dialogue on historical trauma and memory*. Opladen: Barbara Budrich Publishers. https://doi.org/10.2307/j.ctvdf03jc

Gobodo-Madikizela, P. 2002. "Remorse, forgiveness, and rehumanization: Stories from South Africa." *Journal of humanistic psychology* 42(1): 7-32. https://doi.org/10.1177/0022167802421002

Gobodo-Madikizela, P. 2003. *A human being died that night: A South African Story of Forgiveness*. Houghton Mifflin.

Gobodo-Madikizela, P. 2008. Empathetic repair after mass trauma: When vengeance is arrested, *European Journal of Social Theory*, 11(3), 331-350. https://doi.org/10.1177/1368431008092566

Gobodo-Madikizela, P. 2010. Reconciliation: A call to reparative humanism. *In the Balance: South Africans Debate Reconciliation*, 133-139.

Gobodo-Madikizela, P. 2012. Re-membering the past: Nostalgia, traumatic memory and the legacy of apartheid. *Peace & Conflict*, 18, 252–267. https://doi.org/10.1037/a0029078

Govier, T. & Verwoerd, W.J. 2011, 'Responsibility and Responsiveness', *Praxis*, 13(20): 9-23.

Gqubule, T. 2017. *No longer whispering to power: The story of Thuli Madonsela. Jeppestown*, South Africa: Jonathan Ball Publishers.

Grand, S. & J. Salberg (eds.) 2017. *Trans-generational trauma and the other: Dialogues across history and difference*. London: Routledge. https://doi.org/10.4324/9781315466293

Grayson, H. 2018. 'Articulating growth in Rwandan terms: Adapting the post-traumatic growth inventory', *Studies in Testimony* 1:4-30.

Hager, E. 2020. *The Limits of Restorative Justice in Jacksonville*. The Atlantic, July 21, 2020.

Halperin, E. 2017. *Emotions in Conflict. Inhibitors and Facilitators of Peace Making*. New York /London: Routledge.

Hammerich, B., Pfäfflin, J., Pogany-Wnendt, P., Siebert, E., & Sonntag, B. 2008. Handing Down the Holocaust in Germany: A Reflection on the Dialogue between Second Generation Descendants of Perpetrators and Survivors. In C. Van Der Merwe & P. Gobodo-Madikizela (Eds.), *Narrative and Forgiveness: Perspectives on the Unfinished Journeys of the Past*, 27-46. Newcastle: Cambridge Scholars Publishers.

Härle, W. *Ethik*. Berlin 2011. https://doi.org/10.1515/9783110245882

Harrison, R. 2006. *The Black Christ: A Journey of Freedom*. Cape Town: David Philip.

Harrison, R. *The Black Christ: A Journey to Freedom*. New Africa Books, 2008,

Heidegger, M. 1962. Being and Time, trans. Macquarrie, J. and Robinson E. London.

Heidegger, M. 1996. *Being and time: A translation of Sein und Zeit*. (J. Stambaugh, Trans.) Albany, NY: State University of New York Press.

Hermenau, K., Hecker, T., Schaal, S., Maedl, A & Elbert, T. 2013. Addressing Post-traumatic Stress and Aggression by Means of Narrative Exposure: A Randomized Controlled Trial with Ex-Combatants in the Eastern DRC,' *Journal of Aggression, Maltreatment and Trauma* 22: 1545-083X. https://doi.org/10.1080/10926771.2013.824057

Herms, E. 1991. Grundzüge eines theologischen Begriffs sozialer Ordnung, in: Eilert Herms (ed.), Gesellschaft gestalten. Beiträge zur evangelischen Sozialethik, Tübingen, 56-94.

Hewstone, M., Judd, C. M., & Sharp, M. 2011. Do observer ratings validate self-reports of intergroup contact?: A round-robin analysis. *Journal of Experimental Social Psychology*, 47, 599-609. https://doi.org/10.1016/j.jesp.2010.12.014

Hewstone, M., Rubin, M., & Willis, H. 2002. Intergroup bias. *Annual Review of Psychology*, 53, 575-604. https://doi.org/10.1146/annurev.psych.53.100901.135109

Hicks, D. 2013. *Dignity: Its essential role in resolving conflict* (Reprint edition ed.). New Haven, CT: Yale University Press.

Hinton, D.E. & R, Lewis-Fernández. (2010). Idioms of distress among trauma survivors: subtypes and clinical utility. *Culture Medicine Psychiatry*, 34(2): 209-18. https://doi.org/10.1007/s11013-010-9175-x

Hirsch, M. 1997. *Family Frames: Photography, Narrative and Postmemory*. Cambridge: Harvard University Press.

Hirsch, M. 2008. The generation of postmemory. *Poetics Today* 29(1): 103-128. https://doi.org/10.1215/03335372-2007-019

Hirsch, M. 2011. *The Generation of Postmemory: Writing and Visual Culture After the Holocaust*. New York: Columbia University.

Hirsch, M. 2012. *The generation of postmemory: Writing and visual culture after the Holocaust*. Columbia University Press.

Hochschild. A, 1999. *King Leopold's Ghost: A Story of Greed, Terror, and Heroism in Colonial Africa*, Boston.

Hoffman, D. 2011. *The War Machines: Young Men and Violence in Sierra Leone and Liberia*. Durham, 162–93. https://doi.org/10.1215/9780822394488

Hoffman, E. 2004. *After Such Knowledge: Memory, History and the Legacy of the Holocaust*. New York, NY: Public Affairs.

Hogg, M. A. 1993. Hogg MA. Group cohesiveness: A critical review and some new directions. *European Review of Social Psychology*, 4, 85-111. https://doi.org/10.1080/14792779343000031

Hollander. T and Gill. B, 2014. 'Every day the war continues in my body: examining the marked body in post conflict Northern Uganda', *The international journal of transitional justice*, 8(2): 1-18. https://doi.org/10.1093/ijtj/iju007

Hook, D. 2012. Political nostalgia and psychoanalysis: Screened history, fantasmatic memory and retroactive time. *Peace & Conflict*, 18, 225–239. https://doi.org/10.1037/a0029071

Hoy, D. C. 2009. *The Time of Our Lives: A Critical History of Temporality*, Cambridge. https://doi.org/10.7551/mitpress/9780262013048.001.0001

Hume, T. 2017. *Poland's populist government lets far right extremism explode into mainstream*. Retrieved from Vice News: https://news.vice.com/en_us/article/nedyyb/poland-populist-government-far-right-extremism

Hunt, N.R. 2013. 'An acoustic register: rape and repetition in Congo', in Stoler, A.L. (ed.), *Imperial debris: On ruins and ruination*, Durham. https://doi.org/10.1215/9780822395850-002

Hunt, N.R. 2016. *A Nervous State: Violence, Remedies and Reverie in Colonial Congo*. Durham: Duke University Press. https://doi.org/10.1515/9780822375241

IJR calls on prosecuting authorities to intensify their efforts in the Ashley Kriel case, 2018. Retrieved from Institute for Justice and Reconciliation: http://www.ijr.org.za/2018/07/31/ijr-calls-on-prosecuting-authorities-to-intensify-their-efforts-in-the-ashley-kriel-case/

IJzendoorn van, M.H., Bakermands-Kranbenburg, M.J. & Sagi-Schwartz, A. (2003) Are children of Holocaust survivors less well-adapted? A meta-analytic investigation of secondary traumatization. *Journal of Traumatic Stress* 16(5): 459-469. https://doi.org/10.1023/A:1025706427300

Iliffe, J. 1987. *The African poor: A history*. Cambridge. https://doi.org/10.1017/CBO9780511584121

Ilunga A.R and Kalonji, B. 1964. 'Les événements du Kwilu', Etudes Congolaises, 6(3) 8-9.

Index of Public Integrity. 2017. Judicial Independence. Retrieved from Index of Public Integrity: https://integrity-index.org/?yr=2015.

Ingabire, C. 2018. *Youth perspective on reconciliation: Challenges and opportunities in post-genocide Rwanda. African Peacebuilding Network policy briefing note*. Retrieved from: https://www.ssrc.org/programs/view/apn/apn-policy-briefing-notes/

Ingabire, M.C., Kagoyire, M.G., Karangwa, D., Ingabire, I., Habarugira, N., Jansen, A. & Richters, A. 2017. Trauma informed restorative justice through community based sociotherapy in Rwanda. Intervention: *Journal of Mental Health and Psychosocial Support in Conflict Affected Areas* 15(3): 241-253. https://doi.org/10.1097/WTF.0000000000000163

Inglehart, R. 1997. *Modernization and postmodernization: Cultural, economic, and political change in 43 societies*. Princeton, NJ: Princeton University Press. https://doi.org/10.1515/9780691214429

Ishiyama, J., & Laoye, O. 2014. Do Truth Commissions promote trust in the judiciary in African states? *Journal of Asian and African Studies*, 1-17.

Jain, S.L. 'Cancer butch', *Cultural Anthropology*, 22(4): 501–38. https://doi.org/10.1525/can.2007.22.4.501

Jansen, J. D. 2009. *Knowledge in the Blood: Confronting Race and the Apartheid Past*. Cape Town: UCT Press. https://doi.org/10.1515/9780804771160

Jean-Luc Nancy, *The Sense of the World*, trans. by Jeffrey S. Librett, Minneapolis: University of Minnesota Press, 1997.

Jilovsky, E., Silverstein, J. & Slucki, D. (eds.) 2016. *In the shadows of memory: The Holocaust and the third generation*. London: Vallentine Mitchell.

Kagoyire, M.G. & Richters. A. 2018. 'We are the memory representations of our parents': Intergenerational legacies of genocide among descendants of rape survivors in Rwanda. *Torture* 28(3): 30-45. https://doi.org/10.7146/torture.v28i3.111183

Kagoyire, M.G., Vysma M. & Richters, A. 2018. The ghosts of collective violence: Pathways of transmission between genocide – survivor mothers and their young-adult children in Rwanda. Submitted for publication.

Kalema, E.M. 2018. 'The Mulele 'rebellion', Congolese political regimes, and the politics of forgetting', *Cahiers d'Etudes Africaines*, 4:233. https://doi.org/10.4000/etudesafricaines.26915

Kellermann, N.P.F. 2001. Transmission of Holocaust trauma: An integrative view. *Psychiatry*, 64(3): 256-267. https://doi.org/10.1521/psyc.64.3.256.18464

Kellermann, N.P.F. 2013. Epigenetic transmission of Holocaust trauma: Can nightmares be inherited? *The Israel Journal of Psychiatry and Related Sciences*, 50(1): 33-39.

Kenney, H. 1980. *Architect of Apartheid: H.F. Verwoerd – an Appraisal*. Johannesburg: Jonathan Ball.

Kiangu, S, 2009. *Le Kwilu à l'épreuve du pluralism identitiare* (1948-1968). Paris.

Kidron, C. A. 2009. Silent legacies of trauma: a comparative study of Cambodian Canadian and Israeli holocaust trauma descendant memory work. Remembering violence: anthropological perspectives on intergenerational transmission, 185-220.

Kidron, C.A. 2010. Toward an ethnography of silence: The lived presence of the past in the everyday life of Holocaust trauma survivors and their descendants in Israel. Current Anthropology 50(1): 5-27. https://doi.org/10.1086/595623

Kidron, C.A. 2012. Alterity and the particular limits of universalism: Comparing Jewish-Israeli Holocaust and Canadian – Cambodian genocide legacies. Current Anthropology 53(6): 723-751. https://doi.org/10.1086/668449

King Jr, Henry T. 2002. "The legacy of Nuremberg." *Case W. Res. J. Int'l L.* 34.

Klaassen, J. A. 2001. 'The Taint of Shame: Failure, Self-Distress, and Moral Growth', *Journal of Social Philosophy*, 32 (2), 174–196. https://doi.org/10.1111/0047-2786.00087

Kleber, R.J. 2014. Transfer of psychotrauma to the next generation? Inside insights from scientific literature and empirical research, in E. Captain & T. Mooren (eds.) *Family, generations and war: Historical, psychological and artistic views*, 118-141. Amsterdam: Nationaal Comité 4 en 5 mei.

Klein, M. 2002. *Love, Guilt and Reparation and Other Works 1921-1945*. Free Press.

Klein, Melanie. Notes on Some Schizoid Mechanisms. *Journal of Psychotherapy Practice and Research*, 5(2): 164-179.

Knowles, H. 2019. "Amber Guyger was hugged by her victim's brother and a judge, igniting a debate about forgiveness and race." The Washington Post, October 3, 2019. https://www.washingtonpost.com/nation/2019/10/03/judge-botham-jeans-brother-hugged-amber-guyger-igniting-debate-about-forgiveness-race/

Kohut, H. 1978. Introspection, empathy and psychoanalysis. In P. Ornstein, H (ed.), *The Sense for the Self: Selected Writings of Heinz Kohut: 1950-1978* (Vol. Vols. 1 and 2, 205-232). New York: International Universities Press.

Koselleck, R. 2004. *Future Past: On the Semantics of the Historical Time*, trans. Keith Tribe. New York.

Kundera, M. 2000/1983. Únos západu aneb tragédie střední Evropy (1983). In M. Havelka, & L. Cabada, Západní, východní a střední Evropa jako kulturní a poitické pojmy, 101 - 114). Prague: Metropolitan University Prague.

Kusá, D. 2018a. Režim pamäti a spravodlivá spoločnosť. *Filosofický časopis*, 66(2).

Kusá, D. 2018b. Legacy of the past and the quality of democracy. *Survey Report*. Bratislava International School of Liberal Arts.

Lebert, S. & Lebert N. 2000. *My father's keeper: Children of Nazi leaders – An intimate history of damage and denial.* Boston: Little, Brown and Company.

Levine P. 2015. *Trauma and Memory: Brain and Body in a Search for the Living Past: A Practical Guide for Understanding and Working with Traumatic Memory*. Berkeley, CA: North Atlantic Books.

Lifton, R. J. 1986. *The Nazi Doctors: Medical Killing and the Psychology of Genocide.* Basic Books.

Little, A. & Verwoerd, W.J. 2013. *Journey through Conflict Trail Guide: Introduction*, Trafford Publishing.

Livingston, J. 2008. 'Disgust, bodily aesthetics and the ethics of being human in Botswana', Africa: *Journal of the International African Institute*, 78:(2): 288–307. https://doi.org/10.3366/E000197200800017X

Loraux, N. 2005. La Cité divisée. L'oubli dans la mémoire d'Athènes, Paris.

Mabasa, N. 2018. Rise of the EFF youth: EFF Students Command brigades take university SRC elections by storm. Retrieved from The Daily Maverick: http://firstthing.dailymaverick.co.za/article?id=127372#.W-SukHRKjOR

Mackenzie, B., & Steinberg, C. 2015. Recognising the academic and political purposes embedded in history textbook assessment tasks. *Yesterday and Today* (14), 125-150. https://doi.org/10.17159/2223-0386/2015/nl4a6

Malabou, C. 2012. *The Wounded: From Neurosis to Brain Damage*, trans. Miller, S. New York.

Marchal. J, 2008. *Lord Leverhulme's Ghosts: Colonial exploitation in the Congo*. London 2008.

Margalit, A. 2017. On Betrayal. Cambridge, Massachusetts: Harvard University Press. Margalit, A. 2002. *The Ethics of Memory*. Cambridge, Massachusetts: Harvard University Press.

Mark, J. 2010. *The unfinished revolution: Making sense of the communist past in Central-Eastern Europe*. New Haven and London: Yale University Press.

Martinon, J.-P. 2007. *On Futurity: Malabou, Nancy and Derrida*. New York, 2007. https://doi.org/10.1057/9780230222977

Mattes, R., & Richmond, S. 2015. Are South Africa's youth really a 'ticking time bomb'? (M. Bratton, Ed.) *Afrobarometer*.

Mbembe, A. 2001. *On the Post colony*. Berkeley.

Mbembe, A. 2006. 'Variations on the beautiful in Congolese worlds of sound', in Nuttall. S (ed.), *Beautiful/Ugly: African and Diaspora Aesthetics*. Durham.

Mbembe. A, 2013. *Critique de la raison nègre*, Paris.

McEvoy-Levy, S. 2016. *Troublemakers or peacemakers? Youth and post accord peacebuilding*. Notre Dame: University of Notre Dame Press.

McGlothlin, E. (ed.) 2006. *Second-generation Holocaust literature: Legacies of survival and perpetration*. Rochester, NY: Camden House.

Meagher, R. E. 2014. *Killing from the Inside Out: Moral Injury and Just War*. Eugene, Oregon: Cascade Books.

Meier, B. P., & Hinsz, V. B. 2004. A comparison of human aggression committed by groups and individuals: An interindividual–intergroup discontinuity. *Journal of Experimental Social Psychology*, 40, 551-559. https://doi.org/10.1016/j.jesp.2003.11.002

Melchior-Bonnet, S. 2001. *The mirror: A History*, trans. K. H. Jewett, New York.

Meyer-Fong, T, 2013. *What Remains: Coming to terms with Civil War in Nineteenth Century China*. Stanford. https://doi.org/10.11126/stanford/9780804754255.001.0001

Molefe, T. O. 2014. *Reconciliation ideology, or why I will not let Adran Vlok wash my feet*. Retrieved from The Reconciliation Barometer Blog: http://reconciliationbarometer.org

Morelli, S. A., Rameson, L. T., & Lieberman, M. D. (2014). The neural components of empathy: Predicting daily prosocial behaviour. Social Cognitive and Affective Neuroscience, 9: 39-47. https://doi.org/10.1093/scan/nss088

Morrison, T. 1987. *Beloved*. New York: Plume.

Možný, I. 1991. *Proč tak snadno?* Prague: SLON.

Münyas, B. 2008. Genocide in the minds of Cambodian youth: Transmitting (hi) stories of genocide to second and third generations in Cambodia. *Journal of Genocide Research* 10(3): 413-439. https://doi.org/10.1080/14623520802305768

Nancy, J.L. 2000. *Being Singular Plural*, trans. Richardson, R.D. and O'Byrne A.E. Stanford.

Nancy, J.L. 2005. *The Ground of the Image*, trans. Fort, F. New York.

Ndaywel è Nziem, I. 1998. *Histoire générale du Congo: de l'héritage ancient à la République Démocratique du Congo*, Bruxelles, 610-19.

Neumayer, L. 2019. *The criminalization of communism in European space after the Cold War*. Milton Park and New York: Routledge. https://doi.org/10.4324/9781351141765

Neuner, F. Onyut P.L, Ertl, V., Odenwald M., Schauer. E & Elbert T. 2008. 'Treatment of posttraumatic stress disorder by trained lay counselors in an African refugee settlement: A randomized controlled trial.' *Journal of Consulting and Clinical Psychology* 76: 686-94. https://doi.org/10.1037/0022-006X.76.4.686

Ngewu, C. 1998. *Truth and Reconciliation Commission Final Report, Volume 5, 1998*. Cape Town: The Commission.

Nichols, Bryan K., and Medria L. Connolly. 2019. "*Transforming Ghosts into Ancestors: Unsilencing the Psychological Case for Reparations to Descendants of American Slavery.*" https://static1.squarespace.com/static/50ff32e1e4b067187f08016a/t/5d262a2beb582b00011b0af7/1562782252202/Reparations+-+Nichols+and+Connolly.pdf

Nietzsche, Friedrich. Vom Nutzen und Nachteil der Historie für das Leben (1874), in: Friedrich Nietzsche, Sämtliche Werke Bd. 1. Kritische Studienausgabe, Giorgio Colli and Mazzino Montinari (eds.), Berlin 1988.

Nobus, D. 2000. *Jacques Lacan and the Freudian Practice of Psychoanalysis*. London: Routledge.

Nou, L. 2013. Living in his father's shadow: Exploring healing justice and reconciliation in Cambodia with Duch's son. *Asian Journal of Social Science 41(1)*: 29–66. https://doi.org/10.1163/15685314-12341279

Ntigurirwa, H. 2018. *The Dilemmas and the Cost of Re-humanisation*. Paper presented at the Post-genocide Rwanda: Research Workshop, London School of Oriental and African Studies / Aegis Trust.

Nussbaum, M. 2001. *Upheaval of Thought: The Intelligence of Emotions*, Cambridge. https://doi.org/10.1017/CBO9780511840715

Nussbaum, M. 2011. *Creating Capabilities: The human development approach*. Cambridge, MA and London, England: The Belknap Press of the Harvard University Press.

Obotela Rachidi, N. 'L'université face à une jeunesse en quête de modèle', in Ndaywel è Nziem, I. (ed.), L'université dans le devenir de l'Afrique: un demi-siècle de présence au Congo-Zaïre (Paris, 2007), 253–61.

Opladen & Farmington Hills, 1997. MI: Barbara Budrich Publishers (Revised edition, first edition in German 1997).

Orange, D. 2018. 'Traumatised by Transcendence: My Other's Keeper' in Eric Boynton & Peter Capretto (eds), *Trauma and Transcendence: Suffering and the Limits of Theory*, New York: Fordham University Press.

Parens, H. 2009. Aftermath of genocide: The fate of children of perpetrators. *Journal of Applied Psychoanalytic Studies* 6(1): 25-42. https://doi.org/10.1002/aps.187

Pásztor, D. 2018. Pithart: Česi sa sekli, Slovensko je na tom lepšie, dokážete sa postaviť zlu [Pithart: Czechs made a mistake, Slovaks are doing better: you are able to stand against evil]. Retrieved from Denník N: https://dennikn.sk/1276238/pithart-cesi-sa-sekli-slovensko-je-na-tom-lepsie-dokazete-sa-postavit-zlu/?ref=mpm.

Perroud, N., Rutembesa, E., & Paoloni-Giacobino, A. 2014. The Tutsi genocide and transgenerational transmission of maternal stress: Epigenetics and biology of the HPA axis. *The World Journal of Biological Psychiatry* 15(4): 334-345. https://doi.org/10.3109/15622975.2013.866693

Pew Research Center 2018. Eastern and Western Europeans Differ on Importance of Religion, Views of Minorities, and Key Social Issues. Retrieved from Pew Research Center: http://www.pewforum.org/2018/10/29/eastern-and-western-europeans-differ-on-importance-of-religion-views-of-minorities-and-key-social-issues/

Pierre, M.L. 1985. *Mulele ou la seconde vie de Lumumba*, Bruxelles.

Pogany-Wnendt, P, 2019. Der Wert der menschlichkeit: Psychologische perspektiven für eine humanisierung der Gesellschaft. Psychosozial. https://doi.org/10.30820/9783837976212

Prager, J. 2016. Disrupting the intergenerational transmission of trauma: Recovering humanity, repairing generations. In P. Gobodo-Madikizela (ed.) *Breaking intergenerational cycles of repetition: A global dialogue on historical trauma and memory*, 12-26. Opladen: Barbara Budrich Publishers. https://doi.org/10.2307/j.ctvdf03jc.7

Radstone, S., & Hodgkin, K. 2011. *Regimes of memory*. New York: Routledge.

Ramaut, P. 2014. 'Les fantômes de la guerre 14', in A. Dartevelle & P. Ramaut, Trois journées d'août, pp. 31-41. Liege: RTBF Derives.

Ranciere, J. 1999. *Disagreement: Politics and Philosophy*, trans, Rose, J. Minneapolis: University of Minnesota Press.

Ray, M. 2016. *Free fall: Why South African universities are in a race against time. Johannesburg*, South Africa: Bookstorm.

Republic of South Africa. *Constitution of the Republic of South Africa Act 200 of 1993*. Government Printers: Pretoria.

Richters, A. 2015. Enhancing family and community resilience and wellbeing across the generations: The contribution of community based sociotherapy in post-genocide Rwanda. *International Journal of Emergency Mental Health and Human Resilience* 17(3): 661-663. https://doi.org/10.4172/1522-4821.1000258

Richters, A. Rutayisire, T., & Dekker, C. 2001. Care as a turning point in sociotherapy: Remaking the moral world in post-genocide Rwanda. *Medische Antropologie* 22(1): 93-108.

Richters, A., Rutayisire, T., Sewimfura, T. & Ngendahayo, E. 2010. Psychotrauma, healing and reconciliation in Rwanda. *African Journal of Traumatic Stress* 1(2): 55-63.

Ricoeur, P. 1990/1983. *Time and Narrative, I (Vol. I).* (K. McLaughlin, & D. Pellauer, Trans.) Chicago and London: The University of Chicago Press.

Ricoeur, P. 1992. *Oneself as another.* (K. Blamey, Trans.) Chicago and London: The University of Chicago Press.

Ricoeur, P. 1995. *'The Memory of Suffering', Figuring the Sacred.* Minneapolis: Fortress Press.

Ricoeur, P. 2004. *Memory, History, Forgetting.* (K. Blamey, & D. Pellauer, Trans.) Chicago: The University of Chicago Press. https://doi.org/10.7208/chicago/9780226713465.001.0001

Rieder, H. 2014. Legacies of the 1994 Rwandan genocide: Organised violence, family violence, mental health and post-conflict related attitudes examined among families of genocide survivors and former prisoners. PhD Dissertation Universität Konstanz.

Rieff, D. 2011. *Against remembrance.* Melbourne: Melbourne University Press.

Roberts, R. C. 2003. Emotions. *An Essay in Aid of Moral Psychology*, Cambridge. https://doi.org/10.1017/CBO9780511610202

Robjant, K and Fazel, M, 'The Emerging Evidence for Narrative Exposure Therapy: A Review,' Clinical Psychology Review 30 (2010): 1030-39. https://doi.org/10.1016/j.cpr.2010.07.004

Rosenthal G. (ed.) 2010. The Holocaust in three generations: Families of victims and perpetrators of the Nazi regime. https://doi.org/10.2307/j.ctvddzxt6

Rosenthal, G. 2002. Veiling and denying the past. *The History of the Family* 7(2): 225-238. https://doi.org/10.1016/S1081-602X(02)00093-3

Rothberg, M. 2014. Beyond Tancred and Clorinda: Trauma studies for implicated subjects. *The future of trauma theory: Contemporary literary and cultural criticism*, 2076-0787.

Rudahindwa, S., Mutesa, L. Rutembesa, E. et al. 2018. 'Transgenerational effects of the genocide against the Tutsi in Rwanda: A post-traumatic stress disorder symptom domain analysis', *African Academy of Sciences Open Research* 1:10. https://doi.org/10.12688/aasopenres.12848.1

Rupnik, J. 2002. Coming to terms with the communist past: The Czech case from a comparative perspective. (Tranzit, Ed.) Tr@nsit Online (22). Retrieved from Tr@nsit Online: http://monumenttotransformation.org/atlas-of-transformation/html/c/ coming-to-terms-with-the-past/coming-to-terms-with-the-communist-past-the-czech-case-from-a-comparative-perspective-jacques-rupnik.html.

Sachs, A, 2011. *The strange alchemy of life and law.* Oxford University Press.

Samolsky. R, 2011. *Apocalyptic futures: Marked bodies and the Violence of the text in Kafka, Conrad, and Coetzee*. New York. https://doi.org/10.2307/j.ctt14bs07v

Samuels, R. From the discourse of the university to the discourse of analysis. *Psychoanalysis Culture Society*, 23, 68–76 (2018). https://doi.org/10.1057/s41282-018-0071-6

Sansal, B. 2011. *An unfinished business*. London: Bloomsbury Publishing.

Sarabwe, E., Richters, A. & Vysma, M. 2018. Marital conflict in the aftermath of genocide in Rwanda: An explorative study within the context of community based sociotherapy. *Intervention: Journal of Mental Health and Psychosocial Support in Conflict Affected Areas* 16(1): 14-21. https://doi.org/10.1097/WTF.0000000000000147

SARB 2017. 2018. South African Reconciliation Barometer Survey Report 2017. Retrieved from Institute for Justice and Reconciliation: http://www.ijr.org.za/home/wp-content/uploads/2018/03/IJR-Barometer-Report-2017-WEB-final.pdf

Sartre, J.-P. 1956. *Being and Nothingness: An essay on Phenomenological Ontology*, trans. Barnes, H.E. Secaucus, 4-5.

Saxe, R. 2006. Why and how to study Theory of Mind with fMRI. *Brain Research*, 1079, 57-65. https://doi.org/10.1016/j.brainres.2006.01.001

Schaal, S, Elbert, T and Neuner, F, 2009. 'Narrative exposure therapy versus interpersonal psychotherapy. A pilot randomized controlled trial with Rwandan genocide orphans. *Psychotherapy and Psychosomatics* 78: 298-306. https://doi.org/10.1159/000229768

Schauer. M, Elbert, T. and Neuner, F. Narrative Exposure Therapy: A Short-Term Intervention for Traumatic Stress Disorders after War, Terror, or Torture (Gottingen: Hogrefe & Huber, 2005).

Schoenbrun, D. 2007. 'Violence, marginality, scorn and honour: language evidence of slavery to the eighteenth century', in Médard, H and Doyle. S. (eds.), Slavery in the Great Lakes Region of East Africa. Oxford, 38-75.

Schwab, G. 2010. *Haunting legacies: Violent histories and transgenerational trauma*. New York: Columbia University Press.

Sedikides, C., Wildschut, T., Arndt, J., & Routledge, C. 2008. Nostalgia: Past, present, and future. *Current Directions in Psychological Science*, 17: 304–307. https://doi.org/10.1111/j.1467-8721.2008.00595.x

Sen, A. 2011. *The Idea of Justice*. Cambridge, MA: Belknap Press.

Sereny, G. 2011. *Into that darkness: An examination of conscience*. Vintage.

Shklar, J. 1990. *The Faces of Injustice*. New Haven: Yale University Press.

Snyman, G. 2011. 'Empire and a Hermeneutics of Vulnerability', *Studia Historiae Ecclesiasticae*, 37 – Supplement: 1-20.

Sommers, S. 2017. Getraumatiseerde gezinnen: Temmen van draken en monsters (Traumatised families: Taming dragons and monsters). Presentation study-day on Ethnopsychiatry of the Section Transcultural Psychiatry of the Dutch Society for Psychiatry. Amsterdam 15 December 2017.

South Africa 1996. Truth and Reconciliation Commission Human Rights Violations Hearing Transcript, Bisho Massacre, Day 2, 1996. https://www.justice.gov.za/Trc/hrvtrans/bisho2/gqozo.htm

South Africa. 1998. *Truth and Reconciliation Commission of South Africa report*. Cape Town: The Commission.

Starobinski, J. 1989. *The Living Eye,* trans. Goldhammer. A, Cambridge, MA.

Steyn, M. 2012. 'The ignorance contract: Recollections of apartheid childhoods and the construction of epistemologies of ignorance', *Identities,* 19(1): 8-25. https://doi.org/10.1080/1070289X.2012.672840

Summerfield, D. 2002. Effects of war: moral knowledge, revenge, reconciliation, and medicalised concepts of "recovery". Bmj, 325(7372), 1105-1107. https://doi.org/10.1136/bmj.325.7372.1105

Swartz, S. 2016. *Another Country: Everyday Social Restitution.* Cape Town, Western Cape, South Africa: HSRC Press.

Tankink, M. & Richters, A. 2017. Silence as a coping strategy: The case of refugee women in the Netherlands from South-Sudan who experienced sexual violence in the context of war, in P. Wilson & B. Drozdek (eds.) *Voices of trauma: Treating survivors across cultures,* 191-210. New York: Springer. https://doi.org/10.1007/978-0-387-69797-0_9

Tapscott, C. 1977. '*The Effects of the Structure of Local Government on Crime*', Unpublished Masters dissertation, Department of Public Administration, University of Cape Town, South Africa.

Tavuchis, N. 1991. Mea culpa: A sociology of apology and reconciliation. Stanford University Press.

Teege, J. 2015. *My grandfather would have shot me: A black woman discovers her family's Nazi past.* London: Hodder & Stoughton.

Todd, A. R., & Galinsky, A. D. 2014. Perspective-taking as a strategy for improving intergroup relations: Evidence, mechanisms, and qualifications. *Social and Personality Psychology Compass,* 8, 374-387. https://doi.org/10.1111/spc3.12116

Truth and Reconciliation Commission of South Africa. 1998. *Truth and Reconciliation Commission Final Report 1998.* Government Printers: Pretoria.

Tutu, D. 1999. *No Future without Forgiveness.* London: Image. https://doi.org/10.1111/j.1540-5842.1999.tb00012.x

Ulrich Schnyder, et al. 2015. 'Psychotherapies for PTSD: What do they have in common?' *European Journal of Psychotraumatology* 6: 28186-96. https://doi.org/10.3402/cjpt.v6.28186

Vagovič, M. 2017. Sudca Harabin rozdeľoal a panoval. Dobu temna vystriedala apatia [Judge Harabin divided and ruled. The dark era was replaced by apathy]. Retrieved from Aktuality.sk: www.aktuality.sk/clanok/547661/sudca-harabin-rozzdeloval-a-panoval-dobu-temna-vystriedala-apatia

Van de Loo, S. 2009. Versöhnungsarbeit. Kriterien – theologischer Rahmen – Praxisperspektiven, Stuttgart.

van der Heiden, L., Scherpiet, S., Konicar, L., Birbaumer, N., & Veit, R. 2013. Inter-individual differences in successful perspective taking during pain perception mediates emotional responsiveness in self and others: An fMRI study. *Neuroimage*, 65, 387-394. https://doi.org/10.1016/j.neuroimage.2012.10.003

Van der Kolk, B.A. 2014. *The body keeps score: Brain, mind and body in the healing of trauma*. New York: Viking Penguin.

van IJzendoorn MH, Bakermans-Kranenburg MJ, Sagi-Schwartz A.J. 2003. Are children of Holocaust survivors less well-adapted? A meta-analytic investigation of secondary traumatization. *Trauma Stress*. (5): 459-69. https://doi.org/10.1023/A:1025706427300

Verwoerd, W. J. & Little, A. 2018. 'Beyond a Dilemma of Apology: Transforming (Veteran) Resistance to Reconciliation in Northern Ireland and South Africa', in B. Kröndorfer (ed.) *Reconciliation in Global Context, SUNY* (State University of New York) Press.

Verwoerd, W. J. 1997. *My Winds of Change*, Johannesburg: Ravan Press.

Verwoerd, W. J. 2019. *Verwoerd: My Journey through Family Betrayals*, Cape Town: Tafelberg.

Verwoerd, W. J., 2001. 'On Our Moral Responsibility for Past Violations', *Alternation*, 8 (1): 219-242.

Villa-Vicencio, C. 2015. The South African Transition: Then and Now. In V. Tismaneanu, & B. C. Iacob, *Remembrance, History, and Justice: Coming to terms with traumatic pasts in democratic societies*, 311-327. Budapest & New York: Central European University Press.

Von Buchholtz, J. 2014. *A Collage of Thoughts and Images on Silence*. from www.jungatlanta.com.

Walker, J. 2013. "Referred pain: The Act of Killing and the production of a crime scene." *Film Quarterly* 67(2): 14-20. https://doi.org/10.1525/fq.2014.67.2.14

Walker, M.U. 2006. *Moral Repair: Reconstructing Moral Relations after Wrongdoing*. Cambridge University. https://doi.org/10.1017/CBO9780511618024

Walkerdine, V, Olsvold, A, & Rudberg, M. 2013. 'Researching Embodiment and Intergenerational Trauma using the work of Davoine and Gaudilliere: History walked in the door,' *Subjectivity* 6: 272-97. https://doi.org/10.1057/sub.2013.8

Warnier J.-P. and Bayart J.-F. (eds.), Matière à politique: le pouvoir, les corps et les choses (Paris, 2004)

Waters, A. 2018. *Coming of age in the 'lost' history of communism: Teaching the post-wall generations*. Retrieved from Academia.edu: https://www.academia.edu/7756806/Coming_of_Age_in_the_Lost_History_of_Communism_Teaching_the_Post-Wall Generations.

Weisman, R, 2014. *Showing Remorse: Law and the Social Control of Emotion*. Ashgate.

Werbner, R and Ranger, T. 1996. (eds.), *Postcolonial Identity in Africa*, London.

Wijaya, Elizabeth. "To See Die, Again: The Act of Filming and The Act of Killing." *Parallax* 22(1): 81-95. https://doi.org/10.1080/13534645.2015.1135520

Williamson, C.M. 1997. *Quoted in TRC Report, Vol 1:131*, Cape Town.

Wolterstorff, N. 1987. 'The wounds of God: Calvin's Theology of Social Justice', *The Reformed Journal*, 37 (6): 14-22.

Wolynn, M. 2016. *It didn't start with you: How inherited family trauma shapes how we are and how to end the cycle*. Penguin Books

Wondo Omanyundu, J.-J. 2013. Les armées au Congo-Kinshasa: Radioscopie de la Force Publique aux FARDC. Saint-Légier.

Young, A, 2007. 'Posttraumatic Stress Disorder of the Virtual Kind,' in Trauma and Memory: Reading, Healing, and Making Law, (eds). Sarat, A, Davidovitch, N & Alberstein, M. Stanford: Stanford University Press.

Zaki, J., & Ochsner, K. N. (2012). The neuroscience of empathy: Progress, pitfalls and promise. *Nature Neuroscience*, 15, 675-680. https://doi.org/10.1038/nn.3085

Zimmermann, Ruben. Pluralistische Ethikbegründung und Normenanalyse im Horizont einer 'impliziten Ethik' frühchristlicher Schriften, in: Friedrich Horn et al. (eds.), *Ethische Normen des frühen Christentums. Gut – Leben – Leib – Tugend, Tübingen* 2013, 3-27.

Žižek, S. 2006. *The Parallax View*. Cambridge. https://doi.org/10.7551/mitpress/5231.001.0001

Notes on Contributors

Jane Abatoni is a founding member and Executive Secretary for the Rwandan organisation of professional counsellors, Jane Abatoni Gatete is a peace builder and human rights activist with over 20 years working in the psychosocial field, peace building and conflict management in post conflict settings. She is a trained and practising professional counsellor, one of the ARCT-Ruhuka Senior Trainers and Clinical Supervisor for professional counsellors. She holds an MA in Peace Studies and Conflict Transformation from the University of Rwanda. She has worked as Chairperson for the Rwanda Youth Healing Centre, as 1st Vice-President for Profemmes Twese Hamwe (PFTH), an umbrella organisation that promotes women and children's rights, served on the East African Sub Regional Support Initiative for Advancement of Women (EASSI), and on several committees and commissions at local and regional levels, especially those on women and children's rights.

Jaco Barnard-Naudé is Professor of Jurisprudence, and co-director of the Centre for Rhetoric Studies at the Faculty of Law at the University of Cape Town. He is the British Academy's Newton Advanced Fellow in the Law School at Westminster University, London. He holds a National Research Foundation (NRF) rating and is a past recipient of the UCT Fellows' Award. He is a respected book and film critic in South Africa and a frequent speaker at international academic gatherings. His research concentrates at the intersections of critical theory, psychoanalysis, cultural theory, law and literature.

Andrea Bieler is Professor of Practical Theology at the Divinity School of Basel University in Switzerland. She is an Advanced Career scholar in the Enhancing Life research network at the University of Chicago. Her project title is: Enhancing Life in the Aftermath of Atrocious Violence. Exploring the Religious and Cultural Imaginary. She is interested in historic trauma as a hermeneutical category in practical theological reflection and in social as well as aesthetic practice. She is author / editor of 13 books and numerous essays, including *After Violence. Religion, Trauma and Reconciliation*, and *Horizonte einer Theologie der Seelsorge*. She produced a film on the Institute for Healing of Memories in South Africa in co-operation with Ralf Bieler.

John Brewer is Professor of Post Conflict Studies in the Senator George J Mitchell Institute for Global Peace, Security and Justice at Queen's University Belfast. He was awarded an Honorary DSocSci from Brunel University and is a Member of the Royal Irish Academy, a Fellow of the Royal Society of Edinburgh, a Fellow in the Academy of Social Sciences and a Fellow of the Royal Society of Arts. He has held visiting appointments at Yale University, St John's College Oxford, Corpus Christi College Cambridge and the Australia National University. He has been President of the British Sociological Association. He is Honorary Professor Extraordinary at

Stellenbosch University and is a member of the United Nations Roster of Global Experts. He is the author or co-author of sixteen books and editor or co-editor of a further six.

Shari Eppel is the director of Ukuthula Trust, which focuses on community reconciliation processes. In the 1990s, she was the primary author of what remains the only substantial history of the post-independence 'Gukurahundi' massacres. She has authored more than thirty human rights reports in the last twenty years, as well as publishing internationally on torture, government demolitions, humanitarian disasters affecting rural families in Matabeleland. Since the 1990s, she has spear-headed ad hoc exhumations and reburials, for purposes of 'healing the dead'. She acquired a Masters in Forensic Anthropology in 2014 and is currently training a forensic anthropology team for Zimbabwe, as well as doing her Doctorate. Shari Eppel was a recipient of the Barbra Chester Award in 2000.

Melike Fourie is a Research Associate leading the neuroscientific investigation of empathy in the Historical Trauma and Transformation Unit at Stellenbosch University. She holds an MSc in cognitive neuropsychology from University College London (2006), and a PhD in affective neuroscience from the University of Cape Town (2011). Her research interests fall within the domains of social psychology and social neuroscience, with a particular focus on intergroup relations and identifying and characterising the factors that affect how we see and respond to members of social (racial) outgroups. She believes a deeper understanding of implicit brain processes that drive behaviour is key in this undertaking.

Pumla Gobodo-Madikizela is Professor and Research Chair for Historical Trauma and Transformation in the Faculty of Arts and Social Sciences, Stellenbosch University and the 2020/2021 Walter Jackson Bate Fellow at Harvard University's Radcliffe Institute for Advanced Studies. Her work focuses mainly on two strands of research. The first is exploring intergenerational repercussions of oppression and institutional violence. For her second research area, she expands her earlier work on the relationship between remorse and forgiveness after historical trauma and examines what she terms "reparative humanism." She is the author of the critically acclaimed book, *A Human Being Died that Night: A South African Story of Forgiveness.* Among her edited and co-edited books are *Breaking Intergenerational Cycles of Repetition: A Global Dialogue on Historical Trauma and Memory*, as editor, and *Post Conflict Hauntings: Transforming Memories of Historical Trauma* as co-editor.

Nancy Rose Hunt is Professor of History and African Studies at the University of Florida since 2016. Her work pays particular attention to subaltern politics on a global scale with a focus on the history and anthropology of health, medicine, reproduction, childhood, humanitarianism, and forms of trauma in Africa. *A Colonial Lexicon: Of Birth Work, Medicalization, and Mobility in the Congo* received the prestigious Herskovits

Prize. *A Nervous State: Violence, Remedies, and Reverie in Colonial Congo* received the Martin Klein Prize from the American Historical Association. She is currently preparing a history of anthropology in ex-Belgian Africa from Mary Douglas and the IRSAC anthropologists to the present. Hunt's articles have appeared in numerous journals and publications, including Past & Present, The Lancet, History Workshop Journal, Somatosphere, Africa, Journal of African History, Signs, and Contemporary Anthropology.

Angela Jansen is PhD candidate at Stellenbosch University in South Africa. She has a BA in Cultural Anthropology and a MSc in International Development Studies, with a specialisation in Holocaust and Genocide Studies. She has worked with different NGOs in the Netherlands, Haiti and Cameroon. Since 2013, she has been working as a Programme Manager for Community Based Sociotherapy Rwanda. In line with her work, she conducts research within the Rwandan context, focusing on narrative identity among perpetrators and intergenerational dynamics.

Marie Grace Gasinzigwa Kagoyire is a PhD candidate at Stellenbosch University. She is a public health professional with a background in professional counselling and social sciences. She is a Participatory Action Researcher in Community-Based Sociotherapy Rwanda. She has experience in working with women victims of rape through group counselling and qualitative research and in psychosocial counselling and clinical supervision in the mental health field. She is a member and the vice chair of the Rwandan Association of Trauma-counsellors (ARCT-RUHUKA). Her research interests are silencing of past memories and transgenerational transmission of trauma in post-genocide Rwanda.

Emery Kalema is a senior researcher and a postdoctoral fellow in Studies in Historical Trauma and Transformation at Stellenbosch University, South Africa. He holds a PhD in History from the University of the Witwatersrand (2017). His research interests include power and politics, body and embodiment, violence, memory, trauma and suffering, as well as the post-colony. He is currently working on a book project, based on his doctoral dissertation, tentatively entitled, *Violence and Memory: The Mulele 'Rebellion' in Post-colonial Congo*. The book focuses on the 'imaginaries of suffering' and the relationship between power, memory, and suffering. He is also planning to conduct a set of philosophical reflections around the theme Memory as Freedom and Right.

Diogene Karangwa is a Rwandan with a Master of Science in Project Management from Jomo Kenyatta University. In addition, he has an internationally recognised certificate in Group Analysis from the Institute of Group Analysis (IGA-UK) and certificates in Genocide and Mass Atrocities Studies and in Human Rights by Aegis Trust and Conflict Management by Community Based Sociotherapy. He has worked for four years as a Participatory Action Researcher in Community-Based Sociotherapy

Rwanda, with interests in intergenerational transfers, mixed marriages, psychosocial dynamics and economic development. He is also a part-time Assistant Lecturer at the University of Tourism, Technology and Business Studies (UTB). Since September 2017, he has co-ordinated the community-based sociotherapy project Foundation of Sustainable Peace-Breaking the Cycle of Intergenerational Trauma and Violence.

Dagmar Kusá serves as the country expert on citizenship at the European Democratic Observatory (at EUI) and co-organizes a global annual Muslim-Jewish Conference. She is the Vice President of the Helsinki Committee for Human Rights in Slovakia. Prior to BISLA, she worked in the Slovak Helsinki Committee for Human Rights and served on its board of directors. In 2008/2009, she worked at EUROCLIO, the European Association of History Educators in The Hague. Since 2004, she has been the programme director at the International Center for Conciliation in Boston, where she remains affiliated as a Senior Fellow and trainer in identity conflicts transformation. Her primary academic interests include the political use of collective memory, ethnic identity, citizenship and minorities, and manifestations of cultural trauma in public discourse. Her current research focuses on the quality of democracy in countries transitioning from totalitarian or authoritarian regimes and its relation to the institutional choices of addressing the past, particularly in South Africa and Central European transitions.

Samantha Lakin is a PhD candidate at the Strassler Center for Holocaust and Genocide Studies, Clark University. She currently serves on the Board of Directors of the Fulbright Association and the Board of Trustees of Survivors Fund (SURF). She serves as a Senior Research Fellow at the Institute of Research for Dialogue and Peace. She has also held contracts in the justice sector in Northern Uganda, Nigeria, Burundi, and Rwanda for organisations including Aegis Trust and the Kigali Genocide Memorial, Refugee Law Project, Never Again Rwanda, and the US Embassy. She is a published author and an active public speaker on social justice issues.

Martin Leiner holds a Chair in Systematic Theology/Ethics at the Faculty of Theology at Friedrich-Schiller-Universität (FSU) Jena, Germany, since 2002. He studied Protestant Theology and Philosophy in Tübingen. Under the supervision of Prof. Gerd Theißen, he earned his PhD in 1995 from Heidelberg University on Psychological Exegesis of the New Testament. From 1998-2002 he was professor of Protestant Theology at Neuchâtel university and directed the Ethics Centre of the University of Geneva from 2000 to 2002. In 2013, he founded the Jena Centre for Reconciliation Studies (JCRS), which works on reconciliation processes worldwide with a transdisciplinary perspective.

Eric Ndushabandi is the Director of the independent think-tank, the Institute of Research and Dialogue for Peace (IRDP) in Rwanda. He teaches Political Science at the University of Rwanda where he served as the vice-dean of the School of Political,

Administrative and Social Sciences. His research focuses on memory, policies, and identity questions in post-conflict (genocide) reconstruction processes. He is an associate researcher at the Centre de Recherche en Science Politique (CRESPO) at Université Saint-Louis Brussels. He is also a member of the Belgian Association of Political Scientists (ABSP). He has been awarded the Erasmus Scholarship for Academic Exchange at Lund University, Sweden. In the East African region, Professor Ndushabandi has initiated a regional research network on peace and security, bringing together researchers and academics from the Democratic Republic of the Congo (DRC), Burundi and Rwanda. He is currently the chairperson of the board of the Media High Council (MHC) and a board member of the Rwanda Broadcasting Agency (RBA). He is in the process of publishing a book on *Policy of Memory in Rwanda*.

Kopano Ratele is Professor in the Department of Psychology in the Faculty of Arts and Social Sciences at Stellenbosch University. He is the former Director of the South African Medical Research Council Men, Injury and Violence Research Unit and Professor at the University of South Africa, where he ran the Transdisciplinary African Psychologies Programme. His work focuses on men and masculinities in intersection with violence, race, income, sexuality, and culture. He is past president of the Psychological Society of South Africa and a member of a number of editorial boards, including Feminism & Psychology, NORMA: the International Journal for Masculinity Studies, and Psychology in Society. His books include *There Was This Goat: Investigating the Truth Commission Testimony of Notrose Nobomvu Konile* (with Antjie Krog and Nosisi Mpolweni), *Liberating Masculinities*, and *Engaging Youth in Activism, Research and Pedagogical Praxis: Transnational and Intersectional Perspectives on Gender, Sex, and Race* (co-edited with Jeff Hearn, Tammy Shefer, and Floretta Boonzaier).

Annemiek Richters is Emeritus Professor culture, health and illness, Leiden University Medical Centre, and staff member of the Amsterdam School for Social Science Research, the Netherlands. She has supported community-based sociotherapy in Rwanda since 2005 in various capacities. Her publications address topics in fields such as gender, culture, violence, trauma, human rights, health and healing, the quality of reproductive health care for black, migrant and refugee women in the Netherlands, the cultural comparison of medicine and women's body politics in the context of globalisation, cultural identity and transcultural psychiatry, and community-based sociotherapy in post-genocide Rwanda.

Christine Schliesser is a theologian and an ethicist at the Centre for Ethics at Zürich University, Switzerland. She is also a research associate at Stellenbosch University, South Africa, and the academic coordinator of the Interfaculty Research Cooperation 'Religious Conflicts and Coping Strategies' at Bern University, Switzerland. Her areas of interest include conflict- and reconciliation studies, the theology and ethics of Dietrich Bonhoeffer, human rights, development studies and the role of theology in the public sphere. Her most recent book is *Alternative Approaches in Conflict Resolution* (edited with Martin Leiner).

Wilhelm Verwoerd is a senior researcher, Historical Trauma and Transformation Unit, Stellenbosch University, and a Research Fellow at the Beyers Naudé Centre for Public Theology, University of Stellenbosch. He is also a teaching associate at Trinity College, Dublin (Irish School of Ecumenics, Belfast). As a former researcher within the South African Truth and Reconciliation Commission (1995-1998) and a reconciliation practitioner in Northern Ireland (2001-2012), he is particularly interested in approaching the dynamics of (re)humanisation / reconciliation from the perspective(s) of former combatants / veterans / perpetrators. He is currently working on a book based on an international '*Beyond Dehumanisation*' reflective learning project with ex-combatants and survivors from the conflict in and about Northern Ireland, Israel-Palestine, South Africa and the USA.

Kim Wale is a senior researcher in Studies in Historical Trauma and Transformation at Stellenbosch University. She is leading the analysis of a large dataset on transgenerational transmission of trauma, one of the initiative's flagship research projects funded by the Mellon Foundation. She completed her PhD at the University of London (SOAS) in post-conflict development. She was project leader of the South African Reconciliation Barometer Survey at the Institute for Justice and Reconciliation. Her first major book was *South Africa's Struggle to Remember: Contested Memories of Squatter Resistance in the Western Cape*.

Sue Williamson is a South African artist who lives in Cape Town, South Africa. She studied at the Art Students' League in New York from 1963-65. In 1983 she was awarded an Advanced Diploma in Fine Art from the Michaelis School of Fine Art, Cape Town (UCT). Williamson's works feature in numerous public collections across the globe, including those at the Museum of Modern Art, New York, USA, Tate Modern, London, UK, Victoria & Albert Museum, London, UK, National Museum of African Art, Smithsonian Institution, Washington D.C., USA, Wifredo Lam Centre, Havana, Cuba, Iziko South African National Gallery, Cape Town, South Africa, and Johannesburg Art Gallery, South Africa. Williamson has received various awards and fellowships such as the Bellagio Creative Arts Fellowship 2011, Italy, Rockefeller Foundation, the Visual Artist Research Award Fellowship 2007, Smithsonian Institution, Washington D.C., USA and the Lucas Artists Residency Fellowship 2005, Montalvo Art Center, California, USA.